CONTEMPORARY
STAGE
DIRECTING

CONTEMPORARY STAGE DIRECTING

George Black

University of Virginia
and
Artistic Director—Heritage Repertory Theatre

Holt, Rinehart and Winston, Inc.

Fort Worth   Chicago   San Francisco   Philadelphia
Montreal   Toronto   London   Sydney   Tokyo

Publisher:	Ted Buchholz
Acquisitions Editor:	Janet Wilhite
Developmental Editor:	Kathryn Lang
Project Editor:	Mike Hinshaw
Production Manager:	Kathy Ferguson
Art & Design Supervisor:	Guy Jacobs
Text Designer:	Harry Rinehart
Cover Designer:	Pat Sloan
Cover Photograph:	Martha Swope
Back Cover Photograph:	Claire Black

Library of Congress Cataloging-in-Publication Data

Black, George, 1935–
    Contemporary stage directing.

    Includes bibliographical references and index.
    1. Theater—Production and direction.   I. Title.
PN2053.B525   1990   792'.0233   90-5138
ISBN 0-03-016633-0

Requests for permission to make copies of any part of the work should be mailed to: Copyrights and Permissions Department, Holt, Rinehart and Winston, Inc., Orlando, FL 32887.

Address editorial correspondence to: 301 Commerce Street, Suite 3700, Fort Worth, TX 76102.

Address orders to: 6277 Sea Harbor Drive, Orlando, FL 32887.
1-800-782-4479, or 1-800-433-0001 (in Florida)

The paper used in this book was made from recycled paper.

PRINTED IN THE UNITED STATES OF AMERICA

1 2 3 4   038   9 8 7 6 5 4 3 2 1

Holt, Rinehart and Winston, Inc.
The Dryden Press
Saunders College Publishing

PREFACE

Working in the theatre can be wonderful and rewarding. When those exciting moments happen in rehearsal and production, being a director is a great experience.

Directing is a subtle and complex art. The craft requires not only talent, but also serious thought and years of practice. Learning about the theatre—about the world at large—is the work of a lifetime. That is one of the things that makes the work—and the profession—so daunting and so attractive. Making a good start is possible for most interested students with the necessary talent and commitment. But there are no shortcuts to mastery in the field.

Of course, few people set their sights on *mastering* the art; that is only natural. Studying and practicing directing has its own rewards. It can teach you to *observe* your world, develop your *intuitions*, broaden your *experience*, and *respond* to it all. You should keep in mind that your greatest progress—and your greatest satisfaction—will come if you *work* at it. If you have some aptitude—and, yes, passion—for the work, you will be rewarded with steady progress.

About this Text

This book attempts to cover as much as possible of the essential material used by skillful directors. Its point of view is one evolved from observation and study of the best contemporary practice. You might find some of it complicated and tedious. If you do, keep in mind that everything here is potentially useful to you as you make progress. But you do not need to master—or even understand—everything presented here to begin to experience what directing is all about. You can start directing scenes almost at once and begin learning from the work. A resourceful teacher can be of incalculable help to you, just as a perceptive coach is to an athlete.

The book is divided into two complementary parts. The first part—Intro-

v

duction and Chapters 1 through 5—is devoted to the *idea* of directing and the understanding of and response to the script. The second part of the book—Chapters 6 through 12—builds on the ideas explored earlier and suggests *methods* for the director actually working in the theatre. Both parts of the text are synthesized in Chapter 13, which deals with the evaluation of the director's creative work in making a production.

THE STUDY OF DIRECTING

It is possible to divide the material into two useful courses, but the essential idea of a director *making* a production by working through a text should never be lost. Therefore, the best approach for a first course in directing probably is to concentrate on the techniques for *making a production*. A student who directs two or three scenes for a class will have a good introduction to the work—especially if one or more of the scenes is reworked and presented again after comment and analysis in a classroom or studio setting. Appendix A suggests some approaches to this kind of *scene work* for both beginning and advanced practice.

"Letting the work teach you" is an idea repeated throughout this book. Real improvement in a director's skills begins when the work leads beyond the nuts and bolts of "getting a show up" into the need to understand the theory behind the methods. Even in a first course, the director will learn to work better if introduced to the ideas and principles that consciously or unconsciously influence *everything* he or she does in the rehearsal hall and on the stage.

FEATURES WORTH NOTING

Several chapters contain in-depth discussions of plays ranging from the classic *(Macbeth)* through the early moderns *(Hedda Gabler)* to the contemporary *(Master Harold . . . and the boys)*. Most of these discussions are self-contained and do not require outside reading. However, reading five of the plays may yield a better understanding of the text discussions.

Of course, reading plays goes with the territory; every good director must know dozens of plays. Such knowledge helps in evaluating and choosing plays—and in understanding what theatre is all about. Nevertheless, each instructor is the best judge of the reading requirements for each class. The following list shows the chapters featuring the in-depth discussions and the corresponding plays; the five plays shown in **boldface** are those the instructor may want to consider assigning as additional reading:

- Introduction—*Hedda Gabler* by Henrik Ibsen
- Chapter 2—*The Maids* by Jean Genet

- Chapter 3—*Death of a Salesman* by Arthur Miller; **Macbeth** by William Shakespeare; **The Foreigner** by Larry Shue
- Chapter 4—*The Masterbuilder* by Henrik Ibsen
- Chapter 5—*The Cherry Orchard* by Anton Chekhov; *A Midsummer Night's Dream* by William Shakespeare; *The Homecoming* by Harold Pinter; *Ghosts* by Henrik Ibsen; **Miss Julie** by August Strindberg; **The Visit** by Friedrich Dürrenmatt
- Chapter 8—**Master Harold . . . and the boys** by Athol Fugard; **The Foreigner** by Larry Shue
- Chapter 11—*Macbeth* and *Richard III* by William Shakespeare; *Master Harold . . . and the boys* by Athol Fugard; *True West* by Sam Shepard
- Chapter 12—*Hedda Gabler* by Henrik Ibsen

Brief biographical notes on certain directors are highlighted throughout the text. There are certainly many more important and influential directors—past and present—than are cited. Because directors as a group are not widely known, the biographical notes give indications, at least, of the scope of the profession and some of its important exponents.

Appendix A outlines ideas and approaches for doing *scenework*. Appendix B discusses some of the special challenges and rewards of directing *musical* productions; C examines the prospect of *jobs* and *careers* for directors, and D provides a short list of useful organizations and resources.

A Glossary of dramatic and theatrical terminology includes many terms in general usage and some that are specialized or particular to this text. A list of References gives sources cited in this text along with a few titles recommended for study and, perhaps, addition to your professional library.

End Note

The serious study of directing will challenge you in a variety of ways. Because it is essentially a *collaborative* venture, few things can be as satisfying as a production artfully conceived and executed by a dozen or more people working together creatively. The days when the director could be a dictator are virtually gone. Today, successful directors are skillful at communication and motivation; they are team leaders. They are also better educated, more informed about art and politics, and more cosmopolitan in their outlooks than only a few years ago. Directing has become international. In the U.S., directors from Britain, Eastern and Western Europe, an the Orient are working extensively and influencing the American Theatre profoundly. Just as surely, American directors are working in leading theatres around the world. As a result, directing is the most exciting field in the contemporary theatre. It is a wonderful time to learn about directing—a great time to *be* a director.

Acknowledgements

Many people inspired this book—from Tyrone Guthrie, who showed me the director should be an artist; to Karl Eigsti, who changed my ideas about the workings of imagination in a single afternoon's conference on a set design; to Alan Schneider, who encouraged me to be as daring as I can. Of equal importance are literally dozens of students, actors, designers, directors, and friends—many more than I can reasonably list here. Many continue to spur me on and teach me things even when they don't realize they're doing it. My family, of course—Margaret and our daughters, Annamarie and Claire—supported me in ways that cannot be measured or repaid.

Two brilliant designers contributed by challenging, delighting, and amazing me through dozens of collaborations: Charlie Caldwell, whose artistry in designing magnificent sets is surpassed only by his talent for being a great, witty person; and Gweneth West, who actually provoked me into starting this book and is continually opening new ideas and possibilities with her perceptive and splendid costume designs.

In getting the book into shape, my editor Kathryn Lang was indispensable and a model of forbearance and tact. Among the dozens of people who helped me particularly with the manuscript or encouraged me when I really needed it were virtually all my colleagues at the University of Virginia, especially John Frick, Betsy Tucker, and Richard Warner—who tested some of the material in their own work—along with David Weiss and LaVahn Hoh, who tried to keep me on track with the technical material. Barbara Peeks helped with insights into pedagogy, and Paulina Shur supplied much needed help with some translations. Of great service also were the following reviewers who helped the text during several revisions and provided dozens of useful comments: Edward Amor—University of Wisconsin at Madison; Vincent Angotti—University of Evansville; Sally Askins—Texas Tech University; James Christy—Villanova University; Gaylan Collier—Texas Christian University; Ken Cox—Oklahoma State University; William Dobkin—Arizona State University; Corwen Georges—Wittenburg University; Michael King—Northern Kentucky University; Stanley Longman—University of Georgia; Jack McCullough—Trenton State College; Norman Myers—Bowling Green State University; Richard Palmer—College of William and Mary; James Panowski—Northern Michigan State University; Maarten Reilingh—Middle Tennessee State University.

CONTENTS

PART ONE: IDEAS

PART TWO: METHODS

CONTEMPORARY
STAGE
DIRECTING

PART I

IDEAS

Real performance is as creative an act as composition . . .

—**Suzanne Langer,** *Feeling and Form*

INTRODUCTION

The Search for the Great Production

Everyone who works in the theatre—certainly everyone who wants to be a director—has seen at least one production that made a deep and lasting impression, an impact so strong that its images never fade completely. It was magic of the sort that only the modern theatre can express. As theatre artists we want to participate in that sort of creation. As directors we want to make such productions. The more deeply we explore the process, the more we understand the craft of directing and its potential, the more we are frustrated by our limited ability. It is a cruel paradox. The more we learn, the farther away the goal seems to move. We still want to create the kind of magic we once experienced in the work of others.

There is no golden path to creativity. There is no one way to understand either the complex feelings and meanings lying dormant in a playtext, or the kind of imagination required to express those intuitions fully in a production. What we can do is attempt to participate in the creative process. We can attempt to focus our own energies by trying to understand what makes a production powerful and the ideas, methods, and impulses at work in creating it.

Great productions—whether they are classic or contemporary, tragedy or comedy, melodrama or farce—seem to have several things in common. A great production has *integrity:* every element is right; nothing is out of place. It is *elegant:* the pieces fit together without strain or effort. It has a sense of *inevitability:* it must be the way it is; any alteration would be amiss. It is *unique:* other productions may resemble this one in some ways, but they never capture the same quality or produce the same effect. It is *compelling:* it engages; it entertains; it ensnares. It *reverberates:* the images return again and again. And it is *beautiful:* its images and patterns form a coherent structure that communicates not only meaning but aesthetic satisfaction as well. That beauty is neither incidental nor affected; it is what makes the production wonderful.

The artist responsible for this sort of achievement is the person we call the modern director. How do directors create great productions? By exploring that process, we can hope to tap the springs of creative direction in ourselves.

The Director's Creation

1. An open stage, vast and black, platforms arranged asymmetrically rising abruptly in the distance. Shafts of light piercing the darkness. A high-pitched whine is heard, growing in intensity. Slowly, a beam of light picks out a solitary figure, tall and imposing: a statuesque woman—pale porcelain skin, auburn hair, long gown of green velvet. The sound builds, filling the space, coming from every direction. The woman's face is serene but implacable. The light on the woman peaks, starts to fade away. Objects glide silently into view. A gas chandelier, an oil portrait, a tiled stove, settee, chairs, a curtained archway. The sound dies away as light—seeming to radiate from the chandelier—begins to define the space on the platforms. The curtains part, and an elderly woman in gray comes in briskly, chattering, "Oh, I don't think they are up yet!" (Translated by Geir Jensen)

2. A thrust stage, a polished wood floor with oriental rugs. Upstage, a wall with dark wood wainscoting below a rich brocade paper in tones of burgundy. Notes of a piano are heard in the distance as the lights go out; then the sound grows clearer, closer. A light picks out a young woman in riding clothes seated on stage playing the piano, and yet the direction and source of the sound are still ambiguous. Another shaft of light finds a display case with a brace of dueling pistols.

More light, pale and smoky, pervades the room. The shadowy figure of a man, also in riding clothes, crosses to the woman. She takes his arm and both exit through French doors with pale blue light filtering in. The sound of the piano continues for a moment, then falls away as the lights change and the room darkens. The curtains in the archway upstage are thrown open allowing some light to spill onto the stage floor. A woman in a maid's cap moves briskly to the French doors and throws open the curtains, bathing the stage in bright, amber light. An elderly woman steps into the archway. "Oh," she says brusquely, "I don't think they are up yet!"

3. Curtain rises to reveal a handsome, spacious room. Dark green walls, polished mahogany. Through French doors at right is seen the roof of a verandah shaded by autumn foliage. Morning light streams through the doors. Down right a porcelain stove, and a high-backed chair with ottoman; down center a round table flanked by two straight chairs; down left a small sofa. An upright piano stands against the wall upstage, and an oil portrait hangs on the wall above. What-not shelves with knickknacks flank an archway up center. A nice-looking woman of 65 dressed in a grey suit turns to the middle-aged maid following her and says in a low voice, "Oh, I don't think they are up yet!"

Each of these scenes might be from the opening moments of *Hedda Gabler* interpreted by a contemporary director. Each scene bespeaks an intensely personal vision, honestly conceived and artistically rendered by different artists. The three productions all purport to be unique, and yet each calls itself *"Hedda Gabler* by Henrik Ibsen." How we deal with this apparent paradox is one indication of our attitude towards the nature of modern theatrical creation. What may be obvious, but nonetheless critical to our understanding, is that each of the productions grows out of a distinctly *modern* directorial sensibility. It is only in the modern theatre, defined in large measure by the modern director, that this paradox could arise.

Is there one *Hedda Gabler,* a definitive production that Ibsen conceived and towards which ideal directors, actors, and designers strive? If and when that ideal production is achieved, will we then be able to say that the playwright's artistic impulse has been realized, that the proper medium of theatrical expression has been found and the work of the playwright's art, *Hedda Gabler,* lives in the theatre at last?

Or are there many *Heddas,* many different works of theatre art, each with its own distinctive life and special validity?

We try to have it both ways. On one hand, we persist in claiming that it is the playwright's unique creation in which we wish to participate as collaborators or as audience, that the play as a work of art is created by the playwright as a complete structure. But do we act with conviction on this premise? Or do we see different productions of *Hedda Gabler,* or *Hamlet,* or *Cat on a Hot Tin Roof* because we suppose that although we might never see the *definitive* production of the author's creation, we might be able to pick up an insightful moment here, a riveting performance there, until we can at least create that perfect production in our own heads?

Although we may say that Ibsen's vision—if truly realized—alone deserves to be called *Hedda Gabler,* our actions betray us.

We produce *Hedda Gabler* and *Hamlet* and *Cat on a Hot Tin Roof,* or we go to see these productions again and again, because we expect a *different* artwork from the versions we have known before. We expect to create, or encounter, not the *same* play but a *new* one. We view each production as a new work of art— not a version of one already achieved—since its aim and function is to create something unique.

A theatrical production, like any art, creates what aesthetician Suzanne Langer terms "perceptible forms expressive of human feeling." (*Problems of Art,* p. 80)

Certainly the number and vitality of new productions testify to the extraordinary life and energy to be found even in scripts that have become standards. Every new production expresses something different about a play—no matter how many times the play has been performed. Each new production is a unique artistic expression.

Who is the artist, then, who creates the theatrical production? We understand that the playwright's vision or intention (or whatever we care to call it) cannot be fully achieved by a single production or a single approach. If it were, we would expect to see that one production. We might suppose that after hundreds of years and thousands of attempts to learn the lessons, some company could put it all together and show us in one shining event *Hamlet* as it was meant to be played! Or we might expect some modern playwright-directors to achieve the ideal by directing their own works.

But we know we look in vain for these transcendent definitive events. We acknowledge that neither the playwright's insights nor the experience and scholarship of centuries—as valuable as these things may be—can bring that definitive production into being.

Playwrights tell us all they know about the play when they complete their playscripts. Contemporary playwrights Samuel Beckett and Harold Pinter are not being perverse when they confess an inability to go further in identifying Godot or the "weasel behind the cupboard." The great modern director Tyrone Guthrie came to understand that playwright James Bridie was stating a simple fact when he said he did not know any more about his play than what he had already written.

TYRONE GUTHRIE 1900–1971 (Great Britain)	London; New York; Stratford-upon-Avon; Stratford, Ontario; Minneapolis. *Troilus and Cressida, Hamlet, Othello, The Tenth Man, Candide.* Founder of the Guthrie Theatre, much-honored, and one of the most influential modern directors in the English-speaking world.

What, then, of theatrical tradition? Even if we grant the playwright has gone as far as possible in creating the playscript, we must admit the value and import of tradition and history in leading us towards a more perfect production. In a limited sense, this is a valid admission. Insofar as craft is concerned, we do draw upon previous achievements. We can draw even insight and inspiration from other productions. But we cannot create an artwork based solely on tradition and evolution. We cannot improve up this year's model of *Hamlet* in the manner of product manufacturer—not, that is, if we are artists. An artist bases his or her work upon a fresh image, a new interpretation, a special vision or feeling from which to create new forms. Now these forms will inevitably draw from the past productions and conventions; elements might recur in what seems to be simple repetition. But if the new work is truly an artwork, these borrowed elements have been fundamentally changed and informed by an overriding artistic impulse. Without this transformation, we are left with a hodgepodge. Tyrone Guthrie called it warming up "cold pudding, and cold second-hand pudding at that."[1]

Yet the playwright's script is the primary source and inspiration of most productions. Understanding and interpreting the script imaginatively is the director's first essential task.

After the script, the director deals most intensely with actors.

Most directors acknowledge that the actor is the core of the play in production—its central and most dynamic element. It is the actor, after all, who defines "live" theatre. There is yet another component to the director's task. Beyond working with script and actors, the contemporary director must know how to employ and integrate all the production elements. The director who cannot read a script intelligently and respond to it imaginatively is radically impaired. The director who does not understand the actor's process—who cannot master a vocabulary for working with the chosen performers simply cannot hope to create effective, expressive productions. But then, neither can the director who cannot grasp the creative languages of playwrights and designers.

These, then, are some of the *elements* the director *must* be prepared to use: the *script,* the *actors,* the *design* of the production.

Still, this still leaves two unanswered questions. First, what is the *product* of the director's work? And, second, what are the *methods* that stimulate the director to create intelligent and exciting work? We can begin exploring these issues by looking at how the idea of the director came to be.

[1]From remarks recorded by Folkway Records in New York in 1962 during rehearsals for *Gideon,* by Paddy Chayefsky.

The Director: A Biography

We have some idea of how to define the modern director because the first one was immediately recognizable. We can even fix the time and place with some precision: the date is May 1, 1874; the city, Berlin. The first modern director was George II, Duke of Saxe-Meiningen, and the date marks the occasion of the debut of his company, the Meininger. As Toby Cole informs us in her indispensable "The Emergence of the Director" (*Directors on Directing*, pp. 3–77), the Duke's contribution was to invest in a single artist the task and responsibility of making a production that would reflect a unified and coherent aesthetic vision.[2]

GEORGE II 1826–1914 (Germany)	Duke of Saxe-Meiningen, the founder of the Meininger Company. The first modern director.

The step was revolutionary and radical. With this approach to theatrical production, the Duke defined the modern theatre. He did so by responding to the multiplicity of styles, forms, and fashions that had fragmented the European theatre for almost two centuries. Where before, the various elements of the theatre—acting, scenery, movement, costumes, music, properties, text—had maneuvered and jostled for attention and acclaim, the Duke undertook to establish a single, controlling vision. The modern director was born—as the theatre itself—full-blown and brash.

The Duke was an artist and designer—what we might call a scenographer—and was willing and eager to unify the visual elements of the production. But he went beyond that, attempting to integrate *all* the elements of theatrical production. The Duke realized that the theatrical event could itself be an art work, going beyond a good performance by a star in a powerful role complemented by attractive scenery and costumes. He approached the actors in a new way—as individuals and as groups; he found he could move and arrange them into static and kinetic patterns and have them make sounds of varying rhythms, pitches, and timbres. He saw that he could unify the visual elements of the scenery, lighting, and costumes in such a way so as to be not only "historically correct," but to *say something* about the play. All these elements needed direction, control, modulation—a single vision—which the Duke was able and willing to supply.

---

[2]There seems little doubt that Ludwig Chronegk, the Duke's principal collaborator, was a critical figure in the process of defining the director, as Max Grube makes abundantly clear in *The Story of the Meininger*. The Duke nonetheless remains the *image* of the nascent modern director in the sense we are discussing it here.

Not everyone approved of what he was doing, but virtually everyone recognized that he was doing something new and different.

After the Duke, the director's job needed nothing but refinements, and a few changes in focus. Many of these modifications were accomplished with a great deal of uncertainty and divisiveness—much of it well-meaning and intelligent. Some of these efforts were complicated by a fair amount of blundering and ineptitude. Beginning around the turn of the century, Edward Gordon Craig became the most important spokesman on behalf of the director.

EDWARD GORDON CRAIG 1872–1966 (Great Britain)	A designer and theorist, Craig profoundly affected the shape and concerns of the modern theatre by alternately inspiring and infuriating his contemporaries with notions of the absolute importance of the director and (apparent) subordination of the actor. Wrote *The Art of the Theatre*.

Craig grasped the significance of the *idea* and many of its implications, and he was eager to push the possibilities to the limits. "The artist of the theatre," he proclaimed the director, offending just about everyone. Worse, in an effort to demonstrate this *new* art of the theatre, he failed more often than not to illustrate his ideas with successful productions. The notion of the *Übermarionette*—the "actor-as-marionette"—still infuriates many people. His impractical scenic designs offended Lee Simonson, one of the most thoughtful and influential scene designers of the time, and his interpretations of Shakespeare confounded Constantin Stanislavski, who would himself emerge as one of the modern theatre's greatest innovators as leader of the Moscow Art Theatre. But for all his visionary hyperbole, Craig pushed his idea of the director as artist to the forefront of theatrical thought and practice. The idea of the *regisseur* (the continental term for "director") has inspired the great theatricalist directors from Stanislavski's contemporaries to today.

Saxe-Meiningen and Craig saw the theatre as *theatrical:* poetic and grand. At around the same time, however, playwrights were beginning to write *realistic* plays that called for different directorial sensibilities.

ANDRÉ ANTOINE 1858–1943 (France)	Founder in Paris of the Théâtre Libre, which became the model for the "Free Theatre" movement in Europe early in the century. Father of the realistic/naturalistic style of directing.

Andre Antoine established the pattern and aesthetic of the realist directors[3] at the *Théâtre Libre* in Paris. Antoine found that the use of actual furniture and props with his untrained and unsophisticated performers gave him the opportunity to dictate and modulate effects towards a non-theatrical statement suitable for the sorts of plays he wanted to produce. The very exigencies of his situation—little money, few technical resources, no professional actors—suggested the approach to production and ultimately defined the aesthetic that typified his

For more than one hundred years, the realistic "fourth wall" staging pioneered by Andre' Antoine has continued its popularity as demonstrated in this premiere during the 1988–1989 season.
Play: *Abundance* **Author:** Beth Henley **Theatre:** South Coast Repertory **Director:** Ron Lagomarsino
Costumes: Robert Wojewodski **Set Designer:** Adrienne Lobel **Lighting:** Paulie Jenkins **Actors (l to r):** Belita Moreno, Bruce Wright, Jimmie Ray Weeks, O-Lan Jones (Photo by Ron M. Stone)

style. As a director, Antoine was behaving fundamentally in the same way as the Duke: he was consciously imparting a particular vision to a production by integrating and modulating all the production elements.

Antoine achieved the illusion of the "slice of life," for example, through his celebrated *fourth wall* technique. By rehearsing a scene as if it were in an actual room and following only the logic of character, action, and architecture, An-

[3]The designation "realist" is used loosely here, although it is probably more accurate to say "naturalist." For our purposes, and from the perspective that the two modes have more or less merged over the years, it is fair to consider Antoine's work as setting the pattern for realist directors. While the convention is to designate the theatricalist modes as "non-" or "anti-" realist, it is sometimes more useful to think of realists as non or anti-*theatricalists*.

toine could convince himself of the naturalness of the staging. Then, by removing one wall (i.e., by selecting the viewing angle of the audience), he could create the illusion of a non-theatrical presentation. This, of course, is the fundamental creative decision made by Saxe-Meiningen in designing *his* stagings to bring together text, actors, design elements, and action to achieve a deliberate and controlled artistic form. The effects these directors produced were different in intention and result, but both men were on the same track in defining the working philosophy of the modern director.

It remained for Constantin Stanislavski to make the last important refinement, the full incorporation of the actors' contributions to the production scheme. Like the Duke, Antoine had worked with actors who were essentially amateurs, training them as he wished and subjugating them to his directorial vision. Unlike Saxe-Meiningen and Antoine, however, Stanislavski approached the task of the director from the perspective of the actor—specifically the *professional* actor.

CONSTANTIN STANISLAVSKI 1863–1938 (Russia)	Co-founder and director of the Moscow Art Theatre. *The Seagull, The Cherry Orchard, The Lower Depths*. A seminal figure in the contemporary theatre, Stanislavski developed his *System* of actor training and defined the dominant modern directorial approach to actors. Wrote *An Actor Prepares, Creating a Role, Building a Character, My Life in Art*.

An actor himself and a keen observer of the art, Stanislavski was clearly inclined towards the notion of the actor sharing with the playwright in the real creative act of theatrical art. He had seen it. He had thrilled to many of the great actors of the nineteenth century, including the fiery Tomasso Salvini and the incomparable Eleanora Duse. Stanislavski knew what a great performer could do with a character. Armed with that knowledge, he set about discovering a way to harness the creative potential of the actor and the ensemble. What he discovered, of course, was popularized in the *System* of actor training that bears his name. What he accomplished goes beyond the bounds of actor training or even the ideals and techniques of ensemble acting. Stanislavski understood and worked towards the inclusion of the actor's creativity in the bank of materials upon which the modern director can draw. With Stanislavski's contribution, the definition of the modern director was complete, the full range of the director's materials had been discovered and explored.

The Director's Art

If there is an art of the theatre, then that art lives in the theatre—at a performance. And if that performance, that production is an artwork, then—in the modern theatre, at least—the director is the artist who makes it.

> **The director is the artist of the theatre. Using the materials at hand provided by the other theatre artists who collaborate in the process, the director's vision and craft gives form to the theatrical expression of the production.**

For some people, the preceding statement is sure to provoke controversy. From the time of Aristotle, theatrical art has suffered from the persistent notion that its only fundamentally artistic element is the text, and that is, quite obviously, a piece of *literature*. As a result, students from high school through graduate school are taught that plays are essentially works of literature to be approached and appreciated in the same way as novels and poems—as complete and fully realized on the printed page. Asked to articulate the argument, one might state:

> The only artist in the theatre is the playwright whose imaginative conception, characters, and *words* form the indispensable core and kernel of a theatrical production. Besides, *"Littera scripta manet"*—"The written word endures." Plays are literature. They can be bound into volumes, gathered into libraries, pored over and savored by general readers as well as critics and scholars. Productions, on the other hand, are ephemeral and virtually always flawed by some intellectual, artistic, or technical ineptitude. A play in performance is best left to the unlettered, to those without the intellect, education, or energy to read the text with the requisite insights and sensitivities.

Theatre people demur, of course, maintaining that a playtext is incomplete until it is in production. Indeed, classes in dramatic literature inevitably begin with some maxim about plays written to be performed, the shape of the Globe Theatre ("Wooden O and all that"), the Elizabethan actor Richard Burbage (it's almost inevitably a course in Shakespeare). Then (just as inevitably) all that quaint and interesting historical trivia is put to one side, and the plays are studied *seriously*, that is, as literature.

Aside from the obvious fallacy of approaching one element of a performance art (the text) as separate from and basically unrelated to its other essential components, what real harm comes from the idea that plays are literature? There are many. Most damaging is the idea that a play can be best and most fully perceived and appreciated by *reading* and that performance is somehow a vulgarization of a sacred text (as it was in Medieval Europe). Euripides, Shakespeare, and Moliere might disagree, but some critics argue that these great playwrights were victims of the demands of their own popular cultures.

If, however, we believe that theatre-worthiness is the essential mark of a good script, the only valid and convincing test of that quality must be in the theatre, in production.

We can say with confidence that all theatre collaborators are properly artists. The playwrights surely: they create the texts. The designers surely: they create the costumes, the sets, the lights. The actors surely: they create the performances. The directors surely: they create the productions.

Because we call these people artists, we do not mean they are incapable of poor work. There is bad art in the theatre just as there is in any other creative enterprise. There are most certainly bad directors. Directors who think of themselves a creative artists are no more immune from doing bad work than painters, composers, or playwrights. A definition that denies the creative function to the director, though, can lead to a fundamental misunderstanding and cheapening of the work itself.

Still, to suggest that the understanding and acceptance of the director's creative function is proof against excess and stupidity is obviously wrong. Everyone has a story of that genuinely awful production by that impossibly arrogant director that stand as an ugly monument to the vulgarity and insensitivity of the today's theatre. That production (again, it's almost certainly Shakespeare) wrenched the play out of its proper and intended place and time, undermined the audience's reasonable expectations, and generally distorted plot and character to the point of unrecognizability. What is worse, the production flew in the face of what we know and understand to be the intentions of the playwright. The result is theatrical disaster and more challenges to the director's claim to creative interpretation.

Every theatergoer of taste has experienced some kind of revulsion upon seeing a monumental miscarriage of theatrical license. But the case does not stand. If the director is prohibited from bringing a strong creative impulse into play, we may reduce the number of disasters, but we also lose the prospect of epoch-making productions of contemporary directors like Tyrone Guthrie, Peter Brook, and Jerzy Grotowski. Furthermore, we must then ask other inevitable questions. Why should the theatre be held to different standards from the other arts? What is an acceptable ratio of outrages to masterpieces? And should the theatre—not music, painting, dance, or sculpture—be denied the prospect of masterpieces because so many efforts are artistic disasters?

JERZY GROTOWSKI 1933– (Poland)	Theatre Laboratory, Institute for Research into Acting. *Akropolis, Dr. Faustus, The Constant Prince.* Originally committed to exploring the mythic and religious implications of great Polish and international classics; now moving away from performance and into anthropological study. Wrote *Towards a Poor Theatre.*

The case against the idea of the director-as-artist fails in yet another way, even assuming one would be willing to forego the few great productions for the chance to be free of the genuinely awful. Suppose we required the director to eliminate or neutralize any strong imaginative visions and impulses. We might *require* the director to bring the text to life upon the stage, to follow scrupulously the playwright's vision, and that vision alone. Then, we must confront the fact that such an approach is quite clearly impossible. Every director, of necessity, makes hundreds of decisions based on interpretation and formed in terms of imagination and craft, and each of those decisions marks the production in unique way. Nonetheless, the ideal of the director as a neutral agent represents a kind of theatrical fundamentalism that is probably still the dominant sect across the broad spectrum of contemporary American theatre, most certainly among reviewers and critics.

The influence of this viewpoint is widespread. For every overblown, artsy production of the type just described, every serious theatergoer will have the opportunity to witness ten—perhaps twenty—bland, conventionalized renditions. "Deadly," Peter Brook terms it. In *The Empty Space*, Brook spells it out:

> The Deadly Theatre can at first sight be taken for granted, because it means bad theatre. As this is the form of theatre we see most often, and as it is most closely linked to the despised, much-attacked commercial theatre it might seem a waste of time to criticize it further. But it is only if we see that deadliness is deceptive, and can appear anywhere, that we will become aware of the size of the problem. (p. 9)

PETER BROOK 1925– (Great Britain)	Paris, London, New York. *King Lear, A Midsummer Night's Dream, The Mahabharata, The Cherry Orchard*. Formerly co-director of the Royal Shakespeare Company and co-founder (with Jean-Louis Barrault) of the International Centre for Theatre Research, his productions and writings have been among the most important influences on contemporary Western theatre.

Playwrights write for production. That is admittedly a dangerous game. Playwrights hope for honest, intelligent, and imaginative people to make productions of their plays. They know they will not always get that. They also know that the real hope and test of what they write depends on the people who work together to produce the play. The imaginative, creative director is the best person to turn to if the play is to have a chance of fulfilling its promise.

We are left with the paradox of the *Hedda Gablers*. If there are different productions, each with its own artistic integrity, then it is clear that the playwright—while contributing an essential element to each production—has not created the productions. Nor are the fundamental differences in the productions accounted for by a process of evolution or the chance result of simple cooperation. The explanation lies clearly in the work of the director and the contributing artists and craftspeople. The playwright begins with an impulse or a feeling that is transmuted into the expressive form of a play; the director begins with a response upon confronting the playwright's work. When a director give form to impulses resulting from that confrontation, he or she creates a production.

This confrontation accounts for the many productions of *Hedda Gabler* that may be vastly different and yet remain valid and artistic renderings of Ibsen's play.

This is not to say that *any* rendering of *Hedda Gabler* must be considered either valid or effective. The creation of an image or interpretation and its imposition on a play constitute no necessary claim to validity. There must be an *essential* relationship between the created form of the play and the created form of the production. It is in an honest and imaginative confrontation between director and text, and drawing upon the creative contributions of actors, designers and technicians, that a truly artistic and theatrically effective production can result.

> **Our goal in this text is to develop methods to stimulate the director's imagination and techniques for translating the resulting images into production elements.**

DISCUSSION

1. What would be the implications in terms of your audience and the *idea* of contemporary theatre if you could direct an Ibsen play *exactly* as the playwright had envisioned it?

2. What happens to the plays themselves when directors can do *anything* they want and pawn that off as the playwright's intention?

3. In this chapter begins a list of important directors in the American and European theatres. Mention any productions by these directors, or other facts that you have discovered from other sources.

To begin with, the playwright is the director's

closest collaborator.

—**Harold Clurman,** *On Directing*

THE DIRECTOR, THE PLAYWRIGHT, AND THE THEATRICAL EVENT

HAROLD CLURMAN 1901–1980 (U.S.)	Broadway. *The Member of the Wedding, Bus Stop, Waltz of the Toreadors.* Founding member and chronicler of the Group Theatre. Director and critic. Wrote *The Fervent Years* and *On Directing.*

Defining the director's task is a difficult and subtle job. We will try first to come to an understanding of where the director stands in the creative process, particularly as he or she relates to the playwright and the playscript.

The explanations that follow define five possible functions of the director in the process of making a production. The first two are broadly "editorial" in describing the place and function of the director as subservient to the playwright or the playscript. The remaining three view the director's place and function as "creative"; the playscript is viewed as one element among many the director uses in composing a production.

Editorial Direction: Two Cases

A director who sees the work only as an intermediate step between playwright and audience, who views herself or himself simply as an interpreter and faithful translator of the written word, need meet only two criteria: fidelity and clarity. Indeed, directors and critics who view theatre art as a subspecies of literature are apt to look upon anything in a production beyond fidelity and clarity as self-serving and vulgar adulterations of the artwork.

The most obvious type of "editorial" direction is that in which

1. the director is a functionary, a medium through which the playwright communicates more or less directly with the audience. In such a case, the director functions as an editor or proofreader, charged with ensuring that a "clean copy" of the playwright's creation reaches the public. In fact, some successful and respected directors have described their work in exactly these terms.

2. In another type of "editorial" relationship, the director is seen in a less passive role—as one who attempts to improve clarity, style, and effectiveness in the manner of a creative editor. In such a situation, the director becomes more than the medium of the playwright's communication, and yet remains less than an authentic creative artist.

The *editorial* director aims at communicating the playwright's intentions to an audience through the clear and faithful presentation of a playscript in the theatre. Such direction also might be called "anecdotal," since it presents the play's incidents in a straightforward manner.

Editorial direction, by subjugating the director to the playwright, puts close limits on directorial choices. Indeed, a director working in such a mode eliminates his or her own choices and possibilities by deferring to the instructions of the playwright.

PRINCIPLES OF EDITORIAL DIRECTION

Adherence to Existing Theatrical Conventions

The director employs those conventions in place at the time of production. If the play's composition is of a different time or place, the conventions at the time of composition or original production are often employed, though almost invariably altered and modified by existing conventions. Thus the productions of England's William Poel around the turn of the century can be said to have replaced conventionalized nineteenth century *pictorial style* staging of Shakespeare with conventionalized nineteenth century *Elizabethan style* staging. One convention replaced another.

A writer such as Shaw encourages the director to employ the editorial mode by means of extensive notes and detailed descriptions of characters, costumes, and settings.
Play: *You Never Can Tell* **Author:** George Bernard Shaw **Theatre:** South Coast Repertory **Director:** David Emmes **Set Designer:** **Cliff Faulkner** **Costumes:** Shigeru Yaji **Lighting:** Peter Maradudin **Actors (l to r):** Tom Harrison, I.M. Hobson, Sally Spencer (Photo by Ron M. Stone)

Direction in the "editorial" mode aims at delivering the playwright's image of the play in production. Here the casting of the actor playing Bo, his costuming, his body language and the set all contrive to create that image.
Play: *Bus Stop* **Author:** William Inge **Theatre:** Heritage Repertory Theatre **Director:** Robert Ingham **Set Designer:** Charles Caldwell **Costumes:** Rosemary Ingham **Actor:** Steve Andresen **Lighting:** Michael Rourke

Adherence to Stage Directions

The director rigidly follows pre-existing stage directions; these may be the work of the playwright, an editor, or even a stage manager who recorded the directions of an early production. The assumption here, as in the case of theatrical convention, is that there is a "right" way, and that way is most likely to be the one closest to the playwright in time and space.

Evenness of Execution

The director makes an effort to balance production elements and performances so that no single component calls attention to itself and distracts from the unfolding of incident in the play.

Immediate Justification

The director emphasizes causal relationships and holds the laws of probability sacred.

Neutrality

The director tries to avoid, submerge, or disguise directorial bias, personal style, or point of view.

Editorial direction at its best results in clearly executed productions that give the playscript an uncluttered linear theatrical structure with no frayed edges or discordant elements. Like a good editor, the director in this mode delivers a "clean copy." The playwright seems to have a direct and unencumbered communication with the audience. Can such an approach be faulted? Its aims seem honest and sincere. Most playwrights would probably suggest this is the only defensible approach. Most directors would applaud the goals and quibble with only a few of the means.

> **Some of the methods implicit in the *editorial* mode are so obviously effective and valid that directors, regardless of their theoretical or artistic pretensions, ignore them at their own hazard.**

The editorial approach is ideally well-crafted, straightforward, and professional. The resulting production may well communicate—and do so with great effectiveness.

Creative Direction

There is yet another approach to posit, one that regards direction as something other than communication of the playwright's presumed intent through a theatrical medium and the director as something more than a functionary. We call this approach "creative."

> Creative direction alters the relative positions of director and playwright in a radical way because it is based upon the following assertion: *The director is the artist who creates an artwork—the theatrical production.*

Now, entirely different structures emerge:

WORKING THROUGH THE SCRIPT

The director is seen as an artist whose impulse to create mandates working through the selected medium, in this case the playscript.[1] The script becomes simply one element of the theatrical medium; although it is a work of art in itself, it is not considered a piece of *theatre art* until it is produced.

RESHAPING THE TEXT

The director using greater discretionary powers, may employ the script as raw material for the production, and the text may be altered to suit the director's choices.

Here the playwright's original script is put at the service of the director. The director uses improvisation or other means to find a new impulse or direction. The playwright may then be employed to shape those discoveries into sce-

---

[1]The fact that often the director is employed by a producer *after* the script has been chosen does not invalidate this basic notion any more than the fact that he was commissioned to do a portrait invalidates Leonardo's function as artist in that case.

Whether the director's interpretation of the script is apparently conventional (as in this *Oedipus*) or unexpected (as in this *Uncle Vanya*), every production is unique.

Play: *Oedipus* **Authors:** Adapted from Sophocles by Abigail Adams and Lee Devin **Theatre:** People's Light and Theatre Company **Director:** Abigail Adams **Set Designer:** James F. Pyne, Jr. **Costumes:** Marla J. Jurglanis **Lighting:** James F. Pyne, Jr. **Actors (l to r):** Stephen Novelli, Alda Cortese (background), Carla Belver (Photo by Gerry Goodstein)

Play: *Uncle Vanya* **Author:** Anton Chekhov **Theatre:** The Guthrie Theater **Director:** Garland Wright **Set Designer:** Douglas Stein **Costumes:** Martin Pakledinaz **Lighting:** Marcus Dilliard **Actors (l to r):** Richard Grusin, Cristine Rose, Stephen Yaokam (Photo by Michael Daniel)

narios, or dialogue scenes. Examples of this approach have been observed in the work of New York's avant-garde Performing Garage and the Living Theatre, and in some of the productions of Britain's Joan Littlewood (as described in the case of Frank Norman's *Fings Ain't Wot They Used T'Be*, in *Directors on Directing*, pp. 393–94).

JOAN LITTLEWOOD 1913– (Great Britain)	London fringe theatres—Theatre Workshop, and others. *The Hostage, Oh, What a Lovely War, A Taste of Honey.* Famed for social/political consciousness and work with ensemble improvisational technique.

WORKING WITH THE PLAYWRIGHT

Finally, there is a kind of creative direction that presumes joint control of the production elements by playwright and director.

Many view this as the proper working relationship. Ideally, the two artists share the creative work in design and rehearsal decisions. They hope the production resulting from their interaction is finer than either alone could have achieved. In most first productions of a play where the director has an established reputation, this relationship is the one that promises the best hope of success. (It is the working method of choice for producing new plays.)

In deciding whether to function in the editorial mode or the creative mode, the director defines his or her relationship to the task, to the medium, and to the contributing artists.

DEFINING THE WORKING METHOD

	→	**The Task** *(To edit or create)*
THE DIRECTOR *defined in relation to:*	→	**The Medium** *(The relative inviolability of the script, the theatrical space)*
	→	**The Collaborators** *(Actors, designers)*

In defining the relationship of the director to the playscript, and thus to the playwright, we make some fundamental decisions about philosophy and method. The last two cases described above represent opposite poles of creative direction—from one completely free of constraints imposed by the script to another where the need for the playwright's direct participation and approval is essential. While these two working methods are in use, the most common is what we have called "working through the script." Of the three "creative" possibilities, this approach has the broadest implications and most useful applications. It is the method we will concentrate on throughout this textbook.

Principles of Creative Direction: *Working Through the Script.*

Considering the playscript as a vital and inviolable element of the medium, the creative director usually accepts a number of working principles:

1. **Respect for the script.** Since the director *chooses* the script as the basis for the production, he or she respects the integrity of that material. Therefore a director will cut or alter a text only in extreme circumstances and after serious consideration. Even then, the director understands that alteration is probably the result of the director's shortcomings rather than those of the script. Also, changing the text too early in the process of preparing the production can sometimes cause more problems than it cures. This is especially true when dealing with plays by master playwrights.

2. **The playscript as the source of the production.** The playscript deserves respect not only in the matter of its expression—words, scenic progression, plot, incident, and the like—but also in its *expressive force*—its inner life, its symbology, its patterns and rhythms. This expressive force is neither as self-evident nor as constant, as *expression* can be thought to be. Since the expressive force of a playscript works on and through an interpreter, the director, it changes from person to person and from time to time. These changes may seem profound and sweeping, but are never truly *radical* if the playscript itself has not been violated—that is to say, if the script itself provides the expressive force or inspiration for the production. Thus *Hedda Gabler* may be produced in a variety of forms which, though they vary immensely, are *all* potentially valid artistic statements of the same play.

3. **The director's imagination and craft as the medium of expression of the production's meaning.** The director works with available materials and collaborators; they influence, in turn, the created form of the production. Indeed, a single director may produce the same playscript in a variety of forms reflecting either a change in materials or perspective, or both. A change in materials can involve any of the production elements: cast, designers, or theatre. A change in perspective can be marked by a shift in public or private interests, by new information, by different philosophical or aesthetic considerations, or by any other change in the director's knowledge or sensibilities. In every case, though, the production that appears upon the modern stage is the result ultimately of imagination and interpretation.

The Director's Resources

The director, wishing to work in a creative mode, should possess a wide range of talents and capabilities. The following list, while not exhaustive, is indicative of that range:

- **Craft Skills:** textual analysis, staging dynamics, performance rhythms, performance structure.
- **Imagination:** specifically, the capacity to find and communicate imagery (that is, by analogy and metaphor), and to evoke those images in the theatre.
- **Collaborative Sense:** essentially interpersonal skills, including the ability to use the resources and techniques of actors, designers, and technicians.
- **Actor Coaching Skills:** the ability to draw from the actor's creative and satisfying performances through a combination of sensitivity, insight, and grasp of the actor's methods and tools.
- **Theatrical Knowledge:** a working grasp of dramatic literature and theatrical periods and styles.
- **Broad Sensibilities:** a consciousness of the world beyond the theatre, including a knowledge of and sensitivity to the other arts, and extending to such fields as science, politics, and society.
- **Organizational and Executive Skills:** including an ability to identify and deal with administrative and public relations problems as well as artistic ones.
- **Ego:** essentially, the artistic temperament—the self-security necessary to make and, in some cases, defend creative judgments.

Obviously, the development of even a fraction of one's potential in all of these areas is the work of years, but the work is necessary and the rewards as limitless as the task.

The Director's Medium

> If theatre is an art realized in production, then the modern director is the artist who makes it.

The above statement in no way denigrates or minimizes the contributions of the playwright, the actors, the designers, or anyone else. Their contributions to the production are indispensable and affect the production in the most profound ways. The work of these artists provides the *material* the director uses in composing a theatrical production.

An art to be experienced in the fullness of a performance, theatre has its own unity and integrity. It is, according to Suzanne Langer, "neither a hybrid product pieced together at the demand of many interests, nor a synthesis of all the arts—not even of a more modest several." (*Feeling and Form,* pp.365–66) A theatre performance moves in time and space, its expressive force the result of images made of visual, aural, and kinetic compositions and patterns. These the director shapes in rehearsals and conferences with fellow artists.

In *blocking* the action of a scene with the actors, the director is involved in one of the most intricate and subtle of creative tasks. At one level, there is the attempt to meld the anecdotal requirement of the text, the visual elements of the design of set, lights, and costumes, and the physical and emotional requirements—the very *presence*—of the actors. To the director falls the job of orchestrating all these elements so that each scene appears to be unified, clear, and coherent. A seamless and objective production is the ultimate goal of the editorial mode of directing. Like the musician who hits all the notes in the correct sequence and tempos, the editorial director is a fair technician or craftsperson, but such a director's work often lacks a compelling vision. Most good directors, like most good musicians, seek to express feelings in their work beyond mere accuracy and clarity. The musician uses the qualities and possibilities of the instrument, the musical composition, personal passion, and technical resources to coax forth a performance that is honest, individual, and artistic. Creative direction goes beyond the editorial to form a production that expresses a unique and personal vision or feeling.

Again, it is important to note that it is virtually impossible to do otherwise. In *Understanding Playscripts,* Roger Gross describes "The Fallacy of Neutral Performance"—the mistaken notion that a performance can somehow take place without interpretation. (pp.17–18) The *creative director* accepts the fact that neutrality is impossible and welcomes the challenge to interpret and communicate feeling and meaning through the theatrical medium. The creative director establishes a structure of images and patterns for a production and uses the expressive means at hand, namely the visual, aural, and kinetic elements of the production.

THE DIRECTOR'S VISUAL DESIGN

The modern director is responsible for the visual unity and the aesthetic statement of the *look* of a production as surely as was the Duke of Saxe-Meiningen. Unlike the Duke, however, the contemporary director might not personally create the designs. The modern director must participate in the designs to make certain they are integrated into the total production design and be more than merely anecdotal and decorative. The director must integrate the visual elements of the production into the theatrical creation much as the painter uses color, line, and mass and the sculptor uses volume, space, and texture to produce and modulate their own artistic expressions.

Play: *The Merchant of Venice* **Author:** William Shakespeare **Theatre:** The Shakespeare Theatre at the Folger **Director:** Michael Langham **Actors (l to r):** Kelly McGillis, Marcia Cross (Photo by Joan Marcus)

Play: *Tonight at 8:30* **Author:** Noel Coward **Theatre:** Alabama Shakespeare Festival **Director:** Daniel Kern **Set Designer:** Robert Wolin **Costumes:** James B. Greco **Lighting:** Karen S. Spahn **Actors (l to r):** Ty Smith, Barbara Beatty-Shrawder (Photo by Scarsbrook)

The directors of these productions have collaborated with their designers and actors to give each production a particular look, sound, and movement. These elements express the production's meaning and effect.

THE DIRECTOR'S AURAL DESIGN

The creative director also functions as a musician, controlling tempo, rhythm, pitch, harmony, and dissonance. Perhaps the least appreciated of the elements, the *music* of a performance is one of the most subtle and pervasive. This *music* is in no way limited to conventional and obvious musical statements. It extends to sound effects, the pitch, quality and use of the actor's voices, even to the timing of exits, entrances, curtains, lights. Jacques Copeau notes that "a good script, a play that is well written for acting on the stage, contains time spans—movements and rhythms—comparable to those in music." (Quoted in *Directors on Directing,* p. 222) Indeed, a production—occurring in time—creates its own music, a powerful and persuasive element in communicating the meaning and force of the performance.

THE DIRECTOR'S KINETIC DESIGN

The choreographer creates moving images in space and time to express powerful emotions. The director does the same, even if not in so obvious and abstract a way. For the director, the kinetic elements of production—actors, scenery, props, lights, and sometimes even the audience—blend with and complement the aural and visual elements to produce what we recognize as a theatrical creation.

A directorial vision of the play is expressed in every element of the director's design through the collaboration of all the designers and actors.
Play: *Hamlet* **Author:** William Shakespeare **Theatre:** The Guthrie Theater **Director:** Garland Wright **Set Designer:** Doug Stein **Costumes:** Ann Hould-Ward **Lighting:** Jim Ingalls **Actor:** Zeljko Ivanek (Photo by Joe Giannetti)

Although the choreographic function of the director is seldom noted, its importance cannot be overlooked. It is no accident that many of today's best-known and most influential stage directors are choreographers. Their sensitivity to the visual, aural, and, especially, the kinetic design of theatrical production is much more keenly developed than that of the conventional stage director.

The Theatrical Event

"I can take any empty space and call it a bare stage."
—Peter Brook

Let us experiment with Peter Brook's notion. Suppose you are seated in a theatre. *There is nothing going on, no set on the stage, no props, no light except for the bare-bulb worklight. You look up and see someone—a technician or stagehand, probably—walk across the stage from left to right and disappear into the wings.*

What has happened? Nothing much. A bit of life perhaps, but it didn't *mean* anything.

But—suppose that once again you are seated in the same theatre. Before you is an empty space. Then the dim glow of the lights overhead fades to darkness for a moment, and a bare-bulb worklight begins to glow. Someone enters and walks across the stage and disappears into the wings.

This time, you have seen an act of theatre. Someone has taken an empty space and called it a stage. And you have understood. Now—somehow—the action you have witnessed *means something*. Brook says, "A man walks across this empty space whilst someone else is watching him, and this is all that is needed for an act of theatre to be engaged." (p. 9)

We agree, but we are faced with a clear paradox. How can it be true in the second case and not in the first?

There is one essential difference. In the second instance, someone has announced a creative intention to make an expressive statement and translated that intention into a form—in this case a theatre piece.

> TO MAKE THEATRE: The essentials are place, actors, action, audience, AND *an agreement that there is to be a theatrical event*.

In the first instance above, all elements but the last are present, and so the result has no meaning—at least in terms of art. In the second, the agreement is engaged. The director has said, "Here it is; it is beginning now. Watch." We do, and what we see and hear becomes significant. In the first case, the direction, the tempo, the quality of the person's cross is meaningful only in terms of the person doing the action. Perhaps she is going to get a wrench, or to leave a note. These possibilities might engage our attention and interest; they might even be important. But they have no other meaning. In the second case, though, everything is charged with significance. We find ourselves paying close attention not only to *what* is happening but *how*. Now, whether the cross is left to right or right to left becomes important; so does the tempo and rhythm of the move, and the sound (or lack of it). Suppose an offstage noise is heard. Is it part of the scene or not? We make a quick judgment. If it is part of the theatrical event, it means something. If not, it is simply a distraction—an accident. In some cases theatre can cease for a longer period of time. Almost everyone has seen an instance of a suspension of the theatrical event. Perhaps an actor forgets a line or fails to make an entrance, or something outside the theatrical event takes over—something happens in the audience or outside the theatre that intrudes upon and destroys the created act for a time. Such events merely underscore the fact that the created form is making specialized demands upon our attention.

How and why does this phenomenon exist? Anyone who wants to work seriously in the theatre must consider it, especially someone who wants to be a director.

This little experiment leads to some radical assumptions about the creation and communication of theatre art.

First, *the work must be defined*. There are specific limits of time and space analogous to the length of a symphony or the frame of a picture. The theatre event begins and ends where the artists specify. In the second example we proposed, there is no theatrical act until the signal is given; it did not exist offstage, and it will not continue after the final curtain (or whatever convention marks its end).

Second, *every element of the theatrical event has significance*. Within the established frames of time and space, nothing is incidental or meaningless. If something occurs that is irrelevant to the created form, the theatrical event ceases. The level of consciousness and attention of everyone present is changed until the irrelevancy is past.

Third, *each theatrical event is unique and exists only in the present*. Because there is a flow of energy from performer to performer, from audience member to audience member, and from audience to performer and back again, the exact circumstances of any given performance can never be replicated.

End Note

Every director planning a production sets up a working relationship with the play and also with the *very idea of theatre*. As you learn about the art of theatrical directing, you will constantly be faced with essential philosophical questions. "What does this mean?" "How does it mean?" "How can I get this actor or designer to create something true and exciting?" "If I change this part of the performance, does that violate some principle I ought to respect?" "What if I can't think of myself as an artist, but I still want to direct plays?"

I have written an armature, inside which, possibly, are the deepest ideas which have never quite formulated themselves in my consciousness. If, as I hope and believe, I am a poet, there will be something in these, but I am the last person to know what it is.

—James Bridie

2 THE PRODUCTION MATRIX

The director designs and shapes the visual, aural, and kinetic patterns of the production using text, actors, designs, and technical resources. The complexity and subtlety of this task demands some sort of plan or reference to lend it form and coherence.

Metaphors and Models

In our efforts to understand and work with abstractions in a wide range of activities, including theatre, we invariably use *metaphors* and *models*.

> A *metaphor* is a perceived likeness that, when expressed, communicates a new and different way of knowing or viewing a subject.

> A *model* is a construct that enables us to see things from a certain perspective, to perceive relationships, and to predict results.

Metaphors allow us to express and order processes and phenomena that we cannot control or communicate in any other way.

There are *models* relating to science, mathematics, and philosophy. Scientific models may be purely theoretical, or they may actually take on three-dimensional form. For example, in their search to understand the structure of the DNA molecule, scientists James Watson and Francis Crick assembled many three-dimensional models hoping to find the one structure that answered all the tests. At one point, they had constructed a model that seemed perfectly adequate. In spite of all the scientific justifications for the validity of their hypothesis, however, Crick had a serious misgiving about the structure they had devised. It was not "pretty."

The scientist's intuition proved correct. The model was faulty. Crick knew that all natural structures and processes are based on an order and integrity that endows them with a natural elegance. His suspicion that the theoretical construct lacked this quality was far from frivolous; it was profound. Like Crick, Watson was convinced that the satisfactory model of the DNA molecule must reflect a natural finesse. When he found a design that was "aesthetically elegant," he concluded, "a structure this pretty just had to exist." (*The Double Helix,* p. 205) Watson was right. The model proved to be scientifically accurate and is, indeed, "pretty."

Directors (indeed, all artists) can draw a valuable lesson from this scientific insight. In making a created form whose very aim and purpose is the ordering and communication of feeling, the integrity of the work—expressed in the elegance and beauty of its form—is essential.

Everyday, we see the importance of conceptual models in the processes of knowing, organizing our knowledge and intuitions, and communicating with others. In the theatre we consistently use metaphors to formulate our intuitions and models to organize and communicate them. The two things work together—content and form—as creative complements.

In the nineteenth century, writer-philosopher Émile Zola and other theorists worked out a behavioral model called Naturalism and a variant called Realism. Playwrights adopted the new ideas with a vengeance. Secure in the notion that objective observation can reveal truth, they began to write plays examining the internal springs of human behavior and the influence of society and the physical environment upon individuals. (One of the most influential of this new breed of playwrights was Henrik Ibsen, whose *Hedda Gabler* was mentioned earlier.) In the theatre, Antoine and Stanislavski translated psychological models into new approaches to acting and production. The residual effects of these pioneering efforts remain firmly in place. Directors since Stanislavski have been so strongly influenced by the use of psychological models that it now has become virtually unassailable. The presumptive foundation for the psychological model in the theatre can be stated thus: *"Plays deal with human action. Psychological and behavioral sciences explain human actions. Therefore, psychological and behavioral sciences can explain plays."* Or, at least, the theories and observations of these sciences suggest how to interpret and understand the plays.

No one can fault this line of reasoning. The psychological model is a powerful and useful one. Among other things, it has given us insights into not only the work of modern playwrights, but of the classical authors as well. The inner working of the human spirit has always been the subject of great playwrights. Shakespeare is the obvious example, but so are such different writers as Molière and Eugene O'Neill. Freud learned much psychology from the Greek tragedians—and not only from Sophocles's *Oedipus*. Certainly Euripides was a master of psychology; one need read only *Medea, Electra,* or *The Bacchae* to be convinced of that.

Still, the insistent, self-conscious use of psychological models to *interpret* plays and characters for production is a modern phenomenon. Other models served for centuries and continue to be explored in the modern theatre. As already noted, at the very time Stanislavski was exploring the frontiers of psychological realism in the Russian theatre, Eugene Vahktangov and Vsevelod Meyerhold were experimenting with theatrical models from "fantastic realism" to "biomechanics."

Eugene Vahktangov 1883–1922 (Russia)	Moscow. *The Dyybuk, Turandot.* Champion of what he termed "fantastic realism," a sort of marriage between Stanislavski's style and the pure theatricalism of Meyerhold.
Vsevelod Meyerhold 1874–1942 (Russia)	*The Inspector General, The Bedbug, The Proposal, The Bear.* Brilliant proponent of theatricalism. Meyerhold experimented with constructivism and an approach to acting he called "bio-mechanics."

Today, the modern director employs an ongoing and vigorous eclecticism, using the wide range of choices that gives the best contemporary theatre its unique energy. Part of what keeps this movement alive is the international quality of theatre today. Influential directors come from all over the world—from Britain, like Trevor Nunn; from Eastern Europe, like Jerzy Grotowski (Poland) and Liviu Ciulei (Romania); from the U.S., like Garland Wright; and from Western Europe, like Pina Bausch (Germany). When such artists as these undertake to direct a production, the possibilities are wide open. Each will find an inspiration and a method that suits the play, the time, the company, the theatre, and the director's own thinking and feeling. The inspiration might be drawn from primitive ritual, from bio-mechanics, from dance, from Kabuki, from almost any source. When we suggest that the modern theatre became inevitable as an outgrowth of fragmentation and the resulting proliferation of choices, this is what we mean.

TREVOR NUNN 1940– (Great Britain)	London and Broadway. *Hamlet, Nicholas Nickleby, Cats, Les Misèrables*. Artistic Director of the Royal Shakespeare Company since 1968.
LIVIU CIULEI 1923– (Romania)	Bucharest, New York, and U.S. regional theatres—Arena Stage and the Guthrie. *Leonce and Lena, The Tempest, Hamlet, A Midsummer Night's Dream*. Noted for visually and intellectually exciting postmodernist stagings of Shakespeare and Chekhov. "Theatre is play."
GARLAND WRIGHT 1946– (U.S.)	Regional theatre: Arena Stage, Artistic Director of the Guthrie Theatre. *K—Impressions of the Trial, Vanities, On the Verge*. Working to create a major acting ensemble dedicated to the classics.
PINA BAUSCH 1940– (West Germany)	The Tanztheater of Wuppertal. *Rite of Spring, Seven Deadly Sins, Bluebeard*. A leading choreographer-director whose dance dramas depict personal and political struggles between the sexes.

The Directorial Matrix

The modern director first finds or creates a *metaphor,* then constructs a *model* to give each production a sense of organic integrity and structure. This notion has been described variously as *concept, image, interpretation,* or simply *ap-*

proach. There is nothing particularly wrong with any of these terms, but none suggests the *metaphor/model* idea that precisely describes how the contemporary director works. One term that has the advantage of freshness and precision in describing this aspect of the director's function is *matrix*. The term is appropriated from Suzanne Langer, who uses it to describe a critical step in the creative process in music:

> The matrix, in music the fundamental movement of melody or harmonic progression which establishes the greatest rhythm of the piece and dictates its scope, is born of the composer's thought and feeling. . . . That is why one may puzzle for a long time over the exact form of an expression, not seeing what is wrong with this or that, and then, when the right form presents itself, feel it going into place almost with a click. Since the emotional content of it is not clearly preconceivable without any expression, the adequacy of the new element cannot be measured by it with anything like the precision and certainty of that intuitive click. It is the commanding form of the work that guarantees such a judgment. (*Feeling and Form*, pp. 122–23)

In directing, we define the term *matrix* as the principal image *(metaphor)* that imparts a fundamental shape or design *(model)* to the production.

A directorial matrix suggests an essential shape for a production that may be expressed overtly, as shown here to surprising effect in an opera usually presented in Baroque settings and costumes.
Play: *Don Giovanni* **Author:** Wolfgang Amadeus Mozart **Theatre:** Boston Opera Theater, Plaza Media, and Austrian Television **Director:** Peter Sellars **Actors (l to r):** Eugene Perry, Ai Lan Zhu (Photo by Ali Schafler)

In short, the directorial matrix expresses the director's guiding structure in creating a production and is analogous to Stanislavski's *spine* applied to an actor's characterization. It is the statement of a metaphor/model that both describes the director's intuition and suggests the form of its expression. It is derived from the director's response to the text in the light of the other production elements—actors, designers, technicians, theatre space, time, and even budgetary constraints. That response is conditioned by personal experience, instincts, and technique. The director employs the matrix as the formative principle underlying the production by making choices and decisions suggested by the matrix or in reference to it.

The paradox of the matrix (as Langer points out) is that by specifying and apparently limiting the range of the director's choices, it actually opens up possibilities by suggesting specific avenues for development. When it is understood that this development very often follows a pattern more *fractal*[1] than *linear,* the director can develop the production using patterns and images that reflect organic creation (sculpture) rather than scientific structure (engineering).

Surely, many directors have felt that "intuitive click" Langer describes—the flash of awareness, a sense of knowing when something is *right.* The matrix—confirmed by that intuitive flash—can illuminate the shape and texture of a potential production and shed light on the details of its expression whenever questions or problems arise. The term *matrix,* used in Langer's sense and applied to the work of the director, can be understood as a sculptor's skeletal framework or mold. In this sense, the matrix is an armature upon which an artwork is built. In the theatre, the directorial matrix settles most ambiguities about the essential form of the production and provides the artist with a reference and guide to the fulfillment of the created form.

DEFINITION AND USE OF THE DIRECTORIAL MATRIX

The Matrix Is

- the skeleton, armature, framework, model, or mold used to give a production a particular form.

---

[1]The term *fractal* is derived from a mathematical concept that can be used to describe the forms of many natural phenomena, including plants, trees, and the shapes and contours of many inanimate phenomena—crystals, mountains, wave patterns. The important consideration of the notion of fractals here is that it can be used to account for the fundamental formative principle of things in nature and in art that display patterns of repetition and modulation to produce a result. A snowflake is one example: basic patterns are repeated, altered in some way, and built by accumulation or branching into the final form.

In Chapter III, we discuss something like *fractals* in considering the action of a single *beat,* a scene, an entire play as repetitions of a underlying structure.

The director employs the fractal metaphor by repeating and modulating forms—positions on stage, business, sound, and movement patterns—in the manner of motifs or *leitmotifs* to create a particular impression or feeling.

- the statement of a metaphorical principle that describes the quality of the basic statement, feeling, action, atmosphere, and relationships in the play in terms that can be realized in production.
- complex, affecting choices and decisions at every level—in the visual, kinetic, and aural elements of design and execution.
- related to notions expressed in other contexts as "concept," "commanding form," "total idea," "expressive form," "directorial design," "organic form."
- a construct that grows out of the play and the director's vision and operates within the promise and limitations of the materials at hand.
- a concept that provides an inevitable and radical connection between the content of the theatrical materials and the created form.
- capable of validation or vindication only in the actual creation of the production.

The Matrix Is Not

- a statement of the director's choice of period.
- a pronouncement of a generalized quality, relationship, or action.
- a declaration of intention or objectives—for or by characters, playwright, or director.
- a description of any element or combination of elements.
- simple—affecting only one aspect of the production.
- imposed arbitrarily without an essential and radical interplay between form and content.
- wholly defensible as an intellectual exercise.

DESCRIBING A MATRIX: SOME MODERN EXAMPLES

Nicholas Nickleby (The Royal Shakespeare Company production, directed by Trevor Nunn and John Caird, 1980): A company improvises the melodramatic narrative of a young man's serial confrontations with good and evil.

JOHN CAIRD 19– (Great Britain)	London and Broadway. *Nicholas Nickleby, Les Misérables.* Co-director with Trevor Nunn at the Royal Shakespeare Company.

The Tragedy of Carmen (produced in the United States at Lincoln Center, directed by Peter Brook, 1982): A primitive folk-tale of passion and betrayal enacted for the members of the community.

Bye-Bye, Birdie (directed by Gower Champion, 1961): A teen-age musical comic book ("Archie Comics") depicting adolescent hero-worship and rejection of parental values.

GOWER CHAMPION 1921–1980 (U.S.)	Broadway. *Bye-Bye, Birdie; Hello, Dolly; 42nd Street.* Brilliant Broadway choreographer and innovative director; winner of two Tony Awards for direction and choreography.

Equus (Broadway production directed by John Dexter, 1973): Modern science confronts the powerful gods of primitive impulses in a ritual arena between the past and the present.

JOHN DEXTER 19– (Great Britain)	London, Broadway. *Equus, M Butterfly, The Threepenny Opera.* Theatrical productions—visually stunning and steeped in myth and ritual.

Tartuffe (Arena Stage production directed by Lucian Pintilie, 1985): In a time-machine world, the devil seduces and shatters humanity over the centuries until the mechanism self-destructs.

LUCIAN PINTILIE 1930– (Romania)	Bucharest, Paris, and U.S. regional theatres—Arena Stage and the Guthrie. *The Seagull, Tartuffe, The Cherry Orchard.* Bold, irascible, and innovative post-modernist director.

Sweeney Todd (directed by Hal Prince, 1979): A Brecht and Weill variation on Victorian melodrama; a case study of social disorder and convolution.

HAL PRINCE 1928– (U.S.)	Broadway. A *Funny Thing Happened on the Way to the Forum, Candide, Company, Phantom of the Opera.* Recipient of more than a dozen Tony awards

as director and producer; principal collaborator of composer Stephen Sondheim.

King Lear (directed by Peter Brook, 1962): The world grinds to a halt and gradually crumbles in a manner inspired by Jan Kott's images of Samuel Beckett's *Endgame*.

A Delicate Balance (directed by Alan Schneider, 1966): Caught in a game that becomes serious, aging children try to hide from the secret terror at the front door.

ALAN SCHNEIDER 1917–1984 (U.S.S.R.-U.S.)	Broadway and Washington, D.C.: Arena Stage. *Waiting for Godot, Who's Afraid of Virginia Woolfe?, A Delicate Balance*. Leading proponent in English of Samuel Beckett and Edward Albee; intensely emotional and intellectual productions.

Richard III (directed by Ariane Mnouchkine, 1981): A Kabuki rendition of the violent use and abuse of power between emperor and samurai.

ARIANE MNOUCHKINE 1934– (France)	Paris: Théâtre du Soleil. *Richard III, L'Age d'Or, Molière*. Bold theatricalism devised with her collaborators *(création collective)*.

(These descriptions are inferences drawn from the images created by each of the productions, not from statements made by the directors.)

UNIQUE ELEMENTS SUGGESTED BY THE MATRIX

The above statements of an inferred directorial matrix carry a strong impression of a unique *quality* or feeling that each production communicated. Specifically, each statement suggests the *created world* in which the play is set, the *dramatic action* of the play, and the *manner* in which the action is depicted. In several cases these things are implicit in *theatrical* metaphors; in others, we see *psychological* forms, *rituals,* and *games.* Note the use of such terms as *improvisation, melodrama, ritual, "musical comic-book,"* and *Kabuki.*

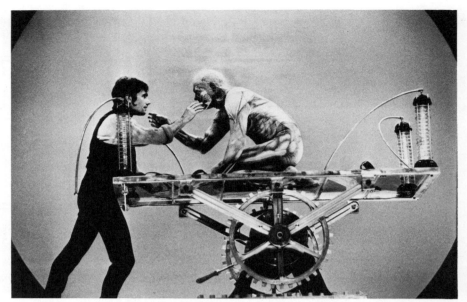

A created world expressing nineteenth century elements in twentieth century forms. Note the ar-chaic machinery executed in sparkling glass and polished metal, the elegant contemporaneity of the costumes and setting.
Play: *Frankenstein—Playing With Fire* **Author:** Barbara Field (from the Mary Shelley novel) **Theatre:** The Guthrie Theater **Director:** Michael Maggio **Costumes:** Jack Edwards **Set Designer:** John Arnone **Light-ing:** Marcus Dilliard **Actors (l to r):** Curzon Dobell, John Carroll Lynch (Photo by Joe Giannetti)

The *created world* invoked carries suggestions, at least, of the environment and atmosphere: possible locales, visual compositions, and color palettes. Going only slightly further, one begins to imagine the lighting, sound, and movement.

Each matrix statement also implies the principal or *core* dramatic action of the play, and suggests, either directly or indirectly, the forces that oppose or hin-der the action.

The *character* of the participants is projected in an image, or implied through the definition of the universe or the action. In *A Delicate Balance,* for ex-ample, the characters are clearly labelled in the matrix statement. In *Sweeney Todd,* they are obviously intended to be the various stock characters of the world of the Victorian melodrama.

EXERCISES AND DISCUSSION

1. In each of the matrix statements above, list the image that describes or implies the three essential elements of *created world, dramatic action,* and *character* of the participants.

2. Formulate a statement of directorial matrix based on a production you have seen. (Try to derive the statement from what you *observed* in the

production, not from your own notions of what the production ought to have done.)

3. From the productions listed above, select one in which neither the play nor the production described is familiar to you. Describe the kind of place the image statement suggests to your imagination. Have another person ask you for details as you make your way through the descriptions. Use reviews, tapes, photographs, or information from people familiar with the production to discover how the play actually was done.

4. Do the same with character and dramatic action.

5. Discuss the similarities and differences between your assumptions and the actual productions discussed in 3 and 4. Evaluate the extent and significance of your discoveries. What do the similarities and differences suggest about the use of a directorial matrix?

THE PRODUCTION MATRIX: ONE EXAMPLE

> The most important test for a chosen matrix is its *suggestiveness*. The matrix should not only organize and integrate, but it should also open up new vistas and provoke a variety of new ideas and directions.

The brilliant Romanian director sometimes moves a great classic into the future and still manages to evoke the distant past.
Play: *Coriolanus* **Author:** William Shakespeare **Theatre:** McCarter Theatre **Director:** Liviu Ciulei **Actors (center):** Peter Francis James (Photo by Clem Fiori)

The director will be reassured and excited by the "clicks" when a provocative matrix sets off chain reactions of ideas and images. Notice in the example that follows how the images suggested by the matrix are translated into *theatrical* elements.

Production Matrix

The Maids by Jean Genet

A "Black Mass" celebrated by priests who perform the ritual—at once erotic, exculpatory, and sacrificial—not knowing its purpose, its forms, or its outcome.

This matrix immediately suggests the images the director uses as the core of a production. The matrix welds those images into a model that is practical in providing specific theatrical ideas and provocative in opening up a range of eloquent possibilities. Notice how the descriptions that follow all flow from the matrix:

Visual Effect: A chapel setting for a requiem, the bed as altar; a funeral parlor, the bed as bier; a boudoir, sleek and sensual, frightening.

Visual Design: Black lacquered furniture and floor, framed mirrors, shiny satin bedspread. Symmetrical or balanced composition with the bed centerstage. Table at the head of the bed, white or gray candles. Whole scheme achromatic except for flowers—huge, voluptuous arrangements of fragrant blossoms. Few set dressing details and those very spare and precisely placed—brush and comb, large book, incense burner, candles. Maids in black, gray, and white. Madame in pearl-gray lace dress. The dress that Claire puts on, a dark red velvet.

Aural Effect: The sounds of religious services, broken from time to time by an urgency or drive that pushes the formal restraint too far, causing a correction or modulation, a beginning again of a shift in tone or style. The maids' voices, raspy or metallic; whiny but capable of catching the quality of Madame's throaty mellow sounds—perhaps like acolytes speaking once in their own voices and then mimicking the priest's tones.

Aural Design: Hushed, measured tones. Chant. Plain and polyphonic. Breathy and urgent, then self-consciously conversational. Bells. Movements composed and modulated deliberately with clear melodic and rhythmic shape and structure. Perhaps a growing, intense and unpleasant chord at the beginning and end of the action.

Kinetic Effect: Ritualized movement—frightening, but fascinating, confusing but in dead earnest. Everything according to the form. The rites may be effective this time, and so they must be performed with care.

Kinetic Design: Careful and precise actions and gestures, patterned and repeated movement. Mirror images. Vesting, divesting, grooming; everything done with great precision and economy. Consciousness of texture, touch and sensation—very erotic.

The production matrix—sometimes intuitively *felt*—provides the model or skeleton upon which the director will form the production. But the intuitive flash does not always come, and it might come without the support of real conviction. In such cases the director needs a methodology to depend upon, the kind of technique that Stanislavski hoped his *System* would provide for actors: "To make inspiration appear more often than is its wont." The following chapters suggest ways to develop such a technique.

DISCUSSION

1. Describe what you infer to be the nature and quality of the "black mass" described in the production matrix above?

2. How has the director used the matrix in designing the production? How does he seem to have elaborated it, used it as a genuine inspiration? Do the theatrical images seem to flow from the director's matrix in ways that seem organic and inevitable?

3. Discuss the play that might emerge from this matrix? (It might be interesting to hear people not familiar with the play reveal their imaginative responses and surmises as to the qualities and particulars of the play—its characters, the nature of its action, atmosphere, and the like.)

SOURCES FOR THE PRODUCTION MATRIX

A director can create a production matrix and its complementary images using any of three sources: 1) the text of the play and its historical context; 2) associations with and allusions to outside sources; and 3) theatrical discovery and invention.

The first source seems obvious—some would claim it to be the *only* valid source of a production. There can be little quibble with the idea that the text is the *first* source of useful images; but only the most conservative and literal of editorial directors will stop there. Every director must use all three sources in some degree. This is not to suggest, however, that the script is merely a framework on which to hang bits of directorial invention. On the contrary, the goal of any honest director is to find a structure for the play that will allow it scope and vitality as a theatrical performance. That structure or *matrix* is what the director seeks as the basis for translating interpretation into theatrical form. Plot is not enough. Characters are not enough. Nor is the play's moral, intention, or theme. None of these—alone or in concert—provides a *theatrical* structure.

Images, however, do. An image is precise and evocative; it can contain a wealth of possibilities and modulations. Images are the stock and trade of the creative artist.

> **For the director, images provide tools and materials as well as inspiration.**

The text of the play is the first and most obviously reliable source for a director in search of new, concrete, and relevant theatrical images. It is of virtually no value to perceive of those images as simply abstract, literary conceits. Again, we return to the point made by Langer:

> A perfectly free imagination suffers from very lack of pressure; it is in the vague and groping state that precedes the conception of the total form. The great moment of creation is the recognition of the matrix, for in this lie all the motives for the specific work; not all the themes—a theme may be imported if it fits the place—but the tendencies of the piece, the need for dissonance and consonance, novelty and reiteration, length of phrase and timing of cadences (*Feeling and Form,* p. 123).

The translation from perception to form is a difficult process. It has become conventional in many theatres for the director to grope through the play in rehearsal and to study the text in private, searching for solutions and decisions regarding specific problems or details. With designers, the director discusses atmosphere, color, line, physical requirements, and occasionally a *"concept"*—usually some more or less logically styled description of a generalized quality. With the actors, the director begins by mentioning period or theatrical style and then concentrates on psychological motivations and details. Somewhere along the way, the *idea* or concept that was referred to once or twice in design conferences and read-throughs may return, having deteriorated into a vague notion that haphazardly surfaces in bits of business, staging, properties, or costume.

Expressed in such a way, it is little wonder that "concept" direction is scorned by so many. Failing in their efforts to achieve a genuine artistic synthesis, many directors opt instead for arbitrarily "conceptual" productions studded with stylistic irrelevancies and anachronisms. No wonder that in the face of such productions, many directors rein themselves in and try to make a virtue of modest noncommitment. The safe stance is passivity; by claiming a desire to hear only the playwright's voice, directors try to absolve themselves of responsibility for their essential task. If the set and costumes look good and the actors are competent, the director is assumed to be adequate. If the production is well received, he or she is assumed to be excellent. Some directors have responded by attempting merely to "put the show on its feet" in a handsome but unobtrusive way.

Public and critics—even theatre workers—are so inured to complacent direction that they often cannot reliably tell the difference between good, bad, or merely indifferent direction.

End Notes

Is it ever desirable—or even possible—to neutralize the director's imprint on a production? As we have seen, it is difficult even to imagine a production *not* marked by directorial interpretation and technique. A director *must* shape a production through casting, as well as an influence on sets, costumes, lights, movement, visual composition, and performance rhythms. But many directors have been uncomfortable with the notion that a play requires *theatrical* interpretation; that is, a translation into visual, aural, and kinetic performance elements that might not agree with the *reader's* expectations. The problem lies in supposing that the meaning, value, and import of a play can be derived solely from the words of the playwright. If this were so, the process of translating the text into fresh and immediate theatrical forms is not only superfluous, it is also necessarily a distortion. But to work creatively, the director must accept the fact that a play must be interpreted to come alive on the stage. This is the what the playwright asks for in writing a script. The director must learn to respond creatively to a playscript by uncovering its underlying theatrical patterns and structures.

To give the play its due as a director, you must be prepared to use your imaginative *and* your intellectual powers, your capacity to make imaginative associations and decisions. In the terminology of contemporary thought, you must use the *right hemisphere* of your brain—its *affective* capabilities—to search out and develop the essential aesthetic patterns and structures required for theatrical creation.

You will not be alone out there in your search for meaning that is not strictly logical. Even the great classical scholar H.D.F. Kitto acknowledges [in *Greek Tragedy*] the limitations of the strictly linear, or *left hemisphere,* approach when he observes that the meaning expressed in the words of a play may be more akin to the meaning of music or painting than to the meaning conveyed in prose discourse. Another classical scholar, Gerald Else, has suggested [In a talk on "Aeschylean Tragedy," Athens: University of Georgia, 1970] that some Aeschylean odes are impossible to render meaningfully into English for the simple reason that they were written for the *sounds* produced by the chorus speaking the ancient Greek text—the sounds of *threnody,* ritualized wailing and lamentation.

Such observations coming from traditional scholars support the notion that true drama is realized in performance and projects a complex sensual experience that can transcend mere comprehension to achieve the fullness of "meaning" held in a playtext. It is through these means that plays project "forms symbolic of human feeling." In production a play uses action which is seen and heard to create an experience of a "virtual future." This experience makes the play completely unlike a literary form—the novel, for instance, which projects a "virtual past." (*Feeling and Form,* p. 307) For the director, the matrix is the key to making the transition from a written text to a theatrical form, and the means of creating an experience of virtual life expressed in consistent and imaginative patterns and images.

The lines of the play are the only guides the good director or actor needs. What makes the play the author's work is that the lines are really the highlights of a perpetual, progressive action, and determine what can be done with the piece on stage.

—Suzanne K. Langer, *Feeling and Form*

3 UNDERSTANDING THE TEXT

The Playwright's Collaborator

A director who undertakes to produce a play becomes an intimate collaborator with the playwright. Although there may be times playwrights might wish to change it, the fact remains: by writing a play, the author has volunteered, in effect, to work with anyone who steps forward. It is the playwright's act of faith—faith in the theatre. A director is obligated to take this act seriously and return the favor—by placing trust in the playwright's text. The director of *The Cherry Orchard* becomes an intimate collaborator with Anton Chekhov, the director of *Henry V* a collaborator with Shakespeare, the director of *The Oresteia* a collaborator with Aeschylus. One need not ascend to these heights to be overwhelmed by the audacity of the modern director's task; undertaking to direct any worthwhile script requires considerable daring. The director who does not acknowledge this fact and its implications is in the wrong business, or doing plays that are either unworthy or misperceived.

> The director must *earn* the right to take a prominent place in theatrical collaboration with the playwright, the designers, and the actors. That right is merited through understanding, imagination, and craft.

The director has an obligation to grasp the playwright's contribution as clearly and fully as possible, because the script—as we have seen—is the source of the production. The imaginative leap from text to directorial matrix comes from the director's impressions of what the playwright has provided. Armed with an *intellectual and imaginative understanding* of the play's meaning and structure, the director can test the validity and viability of the matrix.

Most often the playwright is not present for advice and consultation as preparation and rehearsals go forward. There is only the text. For the director and the other artists working on a production, however, the only completely relevant resource *is* the text itself. In *On Directing,* Harold Clurman puts it this way:

> There is an analogy with performances of music. We do not hear Bach or Mozart precisely as they were rendered in their day. Our audiences probably would not enjoy them if we did. But such an argument would be an evasion: the analogy will not hold. The director discerns a script's style—the production method best suited to convey its quality and meaning—not through the stage directions set down in the script or through discussion with the author himself, but by what an author has actually written: his plot line and his dialogue. The director then translates his understanding of the material into stage language. When Louis Jouvet was told that his Tartuffe was not Molière's, the actor retorted, "Do you have his telephone number?" (p. 33)

A director's understanding must function on many different levels. It must include not only the "what?" and the "why?" but the "how?" as well. The *how* of a play—its method and structure—opens the channels of communication between director and playwright as perhaps no other question can.

The director has feelings, instincts, intuitions about a play. They come obviously from the script, but *how?* What makes this particular combination of words on a page potentially so exciting, or interesting, or effective, or entertaining, or great? The easy answers begin rolling out: Story. Characters. Theme. Moral. Empathy. Dialogue. Action. Message. Theatricality. Plot. Concept. Language. Verisimilitude. Ideas. Finally, we must admit that no single answer is totally adequate to explain the play's effect. Furthermore, no combination of these easy answers provides a satisfactory explanation. To understand how a play works is to understand how all of its elements are assembled into a single expressive form.

> A director who approaches a play with little understanding and appreciation of the cumulative effect of its elements and method is working in the dark.

Shakespeare wrote great speeches. His words are magical; many of his speeches would be recognized as the work of a master even if found only as parts of works lost and unknown.[1] Suppose, for example, only this fragment were found:

". . . time for such a word.
Tomorrow, and tomorrow, and tomorrow
Creeps in this petty pace from day to day,
To the last syllable of recorded time;
And all our yesterdays have lighted fools
The way to dusty death. Out, o . . ."
                              [*Macbeth*, V,v]

The images here are so compelling, the language so masterful, that we may be sure it would occupy the attention of scholars and provoke widespread admiration. There would be intense speculation about the rest of the poem and about its authorship. Critical consensus would be that the fragment was written by a poet of great power and insight.

The true greatness of the speech, however, lies in its worth as a *theatrical* creation. It is not part of a poem but an element of dramatic art. It is *in* a context, not separated from one. It cannot be fully understood or appreciated simply as a poem. Like any element of an artwork, these lines enrich and are enriched by the context in which they occur. Let us examine that context. Here is the scene to the point where our "fragment" begins:

Act V, Scene v. [*Dunsinane. Within the castle.*]

Enter MACBETH, SEYTON, *and* SOLDIERS, *with drum and colors.*

MACBETH.   Hang out the banners on the outward walls.
The cry is still "They come!" Our castle's strength
Will laugh a siege to scorn. Here let them lie
Till famine and the ague eat them up.
Were they not forced with those that would be ours,
We might have met them dareful, beard to beard,
And beat them backward home.

---

[1]To understand some of the discussions that follow, you should read *Macbeth* by William Shakespeare and *The Foreigner* by Larry Shue.

A cry of women within.

What is that noise?

SEYTON.   It is the cry of women, good my lord.   [*Exit.*]

MACBETH.   I have almost forgot the taste of fears:
The time has been, my senses would have cooled
To hear a night-shriek, and my fell of hair
Would at a dismal treatise rouse and stir
As life were in't. I have supped full with horrors.
Direness, familiar to my slaughterous thoughts, cannot once start
me.

[*Enter* SEYTON.]

Wherefore was that cry?

SEYTON.   The Queen, my lord, is dead.

MACBETH.   She should have died hereafter;
There would have been a . . .

Now the speech *begins* to come into its own. The moments preceding it are loud and thundering, filled with drums, screaming, and bravado. Macbeth proclaims his invulnerability. He has already gone through hell: "I have almost forgot the taste of fears." "I have supped full with horrors./Direness, familiar to my thoughts, cannot once start me." Then, suddenly, the mood is reversed, the braggadocio vanishes.

Outside the play, the speech may indeed be poetry, even great poetry. Placed in the context of the scene where it belongs, it is transcendent, incredibly powerful. In that context, we become aware of the sounds and the smells of battle, of a man proclaiming his dæmonic power at one moment and his shock and anger at the next.[2] We are also vaguely aware of echoes from earlier scenes—repetitions of "time," of "tonight" and "tomorrow," of "later" and "hereafter." Promises once filled with hope and vitality are now cruelly snatched away.

When we see what a good actor can do with such a speech in the context of a *performance,* we are even more convinced of the true power of the theatre. If this is *incidentally* great literature, it is *essentially* great theatre, and Shakespeare is first and foremost a great *playwright.* The gorgeous structure of Macbeth's speech, its resonances with earlier parts of the play, its imaginative and technical virtuosity, are self-evident and seem to support the contention that poetic or exalted language is an essential for important drama. While there is no question that Shakespeare uses his incomparable gift for poetic language as an important tool in his dramaturgy, look what a brilliant *playwright* can do with six Anglo-Saxon monosyllables:

"The Queen, my lord, is dead."

[2]See *Metatheatre* by Lionel Abel for a provocative analysis of tragedy, particularly *Macbeth,* for some understanding of what the term "dæmonic" might suggest to the director and actor.

Seyton is a tiny role so inconsequential that it is often cut, his lines given to someone else. Still, this character is charged with delivering news that will effect a violently dramatic and radical change in the protagonist. Seyton's simple, homely statement delivers a sudden, heavy, and deadly blow to a character who moments before was braying his imperturbable strength to the heavens.

This is playwriting of the highest order, poetry of the theatre.

> To understand a play truly is to understand how it is put together, how each element contributes to its form. We must not suppose that by identifying and abstracting key elements we can adequately explain the play; the playwright's synthesis is critical.

DISCUSSION

Begin with a feeling—a reaction to the preceding speech discussed—and create an image for the scene in which Macbeth speaks "Tomorrow, and tomorrow, and tomorrow." Suggest how the actor, the costume, light, set, and sound designers might contribute to supporting the image and communicating the effect.

Reading a Script

What happens when you read a script for the first time? Even while you are responding to it, savoring its depth or cleverness, you probably are experiencing a separate level of intellectual activity: simply trying to understand what is happening and to keep track of the play's twists and turns. "Who are the characters?" "Where are we now?" "Why is this character climbing through the window when the door is open?" "Is what she is saying true?" All these are efforts to follow the action and the characters the playwright has provided, to understand how this play is put together—how it works. Once these and other questions are answered, they can be put aside and the play appreciated for its other values. A director must take a similar path in the effort to understand a text to be staged in the theatre.

One method of approaching the author's text is to apply the instinctive methods of the play reader to the idea of the play as a created "virtual future." The creation of a future implies *given circumstances*[3] (a starting point—the geo-

[3]Stanislavski's term "given circumstances" is especially useful since it suggests certain elements or presumptions granted by the artist to affect the work at hand. The term "context" is used interchangeably.

graphical, physical, social, moral, intellectual conditions in which the play takes place), *action* (a plot or other structure to support the action sequence), *character(s)* (those who act and are acted upon), and *style* (the manner in which the actions take place).

THE FIRST ELEMENT: GIVEN CIRCUMSTANCES

In one sense, the given circumstances establish the complex environment in which every play, every scene, begins. The action of the play springs from this set of conditions that the playwright and the director establish for a production. In attempting to understand how a play works, the director begins with the given circumstances as the necessary framework.

Place is an obvious element. In examining the text, you should note precisely all explicit and implicit indications of place. You must go about the task as if you were a detective looking for subtle clues, realizing that sometimes the playwright will tell you one thing and mean another. To get the most out of your collaboration, you often must press the issue. Is Macbeth truly in the castle called Dunsinane? If not, then where? Is it the literal, historical Scotland? The actual castle? If you answer that the place is symbolic or fanciful, you must be

Some playwrights, such as Pirandello, challenge theatre artists by questioning the very nature of what we know—or think we know. Still, the director and actors must make clear decisions about character and action.
Play: *Six Characters in Search of an Author* **Author:** Luigi Pirandello **Theatre:** Indiana Repertory Theatre **Director:** Tom Haas (Photo by Tod Martens)

ready to be precise about this imagined place. You must continue your search until you are convinced you understand everything the playwright has to say about this matter of place.

Do not be satisfied simply because the playwright names names. Even if the play is set quite deliberately in an actual place, the questions about setting are far from answered. No city is the same from district to district, from block to block, or even from house to house. Shakespeare says Dunsinane, and Elsinore, and Rome, and Illyria; Dürrenmatt says Güllen; Arthur Miller says Salem; Tennessee Williams says Glorious Hill, Mississippi. If you stop as soon as you recognize the name, or locate it on the map, or find a few pictures of the place, you will probably have missed it completely.

Atmosphere refers to the emotional quality or psychological environment existing in the dramatic context. Almost invariably, the atmospheric element of the given circumstances is reflected and communicated by the physical environment of the scene. Most modern playwrights, attuned to conventions of naturalism, take pains to describe the setting and conditions to suggest the atmosphere. Arthur Miller, in the opening of *Death of a Salesman,* evokes the house where Willy Loman lives with his family in a fine mixture of poetic and realistic images. In the long, detailed description, Miller specifies many of the physical details of the environment—a brass bedstead, a silver trophy—and provides vivid impressions of the quality of the ambient light and sound. When the principal character enters, the playwright completes his painting of the atmosphere that opens the play. The flute that began as the curtain rose is still heard playing a plaintive tune, and Willy Loman comes in exhausted and makes his way slowly into his house.

The opening stage directions end with a description of Linda, Willy's wife. Here is a playwright acutely sensitive to the atmosphere of his play. The stage directions create an overwhelming poignancy in the physical world in which Willy and Linda are first seen. Willy's entrance, accompanied by the sound of the flute, completes the overall image: exhausted and emburdened, he heaves a sigh as he puts down the heavy cases.

Before Antoine and the Naturalist/Realist movement, this sort of detailed attention to atmosphere and environment would not have been so obvious and self-conscious. But playwrights have always found a way to include these details. Shakespeare, for example, plants all the essential defining qualities in the dialogue itself. Here is the opening of Act I, scene 2, of *Macbeth*:

KING: What bloody man is that? He can report
    As seemeth by his plight, of the revolt
    The newest state.

A "bloody man," "his plight," a "revolt"—the stage is set. The protagonist of this tragedy is introduced some dozen lines later:

"For brave Macbeth—well he deserves that name—
Disdaining Fortune, with his brandished steel,

Which smoked with bloody execution,
Like valor's minion carved out his passage
Till he faced the slave;
Which nev'r shook hands, nor bade farewell to him,
Till he unseamed him from the nave to th' chops,
And fixed his head upon our battlements."

The images here are unmistakable: *blood, steel, smoke, confrontation, decapitation, impalement*. The vision is complete and implacable. Shakespeare wrote no stage directions—yet what sensitive director could fail to understand the atmosphere pervading this scene?

Play: *Independence* **Author:** Lee Blessing **Theatre:** Actors Theatre of Louisville **Director:** Patrick Tovatt **Set Designer:** Paul Owen **Costumes:** Marcia Dixcy **Lighting:** Geoffrey T. Cunningham **Actors (l to r):** Shelley Crandall, Sylvia Gassell (Photo by David S. Talbott)

Character, action, and given circumstances influence every movement of every scene.

Play: *The Rose Tatoo* **Author:** Tennessee Williams **Theatre:** The Williamstown Theatre Festival **Director:** Irene Lewis **Set Designer:** Hugh Landwehr **Costumes:** Candice Donnelly **Lighting:** Pat Collins **Actors (l to r):** Dan Cordle, Maria Tucci (Photo by Charlie Erickson)

Whether the atmosphere is described or implied, plays from every period carry the necessary information about atmosphere and environment. Directors who are alert to the clues are rewarded with a much clearer and more appropriate sense of atmosphere than they can gain from generalizations about theatrical conventions or images from earlier productions.

Political and Social Environment is often of major importance to the action of the play and the attitudes and behavior of the characters. Societal attitudes and pressures are major players in many of Ibsen's plays, for example. *Ghosts, A Doll House, Enemy of the People, Hedda Gabler* all operate within a clearly established set of social parameters that challenge and restrict the activities or behavior of the protagonists. (See Chapter V for a discussion of the relationship of the playwright's world to the social and political environment in the play.)

EXERCISES

Using two plays from different periods, examine the opening scene of the play and any stage directions or descriptions provided by the author.

1. Specify the clues that establish *atmosphere*.

2. Describe the sense of that atmosphere.

3. Establish the *time*.

4. Define the *place*.

THE SECOND ELEMENT: ACTION

Doing, changing, and developing are all aspects of action. In the theatre, action does not necessarily connote physical movement.

> **For the most part, dramatic action involves a movement of consciousness, a transition from ignorance to awareness, from insecurity to confidence, from anxiety to assurance and so on.**

The action may have its primary focus in a character or in the relationship between characters. In some plays, the action moves from the individual into a larger arena—society, the world, even the cosmos.

The drama's treatment of action is fundamentally different from that in other forms. Novels, for example, depict action that has been completed; they recount events and so create a "virtual history . . . the mode of Memory." Plays depict action moving forward from moment to moment to create Langer's "virtual future . . . the mode of Destiny." (*Feeling and Form*, p. 307) In drama, all possible action—exposition, recollections, even visions of the past—is framed in terms of the present moving ahead. Through the depiction of recollection (an "act" in itself) or even a "flashback," the past is brought into the present and allowed to advance into a future of its own. Both Oedipus and Mr. Alving (in *Ghosts*) call up the past in the effort to understand it, but even as they do, they are themselves in the theatrical present. And their recollections provoke changes that affect their futures.

Every action has structure, beginning with a given *status* or condition of being, a *stimulus* or disturbance, a *response,* and an *adjustment* that results in a *new status* or condition of being.

We can follow this structure through on a very simple physical plane:

> I am sitting in a chair reading (*status 1*). I hear my name (*stimulus*). I answer (*response*), return to my book (*adjustment*) and continue my reading (*new status 2*).

Of course this sequence might continue, resulting in a connected series of actions. Each segment of the series is complete in itself and exhibits a particular intent and form. In the physical world, a discrete particle is called a molecule; in the theatre we call it a *beat*.

On an internal plane the structure can change depending upon the emotional or intellectual interpretation and affect the actor's reading of a line. Consider, for example, the speech from Act V, Scene 5 of *Macbeth*:

Macbeth, whipping himself into a frenzy of power and fearlessness, snaps his demanding question at Seyton: "What is that noise?" (*status 1*). He hears the terse report of the death of Lady Macbeth and is stung by the word "dead" (*stimulus*)→ He responds to the awful irony of the message: "She should have died hereafter;/ There would have been a time for such a word" (*response*). He takes in a breath and feels the impact of the moment (*adjustment*)→ and stoops under its weight (*status 2*). An emotional image of himself and his lady stealthily plotting their dark deeds floods in (*stimulus*),→ and he explodes: "Tomorrow, and tomorrow, and tomorrow/Creeps in this petty pace from day to day,/ To the last syllable of recorded time;/And all our yesterdays have lighted fools/ The way to dusty death" (*response*).→ The violence of the emotion provides a release, almost a sob (*adjustment*),→and Macbeth realizes the futility of his passion (*status 3*).

This set of *beats* can, of course, be phrased differently if based on a different interpretation. The alternative structure will produce an entirely different reading, and the effect will be markedly different from the one already suggested. For example:

Beginning with status 2, Macbeth is swept by a bitter resentment (*stimulus*) at this joke of fate → and sneers a single word, "Tomorrow" (*response*).→ He is struck by the irony (*adjustment*)→and savors it (*status 3*). The idea of an unending cruelty immediately appears like an inexorable climb up an endless stair (*stimulus*)→and he blurts outs "*and* tomorrow, *and* tomorrow," speaking the "ands" with sardonic emphasis (*response*). He pulls up short (*adjustment*)→with the recognition of the image of crawling up the steps (*adjustment*) that he grasps (*status 4*)→and feels a revulsion (*stimulus*).→Then he snarls "*creeps* in this *petty* pace from *day* to *day* to the last syllable of recorded time" (*response*). And so on.

In terms of their rhythms and structures, these two approaches to the same speech, beginning with "She should have died hereafter" and ending with "The way to dusty death," might be shown as follows:

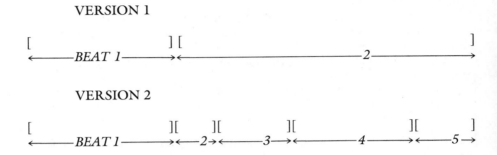

VERSION 1

VERSION 2

Linking a sequence of beats together to complete a movement produces an *action unit* (a conversation or a speech pursued to its conclusion); a series of units results in the larger *dramatic action* (the action of the play). You may know some of these elements by different labels—"inciting action" for "stimulus," "climax" and "denouement" for "response" and "adjustment." Labels aside, the important thing is to recognize the existence of the structure of action and its components. Armed with awareness, you can begin to understand how any action is structured and be better prepared to deal with it.

> Every *action* is composed of four steps proceeding from an original condition or status:
> *STATUS 1: STIMULUS* → *RESPONSE* → *ADJUSTMENT* → *STATUS 2*
> A *BEAT* is a single completed action.
> An *ACTION UNIT* is a compound sequence of related beats that together complete a movement, goal, or intention.
> *DRAMATIC ACTION* is the complex movement structure of the entire play made up of all the action units as embodied in the plot and characters.

THE THIRD ELEMENT: CHARACTER

Characters exist in a play as agents or pawns of the action. In many plays, as pointed out, the characters are themselves the focus; what happens to and within the character can be the embodiment of the total dramatic action. In other plays, most assuredly in classical tragedy, the protagonist—the central character—is defined in terms of a place and function within the universe of the play. The universe, defined by the playwright, might be the family, the society, the nation, the world, or even the cosmos itself. The progression of the protagonist through the play, and the character's ultimate disposition or status, reverberates throughout the entire created world.

The protagonist's course usually begins with a disturbance of the order of the world of the play. It continues through a series of events—usually efforts to restore balance and order. In the course of these events, the protagonist acts and is acted upon. The playwright uses the action of character in the context of the fictive world to create the form of the play—an expression of the *fractal* structure mentioned in Chapter II. The basic, uncomplicated structure of a simple physical action underlies the total, complex dramatic action of an entire play: *status 1* (the situation at the beginning of the play) → *stimulus* (a disturbance) → *response* (efforts to quiet the disturbance) → *adjustment* (the disturbance subsides) → *status 2* (the situation at the end of the play).

|| **Characters exist and are defined in terms of what the play says and implies about them.** ||

As with the other elements we have been discussing, when dealing with characterization we must first look closely and critically at the play and not jump to conclusions suggested by tradition, commentaries, or conventional wisdom. Characters are defined by their own sets of given circumstances, which must be examined and tested if they are to be honest creations. Every character has a history, a biography, that must lead to and justify his or her actions. To presume that a character simply does and says what is prescribed—without reference to a standard of conduct and behavior growing out of the character—is to insult both the playwright and the actor. Obviously, the definition of character is different in every play because the given circumstances are different. But character there must be: an actor cannot play a symbol. Nor must a character in a play have a clear and complete precedent in life. In *The Bacchae,* Dionysus is a character and must be portrayed by an actor. Dionysus is a god, but he is depicted in human form as a living, moving, speaking person whose biography, psychology, and motivations will be inferred from the actor's performance. It happened that way when Thespis, the first actor, stepped out of the chorus and claimed to be a god. Some Greek in the audience doubtless said, "He doesn't act like *my* idea of Dionysus."

The fullness and credibility of any characterization comes from the choices the performer makes and the skill of execution. Any character behaves according to an image we call characterization, psychology, or biography. Every character operates within an ethical system consistent with the characterization. In drama, the application of moral standards from outside the play have led to some outlandish conclusions and maneuverings. We have bent in every direction to justify certain characters as "good" or "bad" or "empathetic"—as if the quality and power of the creation depended upon that judgment. Is Hamlet a *good* character? Macbeth? Mrs. Alving in *Ghosts*? Oedipus? Pentheus or Dionysus in *The Bacchae*? Schill in *The Visit*? The obvious answer is that it depends on what you mean by *good,* and the obvious response is to wonder why it should make any difference. Characters in tragedies and dramas are not alone in this situation. Characters in comedies are subjected to the same tests. Good or bad or empathetic: Horner in *The Country Wife,* for example? Finch in *How to Succeed in Business Without Really Trying*? MacHeath in *Threepenny Opera*? Just about anyone in Aristophanes?

When the World War I drama, *What Price Glory* by Maxwell Anderson and Charles MacArthur, made a hit on Broadway in the '20s, the *New York Times* and other periodicals engaged in extended debates over whether military men should be depicted using vulgar language and whether such language truly reflected the idiom of the modern American fighting man. Even *Harvey,* Mary Chase's perennially popular oddball comedy, has been characterized as immoral because the central character, Elwood P. Dowd, whose best friend is the six-foot rabbit Harvey, is an unrepentant, even exuberant, alcoholic. Since the play shows him in a sympathetic and loving light, since Elwood's alcohol-clouded vision of life and reality is shown as superior to the sober superficialities of those around him, the play—the objection goes—is essentially flawed by its failure to assume an appropriate moral stance.

The ethical and moral standards of a character are drawn by the artist. As a result, each play projects a different set of moral values. How else can one explain the varied moral and ethical systems in *Measure for Measure* and *Twelfth Night, Richard III* and *Othello*? If it is absurd to apply the standards of morality of one play to another, how is it possible to apply an eternally derived standard to any?

‖ **The only fair moral or ethical standard to measure the characters against is to be found in the play.** ‖

The play may present a set of values close to your own; more often it will reflect the values of the society in which the play was originally conceived and created. Sometimes, it will do neither. Playwrights, like other artists, are occasionally outside the mainstream of conventional moral thought—sometimes blatantly and extravagantly so. If this is so disturbing as to make the play or the characters unpalatable to you or your audience, then you are wise to stay away from it. Distorting plays or characters to fit an externally imposed moral standard is as invalid as distorting them for any other purpose.

The Character Dossier

As director, you should be prepared with a relatively complete file on every important character, similar to that each actor might prepare. For the less im-

Character Analysis Outline

	From Text	Inference
I. *Biographical Factors*		
A. Name (actual and assumed)		
B. Age (exact age if possible, even to birthdate)		
C. Physical traits		
D. Family history and relationships		
E. Occupation(s)		
F. Preoccupation(s)		
G. Self-image		
II. *Social Factors*		
A. Class of social status		
B. Social skills		
C. Behavior (both in terms of fashion and manner)		
D. Social relationships or contacts		
E. Romantic relationships		
F. Political life		
G. Social/Professional goals		
III. *Psychological Factors*		
A. Intellectual abilities		
B. Emotional stability		
C. Drive (energy, commitment)		
D. Methods		
E. Limits (moral, intellectual, self-imposed)		
IV. *Character Action*		
A. Status at the outset		
B. Stimulus or initiative		
C. Objectives		
D. Major obstacles		
E. Methods		
F. Manner (Intensity and style)		
G. Setbacks		
H. Achievements		
I. Status at the end		

portant roles in large cast plays, it is probably sufficient to begin with only a few bits of important information. Each entry must be clearly indicated or supported by evidence in the text. Examine what the character says and does, what others say about him, and notes in the author's stage directions. Once again, you are doing detective work at this point, and you are looking for *hard evidence*. After that evidence has been assembled, you will be able to deal with *inferences* that will evolve as you work with the actors.

Charting a Character's Action
EXAMPLE 1—*The Foreigner,* by Larry Shue

We can follow a character's action throughout a play by establishing a sequence of principal plot developments. In this example, we will use Charlie, the eponymous character in Larry Shue's comedy, *The Foreigner*. We will use the criteria listed in section IV, Character Action, above to follow the character's development through the play scene by scene.

Act I, scene 1:   *Action Unit: from non-involvement to involvement.* At the outset, Charlie is deliberately withdrawn, completely convinced that he is dull, ineffectual, and unattractive. He is forced into participation through the act of overhearing the private conversation of Catherine and David.

Act I, scene 2:   *Action Unit: from reluctant participation to the establishment of a non-committed and therefore carefree relationship with Betty, Ellard, and Catherine.* Key moments of dramatic significance showing Charlie's changing attitudes are the breakfast scene, Catherine's sharing of feelings in a long monologue, and Ellard's hilariously touching efforts to help Charlie.

Act II, scene 1:   *Action Unit: from doubts of self-worth and his own capability to confidence gained from his new admirers and his ability to control the opposing forces; these gains are reversed at the end of the act when fear and self-doubt return.* The stimulus for the first step is Froggy's mention of Frankenstein, suggesting to Charlie the vocabulary of his profession as a science fiction proofreader. Using this ability, he is able to unravel Owen and then to turn the tables on David, the more formidable opponent, by means of the "language lesson." At the height of his success, Charlie is reduced to doubt, fear, and insecurity once again when Owen threatens to bring in "the Klan."

Act II, scene 2:   *Action Unit: from shaken confidence to a restoration of confidence, and finally to complete vindication and the love and respect of those around him.* His new-found sense of his own abilities severely shaken at the beginning, Charlie finds new strength in his efforts to bolster Ellard (by invoking a hero with whom Ellard can identify: "King Buddy!"). This strength comes to full power when the lights in the lodge are restored and the grotesque threat of the Klan is seen at face value. Charlie again draws on his knowledge of science fiction—formerly considered a meager resource—to score a complete victory over Owen and David, indeed, over the entire Klan, the "Invisible Empire" of ignorance, impotence, and cowardice. At the end, Charlie is a new person entirely—capable, committed, loved, wanted, and needed—exactly the reverse of the pathetic little character at the beginning of the play.

Charting the character's action in this way clearly reveals the overall pattern of his progression through the play. The movement of *The Foreigner* is a gradual ascent—a rising pattern with intermittent declines, revealing Charlie's growing but fragile confidence in his own abilities and self-worth. At the beginning of the play, Charlie is withdrawn, convinced only of his own worthlessness. By play's end, Charlie is a leader, a complete person. The change, as the analysis implies, happens as Charlie gains the respect and dependence of others—and finally their genuine love.

Similar analyses for the other characters would reveal a parallel development. Ellard and Betty gain self-respect and confidence as Charlie does. Even Catherine finds her self-definition as Charlie and the others find theirs. The total effect of these interrelated patterns of character action suggests the play's overall *Dramatic Action*—a growth and flowering of personality and confidence through the recognition of positive human values, and rejection of the negative values of fearfulness, isolation, and manipulation.

EXAMPLE 2—*Macbeth,* by William Shakespeare

Act I, scene 3:   *Action Unit: Macbeth's appetite for power and station is whetted.* The witches tempt Macbeth with promises of advancement.

Act I, scene 4:   *Action Unit: In Macbeth's conscious thoughts arises an ambivalence between the desire for power and what taking it will entail.* The King is met face-to-face. "Stars, hide your fires;/Let not light see my black and deep desires."

Act I, scene 5:   *Action Unit: Lady Macbeth eagerly urges Macbeth on. He begs delay. Macbeth:* "We will speak further." *Lady Macbeth:* "Only look up clear./To alter favor ever is to fear./Leave all the rest to me."

Act I, scene 7:   *Action Unit: Reversal of the decision to kill Duncan.* After contemplating the enormity of the crime, Macbeth decides against it, saying, "We will proceed no further in this business." Lady Macbeth first shames him with taunts about his manhood and then seduces him with assurances of success. He capitulates. "I am settled, and bend up/Each corporal agent to this terrible feat."

Act II, scene 1: *Action Unit: He decides to commit the murder.* He accepts the invitation of the dagger's apparition, dismisses all further considerations of conscience, and goes resolutely to kill the king.

Act II, scene 2: *Action Unit: Unbalanced by the enormity of his act, Macbeth succumbs to the direction of his wife and remains disoriented.* Lady Macbeth upbraids him for his cowardice and takes the bloody weapons to implicate the sleeping grooms.

Act II, scene 3: *Action Unit: Macbeth gains control of himself and kills the guards.*

Act III, scene 1: *Action Unit: Going still deeper into crime and guilt, Macbeth arranges the murder of Banquo.* "It is concluded: Banquo, thy soul's flight,/If it find heaven, must find it out tonight."

Act III, scene 2: *Action Unit: Macbeth waivers between anxiety and the expectation of being caught in a tide he cannot turn back.*

Act III, scene 4: *Action Unit: Macbeth's fragile balance falls apart when he sees Banquo's ghost.* He again confronts the reality that his future is out of control. "My strange and self-abuse/Is the initiate that wants hard use./We are yet but young in deed."

Act IV, scene 1: *Action Unit: His self assurance returns.* Hecate and the witches seem to promise him invincibility, and Macbeth vows to finish what he started by destroying Macduff and his family.

Act V, scene 3: *Action Unit: After a relapse in confidence and a return of the old fears, Macbeth arms himself in body and spirit for the final confrontation.* "I will not be afraid of death and bane/Till Birnam Forest come to Dunsinane."

Act V, scene 5: *Action Unit: Macbeth goes from a manic boldness to ironic reflection and finally to self-doubt as the prophecies begin to unravel. Having gone too far, he recognizes there is no retreat.* Beginning the scene at perhaps the highest level of his confidence, Macbeth is dealt a deadly blow with the announcement of Lady Macbeth's death. The reversal is radical and marks the beginning of his complete disintegration. From the opening of the scene where he boasts, "Our castle's strength/Will laugh a siege to scorn," to the last lines, "Blow wind, come wrack!/At least we'll die with harness on our back," the impact on Macbeth's confidence is devastating.

Act V, scene 7: *Action Unit: In a frenzy, Macbeth continues killing.* He slays young Siward.

Act V, scene 8:   *Action Unit: His last false hope destroyed, Macbeth finally recognizes his inevitable fate.* "Yet I will try the last."

The action of *Macbeth* is a deadly rollercoaster ride. At the beginning of the play, Macbeth is presented as a man at the top of his powers and status, admired and respected. Yet, from the very outset, Macbeth is ambivalent. He has not called up the witches, but he is both fascinated and repelled by them and their suggestions. Each action unit deals either with his sense of enthusiasm and appetite for the course he has chosen for himself or with anxiety, fear, and revulsion at what he sees as dangerous and unconscionable. Each time his doubts became critical, he is turned away by the witches, by his wife, or by the meanderings of his own tortured mind. The swings occasioned by these reversals give the action pattern of the character its precipitous quality, and the effect of a breathless headlong rush.

Shakespeare's use of the reversal in Act V, scene 5, is especially important. By allowing Macbeth to assert his power once again, and then having it snatched away in a single stroke, Shakespeare demonstrates his absolute mastery of dramatic construction.

Both *Macbeth* and *The Foreigner* move their protagonists through a vertical path. Charlie begins *The Foreigner* near rock bottom, while Macbeth is near the top of his powers. In the end, Charlie is riding the crest, while Macbeth is falling to the depths. In each case, the playwright defines and directs the dramatic action. The characters' fates are not subject to any externally imposed standards of comedy, tragedy, or morality. We would be foolish to regret that Charlies does not end up with the promise of a new job and great wealth, or that Macbeth is not spared to become a wiser, stronger, more admirable human being. These are issues and prospects the playwrights do not raise and so must be counted irrelevant.

Such parallels between these two plays do not suggest that there is any equivalence of significance or merit between them, only that plays of vastly different types and pretensions may display some structural similarities. The power, significance, and importance of these structures are as different from each other as *Macbeth*'s Dunsinane is from *The Foreigner*'s fishing lodge.

TEXT DIVISIONS AND ANALYSIS: THE FRENCH SCENE

For convenience, each of the above analyses uses the structural principle suggested by the published editions: *The Foreigner*'s four scenes in two acts and *Macbeth*'s 28 scenes in five acts. Using the published divisions will usually simplify an analysis of plot action. A problem arises, however, when the suggested divisions do not provide an adequate number of units to make analysis convenient. The complexity of *Macbeth,* for example, would demand many more divisions if *it* were written in two acts and four scenes—a perfectly adequate structure for *The Foreigner*. To circumvent this problem, you might opt for an alternative method of division based on the *French scene*.

The French scene is a division marked by the entrance or exit of a character from the stage; in other words, one French scene ends and the next begins every time the stage population changes.[4]

By using either the published act/scene divisions or the French scenes method, the director may chart the overall dramatic action of a play in much the same way as shown for action units detailing character development. Such an analysis would list each division and its *action*; the *characters* involved; dominant *images* and *key moments, lines,* or *beats*; and script *pages*.

		DRAMATIC ACTION Format for Structural Analysis of ***The Foreigner***			
SCENE	**ACTION**	**CHARACTERS**	**IMAGES**	**KEY**	**PP.**
1	Arrival	Frog., Chas.	Rain, Thunder	"I am boring"	10-14
2	Hear probs	Frog. Betty	Yearning	Lodge condemned	14-20
3	B sees Ch.	+ Chas.	Her delight	" . . . real good"	20-21
4	Settle down	Frog., Chas.	Ch draws in	"I can't do it."	21-22
. . . and so on!					

As you see, the use of French scenes as analytical divisions provides a wealth of detail. You may want to add other categories to the analysis. *Function,* for example, could be used to note how the scene contributes to the overall structure or development of plot or character.

EXERCISES

1–a. Mark a speech or dialogue by identifying the *beats* with brackets. Use marginal notations to indicate the action of each beat.

 b. Mark another copy of the selection to reflect an interpretative difference as shown above in Macbeth's "Tomorrow and tomorrow" speech.

 c. Direct the two versions of the scene for the class.

2–a. Using an act from a contemporary realistic play by Ibsen or Arthur Miller, for example, analyze the action units of each of two principal characters and be prepared to discuss the results.

[4]Dividing a play into French scenes is useful for a director not only for purposes of analysis but also as a convenient method of devising rehearsal times to ensure the most efficient use of the actors' time.

b. Prepare a character dossier for one of the characters, indicating the explicit clues from the text and the inferences required to complete the dossier.

3. Analyze the overall dramatic action and structure of the same act using the principle of the French scene to divide the act into its components.

End Notes

This and the subsequent chapter suggest a plethora of scholarly and imaginative techniques. Every one has potential value as a directorial tool, though not every one will be useful for every director on every occasion. Explore the possibilities and implications of each one, even if you do not immediately appreciate its possibilities. That alone might indicate your need to look into the technique more carefully. Though your own inclinations will shape and refine your method of preparation, you will find that specific plays will *demand* different approaches.

> **It is no more possible to be over-prepared than to be over-rehearsed.**

Good preparation is essential. It is, however, possible to be poorly prepared or poorly rehearsed by spending time inefficiently on details that do not contribute to the accomplishment of the work at hand. Rather than using thorough preparation to make imagination and intuition work more effectively or at a higher level, some directors make preparation more important than production. A good director does not *substitute* research and analysis for insight and creativity.

We started this chapter by noting that the play is the author's medium of communication. Your ability to use a variety of approaches to come to terms with a play is the equivalent of fluency in a number of languages with which to understand the playwright.

Great nations write their autobiographies in three manuscripts, the book of their deeds, the book of their words and the book of their art. Not one of these books can be understood unless we read the two others, but of the three the only trustworthy one is the last.

—John Ruskin

4 EXAMINING THE PLAY'S HISTORICAL CONTEXT

The writing of any play takes place within a certain *context* involving the playwright's life and the historical forces of time and place. By examining these surroundings, we can explore perspectives and elements that might shed light upon the text at hand. We acknowledge from the outset that such factors are *extrinsic* to the play. Even so, an awareness of historical circumstances might provide us with insights on how the play works or how the playwright's vision and craft were influenced by the circumstances in which he or she lived and wrote.

In the broadest sense, plays proceed from the playwright's time and life experience. A play can never be completely cut adrift from its origins—a particular playwright working in a particular context. On the other hand, all plays—most especially great ones—have an independent life. They are self-referring. They have a life, a vision, a morality of their own. We like to say the *Agamemnon* would be a great work of art if we knew nothing of its historical setting or even that it is one of the three plays in *The Oresteia*. Still, there is something compelling in the desire to find out *about* a play, just as we want to know more about a painting or a musical composition. We want to know about the society and the ideals from which the artwork emerged. In our time, particularly, we want to know about the person who produced it. While there is a kind of voyeurism in some of this interest, it is symptomatic of a healthy spirit of inquiry. As playwright Friedrich Dürrenmatt observes: "The artist always represents his world and himself." (*Problems of the Theatre,* p. 22)

Learning about the playwright and the times often can provide keys to understanding a play's structure, intent, and method. It can enlarge the range of our perceptions and give us a means of translating the play from another time, place, and consciousness to our own.[1] The effort to get in touch with the playwright is made for the same reasons we try to get in touch with the designers and actors who are our other collaborators: for the sake of clearer and richer understanding and communication.

> **To explore the playwright's life and milieu is to open the possibility of discovering something significant about the play.**

Exploring a play's historical context often yields new insights, even into a play as well known as this. **Play:** *A Christmas Carol* **Authors:** Charles Dickens (adapted by Nagle Jackson) **Theatre:** McCarter Theatre **Director:** Robert Lanchester **Actors (l to r):** Robin Tate, Mary Martello, George Ede, Deborah Jeanne Culpin (Photo by Randall Hagadorn)

[1]This is not to suggest that this translation requires a change in the period setting in which the production is staged.

To achieve an awareness of historical context, a director should explore the following areas[2] surrounding the play's inception:

1. *The Playwright's Biography*
2. *Sequence, or Relationship to Author's Plays*
3. *Theatrical Conventions of the Time*
4. *Social Conditions*
5. *Author's Commentaries and Contemporaneous Criticism*

The Playwright's Biography

Research into a playwright's personal history often provides a valuable perspective that can enliven or complement a director's insight into a text. Obviously, the playwright's life is an excellent source of information in cases where the work is patently autobiographical, as in Eugene O'Neill's *Long Day's Journey Into Night,* Neil Simon's *Brighton Beach Memoirs,* and Tennessee Williams's *The Glass Menagerie.* Biographical information can also be valuable if we find playwrights working through questions or problems bearing on their personal or public lives in a conscious way—Ibsen in *Peer Gynt,* Stoppard in *The Real Thing*—or in an unconscious way—Strindberg in *The Father,* Samuel Beckett in *Waiting for Godot* and *Endgame.*

A number of useful sources exist. There are, of course, important biographies on most playwrights of the late nineteenth and early twentieth centuries. From one or more of these, a director can find, for example, that as the aging Henrik Ibsen was writing *The Masterbuilder,* he was involved with a much younger woman, Emilie Bardach, and concerned with emerging challenges to his own artistic position by younger artists. Ibsen met Bardach, whom he referred to as "the May sun of a September life," when he was sixty and she eighteen. He took care to note the exact moment of their first encounter and later used that date in a play as the time of the first meeting of Solness, the masterbuilder, and Hilde, the mysterious young woman who comes into his life. This suggests strongly that Ibsen was using his life experience as a direct model for the dramatic event. Although the play confronts the issues of youth and age at many levels, the text never deals explicitly with the ages of the principals. It is, in fact, vague as to details. Of Solness: "He is aging somewhat, but still healthy and strong. . . ." [Act I] Of Hilde: "She is of middle height, supple and delicately built. . . ." [Act I] (Translated by Geir Jensen) Working strictly from the text, with no biographical reference, one could surmise a difference in ages between the two of less than twenty or twenty-five years and conclude that Solness and

---

[2]Even though some of these areas overlap, it is important to consider each for what it might offer in understanding the play itself and not as an exercise in distinguishing one category from another.

Although the goal of the research described in this chapter is *understanding* the play, the aim in Chapter V is to discover images for *interpreting* the play. Chapter V also includes a method involving the examination of other arts contemporaneous with the composition of the play.

Hilde could be fifty and twenty-eight respectively. Indeed, many productions use actors in just this age range. But consider just how radically the play changes when the difference in the ages of the characters, suggested by the biographical reference, is closer to that between Ibsen and Emilie—more than forty years! A director ignorant of the playwright's biography might never even consider the possibility; armed with the historical facts, that same director has opened up the possibility of a different and bolder way to approach the play.

On another level, even more subtle insights are possible. For example, leading British playwright Harold Pinter is an actor and a director, but he is also a writer of radio plays. This last fact alone should provoke a director to *listen* to the sound and music of Pinter's plays with special care. If, in tackling a Pinter play, the director had discovered a special musical or rhythmic insistence, the biographical datum could be an assurance of the validity of the perception. In Pinter's plays—*The Room*, for example—monologues become arias, dialogues may be heard as duets, and so on. This musical structure is created by the playwright-composer and interpreted by the director-conductor, and performed by the actor-musicians. Approached in this way, a special dimension of the work can be grasped. The music of the piece becomes essential to its meaning and may, in fact, inspire a matrix. One such might suggest *The Room* is a jazz set or a rock opera played to frighten or intimidate someone.

In the same way, awareness of Garcia Lorca's talents as a serious painter (he was also a musician and poet) suggest his plays be read with the *eye* as well as the ear. His sensitivity to color and shape, rhythms and harmonies deserve special attention. Garcia Lorca's painterly instincts permeate his work. In his classic *Blood Wedding*, for example, he describes the colors, shapes, and textures in the cave where the Bride lives: large pink flowers, hard white walls, mirrors and fans, and blue jars. The Mother is dressed in black satin with a lace mantilla; the son in black corduroy and a gold chain. The playwright's instincts and talents combine here to communicate his feelings about the effect of the scene in explicit visual terms. Colors and textures become elements of communication. And the painter's vocabulary is all the more obvious once the biographical facts are given full weight.

In describing the colors and surfaces themselves, the playwright is not *prescribing* a color scheme for a production. Rather, he is using the artist's vocabulary to describe something about the *scene*. The quality he describes might well be translated into an entirely different color palette for a production. His stage directions suggest the effect of a clean and virginal space—dainty, feminine, and vulnerable—into which intrude two allied and alien presences: dark, formal, and forbidding. If this is the effect the director finds, this is the quality the matrix should suggest and the designers must understand. The effort to define and reproduce the literal colors in the stage directions is secondary. In fact, one can argue that the literal use of the playwright's colors and textures might produce a different effect entirely. *Blood Wedding,* then, might suggest a matrix built on the images of a series of Spanish surrealist paintings—images rich in color, form, movement, and even sound.

These three cases are useful from yet another perspective. Like most master playwrights, Ibsen, Pinter, and Garcia Lorca were all men of the theatre, involved with the actual production of plays. This information suggests still another level at which to read their plays. One can assume that such writers understand the contributions of actors, directors, and designers, and write accordingly. Other less understanding or tolerant playwrights might write overly prescriptive texts. Gordon Craig, for one, advised against the reading of stage directions on the grounds that many of them were incursions by the playwright into the realms of the director, designers, and actors. Certainly, while Craig's is not the best advice in every case, it might reasonably be adapted as follows: pay the greatest attention to the stage directions and commentaries of the playwrights *who know how the theatre works* through practical involvement, and pay less attention to the others.

> **Read stage directions with an eye to discover the *feeling* rather than the *details* the playwright is trying to communicate.**

Sequence or Relationship of Plays

It often is useful to look at a play as part of the playwright's whole body of work. Sometimes, a chronology gives clues to the playwright's concerns and techniques at the time the play was written. Thus, to find that Shakespeare's first comedy was *Comedy of Errors* and his last was *The Tempest* is to understand something specific and potentially useful about those plays, if it is only a way to explain the youthful exuberance and abandonment of the former and the mellow and mature musings of the latter.

Often, a playwright will treat a theme in several different plays; and the way a subject or theme is handled in related works might illuminate the structure, images, or meaning of the play being studied. Any director about to undertake *Macbeth* would do well to examine other plays—*Richard II, King Lear, Hamlet, Richard III, Henry V*—in which Shakespeare also deals with issues of the divine right of kings, royal succession, the duties of the monarch, and regicide. In the same way, we can find threads that connect Ibsen's moods and preoccupations with the struggle with the sinister forces in our human nature in *Rosmersholm, The Lady from the Sea, Hedda Gabler,* and *The Masterbuilder*.

In some instances, the circumstances surrounding the composition can evoke a special quality that might otherwise be overlooked: for example, that *A Doll House* was written by a frustrated Ibsen who resolved to become "a photographer", or that *Ghosts* was written as a deliberate rebuff to the narrow-minded critics of *A Doll House*. Other instances abound: Shakespeare's writing *Twelfth Night* on the occasion of a wedding celebration; Anouilh's treatment of *Antigone* during the Nazi occupation in France; Molière's acknowledgement of royal patronage in *Tartuffe*.

Theatrical Conventions of the Time

Theatre history can tell us much about how a play works. In plays from a different time or place from our own, we routinely investigate and try to grasp the theatrical spirit—sometimes to mimic, sometimes to look for parallels or images. Even in the case of recent plays, theatrical context is a vital clue. Three elements deserve attention:

1. *the stage itself*—its size and shape, its relationship to the audience, the scenic and costume conventions;
2. *theatrical conditions in general*—the popularity of the theatre or lack of it, the kind of audience, outside pressures or influences, the playwright's status or reputation and that of the producing company;
3. *collaborators in the production*—the actors for whom the roles were written or by whom they were first played, director and designers (if any).

Often, one must know the historical theatrical context of a play in order to recreate the illusion of the original stage production.
Play: *Showboat* **Authors:** Jerome Kern and Oscar Hammerstein 2nd (Based on the novel by Edna Ferber)
Theatre: Paper Mill Playhouse **Director:** Robert Johanson **Costumes:** Bradford Wood & Gregory A.
Poplyk **Set Designer:** Michael Anania **Lighting:** Ken Billington **Actors (l to r):** Richard White, Rebecca
Baxter (Photo by Gerry Goodstein)

It is probably fair to say that Shakespeare in Elizabethan times, or Congreve in Restoration England, or Sam Shepard in the contemporary United States would not have written as they did for a different sort of physical theatre or production method. And so it is important to understand *how* and to what degree the shape of the theatre affected the shape of the play. (An attempt to replicate the original theatre or method is not the point.)

We also can find it useful to discover that *Hamlet* was written for a certain actor and that Molière, himself, played Harpagon in *The Miser*. And how telling to discover that Maurice Valency fashioned his version of *The Visit* for the special qualities and talents of the sophisticated and dazzling acting team of Lynn Fontanne and Alfred Lunt. Such matters as these, of course, require some exploration of theatre history.

Sometimes, we may even discover that theatrical conventions obscured some of a play's essential qualities. In the early 1970's, for example, a number of American and British productions of Chekhov's major plays brought to the surface many comedic qualities that before had only been hinted at. While some of these productions met with critical and popular resistance, their essential validity has since been vindicated. The assertively melancholic versions of *The Cherry Orchard* and *The Sea Gull* that had held the stage since their premieres before the turn of the century have surrendered to the lighter, livelier, and more satiric readings.

Because Chekhov's objections to Stanislavski's interpretation of his plays as *dramas* instead of the *comedies* were well known, it is puzzling that it took so long for the mainstream theatre to recognize their comedic values. Indeed, the plays themselves are filled with farcical comic elements—aimless people squandering their time and money, drunkenness, absentmindedness. The reason lies in the power of theatre to influence perception. The comedic elements in Chekhov were overlooked for decades in large part because of the very success and influence of the Moscow Art Theatre's productions under the direction of Stanislavski.

Stanislavski's great contribution to the art of direction, as we have noted, was his use of the actor's skill and creativity. Part of the "System" of actor training that Stanislavski was developing in his Studio involved the actor's *inner* technique. The System explored the possibilities of the "magic if" (What would happen "if"?), developed techniques of sense and emotional memory, and ultimately produced a feeling of identification of actor with role. Stanislavski's actors sought to avoid or break down theatrical stereotypes, and they found Chekhov's characters tantalizingly complex, humorous, and befuddled; but the characters were always basically fine and eminently sympathetic. Some actions Chekhov had written to be farcical, the actors interpreted as touching. Chekhov could write an action right out of his earlier short farces: Uncle Vanya pursuing the ancient professor around the grounds, firing a pistol at him, and bemoaning the fact that he keeps missing the target; or Trofimoff, so angry and petulant that he stamps out of the room and promptly falls down the stairs. For Stanislavski's actors, though, these characters were to be understood and pitied for their

The Naturalist-Realist movement remains a major force. In these modern productions, the influence of environment on human psychology is evident.
Play: *The Rose Tatoo* **Author:** Tennessee Williams **Theatre:** The Williamstown Theatre Festival **Director:** Irene Lewis **Set Designer:** Hugh Landwehr **Costumes:** Candice Donnelly **Lighting:** Pat Collins **Actors (l to r):** James Naughton, Maria Tucci (Photo by Charlie Erickson)

Play: *Autumn Elegy* **Author:** Charlene Redick **Theatre:** Actors Theatre of Louisville **Director:** Gloria Muzio **Costumes:** Lewis D. Rampino **Set Designer:** Paul Owen **Lighting:** Ralph Dressler **Actor:** Carmen Mathews (Photo by Richard Trigg)

frustrations, not laughed at as they might be in the shallow boulevard theatre. These were characters in *life,* and the stage is the image of life. In life, we may do foolish things *in extremis,* but we do not wish to be laughed at.

The influence of the Moscow Art Theatre was so complete that it established an image for the production of Chekhov that took decades to fade. The total conviction of the performances seemed to brook no alternatives. This was further complicated by translations that reflected the mood and atmosphere of the Art Theatre's interpretations. Few people could appreciate the comedy for the pathos.

In the case of Chekhov, the swing of time's pendulum has restored some of the comic energy about which the playwright had been adamant. This transmutation, which took nearly a hundred years, makes by itself a convincing case for examining the state of the theatre and the state of the playwright's mind at the time of the writing and first production of the play.

Other plays and playwrights have been affected as well. Many of the influential actors, directors, and critics of the nineteenth and twentieth centuries were exposed, in their youth, to romantic, picturesque stagings of Shakespeare and left with the impression that "that's the way it's supposed to be." Tyrone Guthrie suggested that this is because our early experiences in the theatre tend to be idealized. "One seldom sees great acting," he observed, "after one passes the age of eighteen." Among the great moderns, Ibsen has also suffered the assaults of prejudice and unfortunate productions. Distinguished biographer Michael Meyer notes in his *Ibsen* (p. 410), "Few musical scores have so softened an author's intentions as Grieg's *Peer Gynt* suite, which turns the play into a jolly Hans Christian Anderson fairy tale." Perhaps even more pernicious is the much-believed image of Ibsen as a dour moralist grimly writing dull tracts on social standards and responsibility. The plays themselves (in translations faithful to the spirit of the originals) can certainly put these notions to rest, but old prejudices die hard.

The critical point is that our attitudes and predispositions toward a play can be manipulated without our knowledge. Admitting the prime and incontrovertible importance of the text, the director must take all steps necessary to assure that the text is allowed to speak without the distortions of prejudice or unjustified expectations.

Social Conditions

Social conditions and thought should be considered as having potential importance in unlocking a play's secrets. Obviously, plays that deal with social or political subjects or themes invite such scrutiny, but other plays might also benefit. In the case of a play that deals with a time or place other than the playwright's own, a two-pronged investigation is called for: looking at the time of the play's composition and at the time of the action of the play.

> Morality, societal values, politics, art, fashion—all are potential sources of a director's insight and understanding.

Politics, for example, is in the forefront of Bertolt Brecht's plays, both in the environment of the plays themselves and in reference to the situation in the real world outside. *The Threepenny Opera,* although set in an earlier time, is clearly about playwright/director Brecht's world. Likewise, *The Crucible,* which takes place in Puritan Salem, is acknowledged to be Arthur Miller's comment on the McCarthy Congressional "witch-hunts." And the environments of Shakespeare's plays are reflections of the Elizabethan world filtered through the playwright's political sensibilities. Even the work of Molière—considered by some an apolitical writer—carries an acute awareness of social and political realities. One need only examine the celebrated ending of *Tartuffe* to realize that fact. Again, if you are to understand the play's given circumstances fully, you must examine both the social and political environment depicted in the action of the play and the real world in which the play was written.

Author's Commentaries and Contemporaneous Criticism

It is also important—some might say indispensable—to approach any play from the perspective of the playwright's view of the play itself and of the theatrical medium. To understand *The Good Woman of Setzchuan,* it is essential to read the play, to analyze and respond to it. But it would be unconscionable for a director to forego a study of Brecht's essays and discussions of the theatre and politics. This does not suggest that a director must follow the precepts of Brecht's *Regiebuch*—his master plan for the play's production. Brecht did not do that himself when he restaged productions, nor did he intend for others to do so. According to Harold Clurman (p. 40), the playwright was unequivocal: "When I asked Brecht if he felt that his plays had to be staged exactly as he had done them, he answered, 'Certainly not.' " Still, it is clear that a director who understands Brecht's views on theatre and politics will approach the plays infinitely better equipped than one who has slighted or avoided the research. For the same reasons, one might examine Dürrenmatt's *Problems of the Theatre,* Ionesco's *Notes and Counter-notes,* and Shaw's essays and criticism.

BERTOLT BRECHT 1898–1956 (Germany)	The Berliner Ensemble. *Mother Courage and Her Children, The Threepenny Opera, Galileo.* A seminal figure in the modern theatre, affecting playwriting, directing, acting, design, and criticism through his

Some modern playwrights, like Brecht, Dürrenmatt, and Ionesco, have been eager to talk about their plays and their art. Their words on the subject are resources that the serious director must explore. Ibsen's letters reveal a passionate and witty artist who knew the theatre and how to make it work, not a drab social reformer. Here he offers practical advice to the director of a production of his *An Enemy of the People* in 1882. He begins on a diplomatic note: "It is not my intention or wish to attempt to influence *in absentia* either the staging or the casting; but the expression of certain feelings which I hold regarding various aspects of the play can do no harm." (Meyer, p. 504) He goes on to note details of character background, age—even the choice of an east-coast rather than a west-coast dialect. He encourages and inspires in the manner of one who is clearly of the theatre, speaking of the truthfulness of the performance, the necessity for ensemble playing, and two more very practical suggestions: "Throughout the play the stage director must insist that none of the players alters his or her lines. They must be spoken exactly as they stand in the text. A lively tempo is desirable. When I was last at the Christiania Theatre the speech seemed to me very slow." (Meyer, p. 505)

In addition to consulting the playwright's own commentaries, the director also should consider other sources of information about a given play. Indeed, much of what we know about the way plays were done and how they were received comes from the work of commentators and critics who deal with early editions and productions.[3] Diaries and letters as well as formal criticism are of great value in giving evidence of production methods and details as well as a sense of contemporary response to a play.

DISCUSSION

1. What play or kind of play might be exempt from a director's enquiry into historical context? (What about contemporary plays? Fantastical plays? Other types?)

2. If replication of an original production or a recreation of the playwright's original impulse is not the ultimate purpose of historical inquiry, what *can* it be used for?

3. What use to the director is finding out about an original production's actors, designers, director, or theatre when the new production is obviously going to be different?

[3]Another use of criticism as a potential source of imagery is discussed in Chapter V.

A play drawn from myth and another from modern life: each tries to create a meaningful image of the world we share.
Play: *Camelot* **Authors:** Alan Jay Lerner and Frederick Loewe **Theatre:** Theatre Virginia **Director:** Terry Burgler **Set Designer:** Charles Caldwell **Costumes:** Charles Caldwell **Lighting:** Terry Cermak (Photo by Virginia Museum Photography)

Play: *Alone at the Beach* **Author:** Richard Dresser **Theatre:** Actors Theatre of Louisville **Director:** Gloria Muzio **Set Designer:** Paul Owen **Costumes:** Lewis D. Rampino **Lighting:** Ralph Dressler **Actors (l to r):** Walter Bobbie, Steve Rankin, Julie Boyd (Photo by Richard Trigg)

Do a *context analysis* of an assigned play. Use an outline form. The object is to get the necessary facts about the playwright and the times of the play's composition and first production. Point out any discoveries you find useful in making a production matrix.

End Notes

As we said at the outset, every play reflects something of the playwright's life, something of the theatre for which the play was written, and something of the world in which it was written and for which it was produced. If the play deals with other than a proximate contemporary subject or theme, then yet another set of circumstances are brought into the picture. The director must look both at the playwright's time and the period in which the play is set. Often, as with *The Crucible* and *The Lion in Winter*—both modern plays dealing with historical subjects—this is crucial. The examination of these "contexts" will often reveal elements that give special insight or understanding obtainable through no other means. These can be of enormous value to the director seeking ways to understand the play and to provoke ideas for a production.

As a director, on the other hand, you must not succumb to the temptation that you can make a play truthful by unearthing and presenting material or points of view that are merely historically accurate.

Strictly speaking, in the creation and appreciation of an artwork, the simple *facts* of history or science are irrelevant. If it were otherwise, art could not survive. Any play—however great—could be discredited solely on the basis of factual inaccuracies or historical inconsistencies. The function of the play and of the theatre is to tell the truth, not to give the facts. The autonomy of the artwork is essential. That the facts of history or science do not correspond to a play's assertions does not invalidate either history or art.

> No play or production is great simply because it is accurate to the facts; and no play or production is a failure simply because it distorts history or science.

Doing research into a play's historical context is an essential and powerful method for a director bent on discovering the truth about the play. Such research, however, is not the end product. The director's study must not be a substitute for imagination, but rather a stimulus to imaginative interpretation and insight.

List some plays that contain factual errors, such as the historical inaccuracies in Shakespeare's work. Discuss the implications of such errors on the artistic merit of the work. When does adherence to fact become a necessity in the theatre?

Without "shapes" the poet is speechless; he needs words, puppets of the drama, tales. But the unknown "forms" come first.

—G. Wilson Knight

5 SEARCHING FOR IMAGES

A director may well search a text for *meanings*, but as a creative artist, the director must also search for *forms*. Scholars and critics generally treat a text as complete—a fully-realized expression of ideas to be isolated and explained in discursive thought and language. But the director-artist must treat a text as incomplete—a subject awaiting transmutation into a performance artwork.

> The director understands that the goal is not explanation; it is, rather, the creation of expressive theatrical forms.

The director must collaborate with the playwright by going beyond the words of the text to discover the incipient theatrical "forms" in the text, which can be further explored and developed in rehearsal and presented in performance. This can be a complex and daunting task.

In *Drawing on the Right Side of the Brain*, Betty Edwards discusses the concept of competition between the left side of the brain (predominantly logical, verbal, linear) and the right side (spatial, non-linear, intuitive). Her comments put the director's immediate problem into perspective. On the subject of the painter's problems in seeing, Edwards (pp. 76–77) writes:

> Now we are coming closer to the problem and its solution. First, What prevents a person from seeing things clearly enough to draw them?
>
> A part of the answer is that, from childhood onward, we have learned to see things in terms of words: we name things and we know facts about them. The dominant left verbal hemisphere doesn't want too much information about things it perceives—just enough to recognize and to categorize. The left brain, in this sense, learns to take a quick look and says, "Right, that's a chair (or an umbrella, bird, tree, dog, etc.)." Because the brain is overloaded most of the time with incoming information, it seems that one of its functions is to screen out a large proportion of incoming perceptions. This is a necessary process to enable us to focus our thinking and one that works very well for us most of the time. But drawing requires that you look at something for a long time, perceiving lots of details, registering as much information as possible—ideally everything. . . .
>
> The left hemisphere has no patience with this detailed perception, and says, in effect, "It's a chair, I tell you. That's enough to know. In fact, don't bother to look at it, because I've got a ready-made symbol for you. Here it is; add a few details if you want, but don't bother me with this looking business."

But the director *must* look at the "chair" and work beyond the left-brain impulse to "screen out a large proportion of incoming perceptions." Eventually, of course, the director must sort through these perceptions and evaluate their artistic worth. But, initially, any one may hold a key to a powerful element of the play in production, and the director should avoid "seeing" only the literal, the icon rather than the idea.

The techniques and suggestions that follow will encourage you truly to *look* and to develop and use your intuitive, spatial, synthetic, and analogical sensibilities.

Learning to "See": Sources for the Matrix

The dual process of searching a text for images and then creating a matrix for a production comes from two potential sources:

First, the *text of the play* itself, which holds patterns and images that might coalesce into a controlling image for a production;

Second, *associations* the director senses between elements in the text and external images, patterns, and structures.

EXAMINING THE TEXT

To begin the process, the director reads the play—the text—and searches for structures, patterns, and motifs, the materials from which to design a production matrix. The approach to textual analysis suggested below provides useful techniques for exploring a play for the materials and the insights the director needs to shape a production.

Searching For Images And Patterns: The Text

1. Title
2. Character and Place Names
3. Scenic Structure
4. Action Patterns and Motifs
5. Sense Image Patterns and Motifs

Title

The play's title should not be regarded lightly. A title may provide evidence of the play's focus and something of its character and atmosphere as well. One would discover from historical-biographical research, for example, that Ibsen originally intended to entitle his play *Hedda*. Why did he change it—and why doesn't he use the character's married name, *Hedda Tesman*? We must conclude that Ibsen wanted *Hedda Gabler* to make a telling comment on the character herself and on a basic motif in the play: General Gabler's pervasive presence and mysterious influence on his daughter.

After exploring the significance and implications of the title, a director may find it valuable to create an alternative title or sub-title that complements or extends the original. This exercise often proves difficult, probably because it demands a clear subjective choice, but it is an effective way of clarifying one's own feelings about a play. It is not a final commitment, and indeed it can and must be altered if further exploration and analysis warrants.

EXERCISES

1. Analyze the meaning and implications of the title of a familiar play. Consider the fact of any conventions that might have influenced the playwright's choice.

2. Suggest an alternative title that you consider appropriate and compelling for the play as you understand it.

3. Discuss the meaning and implications of your choice.

Character and Place Names

Names in the play, like the title, may hold clues to underlying patterns and impulses that can trigger or support a directorial notion. Playwrights usually devote considerable attention to names, either for their descriptive values—as in the conventions of the Restoration and Eighteenth Century—or for their associative potential. In *A Midsummer Night's Dream,* for example, Shakespeare uses descriptive names for the low-comedy characters (Starveling, Snout, Bottom), names from classical mythology for the superior characters (Oberon, Titania, Theseus), and the names of flowers, insects, and the like for the fairy underlings (Peaseblossom, Moth, Cobweb). The grouping of characters by name is a device used even by contemporary playwrights. In Harold Pinter's *The Homecoming,* all the characters in the family, except Teddy, have names common in Jewish families in Britain. Teddy, as the name scheme implies, is the outcast. Pinter suggests still other underlying patterns. He posits a subtle association of Teddy's wife with her Old Testament namesake, Ruth, the loyal, loving, and dutiful wife. We note, too, that while the names of the two older men have a hard simple snap—Max and Sam—the brothers' names are all diminutive forms: Teddy, Lenny, and Joey. With a little imagination and thought, we recall that Lenny is a nickname for Leonard: the lion, the hunter, the king of beasts. Now aware of the extensive animal imagery in the play, we note that the two other names have animal associations as well: the "Teddy bear," of course, but also the "joey," a young kangaroo, which, incidentally, was often employed in carnival sideshows as a boxer. (In the play, Joey is a prize-fighter.)

Place names can be revealing also. Shakespeare again displays a wide range of choices, from "Vienna" (a city notorious for its degeneracy in the renaissance and the setting for his comedy *Measure for Measure*) to "Illyria" (a make-believe name for the make-believe land of *Twelfth Night,* playfully subtitled: *"or, What You Will"*). Friedrich Dürrenmatt cynically calls the setting for *The Visit* "Güllen," which may be politely rendered as "compost pile."

Playwrights may use names with conscious poeticism, as Tennessee Williams does with regularity ("Alma," "Blanche," "Stella," "Blue Lake Casino," "Glorious Hill, Mississippi"), or they may choose a name simply because it "fits" or sounds right. In any event, the director should explore the implications, associations, and sonorities of names in the play, even when dealing with plays based on actual events and persons. Just as we discovered in our "empty stage" experiment in Chapter I, whatever is used in a play becomes an expressive element and must be perceived as such.

As a helpful start in discovering some of the meanings and derivations of proper names, you might begin with one of the many dictionaries that list them either among the general entries or in a separate section.

DISCUSSION

1. Names have meanings and histories of their own as well as evocative sounds and associations. Discuss methods of discovering some of these aspects and suggest ways of using some of these discoveries in directing.

2. Which playwrights—other than those already mentioned—seem to be especially sensitive to *names* in their plays?

3. Choose a play that deals with historical characters and events and look for the meanings and implications of the proper names. Deal with the exercise as if each name were carefully chosen by the playwright in making the play.

Scenic Structure

Scenic structure is a powerful and elusive element.

H I N T : Pay careful attention to the development and progression of the stage environment. Although rarely consciously noted or commented upon, it is sometimes a most powerful theatrical element.

Scenic structure may consist principally of a pattern of changing scenes, as in *The Cherry Orchard* or *A Midsummer Night's Dream*. In *The Cherry Orchard*, the scenic progression is circular. Note also the progression of time of day as the action of the play proceeds:

Act I: "A room that is still referred to as the 'nursery.' Dawn."
II: "An open country. Sunset."
III: "The drawing-room. . . . It is evening."
IV: "The same setting as in Act I."

(*This and all subsequent* Cherry Orchard *excerpts translated by Paulina Shur.*)

Shakespeare's *A Midsummer Night's Dream* also moves in a circular pattern with the illusion, at least, of symmetry:

Ii: Athens. The palace of THESEUS.
ii: QUINCE's house outside Athens.
IIi: A wood near Athens.
ii: Another part of the wood.
IIIi: The wood. TITANIA lying asleep.

ii: Another part of the wood.
IVi: The wood. LYSANDER, DEMETRIUS, HELENA, and HERMIA
lying asleep.
ii: QUINCE's house.
V: The palace of THESEUS.

One possible interpretation of this structure is that the action moves from the palace to the rustic cottage and successively deeper into the wood until Act III, scene i, after which the steps are retraced, ending (as in *The Cherry Orchard*) where it all began.

In other plays, the progression might be essentially atmospheric. In *Ghosts,* Ibsen builds a powerful image of gathering darkness and gloom intermittently pierced by light until the darkness is relieved at the final curtain. Ironic or not, the theatrical effect is overwhelming in impact, subtle in structure.

Act I: ". . . a gloomy fjord landscape . . . veiled by steady rain."
II: "The fog brought by the rain still lies heavy over the landscape."
"OSVALD: . . . Oh, it's dark—so dark!" "(Regina brings in a lamp and puts it on the table.)"

[*The act ends with the fire from the orphanage lighting up the sky.*]

III: "The lamp is still burning on the table. It's dark outside, just a fire glow off to the left in the background. . . ."

[*Moments before the play ends, this stage direction:*]

"She walks to the table and puts out the lamp. Sunrise. The glacier and the mountain peaks in the background lie in bright morning light."

(Translated by Geir Jensen.)

Some plays, like Ionesco's *The Chairs, The Lesson,* and *The Bald Soprano,* use a rhythmic pattern of development, in which an increasing tempo and intensity builds to a very high climax, followed by a release and, finally, a restoration of something like the original tone and tempo. Though powerful and overtly sexual in the above examples, the rhythmic pattern of a play can be quiet and lyrical as well.

EXERCISES

1. Using a contemporary realistic play, make an outline of the scenic progression. What pattern emerges?

2. Indicate the element (scenery, lights, costume, sound) which makes the strongest statement.

3. Suggest ways in which the statement contributes to the total effect of the play.

Action Patterns and Motifs

Every play has a fabric of substructures that define, complement, and enrich the work. Directors must be able to identify and respond to this fabric as they come to grips with the play. It is the way this fabric is perceived, developed, and presented that most often determines how a production achieves its particular quality and vivacity. The director who recognizes and deals with these patterns and motifs can begin to understand the text as a potentially *theatrical* creation rather than as a restrictedly *literary* one.

Here we search for repeated actions, phrases, or gestures that might elude a casual reader. Gaeff in *The Cherry Orchard,* for example, plays an imaginary game of billiards. By digging deeper, we discover the shots he makes so effortlessly are especially difficult combinations: Gaeff is retreating into a harmless little fantasy where he is capable of marvelous things. This apparently incidental insight might become the major definitive element of the character. Connect this one action to other this type of search can reveal—Gaeff's delight in nibbling chocolates, Firs' clucking over his master's inability to dress himself properly—and Gaeff is seen for what he is in this interpretive light; an overgrown child, clearly incapable of dealing with the world in which he finds himself.

Alert to this perspective on Gaeff, we can find other complementary motifs. Note in the text how often and under what circumstances characters doze off. The play begins with just such an action, and an alert director might sense many other times when what might be simple inattention is actually the character's falling asleep. Perhaps when Firs stretches out at the final curtain, he is bringing this motif to a satisfying artistic completion. Lopahkin dozes at the beginning of Act I while waiting for the family to arrive; Firs dozes at the end of Act IV while the family departs. This supports the circular pattern we noted in the scenic progression of the play.

Chekhov is a master of the theatre; his images are built of theatrical action and implication, not literary conceits. Note, for example, how as the play progresses, almost all the characters weep, invariably for something they cannot have or for which they will not work. The emotions we see displayed are childish, not because they are trivial or stupid—there is not a trivial or stupid character in the play—but because the characters are *childlike.* They live in a world they no longer understand and which they cannot control. Poor Pishtick, and Epihodoff, and Trofimoff: "You are twenty-six or twenty-seven years old," Ranevskaya tells Trofimoff, "but you are still like a second year high school student." [Act III] And poor Gaeff. Firs is constantly scolding him: "You put on the wrong trousers again. What am I going to do with you?" [Act I] It is no accident that the play begins and ends in the nursery. The plight of the characters in the world of *The Cherry Orchard* suggests a directorial matrix based upon the Chekhovian metaphors of childhood and childishness, one making immediate use of the comic sensibilities at work in the play.

In searching the text for patterns of stated and implied action, a sensitive director can find bases for still more directorial structures: the distinguishing elements that give dimension to the work of the actors and designers, the pictorial and kinetic images that inform and invigorate staging and blocking, and even clues that help to solve specific problems. Epihodoff, for example—the clumsy man/child who breaks his toys—can provide the director with a transcendently bittersweet comic effect if it is Epihodoff's guitar that produces the provocative sound of "the breaking string," that delicious theatrical touch that resonates with character, humor, and poignancy. Best of all, the effect belongs to the world of the play and does not appear simply as a melodramatic effect.

DISCUSSION

Every play and every character has patterns of action that can be described and portrayed in various ways. After identifying and describing the elements of action that comprise the patterns you find in any given play or character, discuss your findings and their implications for a director. (In addition to *childishness*, you might consider other behavioral patterns: *animalistic, parental, despotic, compulsive, self-destructive*.)

SENSE IMAGE PATTERNS AND MOTIFS

Theatre exists in time and space and is composed of complex sense stimuli. The playwright understands this, of course, and uses a variety of methods to provide clues to the sense elements of the dramatic events. In many instances, such elements are stated in stage directions or dialogue; sometimes they are merely implied. While it is important to keep the stated elements in the foreground, we must try to uncover hidden clues as our search progresses.

Color images are usually communicated sparingly in stage directions and dialogue—red hair, a green dress, yellow stockings, a chestnut horse. Some playwrights, however, are explicit in their use of color (as noted, Garcia Lorca, in *Blood Wedding*, builds a whole structure of color in his stage directions). When dealing with color, as with all sense imagery, implied or stated, the director should weigh the potentials and the ramifications of any textual discoveries. What colors are called for? How do they complement or clash with the rest of the color scheme? Is there a pattern, structure, or progression revealed in the use of color? What is the aesthetic climate or nuance created? Again, the director's alertness and sensitivity to each sense element is important for its own sake, but in some cases, the imaginative response to color and its use in production can prove to be of surpassing importance.

Light has always been appreciated as a theatrical force and dramatic symbol. Theatre artists from Aeschylus to Shakespeare knew its power centuries before Adolphe Appia suggested, around the turn of the twentieth century, that light was not only an atmospheric determinant but an artistic element and motivational force as well. Certainly, Ibsen knew it and used it powerfully; and Shakespeare was a master of light. *Romeo and Juliet* contains the outline of a lighting plot of the greatest subtlety and power. *Othello, Hamlet, Macbeth, A Midsummer Night's Dream*—these and virtually every other play in the Bard's canon use lighting with distinction and effectiveness. The director who lacks the sensitivity to this pervasive theatrical element in the text is operating with a severe handicap.

O'Neill was acutely sensitive to sound in his plays. In this work, the sound of drums is critical to the production's emotional effectiveness.
Play: *The Emperor Jones* **Author:** Eugene O'Neill **Theatre:** Missouri Repertory Theatre **Director:** George Keathley **Set Designer:** John Ezell **Costumes:** Baker S. Smith **Lighting:** Curt Ostermann **Actors (l to r):** Douglass Stewart, Ben Halley, Jr. (Photo by Larry Pape)

Music and sound, like light, are important simply as incidental or atmospheric effects; but like light, they also can be profound elements in forming the production. In the case of Albert Camus' modern drama, *Caligula,* the director who *listens* to the text might perceive a pattern of dissonant, percussive sounds—gongs, drums, cymbals, clashing swords, breaking glass—that can give a production of the play a jarring, edgy, unsettling quality and define theatrical tone in an especially direct and potent way.

Tennessee Williams, for one, asks for a virtual musical score. He so often includes musical sounds themselves, allusions to musical compositions, and quasi-musical sounds (the street-calls and sounds in *Streetcar,* for example) that a director might organize an entire production in terms of the musicality of individual scenes and characters. In the case of *The Glass Menagerie,* the off-stage music that Tom introduces in his opening monologue is only the beginning. The Paradise Dance-hall is across the alleyway; the gramophone and dance records are important props; Laura and Jim dance to the strains of a waltz. The play, structured as a memory accompanied by music, can be produced as if it were *composed* like music—the scenes as musical movements with appropriate notations, the characters' speeches and conversations as solos, duets, and trios.

Like Williams, Harold Pinter is a musical artist. Treating Pinter's notorious "pauses" and "silences" as musical notations can enhance the emotional and psychological texture of a speech or scene. The director should consider "scoring" playwrights like Pinter and Williams to realize the full potential of their texts in performance. (In Chapter VI, we will discuss the prospect of casting actors in such plays for the *musical* potentials of their voices or personalities).

Touch, taste, and *smell* tend to be determinants of atmosphere and character rather than an overall pattern and structure, but they can be of extreme importance in some cases. For example, Strindberg loads his well-known play *Miss Julie* with these elements. Fragrant tree boughs adorn the room; Kirstin is cooking kidneys for Jean; wine is savored; Julie demands her foot be kissed; the Count's boots are polished. Of course, Strindberg fancied himself writing a naturalistic play, and such imagery doubtless seemed a logical tool for creating the naturalistic environment. But, as inevitably happens, a sensitive playwright has created more than a simple natural setting; Strindberg's creativity produces an entire panoply of sense stimuli. The result? A heightened awareness of sensation, a sumptuously appropriate climate for the eroticism of the play. Understanding how the play works in terms of these sensual elements suggests a focus for the designers of the set, costumes, and properties, as well as the actors who occupy the world created by these images.

Sense elements often help define a character. For example, in the case of Osvald, Mrs. Alving's son in *Ghosts,* Ibsen creates a specific quality of character by having him touch and savor *things:* a chair, a glass of wine, the pipe and tobacco. Unlike his mother and Pastor Manders, who remain physically aloof, Osvald seems to be trying to connect directly to things and to people—notably Regina and Mrs. Alving. By the end of the play, this urgent need to make contact culminates in a hugely satisfying embrace of mother and son. The impulse of the character to make contact is a theme never quite resolved until the climax, a natural rhythm evoked again and again throughout the play. The use of theme and resolution is quite as effective in a theatrical composition as it is in a musical score.

Unlike Peter Brook's theatrical setting, this one presents natural outdoor images. Note the ass's head and the tiny puppet—Moth—at center. Both of these creations were fully articulated and expressive.

Play: *A Midsummer's Night's Dream* **Author:** William Shakespeare **Theatre:** The Virginia Players, University of Virginia **Director:** George Black **Set Designer:** LaVahn Hoh **Costumes:** Monica Weinzapfel **Lighting:** Bruce Auerbach **Actors (l to r):** Jim Ligon, Valerie Chapman

DISCUSSION

Is every playwright sensitive to the sensory elements that become part of his mode of theatrical expression? Indicate the particular elements of the theatrical vocabulary favored by each of the following, citing instances where possible:

A. Eugene O'Neill in *Long Day's Journey Into Night*

B. Neil Simon in *The Odd Couple*

C. Lanford Wilson in *Talley's Folley*

D. Sam Shepard in *True West*

E. Ben Jonson in *Volpone*

Creating the Matrix

The kind of textual analysis suggested previously is an attempt to understand the *aesthetic structure* of the text, to discover *how* the play works so that it may be translated into a theatrical event.

> **The director, who will be forming a production based on the text, should now be asking not *why*, but *how*; not the *meaning*, but the *shape*.**

The director in this mode of analysis and exploration is looking for images, patterns, motifs needed to create a *directorial matrix*. In Tyrone Guthrie's modern production *Oedipus Rex* in Stratford, Ontario—staged as a ritual movement from darkness to light—and in Peter Brook's *A Midsummer Night's Dream* for the Royal Shakespeare Company—produced as a fantastical white circus—we find two famous instances in which patterns discovered in the text suggested images that influenced each director's matrix in unusual and exciting ways. Each creation began with a director's confrontation with a text and the discovery of a key to translate that text into theatrical life.

How do directors form a matrix for a production? The process certainly begins with a reading—or with several readings, as Guthrie suggests—followed by more or less intense study. At some point though, the study evolves into something radically different from the usual study of the scholar searching for clarity and explanation, for content and theme. The artist-director in each case begins probing the text for shapes, colors, textures, sounds, movement. He or she searches for suggestive elements, going beyond the satisfaction of mere explanation. Certain elements attract and engage any director; they come out of the text surely, and, just as surely, they do more than *explain* the text; they open it up and illuminate it.

> **The images do not define the text; they express its feeling in specific forms with a sure (if surprising) integrity.**

The director eventually forms a synthesis of images to make a matrix that then is used to shape the production. The implied components of the white circus are in Shakespeare's play; Brook found them and put them to use. Spinning plates are not in Shakespeare's text, but they belong joyously in Brook's production wedded to the spirit of the playwright by the director's vision and craft. Sophocles knew nothing of the Christian Mass, but Guthrie found parallels enough to permit him to illuminate the ancient ritual in terms of the more modern one.

The method of textual analysis presented in this chapter, then, might yield a directorial matrix—more or less full and fecund—or a collection of images from which the director can pick and choose as he or she forms the production. Those images may consist of colors, shapes, texture, actions, behavioral patterns, and the like that influence the director's creation.

1. Sharpen your own skills, insights, and sensitivity by analyzing a script following the suggested format in this chapter. Consider each component of the method as a *filter* to isolate the particular element or quality you are searching for. There will be some overlapping and subjectivity involved in making many of the decisions. This, of course, should not dissuade you from trying to penetrate the inner workings of the theatricality of the play.

2. Using your discoveries, point out those elements you find most provocative and useful. Try to construct a directorial matrix based on your choices.

Searching for Metaphors

Associative Methods

1. Theatrical Images
2. Other Arts
3. Rituals and Games
4. Psychology
5. Criticism

The text provides, more often than not, all the stimuli the director needs to sense that intuitive "click" to signal the perception of a production matrix. But directors do not limit their explorations to textual analyses. Directors know that insights, perspectives, or experiences from sources other than the playscript, or information about its historical period, can affect profoundly their personal understanding, appreciation, and treatment of a given text in ways the playwright can in no way have envisioned, much less intended.

> **Association and allusion are important tools in the creation and interpretation of any art. In the art of theatrical direction, they are indispensable.**

Dealing with playscripts from another time, another culture, the director feels about for something to hold onto; he or she cannot operate from the perspectives and cognitions that prevailed at the time of Sophocles or Molière, or even of Ibsen and Strindberg.

When Jan Kott asks us to look upon Shakespeare as our contemporary, he is most certainly enjoining us to search our own experience of life and art to make connections to Shakespeare's work that allow us to redefine those plays as masterpieces. Kott asks us, in short, to interpret Shakespeare's forms in the light of what we know and feel today—to use our own experience and contemporary associations to understand the play to the fullest. It is at once an obvious and a radical injunction. At one level, we can strive and study to understand dimly the history and philosophy of the Elizabethans, but there is no way we can experience a play in the way Shakespeare's contemporaries might have done. Even if the scholarship and the sources were clear and unambiguous, they could not provide us with the tools to produce the plays for our theatre

A director must think of a play—even a contemporary, realistic play, but certainly one from a time or place far removed—as being encoded, as needing translation or deciphering. (Note that in one sense the word *matrix* means "an encoder or decoder.") The text needs a key to yield up its treasure. That key is something we *know*, even if only by instinct or intuition. Often it is what the play is *like*.

A directorial metaphor suggests a fundamental likeness. It provides a handle for the director to grab and implies a structural formal principle to be used as the production matrix. "Here," the director says; "This is the feeling, the sense, we draw from this play. Listen to its music and its rhythms. See its shapes and colors. Watch how it moves!" What are those created forms? What moods and thoughts do they provoke?

Sometimes directors tell us out front in their production what they feel the play to be—a circus, a Chagall painting, a Fritz Lang movie, a dance of death— but often they avoid the explicit statement and use the elements of allusion and association in subtle, covert, or indirect ways.

|| Allusion, association—these are natural, inescapable, and powerful tools for any artist. ||

Directors view the technique of associations as a step in a filtering process, as a method for discovering genuine intuitive insights into the material at hand. The procedure is best done without prescription or expectation, but rather freely—even playfully. In so doing, the director attempts to make discoveries and connections that might never be uncovered by the usual linear, critical workings of the mind in a conventional analysis.

SEARCHING FOR THEATRICAL IMAGES

Most naturally, playwrights and directors make *theatrical* connections and references in their work. Theatre metaphors and images are fecund and richly textured. As a directorial matrix, a theatrical image can open up a range of playful or dead-earnest possibilities and suggest a whole vocabulary of formal choices and structures that can at once inspire and discipline a *mise-en-scène*—the total design of the production elements.

First, directors can explore theatrical associations most directly by sifting through the text of a play for clues and hints that at once inspire and discipline the total design of the production. Second, directors can employ a process of systematic trial associations of a play with various theatrical styles or modes, looking for a metaphorical key to unlock the play by providing structures upon which a production matrix can be based.

Theatrical Clues in the Text

The first part of the process might, in some cases, seem redundant; the process of textual analysis might have already yielded information about the theatrical nature or quality of the play's structure. Indeed, in a play like Chekhov's *The Seagull*, where principal characters are actresses and playwrights, those elements would be difficult to overlook. Still, the technique of deliberately *looking* for clues provides a *filter* through which the director examines the play for forms and patterns that suggest the play's *artistic* shape rather than its thematic implications or anecdotal content.

Three cautionary notes on the use of this method of theatrical association:

1. *Do* not *consider the theatrical style for which the text was prepared or in which it is conventionally performed as a potential image for the production.* To do so will almost inevitably close down, rather than open up, the exploration of possibilities. It will also most certainly yield nothing suggestive or imaginative. To approach Sophocles' *Electra* as Greek Tragedy is certainly admirable and direct. It should be inescapable. But such an approach, unmodified by any other principle or perspective, is almost certain to be deadly conventional and lacking real shape or distinction. Such a decision simply tells us something we already know.
2. *Avoid the use of Realism.* Particularly, the director must be wary of *Realism*. We have come to regard Realism as synonymous with truth. "It was very realistic," we say—speaking with the highest approbation. Realism is, however, a theatrical style with its own set of conventions, as arbitrary and evolved as that of any other style. Someone might approach *Electra* as Realism, but to do so would not make the approach honest and true; it would merely involve employing in some way the conventions of the Realistic style. The invocation of Realism is usually a reflex, and its selection often indicates no decision at all.
3. *Do not assume that the selection and use of a specific theatrical style for a directorial matrix means necessarily that the external trappings of that style will be employed in the actual production.* In fact, no obvious or overt statement is necessary. The function of the matrix is to give the directorial design a particular and in-

dividual form. A production of *Electra* based on a matrix of some contemporary psychological theory need not be done in modern dress or with any obvious alteration of time or place. The contemporary bias might be revealed subtly in the layout and use of the stage space, in the relative positions of the actors to one another and to their environment, in the design and finish of costumes and properties, in the motivation of movement, light, and sound, and—most significantly—in the tonalities and rhythms of the performance.

On the other hand, an overt production statement of the director's choice of a theatrical style is the best test of that choice—a chance to discover if, or to what degree, the production concept has validity and interpretive truth. Ultimately, though, the director must decide in concert with his or her collaborators the degree to which the matrix is revealed or concealed in the actual production.

Directors in search of theatrical clues and resonances in the text look for explicit and implicit examples. Among the structures, images, and references directors may encounter:

- *play within a play*—*Hamlet* and *The Seagull* are obvious examples. Consider also *Volpone, The Boys in the Band*
- *playwriting, directing, stagemanaging*—broadly, any kind of manipulation resulting in the playing out of a scenario
- *role-playing*
- *costume, masks, disguises*
- *verbal or action reference*—to the theatre, specific plays, actors, characters

A director can look for these theatrical elements in the same way as for other patterns and motifs in the text; that is, by systematic search and notation.

Free Association: Theatrical Styles

Directors take a more freewheeling approach when they move into the second part of the process: free associations of the director's perceptions of the play with the broadest range of theatrical and period styles. The list of possibilities in the general category of theatrical styles is virtually limitless, including not only the major theatrical periods and styles, but also the work of individual artists and movements. For example, while *cinema* is too broad a concept to serve as a possible matrix, the work of an individual cinema artist—or even a specific film—may prove specific enough to evoke a particular complex of shapes, rhythms, images, and techniques.

Directors must be knowledgeable and observant about the theatre in order to be able to draw on the riches at their disposal. They must be willing to allow their imaginations to work without intellectual censorship, freely scanning the theatrical landscape in search of associations to provoke and challenge their responses to the play. And, perhaps most important, directors must be willing to *accept* the work of the imagination. A good director never uses an association—or an actor or a costume—simply because it is available or because it "might work." On the other hand, to reject an inspiration because it seems silly or difficult to justify is to defeat the genuinely creative process by limiting the power of the imagination with the demands of the intellect.

Following are two examples of the theatrical free association technique, using plays of contrasting periods and styles:

The Visit by Friedrich Dürrenmatt

Associations:
  a. Euripidean Tragedy
  b. The Circus
  c. Morality Play
  d. Grand Opera
  e. Impressionism
  f. Epic Theatre
  g. Expressionism
  h. Romanticism
  i. Cinema-Fellini's *Satyricon*
  j. Commedia dell'Arte

Each of the foregoing associations suggests a strong potential for a directorial matrix—an inner life that can give a particular kind of vitality and a specific set of shapes to a production. Each conveys a certain feeling, attitude, and interpretation. Each can provide the director with a framework and possibility for choices. Any one can be stated more or less obviously in the externals of the production, or used subtly but definitively.

It is undeniably reassuring to be able to identify logical connections between the play under consideration and the potential style/matrix. Between *The Visit* and Euripidean tragedy, specifically *The Bacchae,* there are some striking thematic and anecdotal similarities. Clear parallels can be drawn also between the Dürrenmatt play and the circus. But logical connection is not the point of the associational technique. It aims, rather, at *felt* connections and similarities—at *texture* rather than explanation, at *surprise* rather than evidence. Consider the possibilities for production suggested by two of the associations as they might be applied to the entrance of Claire and her retinue.

1. *The Visit* (Euripidean Tragedy Matrix):
Claire dressed in a long linen caftan, sandals, a braided gold fillet around hair set in long ringlets. Heavy, dark eye shadow and hard, painted lips. Her locomotive monstrous and black, groaning and belching smoke that envelopes her as she steps to the platform. Her fiance in shorts and san-

dals; Bobby, the elderly butler in a too-large morning suit, wears dark glasses and carries a cane of vine-twisted bleached wood. Kobby and Lobby, dressed like Bobby but with shaved-bald heads and brows. They carry white canes.

2. *The Visit* (European Circus Matrix):

The train comes in with bells and whistles. It is painted brightly in quaint 19th century style like a tourist attraction. Claire wears a proper British riding habit cut in an exaggerated fashion, with scarlet tail coat and silk top hat. She carries a riding crop. Pedro, her fiance, is wearing a robe over his tank top bathing costume. His hair and moustache are slicked down. Bobby is in the uniform of a majordomo with much braid and many buttons. Kobby and Lobby, the blind men, have dressed themselves. They wear small, dark spectacles. Everything else is too big or too small—their derby hats, plaid vests, trousers. Colors are loud and the patterns overlarge. Nothing matches. Even their shoes. They fall over their own feet and over each other as they make their way along the platform.

By using the forms suggested by each matrix, the director implements choices and has the potential to produce a lively and vigorous theatrical experience. If the matrix has been chosen well, with honesty and insight, the director has a structure to which to refer, and from which to draw specific ideas and inspiration.

Of course, *The Visit* is undeniably theatrical and broad in theme and treatment. But is it a special case? No. Even narrowly circumscribed realistic plays can be explored through theatrical association.

Miss Julie by August Strindberg

Associations:

   a. Expressionism
   b. Impressionism
   c. Grotowski
   d. Cinema
   e. Improvisation
   f. Neoclassicism
   g. Docu-drama
   h. Chamber Opera

Here, as with *The Visit*, the technique employed is to associate freely with whatever theatrical style or mode comes to mind, accepting or rejecting quickly and intuitively until the most remote possibility is glimpsed. The director's potential for choices for *Miss Julie* are not nearly so varied as for *The Visit*, but some provocative possibilities appear nonetheless.

1. *Miss Julie* (Expressionism matrix):

If life is a dream, then a drama is a dream of a dream even though you have employed it as reality.
—Strindberg, *The Isle of the Dead*

Jean's Dream: Open stage, no walls. Three doors, larger than life, frame the playing area. A tiled stove with a prominent chimney, ice-box, table with chairs, and sink. Colors muted to a virtual gray, the surroundings dark and vast. Details simplified. Kristin also grayed—no clear color in her dress or makeup. Julie the same but clearly upperclass in silhouette and bearing. Only Jean seems to have color in his face, hands, and costume.

The light closes in on Jean and Julie as the play progresses until they leave for the bedroom. As the peasants come through the doors, mysterious blue-white backlight floods in. Their dance is deliberate, erotic, grotesque. They leave quickly, silently. When Julie returns, more color is in her face and clothes. Jean is grayer. Gradually, the light grows brighter until—by play's end—the world is raked by the warm light coming in low and casting long, hard shadows.

> **Julie:** I am asleep already . . . the whole room seems smoky to me—and you look like an iron stove—which resembles a man dressed in black with a tall hat—and your eyes glowing like coals when the fire goes out—and your face is a white patch like cinders. (*The sunlight has now reached the floor and illuminates Jean*) It is so warm and fine."
> (Translated by Geir Jensen.)

2. *Miss Julie* (Docu-drama Matrix):

I took this theme from real life
—Strindberg, *"Author's Foreword"* to *Miss Julie*

Setting small, cramped, full of kitchen utensils and stable gear. Noisy. People outside gathering for the party shouting, singing, making music. Kristin's cooking and cleaning making scraping, sizzling, rattling sounds. Sometimes noise outside and in, making it difficult to hear what's being said. Often—during the most tense and dramatic moments early on—the outside sounds are giddy, full of teasing taunts and laughter. When the peasants spill in, there is little dancing, more an orgy and a drunken search for wine. Quiet for a while, then gradually animal sounds and work noises as dawn's light infiltrates the windows and the chinks in the walls. Costumes of Jean and Julie deliberately discordant in color, maximum quantity of fasteners—particularly lacing—and layers of clothing for Julie but also Jean—shirt, vest, jacket, kerchief, etc. Rhythms of the characters and their speech edgy, syncopated, at times very fast and aimless, at others slow and stumbling.

Notice that in neither case is it necessary to make an explicit stylistic statement in the production about the directorial matrix. The director's choices are nonetheless intimately related to the formative structure. On the other hand, the matrix may overtly affect the outward *style* of the production. An expressionistic set for *Miss Julie* might be obviously distorted in line and color; the lights might change abruptly in intensity, color, and direction to reinforce or comment upon the emotional moment; the servant characters might be costumed alike, perhaps with abstract make-up or masks to make them look alike, robbing them of any trace of individuality. The opening scene of the circus-matrix *The Visit* might employ an unambiguous circus train—the "Zachanassian International Circus"—rolling into the sleepy town and discharging a full-blown circus parade: Claire in her sedan chair in gaudy jewels and ostrich plumes; the eunuches as clowns, perhaps; the black leopard; a band; a menagerie.

In these cases as in every other, the director must question the validity and the effectiveness of the interpretational key.

> Whether its statement is blatant or subtle, the matrix must be connected intimately to the text and not simply applied to it in hopes of some arbitrary novelty.

The concept of an expressionistic *Miss Julie,* stated or implied, depends on the intrinsic validity of the director's imaginative interpretation and the director's skill in employing the forms it suggests. The same is true of the circum-matrix for *The Visit.*

The ability to justify such choices intellectually is obviously not the point at issue, but in some cases justification is possible. *Expressionism* as a theatrical style, for example, grew out of an effort to make the unconscious mind manifest on stage—to show the world of the play as it might appear to the troubled mind of the protagonist. The production assumes the qualities of a nightmare. *Miss Julie* has a number of elements that seem connected to the expressionistic style. The psychologies of the characters are of major importance. The memory sequences Julie and Jean describe are striking and powerful. Julie is in an almost somnambulistic state after the sexual encounter. The play is charged with sexual images and symbols in much the same way as many of the seminal expressionistic plays. And, in fact, Strindberg was himself a potent exemplar for the later expressionist playwrights.

While such justification is reassuring, it is scarcely enough.

> Though the chosen matrix may pass intellectual tests, it may be completely inappropriate or ineffectual when evaluated from the perspective of *theatrical* potential.

Many of Williams's plays—subjective and wide-ranging in space and time—are congenial with the forms and rhythms of Symbolism.
Play: *Eccentricities of a Nightingale* **Author:** Tennessee Williams **Theatre:** Heritage Repertory Theatre **Director:** George Black **Set Designer:** Charles Caldwell **Costumes:** Rosemary Ingham **Lighting:** Michael Rourke **Actors (l to r):** Jeanne Hackney, Howard Korder, Helen Oney, Arthur Greene

The director ultimately must examine the rightness of an expressionistic matrix in approaching *Miss Julie* in terms of the theatrical validity of the choice. Does it illuminate the play? Does it impart a special and inevitable quality? Does it provide a framework of answers and solutions rather than raise more questions and problems? A program note might well try to assure the audience of the intellectual rightness and honesty of the interpretation. The production, however, must stand on its own, must be its own explanation and justification. Directors must always be attuned to the effect of their choices about the production. Good choices make strong statements that inspire designers and actors, that make the play live and coruscate in performance. Poor choices need explanations and excuses.

DISCUSSION

1. How can a theatrical style be an appropriate inspiration on which to base a production? Suggest practical applications.

2. Once chosen, how can a theatrical matrix function without being obviously stated?

Do a complete theatrical analysis of a script as follows:

1. Search of the text: find and briefly identify theatrical allusions and clues (play-within-a-play, etc.)

2. Free associations: make a simple list of the periods or styles that you sense hold some valid potential for approaching the script.

3. Statement of a potential matrix: write a concise description of how the matrix affects the production.

Mention the visual, aural, and kinetic elements, and any unexpected or rewarding possibilities the matrix suggests.

OTHER ART FORMS

Other arts have special value for the director interested in penetrating the puzzle of the playwright's text. In his excellent *Period Style for the Theatre*, Douglas A. Russell (p. xvi) echoes John Ruskin in noting the following principle:

"The arts have always shown the inner life of man in a particular period better than political, intellectual, or social history. For the theatre, the visual arts, in particular, are the key to the inner life of a particular period style."

In fact, all the arts of any period are of peculiar value since they give expression to the ideals and forms in which all artists of the time share.

The director making a production designs the visual, aural, and kinetic patterns that together make up the expressive theatrical form. The director functions as a visual artist (painter and sculptor), a musical artist (composer, conductor), and a kinetic or spatial artist (choreographer, architect). The director's skill in these tasks is rooted in a sensitivity to and knowledge of the ways in which those art forms are expressed.

Like the method of theatrical exploration, the use of other art forms is open-ended and virtually limitless in its possibilities. Beginning again with the text, the director searches for connections and associations with painting (and photography), sculpture, architecture, music, dance—indeed any mode of artistic expression. Once again, the search is for *felt* connections, not logical or strictly symbolic ones. The creative director will explore:

1. Works contemporary with the playwright, especially with the time of the composition of the play;
2. Works contemporary with the time period(s) depicted in the play;
3. Works analogous to the *feeling* of the play, especially modern works.

In the case of Shakespeare's *Julius Caesar,* for example, the director would examine sources from 1) Elizabethan England; 2) Imperial Rome; and 3) modern works that speak with some force and directness to the director's own sensibilities about the play.

This type of search can prove a formidable task. We tend to be distracted by and satisfied with logical connections and congruences: busts or paintings of Caesar and the other principals, photographs and models of the Roman sites or buildings referred to in the play. Such examples can provide telling details and a sense of structure and feeling. Still, such an organized and linear approach to *Julius Caesar* or any other play is self-limiting. Consider how some of the techniques below might open up a director's sensibilities and awareness to potential forms:

- deliberately searching out historical material for which *no* immediate logical connection is obvious; in the case of *Caesar,* this might involve looking at artworks that depict soldiers and statesmen other than those historical figures appearing in the play
- looking for work that is abstract and communicates only a *felt* connection with the play
- going rapidly through sourcebooks and other material to thwart the desire for simple identification or strictly logical connections. (Flipping rapidly through a book of painting, sculpture, or architecture and quickly noting each page is an excellent procedure)
- being alert to connections and resonances of the play with artworks experienced from day-to-day. A moment in a *pas de deux,* for example, in a dance concert might well capture a poignant moment between Brutus and Portia
- cultivating the *habit* of seeing theatrical forms and potentials in other artworks. Seeing Pina Bausch's choreographic creation in *Rite of Spring* could provoke an inspiration for a directorial matrix for *The Trojan Women;* Picasso's *Guernica* for a *Macbeth;* Rodin's *Burghers of Calais* for a *Richard II.*

Work freely and imaginatively. A piece of architecture may suggest a world; a painting might hold the key to the way a character moves; a piece of music could inspire the structure of a dialogue. On one level, this sort of search yields historic and stylistic information; on another it sharpens perceptions of art and of the world; at still another, it shows the director forms that express the feelings dormant in the text.

By and large, the director should be bold in using the images found in these searches. While obviously the painstaking recreation on stage of such a famous painting as *American Gothic* can (and has) become a cliché, such strokes are seldom the problem that many inexperienced directors believe.

|| **When an artwork makes a statement and creates a powerful** ||
|| **and specific feeling, *it is because its form is expressive.*** ||

As long as the use of form is honest, potent, and integrated into the total work, it should be developed and used. When the use of form is superficial, clumsy, or self-conscious, it does not invalidate the technique; rather it indicates the director made a poor choice. As an astute critic once noted "Hacks borrow; artists steal."

EXERCISES

Bring in examples of images from other arts that capture some feeling of a play you wish to explore. (Use photocopies if need be.) A minimum number of examples is suggested in each category. When you have gathered all your images, attempt to correlate your findings and make a coherent matrix for a production. Failing that, describe the particulars of the production that might be guided by your discoveries in the exercise—for example, color, composition, textures, costume, gesture, makeup, movement, and the like.

	PAINTING	SCULPTURE	ARCHITECTURE
A. Works contemporary with the composition of the play	4	3	3
B. Works contemporary with the *action* of the play	4	3	3
C. Analogous works	6	4	3

RITUALS AND GAMES

Because the structures of games and rituals are rich with intimations of hierarchy, significant action, purposefulness, verbal and gestural patterns, and clearly defined relationships, directors use them frequently. In recent years, we have become so attuned to these modes of perceiving and ordering theatrical action that ritual and games have become an indispensable part of our vocabulary of analogs.

The search for ritual and game images in the text may proceed in the same manner as that for theatrical references: systematically filtering through the text to discover obvious and incipient references and actions that relate to rituals and games. Sometimes, of course, the text is rich in those references and clues. Albee's alternations of games with social and religious rituals in *Who's Afraid of Virginia Woolfe?* or Goldman's evocation of chess strategy in *The Lion in Winter* are ready examples.

The analogies discovered in this process may produce either an overall matrix (as with Michael Kahn's hockey metaphor for *Henry V* or Tyrone Guthrie's interpetation of *Oedipus Rex* in terms of the Roman Mass) or an image that suggests a key to the understanding and staging of a particular scene, moment, or even gesture.

MICHAEL KAHN 19– (U.S.)	New York; regional: Café LaMama, American Shakespeare Festival, Shakespeare Theatre at the Folger. *Henry V, The Three Sisters, America Hurrah*. Has headed two Shakespeare Festivals and the Interpretation Department of the Drama Division at the Julliard School.

What remains important is the specificity of the image employed and its power to inspire sound, vital choices that enrich the work. Tossing a ball back and forth is clear enough an image for any exchange of dialogue, but it is neither a vivid nor specific one. Who are the players—children or adult athletes? What kind of ball? What is the game—a pleasant diversion or a special kind of contest? Or is it a racket game? Consider how the choice of table tennis, lawn tennis, racketball, or badminton alters the *dramatic* intensity and meaning of the scene. Specifying the game changes the rhythm and spatial relationships, and even its *weight*. A change can affect movement, breathing, and tempo. And it is not too much to suggest that even the costumes might be affected.

Once again, the artist will meld image and content to create a convincing unity. The hack will be satisfied with noncommitment, incoherence, or cliché.

EXERCISES

Choose a short dialogue scene to experiment with game imagery and its uses and effects by applying some variations (like the ball toss or racket games). Attempt in each variation to create an honest interpretation of the scene. Use each image as fully as your imagination allows to involve stage geography, physical and character relationships, character intentions and objectives, even scenery and costumes. Do not be afraid to make mistakes, but deal honestly with the material. Do not violate the integrity of the text, the characters, or the truth of the action.

PSYCHOLOGY, ANTHROPOLOGY, AND SOCIOLOGY

Since the days of Stanislavski, many directors—especially in America—have built productions on psychological models. We have become so used to the method that we reflexively accept it as "right." Psychology purports to create frameworks and perspectives to explain behavior, which is also the concern of most drama—certainly "realistic" drama. And, because psychology is *scientific,* we are disposed to accept psychological models as *the* valid and honest ones upon which to build productions. We are automatically convinced, for example, of the rightness of the approach of a psychological interpretation even of such plays as *Hamlet* and *Oedipus Rex.*

Note the strong image: sylistic antecedents in Brecht's Epic Theatre and earlier Expressionism.
Play: *The Emperor Jones* **Author:** Eugene O'Neill **Theatre:** Missouri Repertory Theatre **Director:** George Keathley **Set Designer:** John Ezell **Costumes:** Baker S. Smith **Lighting:** Curt Ostermann (Photo by Larry Pape)

Directors also base production approaches on other sciences, notably anthropology and sociology. In fact, any of the scientific disciplines contain vast resources for use in theatrical creation. Their validity and effectiveness are not inherently greater, however, than other models of seeing and ordering life and relationships, such as those we have discussed in terms of the theatre itself, the other arts, and rituals and games.

The most useful scientific models are those that employ clear images and structures. In recent years, for example, some of the aspects of transactional analysis popularized by Eric Berne in books like *The Games People Play* (note the model the *scientist* is using!) proved useful to directors who found the shifting images of child-adult-parent in relationships, or transactions, to be especially precise and provocative. Even works that deal with child development have potential. The insights of Dr. Bruno Bettleheim in *The Uses of Enchantment* deal ostensibly with the interpretation and effects of fairy tales. But his analyses of the structure and workings of myth are rich in theatrical possibilities.

Applying the perspectives drawn from Robert Ardrey's popular anthropological study *Territorial Imperative* to the staging of Pinter's *The Homecoming* yields a range of marvelously suggestive insights and possibilities. From the set design—dank, barren, cave-like—to the primitive manner in which Max commands from his overstuffed chair redolent with fetid cigar smoke, to Lenny's search for his food cache, to Ruth's prowling about until she displaces Max and assumes his commanding position in the lair, the play fairly throbs with animal tensions when it is built on the perceptions in Ardrey's thesis. Also thrown into high relief are the many animal images and references in the play. This directorial matrix highlights the primitive urgency, mystery, and redolence of Pinter's work—qualities that can be made to reverberate in every aspect of the production.

CRITICISM AND INTERPRETATION

By and large, critical writings and commentaries are for information. Some explain particular meanings, backgrounds, and connections that can be found in no other way. Others criticize by applying certain evaluative standards to a work. But a third type *interprets,* attempts to reconstruct and re-express the imaginative experience of a work of art.

This last, interpretive sort of criticism is most useful since, in the process of expressing the results of an imaginative encounter with a text, the commentary might well reveal images, patterns, and structures that could inspire an artist with the insights needed to create a directorial matrix. Jan Kott's *Shakespeare, Our Contemporary* and *The Eating of the Gods* have done just that for Peter Brook (among others) with their vivid and provocative images. As early as the 1930's, the distinguished commentator, G. Wilson Knight, was writing brilliant interpretations of Shakespeare in *The Wheel of Fire and Principles of Shakespearean Production*. (In the former, he anticipates Kott's essay in many ways in "*King Lear* and the Comedy of the Grotesque" and "The Lear Universe.")

In searching through commentaries as part of the research on any play, the director should not seek simply to get at meanings but also to find images that expand and resonate, suggesting forms to express the feelings in the play. Knight himself is eloquent on the point:

> In interpretation we must remember not the facts but the quality of the original poetic experience; and, *in translating this into whatever concepts appear suit-*

able, we find that the facts fall into place at when once the qualitative focus is correct.
(*The Wheel of Fire*, p. 7. Emphasis added)

What should be apparent is that the matrix results from imagination and instinct supported by the intellect. Images provide the raw materials and stimulate the process. Since the director must bring experience and imagination to the work of making a production, the truly creative director looks for ways to develop the innate ability to use those faculties. By being alert to experiences and conscious of ways to employ them in the work of theatrical creation, a director can expand his or her possibilities in limitless ways.

End Notes

The director, as theatre artist, acknowledges the truth that useful images are virtually everywhere. And every director must be sensitive to everything in the world in which we all live. The kinds of analyses outlined in this chapter are meant to broaden the range of image models available to a director who confronts the challenge of translating a text to the stage. The methodologies and approaches are designed to provoke the *imagination* (the image-making powers) of the director, to prompt him or her to create image structures and motifs inspired by the confrontation with the script—to do, in other words, what Stanislavski hoped to do for the actor: "To make inspiration appear more often than is its wont."

PART II

METHODS

But idea itself must always bow to the needs and demands of the material in which it is to be cast.

—**Ben Shahn,** *The Shape of Content*

6 THE DIRECTOR'S FIVE DIMENSIONS

The director works in and through the theatrical medium, manipulating the visual, aural, and kinetic forms of the production to create and communicate feeling and meaning. In every case the director—like every other artist—employs the materials at hand. The director works with a text that must be interpreted and communicated in a *theatrical space,* with elements of *aural and visual design,* and complemented by *actors* who move and produce spoken and other sound.

> **The director works in *five dimensions:* three dimensions of the visual, physical reality; a fourth of movement in time and space; and a fifth of sound.**

111

First, Second, and Third Dimensions

STAGE GEOGRAPHY

Positions on the floor of the stage correspond to the first two dimensions: breadth (lateral positions from right to left) and depth (from near to far, downstage to upstage).

The Stage Grid

These positions are conventionally identified on a proscenium stage as a 15 block grid (see Figure 6–1). Because this concept and terminology is virtually universal, it will be employed throughout this chapter, with the understanding that the *principles* involved, if not the vocabulary, apply as well to non-proscenium stages.[1]

Notice that in looking at the grid, there are only two types of designations: *lateral* (always from the perspective of the actor standing on the stage facing the audience—R [right], C [center], and L [left]) and *depth* (U [up], farthest from the proscenium line, and D [down], closest to the proscenium line). All 15 areas on the grid, then, fix positions both laterally and in depth on the stage.

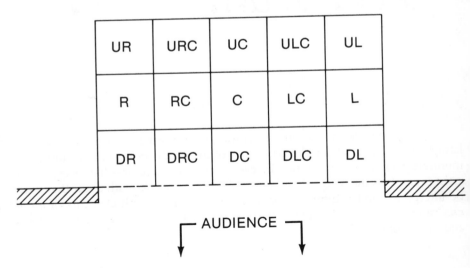

Figure 6–1 Stage Grid

[1]The special qualities and demands of the thrust and arena stage are discussed in Chapter XII—Special Strategies in Staging.

Relative Strength of Positions

The director uses these two dimensions primarily to establish relative strength through stage position. Obviously, *depth* is the more powerful. The closer an object is to the viewer, the more emphatic is its position. In other words, an actor DC (down-center) is a more commanding physical presence than one UC (up-center), if for no other reason than the downstage figure appears larger. The relative strengths of the lateral positions are less clear, although it is fair enough to suppose that the C (center) position is the strongest, because it occupies the position of critical balance in the symmetry of the stage picture. Positions L and R are not as obvious. Conventionally, the R areas are considered stronger than the L areas. Arguably, this judgment is colored by the fact that, in the Western world at least, most writing flows from left to right—from the audience's perspective. In theatrical terminology, of course, that translates to a flow from stage R to L.

Accepting these assumptions about relatively strong and weak positions in the theatrical space, we can posit DC as the strongest *in terms of stage geography* and UL as the weakest. There is some comfort in noting that these two conclusions, at least, conform to theatrical traditions.

DISCUSSION

1. Find and be prepared to discuss the use and importance of compositional principles in different two-dimensional media: newspapers, magazines, posters or displays, paintings, photographs.

2. Analyze the layout of one or more supermarkets to study the intent and effects of the spatial design. Identify the areas that are most and least prominent in terms of audience appeal.

3. Consider any observable patterns in the design of department stores—especially large ones. Is there any accounting for the two-dimensional layout of the main floors?

4. Discuss the implications, if any, of findings from 1–3 above on the use of the two dimensions of stage geography.

EXERCISES

1. Have one person stand on the stage, facing the audience, in first one stage area, then another. Try to evaluate fairly the relative strength of each of the several positions. (Directions should be communicated in stage vocabulary: "up-left," "down-right-center," "left-center," and so on. This will give both parties a chance to achieve some fluency with the terminology.)

2. Put two people on stage, each in a different position (L and R; UL and DC; and so on) to get a sense of the potential of relative stage positioning. (To aid in keeping the exercise a fair one, the actors should be fairly matched in terms of size and visual impact, and should remain still and facing full-front when being evaluated.)

Other Spatial Relationships

Height or elevation is the *third dimension* of stage geography. Putting an actor on a platform or riser suddenly complicates the whole question of emphasis and focus. Even without a platform, an actor who is considerably taller than others on stage is visually a more commanding figure. Director face complications and choices: how, for example, to deal with a stage that is sharply *raked*, rising like a ramp from downstage to upstage (the historical origin of the "up" and "down" designations, since an actor moving away from the audience is, in fact, going "up"). Obviously, the raked stage distorts the usual perception of the third dimension and therefore must be considered when establishing emphasis and focus. The director must also be aware of the relationship of the viewer to the stage. In an auditorium where the audience is well below or above the level of the stage, the viewers' perceptions of relative positions and dimensions differ radically.

DISCUSSION

1. Some directors routinely employ multi-level sets. What are some advantages and disadvantages for the director in using sets with playing areas at different levels?

2. Are certain kinds of plays or approaches either "congenial" or "hostile" to the use of different playing levels?

3. Discuss the circumstances that would suggest the use of a raked stage, and the limitations and the potentials its use would create.

INDIVIDUAL BODY POSITIONS

The positions of the actors' bodies relative to the audience also affects emphasis and focus. For the most part, the operating principle seems to be that the larger the surface area presented to the audience, the more emphatic the position. When the actor faces downstage (full front to the audience), he or she obviously is in the strongest body position.

As the actor makes one-quarter turn, he or she is said to be ¾ *open*. Another quarter turn yields the *profile;* another, *¾ closed;* and finally, *full-back* (completely closed). Traditionally, the apparent relative strengths of these positions (see Figure 6–2) are ranked as follows:

S T R O N G E S T
Full-front
¾ open
Profile
Full-back
¾ closed
W E A K E S T

What happened to our earlier assertion that visible surface area being the sole factor determining emphasis? The process has again been complicated by additional elements. These include 1) *the visibility of the actor's face;* 2) *the line and tension of the body;* and 3) *the psychology of body language.* In some of the exercises that follow, you will have the opportunity to test some of these factors and make some judgments on the influence they exert.

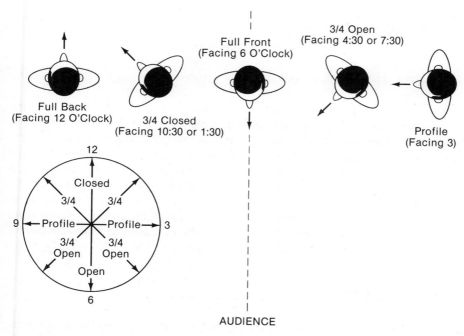

Figure 6–2 Body Positions

RELATIVE BODY POSITIONS

When two or more actors occupy roughly equivalent stage positions (that is, standing slightly R and L of C), their relative strength is determined by their *relative body positions*. Simply and obviously staged, when actor *A* is facing full-front and *B* is facing him or her in profile, *A*'s is the emphatic position, the focus of the scene. In any combination of stronger and weaker positions, the actor in the stronger position is said to have *taken* the scene, the other to have *given* it. When two actors are in body positions of equal strength, the scene is *shared* (see Figure 6–3).

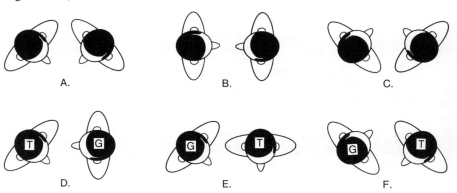

A, B, C ~ "SHARED" ~ Both Actors in Equivalent Body Positions D, E, F ~ One Actor (G) "Gives" ~ The Other (T) "TAKES" the Scene.

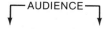

Figure 6–3 Shared and Given Scenes

What directors find fascinating and challenging about these techniques for controlling and modulating focus and emphasis is the fact that, in performance, they are seldom static. Even a brief scene may involve a larger number of shifts in focus, and these must seem to reflect the energy and behavioral patterns of the characters involved in the created world in which they appear. The director is clearly given the responsibility of making certain decisions of emphasis on the gross scale of stage geography, but he or she must also be alert to the subtle shifts that evolve in the dynamics of any scene. Given the pattern of flow from one static picture to another, the director is then confronted with movement, discussed in the next section. (See also Chapter XI on "Side Coaching.")

EXERCISES _____

1. Using two actors, repeat #2 in the Exercises above on "Stage Geography." This time vary the head positions first, then the relative body posi-

Play: *The Duchess of Malfi* Author: John Webster Theatre: The Guthrie Theater Director: Michael Kahn Set Designer: Derek McLane Costumes: Martin Pakledinaz Lighting: Frances Aronson Actors (l to r): Barbara March, Stephen Yoakam

Play: *Richard II* Author: William Shakespeare Theatre: The Shakespeare Theatre at the Folger Director: Toby Robertson Actors: Phillip Goodwin (front), Edward Gero (Photo by Joan Marcus)

Play: *A Thousand Clowns* Author: Herb Gardner Theatre: PlayerStock Director: George Black Set Designer: Charles Caldwell Costumes: Helen Ju Lighting: David W. Weiss Actors (l to r): Michael Zaslow, David Firestone

In each of these scenes, some aspect of the relationship of the two characters is communicated through their relative body positions.

tions. Notice how the line and apparent tension of the body and the visibility of the face affect the focus and meaning of the composition. Finally, give one actor an innocuous hand-held object—a pencil, handkerchief, or the like, and experiment with its effect on the actors' visual focus. How can the object be used to change or intensify focus? When does it disturb or distract?

2. Repeat the two exercises, then add a third actor later in each segment.

   a) On a flat floor, evenly lighted, place the actors—facing D—in different combinations of stage positions. Evaluate their relative strengths in each configuration.

   b) Next, add two platforms, chairs or stools of different heights. Place the actors once more—first in the same then in different body positions. Note the effects.

3. Stage a two character scene that requires little or no movement, attempting to vary emphasis and focus through relative stage and body positions. Using several chairs or other appropriate pieces of furniture, stage the scene *in a single stage area.* Vary the relative heights of the two characters as the scene unfolds. At any given moment, one or both may stand, kneel, sit or lie down on the floor. (Consider such scenes as those between George and Emily or Mrs. Webb and Mrs. Gibbs in Thornton Wilder's *Our Town;* Laura and the Gentleman Caller in Tennessee Williams's *The Glass Menagerie;* or the two Irish teenagers in "Winners," Episode I of Brian Friel's *Lovers.*)

DISCUSSION

Find examples from drawing, painting, or photography that illustrate some of the compositional principles exemplified in the exercises prescribed above (1–3).

THE THEATRICAL ENVIRONMENT

Although we have been concentrating on the actor as a prime compositional element in that never-never land of "all other things being equal," we should underscore the fact that things are never equal. Obviously, the actors perform in a scenic environment that both enhances and complicates the director's task. From an esthetic standpoint, they must be part of the compositional statement along with the scenery, costumes, and lights; they must belong to the visual world of the production. At the same time, they routinely must appear to do only what is dictated by the action of the play, and not by arbitrary artistic or technical demands. In this sense, the design elements are influencing the actors and the entire production at every moment of a performance. And so, while we isolate the actors for the purpose of understanding their function as compositional elements, it is only to be able later to relate them to the larger theatrical scenic and dramatic context. Your skill in these areas will be greatly enhanced if you have sensitized yourself by looking seriously at paintings and other visual resources in the "Other Arts" technique described in Chapter V.

The Fourth Dimension

Going beyond the three dimensions of staging already discussed, the director confronts the fourth: movement. The immediate response to this element is to think of the actors and their blocking; but added to that is a combination of elements that move *actually*—scenery, costumes, and properties—and those that move *virtually*—the lights. And so, while we concentrate here on the movement of the actors, keep in mind that other elements of the production will be parts of its kinetic design as well.

As already noted in the exercises above, movement on stage is immediately engaging; it is sometimes said to "steal focus." While this is not always the case (it may be the opposite, in fact), it is useful to think of movement as one of the most potent devices for attracting focus. Actors and directors learn quickly enough that under most circumstances, only the actor speaking should have compelling movements. Exceptions exist, of course, but they are best used only for extraordinary purposes to distract attention from the speaker, or to call attention to something else on stage.

There are three types of movement. Ranging from the broadest to the most confined, they are *stage position, body position,* and *"business."*

STAGE POSITION

The largest movements involving actors are those from one stage position to another. These movements can be *lateral* (R to C, C to L), *up-and-down stage,* or *diagonal*.

Lateral movements are usually the least emphatic because they involve no change in the apparent size or scale of the character. A lateral cross from L to R is probably slightly more dynamic than the reverse, since such a cross is counter to the pattern of reading in most of the western world.

Up-and-down crosses tend to be either very powerful or very weak. A cross from upstage to downstage achieves the most immediate impact because the scale of the actor (the apparent size) grows rapidly. The reverse movement (D to U) is extremely weak because the scale is reduced quickly. Direct up-and-down crosses are used infrequently, however, because they are essentially *flat* (from the audience's perspective). The cross directly from D to U is invariably awkward for the actor as well.

Diagonal crosses are usually the most emphatic not only because they involve a transition in scale, but also because the diagonal movement projects an impression of greater dynamics and visual interest. Of course, the real power of the diagonal cross is due to its essential up-and-down direction.

Directors must be concerned about more than stage geography and body positions, of course. They must also be alert to the *quality* of any movement through the use of *shape, tempo,* and *rhythm.*

Stage Movement: Principles And Conventions

1. *Single focus* or *emphasis* usually demands only one actor moving at a time.[2] Each individual action must be completed before the next one is initiated. Therefore, each action should have a *finish*. The director may check the control of single focus by supposing a ball is being tossed from actor to actor. Whoever, figuratively, has the ball also has focus and may move. This technique will help ensure a clean control of single focus in any scene.

2. Accepted proscenium stage technique requires the moving actor to cross *downstage* of another actor when *both are standing*. This maintains focus on the moving actor (the expected and usually desirable effect), because the actor making the cross does not disappear even momentarily behind (upstage) of the stationary actor. It also permits the stationary actor to maintain continuous eye contact with the moving actor without having to twist around to follow the movement.

3. When the stationary actor is *seated* on a proscenium stage, however, the moving actor usually crosses upstage, when possible. Otherwise the seated actor is put at the disadvantage of having any reactions (including eye contact) completely hidden during the cross. While this movement seems to guarantee the subordination of the seated actor, it may be employed for the opposite effect if the moving actor is clearly responding to the *controlling attitude* of the seated actor. This relationship is emphasized when the moving actor is moving away from the seated one. For example, a subordinate pleading with a superior crossing upstage of the dominant character seated at a large desk facing front presents an entirely different dynamic from a dominating interrogator encircling an obviously cowed suspect seated on a stool in the middle of the room.

4. *Diagonal crosses,* as we have already noted, are inherently more dynamic than lateral or up-and-down stage moves.

---

[2] A group of characters may be considered an individual actor ir the crowd acts and responds like a single character.

5. *Straight crosses* are generally stronger than curved ones, but *curved crosses* are more graceful and especially useful when the character is costumed in a long train, skirt, or cape.

6. A *punctuated move* is very emphatic. A punctuated move is a cross that is broken, interrupted, or finished deliberately to coincide with a definite character impulse. For example, a character crossing quickly from DL toward an exit UR, might stop sharply three-quarters of the way there and make a one-quarter turn back. Such a movement is particularly powerful because the moving actor carries the expectation that the movement will be continuous and completed. The abrupt halt and turn pulls the focus, which had previously included most of the field of movement, back sharply to the actor alone.

7. Any action that changes an established pattern is emphatic. Such *pattern violation* can upset usual expectation. A lateral curved cross may take on important emphasis if it is employed in the midst of an established pattern of straight diagonal moves. When many elements are moving at once, emphasis can be established by having the focal actor either remain *static* or move *against* the general pattern of movement.

8. A *counter* is a subsidiary move made by one or more actors to accommodate a more important move. When actor *A* crosses from L to R of actor *B,* the actor *B* might take a couple of half-steps D and R as the actor *A* passes. Or the *actor B* could take a few short steps to follow the principal following through with the main cross.

In both these examples, the purpose of the counter is to support the principal physical action and to adjust the position and focus of the actor *giving* the scene in an easy and apparently natural way.

9. The *rhythm* of stage action can be varied by changing *tempo* (or speed of execution); *shape* (straight, curved, lateral, diagonal); *finish* (the softness or crispness of the transitions, best described as the manner in which the actors throw that imaginary ball from one to the other); and *quality* (described in musical notation as "staccato," "legato," "crescendo," and so on).

10. Some actors tend always to make *open turns* on stage. An *open* turn is always *towards* the audience in an effort never to turn one's back to the audience. The opposite, a *closed* turn, though, is not only legitimate but enormously useful to avoid the "stagey" artificial look of an awkward open turn. A closed turn can also give stage action a softer, more natural contour, and provide a natural means of moving the actor into a ¾ closed position or full-back position in order to give the scene definitively to another actor.

To record your blocking decisions in your script, you should use something like a standard shorthand notation method shown in Table 6–1.

TABLE 6–1

BLOCKING TRANSCRIPTIONS

You may record blocking in your script either by making marginal notes or notes on a blank facing page. By referencing the precise place in the text with a caret (^) and a circled number, you can then indicate the exact move or position in a fairly standard theatrical shorthand that follows. The primary aim of such annotation is accuracy and ease of deciphering. By using more or less standard notations, you can achieve both aims.

Some directors prefer to use a separate miniature floorplan for each page of text with numbered arrows keyed to the text numbers. This has the advantage of being graphic, but can become confusing in very active scenes.

② ^	= Text location for notation
X	= Cross
X 4 R	= Cross right four steps
Ent	= Enter
Xit	= Exit
⊃ G	= Turn or Counter
↓ or S̲	= Sit
↑ or Ri	= Rise
Kn	= Kneel
⌒✗—	= Curved cross
Plt	= Platform
Ch	= Chair
//	= Pause or stop
///	= Long pause

(The notations can be used in any logical and consistent combination; e.g., X Ch R /// G S̲ .)

EXERCISES

1.—a. Have an actor cross directly from one stage position to another, then reverse.

    b. Repeat these crosses, having the actor smoothly *curve* each cross slightly upstage before returning to the original lateral plane. Note that one effect of this sort of curved cross is to have the actor finish the cross in a more *open* position than would occur with a straight path.

    c. Without exaggerating the technique, try some compound ("S") curves. This can be done quite subtly and gracefully, elongating the cross for the purpose of timing a line or action, or to suggest an understated indirection quite appropriate to certain personalities or period styles. (You may find it useful to trace the curved path on the floor for the actor to follow until the cross *feels* right.)

2.—a. Have an actor cross from C to DR of a chair placed R, make an *open* turn, then finish the cross to U of the chair.

    b. Make the same cross, this time making a *closed* turn around the chair.

    c. Note the differences in the *phrasing* and *effect* of each of the crosses.

3.—a. Experiment changing the tempo of several crosses. Note, however, that for a cross to avoid the appearance of being forced or unnatural, the actor's speed should virtually never be uniform from start to stop. Especially if the tempo is fast, the actor should begin, accelerate, and then slow down before the end.

    b. Again attempt to control the quality of the crosses, this time with rhythm. Try a variety of methods. Ask the actor to be sullen or happy, apprehensive or confident. Or to move to a rhythm tapped out by the director or another person, or to the rhythm of a piece of music that the actor is asked to call to mind.

    c. Observe people crossing paths in everyday circumstances. Demonstrate the shape, tempo, and rhythm of three or more of the most interesting examples you observed. Try to recreate the movements precisely; do not parody. Discuss the qualities each example communicates and the means through which those qualities are expressed.

The Fifth Dimension

SOUND/RHYTHM

There is a sort of music in every performance, whether or not a musical note is played or sung. The music is produced by the *sounds* of the performance—the sounds of the spoken word, the ringing of a bell, the ticking of a clock, the closing of a door. The quality of these sounds and the way they are composed and played constitues a subtle but very persuasive fifth dimension in the director's repertoire. Much has been made of different playwrights' gifts of language. Shakespeare being the apogee, we assume theatrical music to be a sort of poetry. That indeed it is, but although theatre language is a kind of poetry, it is not necessarily "poetic" in the literary sense. The kind of poetry that produces theatrical music is of a different sort. Relatively few great poets have been great dramatists. Some great playwrights, in fact, have sometimes been characterized as "tone deaf," but all have produced vehicles capable of great music in performance. For example, the charge is often made against Eugene O'Neill, who produced many lines and speeches that are easy to characterize as "non-poetic" or even "tone-deaf," but *Long Day's Journey Into Night* is a modern symphony of the highest order—not so much because the language is elegant, or even careful, but because the language, passion, and sheer theatrical genius weave the incipient music into the very fabric of the text.

"Theatre music" of the sort we consider here is produced when the elements of the play—the contour of the words, the actions, and the sensibilities of the artists involved—come together in compelling theatrical forms. Even in the most prosaic cases, a performance establishes distinctive patterns of sound and rhythm. It is a good bet that every director has said or will say something like "Louder, faster, brighter!" to the assembled company. The Duke of Saxe-Meiningen once had his extras lie on the floor offstage and shout into mattresses to get the muffled, distant quality he felt essential for one scene. Many a successful director has searched feverishly to find just the right sound for the fabled "breaking string" in *The Cherry Orchard*.

Movies and television have made theatre directors more alert than ever to the uses of sound in dramatic productions. Few theatre directors use incidental music the way film or video artists do, but many of the best do "score" stage productions. The sensitive director thinks of casting in terms of voice parts in the manner of musicals or operas (as suggested in Chapter V in our discussion of "Other Arts"). One role might sound best with a light airy voice, another with a rich basso. The voice casting of a production can be every bit as important as the physical casting.

Other elements in "scoring" a stage production are the physical sounds of the action of the play (doors closing, tableware being handled, and so on) and ambient sounds (crickets, traffic sounds, running water, and the like). Good directors realize that while contemporary conventions seldom allow background music in the theatre like that in the movies, a reservoir of possibilities nonetheless exits. The creative director need only experiment with these resources, and with imaginative ways to motivate or justify their use in production.

Characteristics of Sound

Each of the characteristics of sound may be modulated to alter the meaning and effect of any given theatrical exchange, in degrees ranging from subtle to radical.

> *Volume*—loud, quiet
> *Tempo*—fast, slow
> *Rhythm*—regular, staccato
> *Quality*—harmonious, dissonant

DISCUSSION

Describe the "aural" qualities of two similar television shows. Be as specific as possible, analyzing the sound design of each in terms not only of the sounds used (motivated or unmotivated music, ambient sounds, actor- or action-produced sounds, and the sounds of the dialogue itself) but also in terms of the "characteristics" listed above. Comment as well on the atmospheric and emotional effects of the sound design.

EXERCISE

Using any short two-person scene, prepare two or three versions, changing only the *sound* qualities of the performance. The exercise must be done with care; try to make sure that each decision is supported in terms of intention and motivation. Evaluate what happens to the meaning and the effect of the scene as the result of each modulation.

End Notes

It is important to remember that the "five dimensions" with which the director works are neither arbitrary nor superficial. In a very real sense, they define the director's world—the physical realities the director must master in order to communicate meaning and feeling to an audience. The creative director recognizes the importance of these production elements and tries to use them to their best effect. Instead of simply ignoring these facts, good directors use such potential with great imagination and skill.

TABLE 6–2

The Director's Medium

First, Second, and Third Dimensions

Visual Elements [Painting, sculpture, and architecture]: The sum of the work of the technicians and designers (scenery, costumes, lights, and properties) and of the work of the director with the actors (their placement within the *mise-en-scene* and their positions relative to one another). The **look** of the production.

The Fourth Dimension

Kinetic Elements [Choreography]: The movement, the rhythms, and the patterns of movement—actual and virtual—performed by the actors and the set, the stagehands, the curtains, and the lights. The **movement** of the production.

The Fifth Dimension

Aural Elements [Music]: The sounds produced by the actors—in speaking, moving, or in using properties or costumes—and by musicians and technicians employing any method or equipment. The **sound** of the production.

On the other hand, no director can do it alone. Every good director works *with* a company of equally creative collaborators. Honest directors cannot simply impose visual, aural, and kinetic decisions upon actors and designers. The best ones develop the necessary sensitivities and techniques to suggest possibilities and to draw ideas and inspiration from those who are working beside them.

The energy of a particular play, its emotional content, its aura, so to speak, has its own definite physical dimensions. It extends just so far in space and no farther.

—**Robert Edmond Jones,** *The Dramatic Imagination*

7 CREATING THE THEATRICAL ENVIRONMENT

The *theatrical environment* is the created world of the production—the sum of the design elements and the aesthetic rules and logic created for the play. It is also called *mise-en-scene*.[1] While the theatrical environment accounts for *all* the elements of a production, its primary statement—and the one that the actors and director usually confront first and most extensively—is the setting.

In many instances, the director has the assistance of designers who bring particular talents and sensitivities to the job; at other times, the director must do the job alone. In either case, the process begins with the first readings of the

---

[1]"Mise-en-scene" means literally "put-on-stage." In medieval theatre, the person who staged the production was sometimes referred to as the *"metteur-en-scene,"* the "putter" on the stage, a term one occasionally hears still applied to the director in Europe. The term "mise-en-scene" may be used, in the sense that Stanislavski used it, to refer to the placement of the actors in a particular moment. More commonly, it refers to the overall visual image, and it may be applied ultimately to the total design of the production encompassing the work of the actors and the director.

play. Images and impressions start to form as shapes, sounds, and colors emerge. Initally, the director's impressions are those of any skilled and imaginative reader. The director's challenge is to pin down these impressions, to begin the work of creating *art*. While the imagination is fluid, art is solid and hard, with clearly defined contours and textures.

> **The director's and designers' choices of shape, sound, color, texture give theatre art solidity and definition, delineating the contours of the theatrical environment.**

Whether the director is making these choices alone or with the help of designers, he or she must understand something of the mechanics and effects of design decisions, their implications for rehearsals and, ultimately, their impact on the performance.

The Design Collaboration

The procedure for working with the designer or designers of a production has become fairly well standardized, but like most conventional methodologies, especially in the theatre, this one runs the risk of becoming routine and less than productive. Therefore, it is wise to review the goals and methods each time you begin to develop design images for a production.

Directors work with designers throughout the making of a production, most directly in collaborative *design conferences*. Here is a look at a typical design process:

I. FIRST DESIGN CONFERENCE

BEGINNING THE DIALOGUE: The director proposes a matrix, along with any special requirements or limitations that will guide the designers in their work. The goal of this conference is to begin the process of defining the specific physical and aesthetic requirements and qualities of the production. (See *Outline* for this conference suggested below.)

II. PRELIMINARY DESIGNS

ROUGH VISUALIZATIONS AND WORKING SKETCHES: The designers present preliminary thumbnail sketches, color chips, patterns, and swatches for consideration.

Even when the production does not break radically from convention as in this version, the director and the designers must share a single vision in order to create the world in which the performance takes place.
Play: Don Giovanni   **Author:** Wolfgang Amadeus Mozart   **Theatre:** Boston Opera Theater, Plaza Media, and Austrian Television   **Director:** Peter Sellars   **Actors (l to r):** Eugene Perry, Herbert Perry, Lorraine Hunt (Photo by Thomas Ramstorfer)

Thumbnails "Thumbnail sketches," are quick informal sketches used for early suggestions and discussions with scene, costume, makeup, and properties designers. These sketches often reveal in visual terms some feature that are impossible to specify in verbal communication, however precise. The costume designer may establish a particular silhouette, the makeup designer a stylistic approach, the set designer a suggestion of both the atmosphere and the shape of the physical environment. To help define these ideas, the set designer may do both a thumbnail perspective of the set and a thumbnail groundplan (see Figures 7–1 and 7–2). The costume designer also will do thumbnails (see Figure 7–3). The director should respond with thought and sensitivity to these thumb-

Figure 7–1 Thumbnail Perspective   Designer: Charles Caldwell

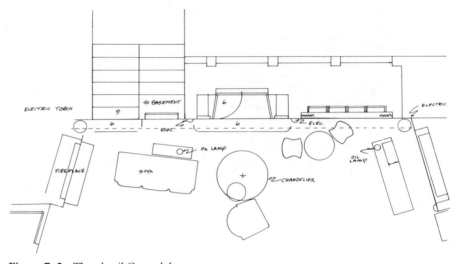

Figure 7–2 Thumbnail Groundplan

nails. Together with the first discussions, they may change the production matrix completely or affect it subtly. Once these preliminaries have been agreed upon, they form the basis for the entire visual statement of the production.

III. INTERMEDIATE DESIGNS

REFINEMENTS OF THE ROUGH SKETCHES: Depending on the earlier conferences, the designers' presentations may include:

Figure 7–3 Costume Designer's Thumbnails

Designer: Gweneth West

A. Set Designer
   1. Ground plan(s) to scale
      a. Horizontal sightlines shown from critical seats
      b. Vertical sightlines shown in section view
   2. Perspective sketches
   3. Front elevations or details
   4. White model
   5. Color samples

B. Costume Designer
   1. Sketches with swatches
   2. Dressing lists

C. Lighting Designer
   1. Light plot
   2. Media samples

D. Makeup Designer
   1. Makeup sketches
   2. Hair and wig sketches

E. Properties designer
   1. Sketches
   2. Photographs (usually including a yard or metric stick to indicate the size and scale of the item)

Elevations   An *elevation* is a two-dimensional scaled view of an object seen directly from the front or the rear. The designer may provide *front elevations* to indicate the scale of a flat or other scenic unit, as well as its detail and finish. *Rear elevations* show the structural elements of the unit and the method of joining to other units. The director is more likely to examine the front elevations to understand the visible details of the design, while the technical director will use both the front and rear for construction and finish. The director will also be interested in *painters' elevations* when these are provided. The painters' elevation is simply a front elevation on which color and texturing techniques are indicated. The scene painter uses these elevations as a guide when painting the scenery.

Section   A *section* is a scale drawing of a vertical segment (or "slice") of a set and its masking depicting the vertical relationsip of scenic elements and to establishing vertical sightlines (see Figure 7–4).

Models   A set designer may opt to provide a *model* instead of front elevations or a sketch. Such a model is constructed to the same scale as the groundplan that defines its layout. So constructed, the model can supplement the groundplan and give the director, actors, and others a sense of the spatial relationships of a design. Because this sort of model is usually left unpainted, it is

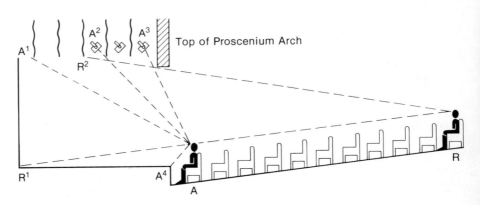

— Seat A sees area A^2 including top of set backwall (A^1) and lighting instruments (A^2 and A^3) and all of the stage floor (R^1 - A^4).

— Seat R sees no lighting instruments but (because of person in seat A) sees none of the stage floor.

Figure 7–4   Section View—Vertical Sightlines

commonly known as a working or "white" model. Many designers and directors prefer the *white model* because it is easier to read than groundplans, sketches, and elevations, especially when the spatial relationships are highly complex or important. To make it even more useful in this regard, the white model should include at least one figure of an actor shown in appropriate scale. The *presentation model* is complete with color, trim, and, often three-dimensional texture. Like the final rendering, which it may supplant, the presentation model tries to communicate accurately the visual impact of the setting.

IV. FINAL DESIGNS

COMPLETED PLANS AND RENDERINGS: Though not necessarily for display, these final designs will reflect the adjustments arrived at in the intermediate conference(s).

Final Sketches   These drawings are made after the initial and intermediate work is completed and the design ideas are ready to be put into the forms agreed upon. The costume designer's drawings will often include swatches, samples of the actual fabrics, and details indicated on the drawings.

Renderings   A *rendering* is a finished depiction in color of a design idea. Its purpose is to communicate the visual impact and significance of the design rather than to provide detailed information. Occasionally, renderings are done after the fact of the design process as presentational items for publication or display. The costume designer's renderings are usually complemented by attached swatches of the actual materials used in each costume depicted.

V. WORKING PLANS AND DRAWINGS

Once the final designs have been agreed upon, the next step is to translate the designs into technical drawings and patterns. *Working plans* and drawings consist of all the appropriately scaled and annotated information necessary for the shops, technicians, crews, and stage manager—the people who build or provide the finished design elements.

Designing the Theatrical Environment

‖ **The best theatrical environment creates the impression that the entire production is the work of a single artist.** ‖

The director usually comes to the first design conference with a directorial matrix in mind. This first meeting is critical, because it sets the director and the designers on a path from which (usually) they do not stray far. Below are some factors and procedures the director might consider in formulating an agenda for that all-important first conference with the designers.

H I N T : Notice how many things discovered in your preparation and research are immediately useable in the design process.

PERIOD

Knowing the historical period is useful, but knowing the precise year or years in which the play is to be set is even better. The director should be prepared to point out specific events that are crucial in the understanding of the period as the director sees it. The director will often ask for "historical accuracy" in rendering the period, but that is of little help. Rather, the director should be prepared to highlight the elements and *qualities* of the period that contribute to the production matrix.

If the period is fanciful, it should be as precise as one based on an historical model—arguably even more precise, if that is possible—so that the designers understand the specific environment they are attempting to communicate. This principle applies to all fantasies, whether they are set in an ancient or a futuristic time.

PLACE

Simply to say "New York" or "London" is to say very little. Once again, the director must give the designers as much guidance as possible by being precise, and by envisioning the contribution of this created *place* to the production matrix. This is not to say that the director must *know* from the outset the exact solution to this or any other problems created by speculation. But, eventually, the specifics of each element must be confronted.

ATMOSPHERE

Every production creates a special mood of ambience that is a major element in communicating the play's feeling as interpreted by the director through the designers and the actors. The description of this *atmosphere* is often phrased in imagistic terms; "light," "heavy," "grim," "bright," and so on. Such terms are translatable into design decisions, and so designers are eager to hear such descriptions. Once again, the director must be willing to specify images and intentions as clearly as possible. It is even possible in this case to use not only verbal images but visual impressions as well. If the director has done the *Other Arts* analysis suggested in the previous chapter, a whole range of visual and aural materials will be readily available for this purpose. The director must take great care, however, to provoke and open up the imaginative processes of the designers, *not* to close them down with prescriptive ideas. It is especially important to deal with terms and images that create and evoke *feelings* rather than dictate *information*.

TIME

Season

"Season," of course, refers to the time or times of year and the prevailing climatic conditions. For suggestions of even richer images than those implied by the seasons themselves, directors might explore the seasonal mythoi suggested by Northrop Frye in *The Anatomy of Criticism* (See Chapter V). A play may move from one season to another in fact or in feeling. Good designers can draw important inspiration from a sensitivity to this movement. *Romeo and Juliet,* for example, may be interpreted as moving from Spring to Summer to Autumn, or, in Frye's terms, from Comedy to Romance to Tragedy. From such an interpretation, a designer might well respond with clear and specific ideas about colors, shapes, and tonalities.

Calendar Progression

The movement of the play from day to day, week to week, year to year.

Times of Day

The movement of the play in time through a given day can be highly suggestive. For example, take note of the movement of *A Long Day's Journey Into Night,* or that of *Ghosts* as noted in the analysis in the preceding chapter.

SCENIC PROGRESSION

The developmental structure of the scenic images in the play. (See Chapter VI on *The Visit* and *The Cherry Orchard.*)

CHARACTER TRAITS

The director should be prepared to present distinguishing elements of each character or group of characters. As with the scenic elements, the director should speak in terms of the character's image, progression, and relationship to the action of the play and to the other characters. These should be images of every kind (not just visual) to clarify and provoke ideas, discussion, and development of character. In this category, of course, the director must consider the contribution of the individual actors as well.

SPECIAL REQUIREMENTS

Unusual design needs should be noted at the outset to give the designers the opportunity to create imaginative solutions. Most often these special elements are physical: the placement of the trapdoor in *The Foreigner,* for example, can be limited by the existing traps or available crawlspace; the placement of the stove in *Hedda Gabler* must allow Hedda to be lit dramatically by the glow of the fire when she burns the manuscript. Occasionally, the requirement is qualitative, calling for a design solution that reflects a special character or makes a symbolic statement. The production team dealing with *A Doll House,* for example, should determine at the outset whether the room of the Helmer household we see reflects Nora or Helmer, and whether Nora's clothes are indicative of her own tastes or her husband's.

THE WORLD OF THE PLAY

The director should address the nature of the created world or universe in which the play is to take place. In some cases, this may reflect certain political or sociological trends or influences; in others, it may disclose a philosophical or metaphysical state. The world of *Hamlet,* for example, has been depicted in countless ways and from innumerable perspectives: as an empire of Machiavellian intrigue; as a crumbling heap of political and moral corruption; and as a Freudian nightmare. Even the world of a light comedy such as *The Odd Couple* has special resonances in each and every production.

Employing the Matrix

‖ **The image of the play, expressed in its matrix, is crucial to the creation of the total design of the production.** ‖

Should the director make an explicit statement of the directorial matrix? There is no hard and fast rule. Some designers—like some actors—may be stimulated and inspired by an imagistic vision that provokes concrete ideas and deeper insights. Others may be confused and even argumentative when confronted by a commanding image to which they do not respond, or one that seems to them trivial or arbitrary.

Initially, perhaps the director's best choice is to employ the matrix as an *implicit, underlying principle* upon which to build and to test the validity of the ideas and images that emerge in design conferences and rehearsals. This will help ensure the designers are not inhibited by a prescribed image and leave the director free to test the matrix against the ideas and images that result from an open, creative dialogue. In fact, it often happens that creative ideas from collaborators seem to "fit" the matrix intuitively. This sort of happenstance is an exciting validation for the director who finds that the instincts of the collaborating artists agree with a clear—if unstated—directorial image.

DISCUSSION

1. Is a director's (or designer's) commitment to "historical accuracy" adequate to ensure a good production design? (You might ask yourself whether asking only for a costume accurately depicting a present-day fashion is adequate guidance to get the design you want for a play set in today's world.)

2. How does specificity in the design process help or hinder the prospects of doing the best work?

3. How should the director and designers deal with elements they want to be *non*-specific or *neutral* as to period, place, time, etc.?

Empty Spaces: Stage Configurations

When beginning to develop the theatrical environment for any given production, the director should consider the unique space in which the production will be mounted. Stage configurations will differ from one theatre to another—in the size and shape of the stage, the auditorium, the acoustics, the sightlines. The technical elements of the theatre will have important effects on the evolution of the theatrical environment. For example, a small proscenium house makes different demands, and holds different possibilities, than a very large house.

But perhaps even more important is the effect of the size, shape, and, especially, the *feel* of the theatre space on the imagistic possibilities. A production moving from an Off-Broadway theatre to a Broadway house must make a successful translation of the original production into the larger space with an entirely different atmosphere. Some productions have survived and flourished as a result; some have evaporated. The result of the move is inevitably a different production, even when the company remains the same in both cases. Tyrone Guthrie, in a letter to authors James H. Clay and Daniel Krempel, noted that the very effect and meaning of his 1956 production of *Troilus and Cressida* had been radically changed by moving it from its original stage at the Old Vic to Broadway:

> Bear in mind that the American production suffered from the incurable disease of being in the Winter Garden Theatre, that is just fine for Ziegfeld Follies, but absurdly too large for a difficult and sublte text. Broadly spectacular effects came off, but subtlety just flew out the window. [*The Theatrical Image,* p. 203]

Because theatre space can be so assertive in its effects on the production, it is good practice for the director to go alone into the theatre where the production will be mounted—even if the theatre is quite familiar—to walk around in the auditorium and on the stage, look around, listen, get the *feel* of the place, just as one tries to get the feel of the play itself.

|| **An empty theatre speaks to the director who is prepared to listen.** ||

And, of course, directors come back for more than one look—after the set is taped out on the stage, and yet again when the scenery starts to go up. This is time well-spent for any director who wants to become more acute in seeing and hearing how the theatre space is "collaborating" with the production the director is attempting to make.

THE PROSCENIUM STAGE

Formally introduced in the 16th century to provide a suitable framework for the new art of painted perspective scenery, the proscenium stage has to date retained its dominance in Western theatre. Oddly, because it was designed to show off *scenery* to the best effect, the proscenium stage was embraced by the Realists, who found instead of a "picture frame" a perfect embodiment of the "fourth wall" ideal of the Realist and Naturalist movements. The proscenium remains the dominant and most influential of the stage forms.

True to its origins, the proscenium provides the best medium for presenting pictorial scenery. The arch establishes clear linear boundaries for the theatrical work, exactly in the manner of the picture frame it emulates. The masking of offstage areas and mechanical paraphernalia facilitates the creation of pictorial and dramatic illusion. The curtain, which can conceal or reveal, works a magic that can be as effective today as when first it was used. The effect of a train rushing towards the camera in the movies may have lost its power to excite—even very young children are immune today—but a theatre curtain rising on a beautiful set or descending silently at the end of a touching scene still works its magic on virtually everyone.

Playwrights and directors regularly condemn this form as dated and inartistic, but the proscenium stage quietly persists. Why? Because it is so adaptable. Its ability to accommodate and enrich virtually any period or popular style of production is what keeps it healthy. No other physical form of the stage has such a record of successful productions from so many periods and styles.

Nonetheless, the proscenium has certain drawbacks for directors. Its very shape—the rectangular frame with the audience viewing from one side—virtually demands a pictorial technique. Many director readily accept this condition with a deliberate two-dimensionality: cross left, cross right; cross center; cross left again. The furniture is also arranged with the same sort of linear precision. Yet this pictorial strength can work against the "feeling" of theatrical *space*. The idea of the stage as *environment* can give way to a series of static two-dimensional visual compositions.

So seductive is the shape that even choreographers succumb, making dances in lines, with little plasticity or vivacity in what is intrinsically a *plastic* (malleable and three-dimensional) artform. The late choreographer Gower Champion gently mocked this propensity of his profession on Broadway by making dances that resembled conventional chorus numbers and then slashing a moving character across, around, and through the predictable lines in a free, exuberant celebration of movement in *space*. He showed that even in the most restrictive of commercial theatre venues, the artist can use wit, skill, and talent to remind us that there is still depth on the proscenium stage.

GOWER CHAMPION 1921–1980 (U.S.)	Broadway. *Bye-Bye, Birdie; Hello, Dolly!; 42nd Street*. Brilliant Broadway choreographer and innovative director; winner of two Tony Awards for direction and choreography.

The insistent pictorial tradition of the stage also contributes to the temptation to fill the stage with scenery. It is as if the picture frame cannot be revealed half-empty; there must be something in every square inch. The best designers understand the fallacy of this notion, but all too many directors and audiences are willing to encourage it. We need only remind ourselves that there is no such thing as an "empty space" on stage. Everything contributes to the overall effect: when the curtain goes up, there is always something there to fill the frame; every inch of the floor space need not be cluttered.

THEATRE-IN-THE-ROUND

Also called "arena staging," theatre-in-the-round has maintained a limited but steady popularity since it was revitalized in the United States in the 1930's. A few major regional theatres in this country, notably Washington, D.C.'s Arena Stage and Houston's Alley Theatre, are outstanding examples of the durability, scope, and effectiveness of the form.

There is little doubt that some companies are drawn to arena staging because it is relatively economical in terms of scenery, and because it allows spaces not designed for theatre purposes to be used with minimal renovation. For small companies trying to establish their identities, the arena form provides the opportunity to show their productions and develop their audiences without a major financial investment.

Beyond simple economics, though, arena staging opens up exciting opportunities for directors, actors, and designers. Theatre-in-the-round is essentially a plastic, sculptural medium. Actors move in a completely open space and must be keenly aware that their expressiveness cannot be projected simply in one direction. Directors and designers are forced to see in three dimensions rather than two. A director who masters theatre-in-the-round can assess a scene or performance from a variety of visual perspectives. In like manner, the designer can develop or refresh the sense of depth, dimension, and spatial quality that all too often can diminish after a long period of work within the framed confines of a proscenium arch. This new sense of space, expressiveness, and plasticity can contribute so markedly to every theatre artist's sensibilities that theatre-in-the-round would be an indispensable training device even if it were not a powerful and expressive performance medium.

Small arena stages have particular value for the relatively untrained performer. The actor—in such proximity to the audience—can give an acceptable performance without a high degree of technical skill. In small-scale realistic plays, particularly, the small arena stage is much more forgiving to small-scale performances than the proscenium house. The reason is obvious: relieved of some of the vocal and character projection requirements, as well as the special physical demands of performing in the proscenium, the untrained actor can concentrate more effectively on the *what* of the performance rather than the *how*. In short, the small arena allows the novice actor to substitute *behavior* for craft, and to create the impression of honesty and lack of pretension that we have come to appreciate in performances for movies and television.

When theatre-in-the-round was in its infancy, the conventional wisdom held that it was only suited to certain sorts of plays and productions, usually small-scale modern comedies with a single interior set. Such plays, it was suggested, benefited from the intimacy of arena staging. But this argument also implies that such intimacy works against plays conceived to be performed on a grander scale, a notion that has been disproved countless times over the years. Dazzling productions of Shakespeare, Moliére, Aeschylus, Brecht, and musicals of all sorts have occupied theatres-in-the-round with stunning success.

THE THRUST STAGE

In a general sense, a thrust stage is a playing platform that encroaches into the audience space (Shakespeare's Globe is typically considered one example). Here, we speak of the thrust stage as one that is viewed by an audience on three sides with some space for scenery on the fourth front.

The thrust stage has a long and noble tradition. Its staunchest supporters are probably U.S. regional theatres dedicated to a classical repertoire. The likely reason is that the thrust combines the freedom, proximity, and plasticity of the theatre-in-the-round with some of the scenic potential of the proscenium stage. But the thrust stage should not be viewed as a compromise between these two. It is, rather, a unique and special form—an eminently *theatrical* space highly adaptable and complementary to plays of the Renaissance and before, as Tyrone Guthrie and his heirs proved so brilliantly in Stratford, Ontario, and Minneapolis. A wide range of modern plays has also found a welcome haven on the "thrust," especially when the theatrical environment has been artistically conceived and executed.

The congeniality of the form to classic plays, ancient and modern, is well documented. The thrust—especially a large one—has the power to invest a work with a special panache, a sense of size and weight difficult to duplicate in any other format. For this reason, it can prove a problem to directors staging lightweight and frivolous plays, which are often not responsive to the space. Interestingly, musicals are the big exception to this rule, probably owing to their energy, theatricality, and sheer audacity.

For discussion of staging techniques for arena and thrust stages and their dynamics, see Chapter XII.

THE "ALLEY STAGE"

With the audience seated on two sides of an elongated playing space, alley staging has usually been a choice dictated by necessity. Having the inevitable two entrances at opposite ends of the playing space limits movement possibilities; having the audience physically on two sides tends to create an opposition in the manner of a football stadium rather than the communal effect of the audience arrangement in arena or thrust stages. And, since most of the playing is back and forth, there is virtually no impression of spatial dimension.

Designing a production for an alley setup is particularly challenging. The director must carefully weigh the implications of the shape of the playing space, the resulting movement of the actors, and the relationship of each segment of audience to the space and the other half of the audience.

ENVIRONMENTAL STAGING

In the 1960's and 70's, a movement to undermine the theatre's accepted conventions resulted in some exciting experiments dealing with the form of the theatre itself. Some of the most dynamic and provocative of these productions involved the design and use of *environments* intended to displace the conventional formalities of theatre architecture and set design. Many of these designs incorporated a theatrical vision that was anti-illusionistic and confrontational; performers and audience shared the same space and could respond openly to one another.

As the notion of environmental staging as a design image has evolved, it connotes the use of a non-traditional theatre space that has been designed and constructed to accommodate a performance. It relies on the immediacy of action and the shared experience of audience and performers rather than on illusion.

The director who envisions an environmental staging for a production should follow the same general principles as for any theatre production. The guiding principles of the *statement or impression* desired, and the *personality* and *logic* of the space all apply when environmental staging is being considered. Directors should, however, note several unique aspects of environmental staging: the space itself plays a distinctly assertive part in the impression created (because it is an *environment* that the audience shares); the audience is probably in a receptive mood because its members *expect* a different kind of theatrical experience; also, like the small arena stage, the environmental stage is forgiving of technical shortcomings.

Many young directors are attracted to environmental staging for most of these reasons. But there is at least one potential drawback: the audacity of the stage form virtually demands ingenuity and audacity from everyone concerned, or a production can look like an interesting promise left unfulfilled.

THE RAKED STAGE

The raked stage is not truly a theatre configuration; it is, rather, a special treatment of the playing area, usually on a thrust or proscenium stage. A "rake" is a platform inclined towards the audience. Typically, the incline is something on the order of one inch of rise per foot in depth; that is, a 12' deep platform touching the stage floor level at the plaster line is 12" high at the back. Originated during the Renaissance to complement the effect of painted perspective scenery, the raked stage is, as noted, the source of our "up" and "down" terminology when speaking of stage positioning. On a rake, an actor is quite literally going "up" and "down."

The raked stage has been enjoying something of a comeback, especially in theatres devoted to a classical repertoire. The raked stage provides a number of advantages for the director.

1. It provides a clearly defined theatrical space—it is unquestionably a stage.
2. It makes movement (and compositions) almost inescapably dynamic because the actors, however comfortable they become, are inevitably working to maintain equilibrium against the gravitational pull. In period plays, this dy-

namic is extremely valuable because it promotes a certain natural improvement in posture and bearing.

3. Vertical emphasis becomes an important tool because it is an easily and naturally controllable element: an actor need not ascend a stair or climb atop a platform, but can simply move upstage a step or two.
4. It is sculptural, and prescribes a "three-dimensional sensibility" in the director, the designers, the actors, and the audience.
5. It can improve sightlines in theatres where some or all of the seats are situated so the audience must look up at the stage.

The raked stage also has several drawbacks:

1. It is a major challenge, in terms of construction, time, cost, and storage.
2. It dominates and dictates other scenic considerations, and complicates scenery and furniture decisions. Conventional scenery and furniture invariably requires modification to accommodate the rake.
3. It draws attention to itself. Everyone is accustomed to flat, horizontal floors; a platform that is deliberately askew demands to be noticed.
4. It is expansive in its symbology and works against a sense of entrapment or enclosure. The incline of the floor pushes the actors literally and figuratively out towards the audience. One result is that the setting is always open-ended. The sense of a restricting "fourth-wall" consequently is less effective than with a flat floor.
5. It sometimes provokes skepticism and anxiety among actors unfamiliar with the form.

DISCUSSION

1. Suggest at least one play suited for production on each of the non-proscenium stage configurations discussed above. Be ready to show how the staging will enhance the effectiveness and the meaning of the play.

2. Suggest three plays that you think would be served well and three that would be served badly by being played on a raked stage. At least one in the first category should be a contemporary, modern dress play, and one in the second should be a period play. Be prepared to discuss your suggestions.

CONSIDERATIONS IN SET DESIGN

At the outset, we make several assumptions about the methods and goals of designing a set:

1. The director should know every scenic convention and should question every one of those conventions when trying to develop a specific design approach to a production.

The theatre is caught between its past and future. Perhaps more than any other art, the theatre of today is built indisputably upon the traditions of the past, and it is always moving inexorably into the future. When a truly epoch-making production comes along, some observers will inevitably sniff that "It's been done before!" And, of course, they are right. Nothing in the theatre can be completely new. The illusion of freshness and vitality comes from the juggling and reassembling of elements that have been around for centuries into forms that capture the spirit and energy of the moment.

In developing a theatrical environment, the director and the designers should be searching for the perfect combination of forms—conventional or not—that express the images and ideas they are attempting to communicate. Rejecting a possibility simply *because it has been "done before"* is as poor a tactic as *doing* it only because it has been done successfully in the past. Creative directors try to re-discover the theatre for themselves every time they start work on a production. Although they may not always find something entirely new and effective, they at least earn a truer and more profound understanding and appreciation of the materials from which theatre is made.

By contrast, some directors are known as "mechanics"—someone skilled in manipulating the most hackneyed of conventions to good effect. The highest approbation for the mechanic's labor is summed up in two words: "It works." Most often those words mean only that the work has achieved an effect at the expense of any honesty or dimension. The notion behind the phrase demeans the theatre as surely as those other refuges of the uncreative soul, the excuses of glitz, show-biz, and "entertainment."

॥   **"It works" is an excuse masquerading as a boast.**   ॥

2. Any attempt at realism *on stage provides nothing more or less than a conventional creation that refers to reality but does not replicate it. "Realism" is neither a justification nor an excuse for shaping something in a certain way.*

Theatre people use few terms as loosely as they use "realistic." Harold Clurman puts it succinctly: "Realism, by the way, is in itself a style—a comparatively new one in theatre history. And there are various sorts of realism." (*On Directing*, 33) To avoid misunderstandings and ambiguity, directors and designers must be sure of what they mean when they use the terms "Realism," "realistic," or "real" as they go about their work. Do they mean:

- something that *actually* exists?
- something that I *personally* have seen or experienced?

- something that is *reported* to exist or to having existed?
- something that *might* exist?
- something that exists *virtually* (i.e., something that is *justified* and *motivated*)?

The last is the only defensible definition for the theatre artist; because in the theatre, the only relevant *reality* is that of the created world on the stage. There, for example, one virtually *never* sees lighting as it exists in the world outside. When we speak of "realistic lighting" in the theatre, we invariably mean lighting motivated and justified within the created world of the production.

> **The theatrical world has a set of given circumstances *necessarily* different from the outside world if only because it *is* a creation.**

The created world of the theatre may indeed *refer* to reality in the world outside, but it is defined and operates by rules and standards that are intrinsically different from those of the outside world. How should awareness of these two realities affect the work of directors and designers? To begin with, they should not use a vague notion of "realism" as an excuse or a justification for sidestepping hard choices in their creative process. They should not exclude something simply because it does not have a clear precedent in the outside world or include something simply because it is "realistic."

Years ago, when "Realism" was all the rage on Broadway in the productions of David Belasco, producer-director Arthur Hopkins (in *How's Your Second Act?*) pointed out that "exact reproduction" is a self-defeating attempt to fool an audience into accepting something as *real* that is patently *fake*. Theatre walks a tightrope, trying to create a truthful *image* of the real world that is at the same time *distinct* from the real world.

> **Although often quoted to prove the opposite, Hamlet tells us "To hold, as 'twere, the *mirror* up to nature"—not *actually* to hold a *magnifying glass*.**

3. *Every setting should be "minimal" in that it should contain nothing superfluous.*

This statement should not be taken to suggest that only "minimalist" settings are valid or appropriate. Like Realism, Minimalism is a mode of expression with a number of established conventions. Do not make the mistake of thinking of "minimal" as an absolute. The set requirements for a spectacle-filled junkyard matrix for a commercial musical like *Cats* are vastly different than those for a spare wasteland matrix for an ironic play like *Waiting for Godot;* yet each should go only as far as necessary and no farther. There is nothing to be admired in overdesigning or in underdesigning.

> **Only a clear directorial matrix can project a reliable standard in the design of any given production.**

As the design for a production evolves, two questions should come up again and again: "What more is needed?" and "What is not needed?" With these questions in mind, the director can approach the process of developing a theatrical environment. To do this well, the director should bring certain minimum skills to the design process, whether or not design collaborators are involved:

- *an understanding of the function and mechanics of the groundplan;*
- *an understanding of the physical elements of the production demanded by the action of the play;*
- *a vision of the aesthetic and symbolic statements of the setting;*
- *choice of movement patterns that the layout will affect;*
- *an ability to interpret plans, elevations, and renderings.*

Set Design Checklist

The process of set design begins with a careful analysis of the playwright's explicit descriptions of the setting in stage directions or notes. This is followed by a close reading of the play to note implicit descriptions that establish requirements of the physical action of the play. These findings should be assembled in outline form for reference as the director considers the following criteria:

1. *What is the* scale *of the setting?*

For most plays, the answer may seem obvious, but that first response can be the result of reflex rather than interpretive judgment. Such plays as *Othello* and *Hamlet,* usually thought to be grand in scale, can be interpreted quite honestly and effectively as small-scale and intensely personal—even domestic—tragedies.

In many circumstances, the size or potential of the theatre space, the budget, the staff, or the acting pool may seem to obviate the possibility of doing certain plays generally thought to be too big or grand. Approaching the play afresh with a matrix that focuses attention intently on personal details and relationships can not only make a production feasible, but also may open up the play to possibilities never before suspected. This does not necessarily reduce the play; it may,

Play: *Hamlet* Author: William Shakespeare Theatre: The Guthrie Theater Director: Garland Wright Set Designer: Doug Stein Costumes: Ann Hould-Ward Lighting: Jim Ingalls Actors (foreground): Zeljko Ivanek

Play: *The Misanthrope* Author: Moliere Theatre: Indiana Repertory Theatre Director: Tom Haas (Photo by Tod Martens)

Play: *Coriolanus* Author: William Shakespeare Theatre: McCarter Theatre Director: Liviu Ciulei Actors (center): Peter Francis James (Photo by Clem Fiori)

Play: *God's Trombones* Author: adapted from James Weldon Johnson Theatre: Ford's Theatre Director: Woodie King, Jr. Set Designer: Llewellyn Harrison Costumes: Judy Dearing Actors (l to r): Trazana Beverly, Al Freeman, Jr., Theresa Merritt

The backwall in each of these scenes makes a complex statement of mood, tone, and style in addition to suggesting time and place.

in fact, inject the work with an intense new life. Conversely, what has usually been perceived as a small-scale play may occasionally benefit from an increase in scale. Obviously, it is not necessary to alter radically the traditional scale of *any* play; it is only wise to consider this most important element carefully before embarking on the actual design of a groundplan. In the end, the director's plan—with or without the collaboration of a set designer—will have a scale, whether or not it is appropriate to the play, its theatrical environment, and the directorial matrix. As in every area of directorial interpretation and technique, a choice *will* be made, whether it is conscious and committed or not.

2. *What is the* location *and* historical period?

Remember that even a fanciful or fantastic play must be defined by these elements. There is no such thing as "non-period" architecture, or "neutral" or "non-period" costumes.

3. *Whose personality or what natural quality should the* setting *or* costumes *reflect*?

If the set presents a room or rooms of a building (or any sort of human environment or habitation), chances are it will reflect the personality of one or more of the occupants. We have already noted in the case of the set for *A Doll House* the importance of deciding whether the room in the Helmer house reflects Nora's tastes or that of her husband, Torvald. Either is a perfectly legitimate interpretation of the text Ibsen has provided, but a strong decision one way or the other will radically affect the statement of the production. Not only will the visual statement of the setting stimulate a certain battery of responses in the audience, the environment will have a significant effect upon the actors in their characterizations and relationships. This fact extends also into the matter of costuming. Whose taste does Nora's wardrobe aim to satisfy? One thoughtful interpretation would be to have her obviously dressing to please Torvald's image of her in the early parts of the play—to have her be a *doll,* and to have her wardrobe reflect her place in the household. Certainly the costume she wears for the tarantella is the paradigm for such a view. When Nora comes into her own, there is little question but that her clothes, as well as her manner, reflect her newfound maturity and sense of personal worth.

Occasionally, a director will claim to be working in a "neutral" setting or, perhaps, in "no" set at all. The stage might be shrouded in black or gray draperies, or the performance might be housed in a "found" space. But this director is playing with words; a space where actors move in a dark and mysterious surround is no more "neutral" than a circus tent. If it creates the impression of actors moving in a great void, the "neutral" setting makes a powerful, aggressive theatrical statement. If the setting is unsuccessful in creating that image, it is still something other than "neutral." And what about the "found" or "natural" space? Just as with the "neutral" setting, a warehouse or an open field is transformed when we "call it a stage."

> **Wherever actors perform is a set, and that set makes an effect on the director, on the actors, on the audience, and—ultimately—on the meaning of the performance.**

In fairness, we should note that what many directors mean when they speak of having no set or a neutral one is actually a non-conventional or non-theatrical set. Directors can create some marvelously effective theatre in unexpected places. It is only important to remember that by eschewing conventional scenery (or costumes, or makeup, or properties, or blocking, or whatever), the director has not created a purer or more honest artwork, but has simply exchanged one set of conventions for another.

4. *What* statement *or* impression *should the setting create?*

Every setting makes a complex statement about the world of the play it envelopes. The statement includes *environment* (the physical and social context), *atmosphere* (the psychic, emotional, and spiritual context), and *symbolism* (the significant and allusory context).

The visual impression of a production can have a powerful influence on the fortunes of plays and productions. Some modern plays owe something of their

Preliminary sketch for the original production.
Play: *Death of a Salesman* **Author:** Arthur Miller **Director:** Elia Kazan **Set Designer:** Jo Mielziner (Courtesy of David W. Weiss)

acceptance as major works to the settings of their first or important subsequent productions. Designer Jo Mielziner's set for *Death of a Salesman*, directed by Elia Kazan, is one of the most famous in the modern theatre. In the opening stage direction to the play, Arthur Miller describes the house of Willy Loman as a tiny, vulnerable building completely overwhelmed by aggressive modern structures. A simple, everyday house is what the text seems to describe, and Miller went on to write a famous essay on the play called "Tragedy and the Common Man." But the set that Mielziner created for the original Broadway production combines the sister elements of *scale* and *significance* to produce a masterfully poetic statement with cosmic implications. Willy's house may be the small and fragile home of a common man, but Mielziner and Kazan place it at the center and focus of an urban universe—a microcosm not only of a social but of an existential struggle.

> Even the simplest and most routine setting—designed for the most trivial sort of play—shapes not only the world of the created incidents and characters but also the theatrical world in which the performance takes place. Every set makes a statement and creates an impression.

5. *How many* entrances *are required or logical? Which is most important of these?*

In dealing with interior box sets, directors think mostly of doorways and archways. With sets depicting exteriors—in some period settings (such as wing and drop sets), and in most non-proscenium configurations—entrances are estabished conventionally by using the openings between the wings, the aisles, or whatever means of access to and egress from the set.

6. *What* other openings (*such as windows in box sets*) *are required or logical?*

These apertures often are used to locate offstage areas or events, as when a character looks through a window to see someone coming from town.

7. *What are the principal* playing areas? *The secondary playing areas? What elements (furniture or other physical objects, platforms and levels, light, stage geography) define these areas?*

The term *playing area* (also called "acting area") is applied to a space where characters are likely to settle to play a scene. In an interior set, a playing area is usually defined by the placement of furniture. In an exterior set, a period set, or on a platform or open stage, acting areas may also be defined by stage geography itself—that is, by the decision that DL will be used for a certain locale and UC for another. The delineation of such areas is often reinforced by selectively focused lighting or carefully chosen set-pieces.

When developing the groundplan for a shallow box set representing a single room, the director should consider at least two principal playing areas—say LC and RC—that could be joined by means of some adjustments of body positions or of the furniture itself (as in Figure 7–5) to produce a secondary acting area. This technique avoids the problem of the actors simply moving from one area to another without smooth and credible transitions, and, obviously, allows a greater fluidity and variety of movement and composition.

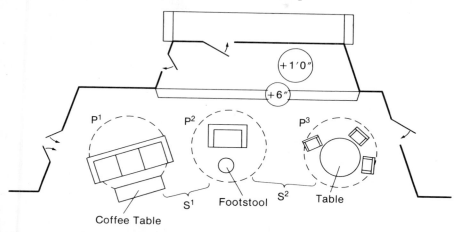

Figure 7–5 Primary and Secondary Acting Areas

In addition to considering the transitional zones between one acting area and another, it is also useful to make each area as flexible as appropriate to the environment and directorial images. A chair or sofa placed against a wall is virtually nevery useful as a primary acting area. Moving the piece away from the wall to allow passage behind it immediately opens up a number of interesting possibilities for movement and composition. For this reason, certain conventions have evolved in the placement of furniture in the box set—notably the placement of a sofa C with chairs at R and L (see Figure 7–6), or of two groupings of furniture balancing the stage picture at R and L (see Figure 7–7). Being aware of these clichés, the director and designer can attempt to achieve effective dynamics rather than surrender to conventional composition.

|| **The groundplan should provide a variety of *bases* to motivate
and justify movement.** ||

Actors find the same comfort in moving and standing *in relation to physical features of a theatrical environment* that people find in their everyday lives. Stand-

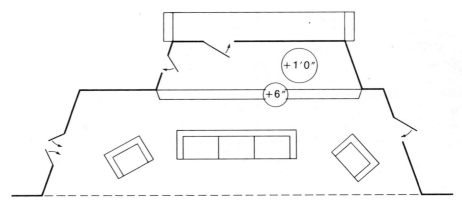

Figure 7–6 Typical Furniture Placement

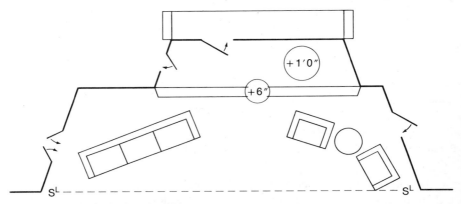

Figure 7–7 Alternative Furniture Placement

ing in the middle of any space without connection and purpose is generally un-comfortable. Standing on a stage with an audience watching intently can take on overtones of an unnatural state. A piece of furniture or other physical feature provides the actor/character with a direction and focus that can be almost magi-cal in promoting relaxation and confidence.

As we have noted, the downstage areas tend to give the actor the greatest emphasis and focus, but the technique of using these areas convincingly in a fourth-wall set seems to elude more than a few working directors. One of the best ways to motivate the movement of characters into the downstage areas is to place furniture there. Unfortunately, furniture placed along the curtain line (however "realistic" that placement might seem) becomes an intrusion between the audience and the performer. The best reasonable compromise is to place the furniture piece—chair, table, bookcase, phonograph—against the wall at DL or DR to motivate the movement of characters into this downstage plane.

8. *Is there any* other important element?

A significant element can be identified by: (a) its function (the windowseat where the bodies are concealed in the comedy-mystery *Arsenic and Old Lace,* for example); or (b) its significance or symbolism (Laura's collection in *The Glass Menagerie*).

9. *What physical feature of the setting should be the* focal point? *What other features are important or desirable in terms of sharing focus?*

Virtually every good set has a focal point to which the eye is naturally drawn. The simplest focal point is a large architectural or natural object placed in a commanding position on the stage, most often upstage center. In a three-walled box set—some variation of the "bent staple" design—the placement of a large doorway, window, staircase, or fireplace in the UC position demands attention because it is in the center of the proscenium frame and because the raked side walls of the set lead the eye directly to it.

However, this composition has become such a cliché that it is a best avoided except for the most obvious and selfconscious of comic or melodramatic purposes. Even the Duke of Saxe-Meiningen assiduously avoided the dead center focal point, and the lessons of the best painters, sculptors, photographers, choreographers, and designers all reflect a search for fresher and more dynamic composition. The balanced central focus is employed only with the greatest care and discretion by careful artists of whatever medium.

10. *What sorts of* movement or compositional patterns *best suit the kinetic or pictorial design of the production?*

The director must decide on the amount and types of movement, as well as visual compositions that best express the character and feeling of the play. Sometimes these are derived from the fashion of the period. Long dresses, robes, and trains almost inevitably dictate curved crosses and crosses that end with "hooks" to let the garment flow gracefully and to keep it from becoming entangled or requiring it to be kicked or jerked around. The groundplan must account for any special limitations or requirements. Close consultation with the costume designer at this point can often forestall many problems with the set or blocking, and alert the director to possibilities and limitations in movement well before the rehearsal work with the actors begins.

Every good production has a sort of choreography that complements and is enriched by the set and costume designs. The movement must come, of course, from the character created by each actor. But the director orchestrates and integrates movement patterns with the sensitivity and participation of actors, set designer, costume designer, and even lighting and sound designers.

The director should try to visualize the *spatial qualities and possibilities* of the set at every step in the evolution of the groundplan. A set with insufficient furnishing will be awkward for the actors and make it difficult for them to execute motivated crosses. A cluttered set for a play that the director visualizes as open and flowing is an obvious contradiction. However, there are no absolutes. Each play has certain physical requirements, but the director and the designers must decide on the specifics of the plan that serve the directorial matrix best. (Note the two possible solutions for *Master Harold . . . and the boys* discussed in the next chapter.)

11. *Does the groundplan have its own discernible* architectural or natural logic?

Perhaps the key idea in stage design is that the set must have its own internal logic. There will inevitably be some painfully literal-minded critics who will claim that such a room never existed and find the whole performance tainted as a result. Even attempting to second-guess and fend off this sort of pinched vision can be self-defeating. As we have noted in the discussion of "realism" above, literalness can be a trap. What should guide the director and designers is an ideal of a self-contained and self-referring consistency and probability. A set must not contradict itself once the logic of the world in which it appears has been estalished.

This does not mean that you may do whatever you want, only that once you make the rules, you must abide by them. Like any artist, the director must have the discretion to interpret *observable reality* and transform it into a *virtual reality*. Different worlds, different rules.

In developing any sort of groundplan, therefore, the director should begin by examining the physical context of the room or landscape that will be seen on the stage. This step not only imposes a logical rigor on the design process, but also may reveal possibilities and suggest details that might have gone unnoticed. The large drawing room that houses Lillian Hellman's *The Little Foxes*, for example, is no doubt a large Southern plantation mansion. But large Southern plantation houses are quite varied in their design and architecture. Choosing the house most appropriate to your vision of the play will help assure that your design for the room within it will be distinctive and effective in communicating your vision of the family that inhabits it.

12. *Do the sightlines allow* adequate visibility?

Sightlines can be forecast on plan and section views of any setting by striking lines from the viewing position (also plotted to scale) past any potential obstructions. In Figures 7–4 and 7–8, the sightlines are drawn and the results clearly shown. Some audience members will not see everything they might; others will see things they should not.

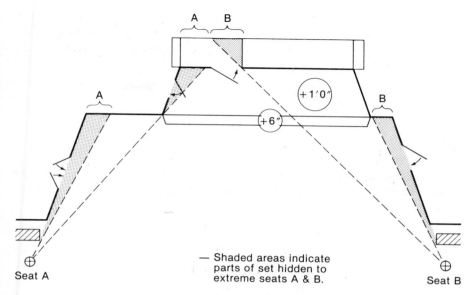

Figure 7–8 Horizontal Sightlines

DISCUSSION

1.—a. Why are scale and significance called "sister elements"?

b. Why do they so often seem to complement each other?

c. Give examples of how they operate either together or independently of one another.

2. Discuss—in terms of the relative *significance* of each—the implications of the three settings described for *Hedda Gabler* in the Introduction to this text.

EXERCISES

1.—a. Prepare a Groundplan Design Checklist outlining the physical requirements and aesthetic considerations for a set design for a scene you intend to direct.

b. Assemble three or four pictures that communicate something of the "feel" or atmosphere you wish the setting to communicate and be prepared to discuss the particular element that you would translate into the scene design.

2. Prepare notes on a play based on the Design Concept Conference Outline with the assumption that you will be meeting with three experienced designers who will do sets, costumes, and lights. Anticipate questions or objections.

End Note

In the next chapter, we explore the actual process of taking the ideas evolved so far and translating them into an actual groundplan.

8 DESIGNING THE GROUNDPLAN

As we have already noted, every director should bring certain minimum skills to the design process. This demands familiarity with *plans,* specifically the *groundplan.* A plan is a representation of an object or area viewed directly from above and drawn to scale. For the purposes of the director, the most common and useful plan is the groundplan, also called the *floorplan,* in which the area depicted is that of a given setting as it is situated on the stage floor. Your familiarity with the conventions and techniques used in theatrical plans is essential. Even if you could be certain of always working with talented and skilled set designers, you nonetheless must be able to *read* plans. Beyond your ability to interpret groundplans, understanding the process well enough to produce a workable plan on your own will greatly enhance your effectiveness in working with designers. And, when that inevitable occasion arises when you must do the job yourself, you will be able to approach the work with reasonable competence.

Developing The Groundplan

We begin with a basic form, the so-called realistic interior setting for a proscenium stage. Ever since André Antoine formulated the idea of the "fourth wall" as the dominant directorial-design aesthetic for realistic plays, the box set has dominated the modern theatre. The box set suggests a room with one wall (the "fourth") removed, leaving the conventional three-walled set. To accommodate sightlines, the two side walls of the set are conventionally splayed open. Sets with squared off angles tend to look more closed than square; this angled treatment offsets the optical illusion and actually can make the open angles of the set appear to be square from the audience's point of view. Adding downstage masking flats, or *returns,* yields the standard box set configuration described as a "bent-staple" set.

By now, of course, the bent-staple has become an overworked convention. Directors and designers routinely alter the shape to produce different "looks" for the audience by adding jogs—sections of interior wall set at angles to break up the unrelieved linearity of the two side walls of the box set (see Figures 8–1 and 8–3). Although the bent-staple is sometimes used for novelty's sake, it works best when supported by the objective of enhancing the theatrical character and environment of the setting.

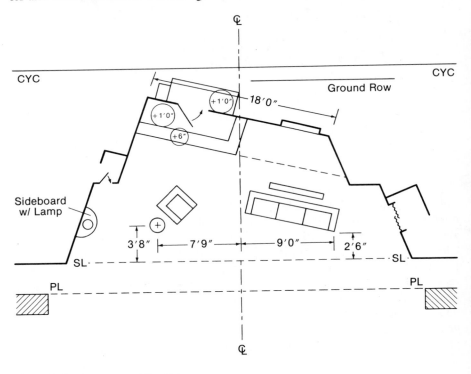

Figure 8–1 Asymmetrical Box Set

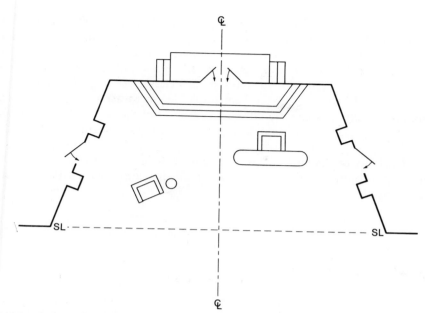

Figure 8–2   Symmetrical Box Set

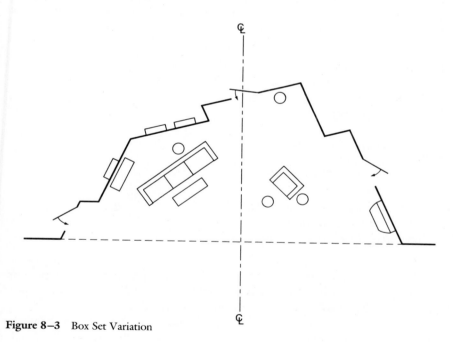

Figure 8–3   Box Set Variation

In Figure 8–2, the use of jogs in a symmetrical composition suggests static balance and, because the jogs are designed as pilasters, a certain stateliness. The addition of such architectural features—complemented by the symmetry of the doors, the unusual depth and height of the walls, and the imposing steps upstage—helps suggest a formal and dignified classical setting. Figure 8–3, on the other hand, uses jogs in the bent-staple design to achieve an improvised ramshackle effect. The entirely different characters of the two compositions are evident in the plans, even though the given structural elements are much the same.

The ability to change the shape or angle of the upstage wall offers virtually limitless possibilities to the director and designer confronted with a "conventional" box set.

Groundplan Checklist

We begin with the list of considerations developed in the set design checklist of the previous chapter. Using this checklist, the director—working alone or with a scenic designer—can begin examining and listing the playwright's explicit and implicit descriptions of the play's action, as well as any special requirement.

1. *Scale*
2. *Location and Historical Period*
3. *Personality*
4. *Statement or Impression*
5. *Entrances*
6. *Other Openings*
7. *Playing Areas and Furnishings*
8. *Other Important Elements*
9. *Focal Point*
10. *Movement and Compositional Patterns*
11. *Architectural or Natural Logic*
12. *Sightlines—Horizontal and Vertical*

The director can now work through a text systematically to develop scenic ideas into an actual plan. (By now you should have read *Master Harold . . . and the boys* and *The Foreigner* to be able to appreciate the discussions below.)

In the following examples, we examine the text of each play for any clues to the requirements of a groundplan. Then we go through the groundplan checklist and arrive at possibilities for a good plan.

Master Harold . . . and the boys
by Athol Fugard

TEXT DESCRIPTIONS

The St. Georges Park Tea Room on a wet and windy Port Elizabeth afternoon.

Tables and chairs have been cleared and are stacked on one side except for one which stands apart with a single chair. On this table a knife, fork, spoon, and side-plate in anticipation of a simple meal together with a pile of comic books. Other elements: a serving counter with a few stale cakes under glass and a not-very-impressive display of sweets, cigarettes and cool-drinks, etc.; a few cardboard advertising handouts . . . and a blackboard . . . ; a few sad ferns in pots; a telephone; an old-style jukebox. There is an entrance on one side and an exit into the kitchen in the other. . . .

The year is 1950. (pp. 5–6)

[During the Action of the Play]

1. [Hally] *Goes behind the counter to the telephone, talking as he dials.* (p. 16)
2. *The telephone rings. Sam answers it.* (p. 35)
3. [Willie] *. . . starts to replace tables and chairs. . . .* (p. 39)
4. *. . . as he [Hally] turns on the lights* (p. 47)
5. *This means another cake on the table. . . .* (p. 47)
6. [Hally] *Heads for the cash register behind the counter.* (p. 49)
7. *The telephone rings.* (p. 52)
8. *SAM AND WILLIE start to tidy up the tearoom. . . .* (p. 61)
9. [Hally] *. . . collects the few coins in the cash register. . . .* (p. 64)
10. *HALLY returns to the counter. . . .* (p. 64)
11. *He* [Hally] *goes to the jukebox. . . .* (p. 66)

IMPLIED ELEMENTS

Three actions recur throughout the play:
1. the cleaning and straightening of the tearoom. Willie, especially, is charged with cleaning the floor and resetting the tables and chairs and their associated supplies;
2. dancing, so important to the resolution of the play, alternates with the cleaning routine throughout; and

3. Hally's eating of the snacks, which takes him to the counter repeatedly, especially in the first half of the play.
(The first two of these actions—cleaning the floors and dancing—require a relatively large area to be clear.)

PHYSICAL REQUIREMENTS OF THE GROUNDPLAN

- Interior
- 2 doors (one exterior, one to the kitchen)
- Serving counter
- Tables and chairs (several)
- Table and chair (for Hally)
- Jukebox
- Telephone
- Cash register
- Food and other sale items

(Although not required by the action or the dialogue of the play, advertising signs and ferns are mentioned in the opening description.)

CHECKLIST

1. **Scale:** The play presents several complex challenges in this regard. A play of intensely personal relationships, it seems at first to be very small and tightly focused. The obvious need to have a fairly large area—room for a few tables and chairs, and the space to move among them—seems to work against the first impression, at least on the surface.

2. **Location and Historical Period:** These are essential and unambiguous. The year must be understood and interpreted in terms of the place. Period research will certainly disclose that 1950 in South Africa was much different from 1950 in the United States. It will also reveal that South Africa then was much different from what it is today, the white government of South Africa having been established only the year before.

3. **Personality:** This will be a critical issue in developing the groundplan and evolving the mise-en-scene. The first impression of the room is, if anything, impersonal. Only two characters appear to have the potential to imprint any sort of style or personality upon the tearoom: Hally's mother and Sam. Putting the first impression to one side, the impact of either of these characters upon the room might be developed in interesting and provocative ways. Sam emerges as the likelier candidate because he is characterized as stylish and competent, and has the opportunity as the play progresses to imprint his personality on the room as well as on the people in it.

4. Statement or Impression: As simple and straightforward as the play seems, its power derives not only from the beautifully realized characters and the development of their relationships, but also from the play's structure, which suggests it is a metaphor for the political and social conditions of the time. This structure is built of contrasts and extremes that are presented and accepted as completely unexceptional and straightforward.

The playwright isolates the tearoom in a rainstorm; the room is at once cut off from the outside yet trapped by it. And inside, Hally is the most confined. He sits bent over his books at the little table while Sam and Willie move about, making changes, even dancing. When Hally describes his childhood memory, it is a linear description:

"Down the corridor . . . telephone on the right . . . past the kitchen . . . into the backyard . . . then into that little passageway, first door on the right and into your room. How's that?" (p. 28).

Sam, on the other hand, describes feelings, stimuli:

"The sound of the big band, Hally, trombone, trumpet, tenor, and alto sax. And then finally, your imagination also left out the climax of the evening when the dancing is finished, the judges have stopped whispering among themselves and the Master of Ceremonies collects their scorecards and goes onto the stage to announce the winners"(p. 46).

Hally's intellectual processes are cramped and rule-bound. When he cannot understand why his life is so confined, Hally dismisses any possibility of change, hope, and acceptance even as Sam begs him to explore and enjoy the space he already has.

While seldom overtly political, and never aggressively so, the play is profoundly political in its portrayals of people trapped in a system that they neither made nor fully understand. The system nonetheless affects them even in their most intimate relationships. This is what the structure of the play, as well as its story, demonstrates. The play moves backwards in time and outward in space to explore the status of the characters' lives in the present time in relationship to the political evolution in the world outside. The past affects the present; the outside affects the inside.

The set design should reflect the idea of being trapped in a large space that is losing its polished image.

5. Entrances: Two entrances are needed: a door to the outside and one to the kitchen.

6. Other Openings: No other opening is demanded either by the action of the play or the dialogue. A window, or windows, would be appropriate here, although such a feature would certainly alter the sense of close confinement. A clear window could complicate things considerably, because this would mean that the persistent rain would have to be visible throughout the performance.

7. **Playing Areas:** Three areas are required: 1) the counter with the snacks, the cash register, and the telephone; 2) Hally's table and chair; and 3) a relatively large area of open floor for the dancing, and to accommodate the other furniture when it is replaced.

8. **Other Important Elements:** The jukebox.

9. **Focal Point:** The counter is the strongest candidate. It has a powerful symbolic function as the seat of control for the business, and since so many things are kept there—snacks, drinks, and ice cream, as well as the cash register and the telephone—it is the busiest place on the set. The other immediate and obvious possibility is Hally's table, which is his base of operations and ultimately the pivot point for much of what goes on in the play.

10. **Movement and Compositional Patterns:** There are essentially two principal patterns to be inferred from the characters and action of *Master Harold . . . and the boys,* and they are of major importance: 1) Hally moves directly to one place and then to another (e.g., to the phone and then to the table). His movement is specific. 2) Sam and Willie, by way of essential contrast, are dancers. Their movements are curvilinear and graceful.

11. **Architectural or Natural Logic:** The simplicity of the set presents few problems. It requires only a rectilinear room in a simple building. No particular architectural features are suggested that would challenge the logic of the layout.

12. **Sightlines:** There is no reason for any portion of this set to be obscured from any seat, nor is there any necesssary reason for anyone to see into the kitchen offstage. The door to the outside is a different matter. If there is to be no window, it is still important for the audience to see through to the outside, if only for the brief moments in which the door is open. Perhaps a full glass door would be in order in the upstage wall so that the park outside could be seen in the rain to establish a sense of the outside world—and of the tearoom as an island on which Hally is marooned.

DECISIONS

1. The most significant challenge presented by the play is to decide the character of the set and the statement it is to make. The range of possibilities is surprisingly wide.

2. Several technical problems must be confronted if a convincing and theatrically effective plan is to be realized.

    a) The two primary acting areas—the table and the counter—leave little possibility for real development or variety. True, both can easily be placed to allow circulation around them. Both the table and the counter are "sittable," and it is quite easy to have a secondary area linking the two (Sam at the counter talking to Hally at the table). The two primary areas need to be reasonably close together, because, for the most part, the play's tone is conversational, one person to another. If the counter becomes the focal point of the set, and the table is close-by, the acting areas are cramped and the stage either assumes a state of static balance or becomes hopelessly lop-sided. These problems would be exacerbated by Hally's only clearly required blocking—going for food (on and behind the counter), for the phone (on the counter), to the cash register (on the counter), and for the comics and the brandy (under the counter). Separating the table and the counter to allow some of the dances to take place in between alleviates part of the balance problem, but does not help much with giving variety to Hally's movement.

b) There must be a clear, logical pattern to the business of Willie's stacking the tables and chairs, cleaning the floors, and resetting the room in a presentable way at the appropriate time. Willie's work, which continues through much of the action of the play, must be so logical and effortless that it draws no unwarranted attention.

Solution A (Figure 8—4)

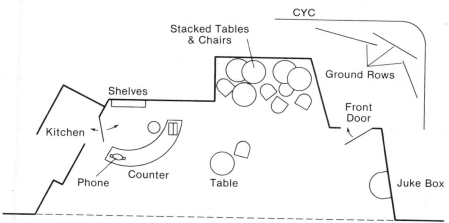

Figure 8—4 Solution A: *Master Harold . . . and the boys*

The configuration meets all the physical requirements of the production and represents a very economical and efficient use of space. The counter is isolated and brought downstage by the jog, which also breaks up the flatness of the upstage wall. The door to the kitchen becomes part of the counter service area, a logical and effective touch because it defines very clearly the management style in the place. One can imagine Hally's mother seated on the stool behind the counter, with easy access to the cash register, the telephone, and the kitchen. The kitchen door has a double-swinging hinge arrangement (as indicated by the double arrow-arcs on the plan) and a window in the upper panel that allows a view of the kitchen activity from the manager's position in the service area. The jog also creates a shallow alcove next to the exterior door that will be used to stack the tables and chairs while Willie works on the floor downstage. The placement of Hally's table quite near C seems natural enough in this arrangement. It provides a prominent stage position for Hally and a ready secondary acting area between the table and the counter as well as the area L where Willie is working and where most of the dancing is staged. The jukebox, the stacked furniture, and the exterior door at the left side of the stage provide compositional balance for the counter area. The door would be glass at the top to allow a clear, if narrow, view of the park in the rain.

This is certainly a workable layout. The placement of the table at C is visually unexciting, but this is alleviated to some degree by the break in the upstage wall, which throws the whole set into an unexpected balance. The placement of the jukebox flat against the L wall is a compromise. The jukebox has such importance in the final moments of the play that it almost becomes another character. In this case, unfortunately, the "character" plays its big scene in a relatively weak position.

The groundplan in this version is designed to establish an image of an existence cobbled together without much foresight or style. The walls are plain and the ceiling rather low (certainly no higher than 10' or 12'). The building is frame construction, and the tearoom was probably added as an afterthought. As a consequence, it serves its purpose rather uncomfortably, but manages to hold together. The image of the resulting groundplan is completely consonant with the given circumstances and with a valid vision of the play and the lives of the characters.

Solution B (Figure 8–5)

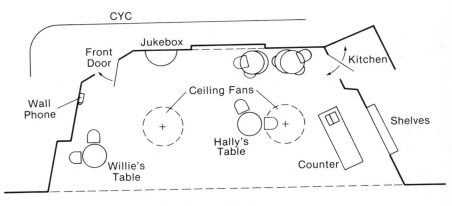

Figure 8–5 Solution B: *Master Harold . . . and the boys*

The radical step of adding a large window to this set changes the look and the statement considerably. The importance of the counter has been greatly diminished by relegating it stage left in a slight inset and moving the telephone completely across the stage and placing it on the wall. The kitchen door, double-swinging, is reasonably accessible to the counter, which is backed by a built-in shelf unit. Hally's table is near the counter, LC. The jukebox, adjacent to the glass panel exterior, is placed against the upstage wall and faces downstage. An additional table and chairs are placed R near the phone (by Willie) shortly after the play begins. The rationale for such an arrangement, as far as the cleaning goes, is that before the curtain rises Willie first pulled all the furniture towards the middle of the room, then cleaned the floors along the walls and the area from the counter to L of center. He then moved the furniture into the positions shown on the plan, and will complete mopping the R half of the room, backing his way towards the door as the play progresses.

This version allows reasonable space for the cleaning and dancing. Furthermore, it motivates crosses both L and R by means of opposing the phone and additional table set-up (which Willie will use to polish some serving pieces and to refill containers) to the counter unit.

While the "bent-staple" look has been alleviated somewhat by the small jogs and the angled exterior door unit, the set retains a rather rigid and formal symmetry. The stage floor is relatively wide and shallow, and the rather grand scale is emphasized by the faded *faux* marble pilasters flanking the large window unit. The walls have wainscoting and picture-molding, all painted off-white and now badly stained and peeling. The ceiling height is 16 feet. There are two slow-turning ceiling fans set in plaster rosettes.

This plan was obviously developed to support the notion of the tea-room as part of a once pretentious colonial building, perhaps a hotel, which has been chopped-up and now furnished and used in an obviously ill-suited manner.

Groundplan II:

The Foreigner
by Larry Shue

TEXT DESCRIPTIONS

The Place: Betty Meeks's Fishing Lodge Resort, Tilghman County, Georgia, U.S.A.
The Time: The Recent Past

(Act I, Scene I)

1. *. . . darkness, rain, and thunder . . . what was once the livingroom of a log farmhouse, now adapted for service as a parlor for paying guests . . . a small counter with modest candy and tobacco displays, a guest register, and a bell. There is also about one sofa too many, a small stove and its woodbin, and a coffee table. . . .* (p. 9)
2. *It is spring. . . . down the hall somewhere, a door closes. . . .* (p. 9)
3. "—see it right from the window." (p. 10)
4. [Froggy] *Taking a key off the wall. . . .* (p. 14)
5. (*Doing as she* [Betty] *says*) "Well—this [spoon]'ll have to go in a drawer. But the others I'll leave right out here. There. Ain't they perty?" (p. 15)
6. "She [Catherine] went on upstairs. . . ." (p. 30)
7. (*Ellard exits into the kitchen.*) (p. 30)

(Act I, Scene 2)

8. (*The following morning. Bright sunlight. Betty enters, pulls up a throw rug in the middle of the floor and stamps a couple of times*) (p. 32)
9. [Charlie] *. . . hurriedly dials the phone.* (p. 33)
10. (*The trapdoor has, of course, opened downward into the floor*) (p. 34)
11. [Catherine] (*Picking up a ragged magazine and reading*) "Princess Diana has given birth to a baby boy, her first. . . . " (p. 36)

(Act II, Scene 1)

12. (*Afternoon, two days later. . . .*) (p. 46)

(Act II, Scene 2)

13. (*. . . Outside the window, darkness. Within, a candle or two illumine the figures . . .*) (p. 71)

IMPLIED ELEMENTS

1. One of the characters, Charlie, must sit unnoticed by other characters onstage. A suitable piece of furniture must be available.
2. Two of the characters, Charlie and Ellard, are served a rather elaborate breakfast. This means several dishes and glasses, flatware, and at least two trays must be brought on stage and suggests the need for a dining table of some sort, at least two chairs, and easy access to the kitchen exit.
3. The electric lights flicker and go off mysteriously. Later (just as mysteriously), they come back on.

4. There is also a trick concocted by several of the characters involving a disappearance through the trapdoor and an invitation by the playwright to elaborate on the basic gimmick.

PHYSICAL REQUIREMENTS OF THE GROUNDPLAN

- Interior
- 2 doors (one exterior [visible porch?], one kitchen)
- Hallway leading to other rooms (door? archway?)
- Window
- Stairway (possibly)
- Counter with displays
- Keyrack (visible?)
- Telephone
- Woodstove and woodbox
- Sofas ("one too many"?)
- Throw rug
- Trapdoor
- Dining table
- Two (minimum) dining chairs
- A sideboard or other device for breakfast implements and for displaying Betty's spoon collection

CHECKLIST

1. **Scale:** This is a very modest room, as we see by the opening stage directions. In fact, it is something of a makeshift. Although some 8–10 people occupy the space at one time in the climactic scene, most scenes involve only two or three people, usually in low-key conversational exchanges.

2. **Location and Historical Period:** Both these factors are clearly stated in the introductory matter and obvious from dialogue in the play. However, the author's insistence on a backwoods location tends to modulate the period statement. While the calendar may, indeed, indicate the recent past, the sense of time in this backwoods locale is surely delayed by a decade or more.

The locale is deliberately remote from the experience not only of the "foreigner," but of the rest of the world as well. To arrive at the little lodge near the lake in Tilghman County, Georgia, the protagonist—we are told almost at once—must fly from London to Atlanta, then go another " 'undred miles south . . . more or less" by jeep (Act I).

3. **Personality:** This is clearly Betty's room. She is the proprietor who, we are told almost immediately, established and continues to run the

place single-handedly. Also repeatedly stated in word and action is that the character continuously has to "make do" with what she has at hand.

4. **Statement or Impression:** The room is modest, and so is the statement of the play. The image of the set should seem to be circumscribed entirely by time and place and the personality of the woman who runs the lodge—friendly and spontaneous. There are two hints, however, that open the possibility of suggesting something beyond the immediately obvious: a) the addition of "U.S.A." to the statement of place, and b) the daring and unusually specific use of the Ku Klux Klan in the context of a generally playful comedy.

Proceeding from these hints—and considering the sweetness of Betty's personality and her revulsion at the meanness and venality of the Klan and its collaborators against whom she must strive—the director and set designer might choose to include in the set decoration some emblems of place: Georgia bumper stickers, for example, among the soft drinks, candy, cigarettes, and fishing accessories. To counterpoise the powerful images of the Klan robes and weapons in Act II, the set might also be dressed with faded patriotic icons: a tiny flag in the pencil glass on the counter, small campaign pictures of Presidents Eisenhower and Kennedy, a group of campaign buttons stuck to a bulletin board. Such elements are easy to justify in such a place and would add a subtle but telling and appropriate symbolism to the statement of the set. They should not be empty gestures, however. They should establish time and place, and provide an identity for the place that contrasts nicely with the "foreigner." They can also provide actors and director possibilities for action and reaction.

5. **Entrances:** Only four entrances are strictly required (as we have noted in the text analysis): a) the door to the outside, b) the door to the kitchen, c) the access to the rest of the house (the hallway), and d) the trapdoor. The outside door is certainly prominent in terms of the play's action. It is through this door that all the outsiders enter and all the antagonists are expelled so dramatically. Although Ellard's re-entrance after his amazing disappearance in Act II makes the trapdoor undeniably important, it is deliberately hidden throughout most of the play. The hallway giving access to the rented rooms is also of great importance since it provides dramatic entrances for Catherine (certainly in Act I), for Ellard and Charlie in Act II, and for the Klan members' exit and reappearance with Catherine near the end of the play. Furthermore, this entranceway marks a critical transition from the public area of the house to the private rooms. "No visitors upstairs," Betty warns Owen on their first encounter, "that's the rules" (Act I).

6. **Other Openings:** One window with a view of the yard and the lake in the distance. (It is not essential that the audience actually see these features.)

7. **Playing Areas:** A minimum of three areas is demanded by the text: a) the furniture—sofa(s) and coffee table near the stove; b) the dining table where the breakfast scene is played; and c) an open area center for the trap-

door and for Charlie's tale in Act II. This last might also open up sightlines for the counter and the hallway access.

8. **Other Important Elements:** a) The counter, and b) the telephone. These might occupy the same area onstage. Each is important in two or three short scenes or exchanges.

9. **Focal Point:** There is no clear contender for this function. The trapdoor is unquestionably the focus at the climax of the play, but part of its effectiveness comes from the fact that it has passed largely unnoticed, having been hidden by a rug most of the time. The window is useful, but never at a genuinely dramatic or important moment. The counter is used only incidentally and never in an important or emphatic manner. The same can be said of the hallway and the kitchen door. This leaves the door to the outside as the strongest of several weak contenders, based on what the text provides directly.

10. **Movement and Compositional Patterns:** The play suggests two obvious compositional patterns: a) shared scenes, tête-a-tête, and b) variations on vertical relationships: parent-child, teacher-pupil.

The movement patterns fall into three categories: a) *linear*—the back and forth, point-to-point movement characteristic of some broad farce; b) an *encircling* or *figure-8* pattern, suggesting stalking and ensnarement; and c) an *explosive* design where the elements move outward as if thrown by an impelling force.

11. **Architectural or Natural Logic:** Several types of structures are possible within the requirements and definitions of the text and the action of the play. The clear implication is that the house is of frame construction and contains four guest rooms, all upstairs. Charlie is using Froggy's old room; Ellard has one room; and Betty makes the point that Catherine and David occupy separate rooms. Betty, of course, lives on the premises and has some sort of accommodations of her own. Assuming a bathroom on the second floor, this could mean at least six rooms on the second floor, not counting the upstairs hallway and stairwell. On the first floor, there are the living room/lobby, the porch (established in the dialogue as being structurally unsound), the hallway (leading where and giving access to what rooms downstairs?), and the kitchen. Since there are several guest rooms upstairs, three possibilities exist: the house is three stories (unlikely from almost any point of view), the downstairs is very capacious while the upstairs rooms are incredibly small, or the house is extraordinarily top-heavy.

This anomaly requires some adjustment and justification as the groundplan is developed, as we shall do later in this chapter.

12. **Sightlines:** Every corner of the main room must be visible to all the seats. This is especially important when there is to be a *coup-de-théâtre* like Ellard's disappearance in Act II. No one must feel that something critical is being hidden from them by accident. Additionally, if the production is to employ the explosive imagery noted above, the explosion is only effective when it is played out in full view of everyone in the audience.

The hallway, on the other hand, is problematic. If it is simply an opening upstage permitting some parts of the audience to see characters moving towards or away from the main room, it can diffuse the effectiveness of entrances and exits. One solution would be to make the hallway opening into a door (not especially likely in what had been a private home rather clumsily converted into a lodge); another would be to conceal the hallway with a curtain (thereby risking an exotic or mysterious statement out of keeping with the personality of the place). A better solution than either of these is to put the arch in a sidewall, with the hallway running off at a perpendicular.

SOLUTION A (FIGURE 8–6)

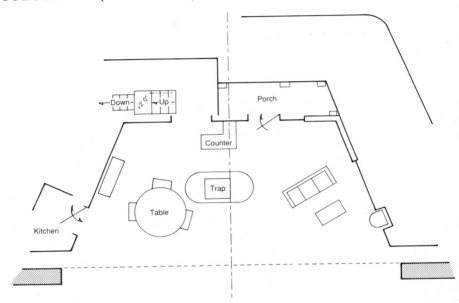

Figure 8–6 Solution A: *The Foreigner*

Problems

The analysis of the set as defined by the text presents a variety of challenges to the director and designer in the evolution of an effective groundplan.

1. The first impression of the set makes little sense architecturally. (See item #12 above.) Many things can be read as probable in the world the playwright posits, but the production must project an acceptable logic for itself.

2. The essential set requirements project a wide, shallow configuration on a single level, with three major, discrete acting areas, R, C, and L. Even

acknowledging the necessity of keeping the room on a small and modest scale, this structure seriously restricts the actors and the director in achieving the desired variety in compositional and movement patterns. (See #10 above.)

3. There is no good visual focal point in the room.

SOLUTION B (FIGURE 8–7)

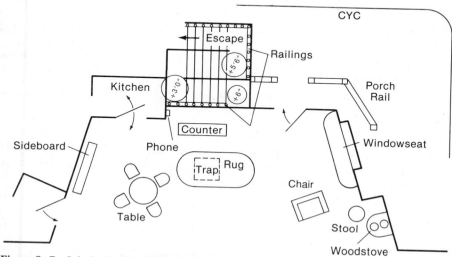

Figure 8–7   Solution B: *The Foreigner*

This groundplan shows another approach to the challenges presented by the play. The basic outline is the familiar bent-staple, with alterations—jogs, platform, and complex stair unit—to relieve the relentless symmetrical balance.

Two major alterations to the basic requirements of the playtext are important: the stair unit UC and the additional door, DR. (The stairs go up, turn on a small landing, then right to another landing, and then left where they disappear behind the up stage wall.)

The stair unit introduces a number of desirable features into the plan, providing: 1) a visual focal point for the room; 2) more effective entrances and exits than the hallway; 3) a better sense of the upstairs; 4) an indication of the fact that the house could have five bedrooms and still be quite modest in its scale and character; and 5) the ability to achieve greater variety in vertical compositions through the use of the several natural levels of the stairs and the small landings.

The door, DR, is not in any sense nearly as powerful an addition as that of the stairway. In fact, it goes almost unnoticed. Still, it has (for the director and designer of this production at least) a compelling logic. The door serves as access to Betty's quarters. The loss of the hallway cuts off the first floor of the house even more. The extra door leading off right and the kitchen door going off upstage give an added dimensionality to the house's first floor and eliminate the need for Betty's quarters to be upstairs. This also creates the impression that the proprietor/manager is in a space separate from the guests and closer to the kitchen, the main entrance, and the telephone.

DISCUSSION

1. Compare the layout of the acting areas of the two groundplan versions for *Master Harold . . . and the boys* shown in the examples.

2. Compare the movement patterns of the two as they relate to the director's analysis.

3. Discuss the additions in the groundplan for *The Foreigner*. Do the visible stair unit and the additional door (R leading to Betty's quarters) violate the integrity of the text or the principle of using the minimum requirements for a setting?

Drawing a Groundplan: the Fundamentals

The theatrical groundplan is based on a number of standards and conventions that assure accuracy and efficiency. The most fundamental of these conventions is *scale*. Scale is the relationship of the dimensions of the drawing to those of the object depicted. The relationship can be stated as a ratio (1:12, 1:24, or 1:48) or, more commonly, as an equation ($1'' = 1'0''$, $\frac{1}{2}'' = 1'0''$, or $\frac{1}{4}'' = 1'0''$). Standard scales for drafting theatrical groundplans are $\frac{1}{2}''$ and $\frac{1}{4}''$, which is to say that $\frac{1}{2}''$ (or $\frac{1}{4}''$) on the drawing represents one linear foot ($1'0''$) on the stage floor. The actual size of a $1''$ scale drawing ($1'' = 1'0''$) will be the $\frac{1}{12}$th the size of the actual object; $\frac{1}{2}''$ scale will be $\frac{1}{24}$th; $\frac{1}{4}''$ will be $\frac{1}{48}$th; $\frac{1}{8}''$ will be $\frac{1}{96}$th and so on. The largest scale mentioned ($1''$) will naturally yield the largest drawing and show more detail more accurately than the smaller scales. For a fairly large theatre, however, the $1''$ scale plan drawing is physically too large for convenience. A $1''$ scale plan for a theatre with a proscenium opening of forty feet and offstage space of eighteen feet left and right would have to be drawn on a piece of paper over six feet wide. A $\frac{1}{8}''$ plan could depict the same stage area on a sheet only $10''$ wide. The small scale drawing, while undeniably easier to handle would, of course, be much more difficult to read accurately. After all, at

⅛" scale a stage measurement of 4" (a not inconsiderable dimension) would have to be drawn as ¹/₂₄"! The reasonable compromises, therefore, are the ½" and ¼" scales. Relatively small or complicated settings are better drawn at ½"; larger, simpler ones at ¼".

The common instrument for measuring theatrical plans is the architect's scale, which has all the necessary scale measurements. The most useful architect's scale, whether the familiar triangular rule or the flat, provides both open and divided elements (Figure 8–8). The open scale allows gross measurements in one foot increments to be made quickly, while the divided permits finer measurements to fractions of an inch.

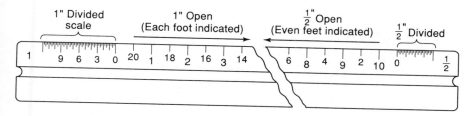

Figure 8–8 Architect's Scale

SETTING LINES

A useful convention in drawing groundplans is the use of setting lines to provide references for measurements, both on the plan and on the stage floor itself. On a proscenium stage, two such lines are commonly employed: the *center line* (CL), running up and down stage center and dividing the stage into left and right halves, and the *set line* (SL), running across the downstage opening of the set from one set return to the other. (As explained below, setting lines are drawn as dimension lines.) Sometimes the *plaster* or *proscenium line* is used instead of the *set line*. The plaster line (PL) is defined by running a line along the back edge of the proscenium wall from one side of the arch to the other and therefore perpendicular to the center line.

Lateral distances (left and right stage) are measured from the center line. Depth (upstage) is measured from the set line or the plaster line. The placement of any spot on the stage thus may be accurately plotted, on paper and on the floor, by striking two lines on the perpendicular from the CL and SL (PL) to the desired spot.

On non-proscenium stages, the locations of the setting lines are not standardized, but the same sort of logic persists: the establishment of two perpendicular lines of reference.

OTHER GROUNDPLAN CONVENTIONS

Note how the following are indicated on the groundplan (Fig. 8–1):

Center line: line of alternating long (1″) and short (¼″) dashes separated by spaces (⅛″) that divides the stage into L and R halves. Marked *CL* at either end.

Set line: a line composed of long (½″) dashes separated by short (⅛″) spaces running L-R that marks the downstage limits of the set. Marked *SL*.

Walls: triple width, dark solid lines.

Dimension lines: light, single-width lines with arrowpoints at the extremes that touch short *extensions,* denoting the limits of the outline of the object being measured. Dimension lines are usually broken in the middle for the numerical dimension to be given in feet and inches.

Object on floor: double-width, medium solid outlines, occasionally with structural details (as for a chair or sofa).

Objects overhead: dotted outlines.

Windows: rectangle abutting a wall, showing proper depth of the construction.

Doors: solid lines at an angle as if the door were open and an arc terminating in an arrow-point indicating the hinged swing as the door shutter moves towards the door frame; this frame should be indicated by the appropriate thickness piece.

Elevation: small numerical dimension enclosed in a small circle with plus (+) or minus (−), indicating measurement from the stage floor.

Draperies: solid wavy lines; draperies hung in pairs to overlap as in a window or door frame are drawn so the overlap is evident.

Setting lines: dimension lines indicating distances from the center line or the plaster line; these lines indicate the exact position of the object on the floor rather than the actual dimensions of a piece of scenery. Most objects can be fixed in place by the establishment of two points; a round object, however, can be fixed by a single center point.

EQUIPMENT

The absolute minimum equipment for basic drafting is a *pencil, paper, and a scale.* With the following tools and equipment, however, the work will probably be more accurate and presentable and, almost certainly, more efficient and comfortable to produce.

- architect's scale
- T-square, 24″ or longer
- 60°/30° acrylic triangle, 8″ or larger
- 2 pencils, 1 HB, 1 2H (for darker and lighter lines)
- drafting paper, plain or with light blue gridlines
- eraser, artgum or kneaded
- drawing board, 18″ × 24″ or larger

- a compass
- drafting or masking tape

Additional useful equipment includes:
- pencil sharpener
- erasing shield
- dividers

Notes on Drafting Supplies and Equipment

The *architect's scale* is obviously very important. It need not be expensive, but it must have ¼″, ½″, and 1″ divisions. It must be easily readable. Look for sharply defined markings, especially with the divided scale. The 6″ long flat scale, which usually comes with a sheath, is quite handy for a director but easy to misplace. The familiar triangular scale is more readily available and easier to keep track of, especially while you are working.

The *T-square* may be wood with a clear plastic edge or entirely clear plastic. It must be long enough to extend past the far edge of the paper you will be using.

HINT: **Triangles of fluorescent acrylic are much easier to keep track of when you are drafting.**

The *paper* may be translucent or opaque, and must take erasures well. Translucent paper will be especially helpful in tracing a finished version of the rough draft. Paper is available in a variety of grades and cut sizes in pads. A good size for most needs is 14″ × 17″. It is acceptable to use a very inexpensive paper for the rough layouts as long as it will take corrections well and not disintegrate when something is erased more than once.

The *drawing board* must have square corners. A metal edge will help the board remain true longer, but a plain edge is acceptable. With care, an inexpensive but serviceable board may be cut on a table saw from a piece of plywood or tempered masonite, then padded with a piece of smooth poster board or several thicknesses of paper.

If you use wooden *pencils,* a battery-operated electric sharpener is a great convenience. Conventional drafting pencils require a lead sharpener of some sort, but the mechanical pencils with ultra-thin (.2mm–.9mm) leads need no special sharpening or pointing accessories, just a good supply of leads.

An *erasing shield* is very inexpensive and very useful. One with elongated slots in various sizes can serve as a lettering guide.

Dividers are very useful for marking repeats of a dimension on the paper and for transferring critical measurements from scale to paper or vice versa. The *compass* can be used in the same way.

1. Using an architect's scale and a simple compass, draw the following:

FIGURE	SCALE
a. Square 6'0"	¼"
b. Rectangle 4" × 8'6"	½"
c. Right Triangle 5'9 ½" (base) × 4'7" (height)	1"
d. Circle 5'8 ¾" (diameter)	1"
e. Square 6'4 ½"	½"
f. Rectangle 2'8" × 6'9"	⅛"
g. Semi-circle 17'6" (radius)	⅛"
h. Rectangle 2'4" × 7'2" with an inside border of 0'6" on one long and the two short sides	½"

i. In each of the squares and rectangles, draw a diagonal; measure it and note the measurement. Be sure to retain the correct scale when doing this measurement.

j. Label each of your drawings with the appropriate dimensions and scale. (If you place the erasing shield with the slotted openings horizontal on the T-square, you can use a sharp pencil to write block letters within the slots to achieve uniform lettering in different sizes without drawing guidelines on the paper.) Compare the relative sizes resulting when a different scale is employed. Note also the relative ease of making accurate measurements in inches and fractions depending upon the scale.

2. Draw a plan of an actual room (either ½" or ¼" scale, as directed), including the furniture. You should select a room that is simple in shape and furnishings. (To do this preliminary exercise, you will probably want to get at least some of the items of equipment listed above.)

3. Cut or find a disc of card, plastic, or metal scaled to 18–24 inches in diameter. Using the disc to represent a person, move it around on your plan in what seems on the groundplan to be a logical traffic pattern. Note and discuss whether the pattern suggested by the plan reflects the way a person actually moves in the room.

DRAWING A GROUNDPLAN

As noted, a director must bring to the design process the ability to understand the drafting process well enough to draw a serviceable groundplan. Not only will this capability allow you to read and interpret plans provided by others (an indispensable skill), it will also serve you well in those inevitable situations early in your directorial career when you must develop your own design without trained assistance. When you are working with trained designers and technicians, the ability to read and interpret plans will help ensure your grasp of the technical elements with which you are dealing, earn the respect of your collaborators, and demonstrate your own respect for their process. As an added benefit, producing a good plan will enhance your sense of spatial relationships and your familiarity with the setting and the stage on which it is placed. Approach the process systematically and take pride in doing it well.

While we will use an arbitrarily defined groundplan for the exercises that follow, you may assume you will be interpreting design decisions that produced a rough sketch of your proposed plan—a thumbnail, if you wish. Later, when you are developing your own plan, you will inevitably be tempted from time to time to use the plan "in the back of the book." Many acting editions are available with a more or less crude groundplan version, usually of the original production. As long as the plan is provided without restrictions, there is nothing to stop you from using it in your process. Be aware, however, of the inescapable pitfalls of using the "back of the book" groundplan: 1) The plan is almost always an interpretation drawn by the stage manager of the original production for use in the prompt script. 2) It is almost never drawn to scale. 3) The stage for the production for which the plan was developed probably has no correlation to the stage you will be using. 4) The images the original director and designer had in mind are obviously different from the ones you might develop on your own. 5) A groundplan developed for someone else's specific production certainly will be less responsive to your production than one you develop yourself.

EXERCISE

The steps described here are meant to help a director working without trained design or technical assistance to produce a reasonably accurate and workable groundplan. They will not make you an expert in drafting for the stage. Taking available courses or training in any phase of technical theatre and design will improve your drafting and other design skills, thereby making you a better director.

1. Select a sheet of paper large enough to leave a comfortable margin (say 2″) around the completed plan. Once you have justified the paper on the board using the T-square, attach it to the board with a small strip of tape in each corner.

H I N T : After attaching one corner, pull the opposing corner and attach it; then repeat with the other corners so that the paper is taut and unwrinkled.

2. Measure or use the dividers to find the centerline of the paper. Make one tick mark with a pencil to establish it. With the T-square snug to the left side of the board (for a right-hander) and the short edge of the triangle resting on the T-square's blade, draw broken line of alternating long and short dashes through the tick mark to within 2" of the bottom and top edges of the paper to establish your centerline.

H I N T : In drawing the centerline and the set line, use the marks on the open scale to achieve a regular pattern.

3. Using the ½" or ¼" scale, establish the set line horizontally across the centerline, 1" up from the end of the CL. The set opening measures 32'6". Use the dividers or the scale to measure equal halves of the opening (16'3") L and R of CL and make a tick at each point. Connect the ticks with a line of long dashes separated by short spaces.

H I N T : All directions refer to stage geography.

4. With the T-square still in position, mark a distance of 3'6", extending the set line *offstage* on either side. Draw from each of these ticks back to the near end of the set line using the softer, darker pencil to make solid lines. You have now shown the returns on the set. This kind of line will be used for all the solid walls of the set.

5. From the set line, measure up the centerline and make a tick at 14'3". Move the T-square to that mark and measure over R 13'9". Connect that point with a light line to the R return at the set line. You have lightly indicated the R wall of the set.

H I N T : Use your triangle as a straightedge, resting the base of the 90° triangle on the T-square to draw verticals and diagonals on your plan.

6. Measure up from the DR corner along the wall. Make a tick first at 6'0", then another at an additional 2'6". Draw a darker line from DR to the first mark, skip the intervening 2'6" space and continue the line to the end of the light line. Erase the light line left in the 2'6" opening and put a perpendicular line 0'8" long at a right angle on each end to indicate the offset of the door frame in the wall.

7. To indicate a door in the R opening, measure and draw a line 2'6" from the upper end of the opening at an angle going offstage to show the door, hinged upstage and opening off.

HINT: If you have dividers, place the points at each end of the opening, pivot the lower one out and make a mark with the point to establish the door.

If you have no dividers, you may want to use a compass or a piece of scrap paper and make ticks for the door's dimension. Now set the compass point on the hinge point of the door and strike a light arc from the door back to the door opening. At this end of the arc, draw an arrow point, a "V," ($\rightarrow$) to indicate the doorswing clearly.

8. Now, from the upstage end of the R wall, use the T-square to draw a solid line for the backwall 16′0″ long and parallel to the proscenium line. From either end of this wall mark off 4′0″. Draw another line 8′0″ parallel to the wall 6″ upstage; then join the ends of this line to the marks on the wall, leaving a rectangle measuring 8′0″ by 0′6″ deep—a large picture window.

9. Measure up the CL 10′0″ and then towards L 11′6″. From the L return, draw a light line to this mark; then plot a 4′0″ opening that starts 2′6″ down along the wall from the upstage end. This will be an open archway. Erase the opening; draw solid lines with the end marks in the opening and overlapping curved lines in the opening to indicate a curtain.

10. From the upstage end of the L wall, draw a solid line 4′0″ onstage parallel to the proscenium line. Complete the set walls by connecting the onstage end of the 4′0″ jog to the L end of the upstage wall.

11. Draw a rectangular riser 6′0″(w) × 2′0″(d) × 1′0″(h) abutting and centered in the window unit URC. Running on 3 sides (L, D, and R) of this platform is a step unit 1′0″(d) × 0′6″(h).

12. Draw a right angle book of two flats, each 5′6″ wide, and place them as offstage masking for the L archway. Usually, one end of the "book" is attached at right angles to the wall of the set upstage of opening. This adds stability to the masking and to the wall itself.

13. Decide on the masking needed for the door R and the window unit and indicate these on the plan. Try to ensure that the masking is wide enough and appropriately placed to mask adequately, to allow free access by the actors, and to continue the logic of the rest of the set.

14. Place the following furniture in the plan and draw the setting lines necessary to place each piece accurately: a) a round table (3′0″ in diameter) with two chairs; b) a two-cushion sofa 6′9″ long and 2′4″ deep placed in any position not parallel to the proscenium line; c) a sideboard (d) 2′6″(w) × 1′8″(d) centered against the 4′0″ jog LC. It is not necessary for *this* exercise to dimension the furniture or to label any element that may be ambiguous.

15. Complete the plan by drawing a 2″(h) × 4″ box (actual measurements) in the lower right-hand portion of the sheet. Label with the following information: a) PRACTICE GROUNDPLAN; b) Scale: ½″ = 1′0″; c) Drafted by: _____; d) Date. (Use the eraser shield for the lettering if you like.)

End Note

Always check your groundplan to be sure that it provides reasonable playing areas, that it has architectural logic, and that someone else can interpret it accurately enough to lay out the plan on the floor of a stage or a rehearsal hall. Setting lines should be provided for the walls and dimensions for the major scenic units.

As you look at the finished plan, be sure the major scenic elements comprising the outline of the set and backing units are drawn with the *heaviest* lines and so appear visually dominant; the furniture pieces and the labels should be next in prominence. The dimension lines and their extensions, on the other hand, should be lightly drawn to distract as little as possible from the object outlines; however, the dimension numbers (in feet and inches) and the arrowpoints should be darker than the dimension lines to which they relate. Finally, make sure the labels are oriented so that it is not necessary to turn the paper constantly to read them.

Although auditioning is never an ideal situation in our theatre, an intelligent actor can give some inkling of what is needed to be known. . . . Of course, it goes without saying that the people listening to the audition must be intelligent, too, and not expect a finished performance.

—**Robert Lewis,** *Method or Madness*

9 AUDITIONS AND CASTING

Casting a production is one of a director's most exciting challenges. In a relatively short time, you must choose the essential elements in the artistic statement of the production, the people who will be your closest collaborators, and the artists the audience will most clearly recognize.

Although there is no way to guarantee getting the best company for a show, there are some things you can do to assure engaging the best people available for the job at hand. You should have, first, a clear notion of what the production will need and, second, an idea of how best to use the audition format to evaluate the potential of the actors who attend.

Obviously, you must have some idea of what sorts of actors are needed *in terms of the acting pool from which the cast will be drawn*. In most cases, the director will have the good sense to evaluate the prospects for casting even before the play is selected and announced.

‖ All casting situations are not created equal, and none is ideal. ‖

Each production is unique. For this reason, directors must be willing to adapt any idealized concept of the characters to the reality of the actors who ultimately might be cast. The best tactic for making the best choices is to be flexible enough to recognize—and cast—the best *available* people.

Casting requires a combination of theatrical instinct, knowledge of the text, the demands of each role, the available pool of actors, and realistic expectations of what can be accomplished in the rehearsal.

Defining Each Role

A director should take the time to consider the requirements for each role. You will want to review the requirements for each role. You will want to review the Character Dossier discussed in Chapter III. Making an index card with information on each role will assure a good grasp of the casting requirements. This table should include information drawn from the character dossier, supplemented with special casting considerations:

- the character's name
- the character's age
- the character's physical description
- the character's profession
- the character's personality
- principal plot actions
- acting demands—technical and emotional
- special personal qualities or requirements
- qualities relating to other actors (stature, coloring, voice placement or range, and so on)
- elements of the director's matrix

With this preliminary work in hand, the director may note potential actors for each role during the initial audition sessions and use the cumulative results to select actors and determine strategies for call-backs before making final casting decisions.

Casting Priorities

Before deciding on the assignment of roles, the director must set priorities first about the *entire cast* and then about any *individual actor's* suitability to a particular role. What priorities apply? Is *one* role so important that everything hinges on it (as might be the case in *Hamlet*)? Or must the director focus first on a *set* of two or more characters who are intimately related or mutually dependent (as with Romeo and Juliet or members of the family in *Life with Father*)? Or is every role—based on the directorial matrix—of near-equal importance?

> **During the audition process, many directors devise lists of possible casts, realizing that until priority roles are set, the choices remain fluid.**

Once decisions are made about a certain individual or group, possible choices for the rest of the company begin to diminish. When there are three possibilities for Romeo, there might be five for Mercutio. Once Romeo is set, however, some of these other possibilities may suddenly seem less appropriate. It is good practice to project as many possible different casts as seem plausible when you prepare for call-backs. In that way, you remain flexible and open in your considerations until the final decisions are made.

Evaluating Individual Actors

No matter what the role or its relationship to another, you must still consider the possibilities of each individual actor. Using guidelines similar to those below will help the director give full consideration to each contender:

1. Presence
   a) stage *persona* (Who is this person on stage? What sort of statement does he or she make by simply being on stage?)
   b) command of the stage (Does the person seem to demand attention naturally? Or seem neutral? Or seem negative?)
2. Acting
   a) responsiveness to the material
   b) characterization and insight
   c) adaptability to directorial suggestion
3. Physical Characteristics
   a) height, weight, build
   b) color of hair, eyes, complexion
   c) carriage, posture, flexibility
   d) special qualities—physical rhythms, projection of personality
4. Vocal Characteristics
   a) quality—pitch, timbre, flexibility
   b) projection and clarity
   c) control—timing and phrasing
   d) special qualities—personality, placement, tonal range

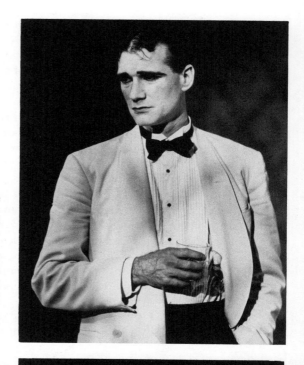

Often, casting considerations hinge around very specific qualities required for a central character as here for the role of F. Scott Fitzgerald.

Play: *Zig Zag Zelda* **Author:** Drury Pifer **Theatre:** People's Light and Theatre Company **Director:** Drury Pifer **Set Designer:** James F. Pyne, Jr. **Costumes:** Chelsea P. Harriman **Lighting:** James F. Pyne, Jr. **Actors (l to r):** Peter Delaurier (Photo by Gerry Goodstein)

Not only should each actor be appropriate for a role but also in terms of the overall production; that is, each actor must complement the other.

Play: *The Duchess of Malfi* **Author:** John Webster **Theatre:** The Guthrie Theater **Director:** Michael Kahn **Set Designer:** Derek McLane **Costumes:** Martin Pakledinaz **Lighting:** Frances Aronson **Actors (l to r):** Barbara March, Daniel Southern (Photo by Michael Daniel)

5. Relationship to Others
   a) physical (How does the actor *look* with others who may be cast?)
   b) character dynamics (How does the actor interact *as a character* with the other characters being auditioned?)
   c) personality dynamics (How does the actor respond *personally* to the director and the other actors?)

The Audition Structure

Armed with a clear idea of what is needed for the show, the director must then decide on how to make the best casting choices.

THE PROFESSIONAL AUDITION

The director auditioning professional actors is faced with a set of procedures and problems different from those encountered in a non-professional situation. For one, dozens of professional actors are usually available for a given role. Next, if auditioning includes members of Actors' Equity Association (AEA), certain rules govern virtually every phase of the process, for example, how many actors must be seen, how long an audition or interview must run, how many call-backs are allowed before the actor must be compensated, and so on.[1] Typically, actors respond to a casting notice in one of the "trades." These publications are published in almost every city with professional theatre activity.

The casting notice usually details the roles available, the contract or terms under which the actor will be signed, and the details of the audition procedure. Most often the actor is required to send a *headshot* (an 8" × 10" black and white photograph) and a *resumé* of theatre experience. The director then invites to the audition the actors that best fit the requirements of the production. Large theatres are turning more and more to *casting agents* who do this preliminary screening. This is becoming common practice with regional theatres that audition in New York, Chicago, Los Angeles, and similar centers on a restricted time schedule.

Many professional auditions begin with a brief interview and a memorized monologue the actor has chosen. If the director is impressed with this display, the next step might be a cold-reading from the script and perhaps an improvisation. Finally, the director might ask the actor to prepare or memorize a particular speech or scene for a final call-back.

---

[1] A director planning to audition Equity actors should contact the Association for information on the relevant regulations. See Appendix D for AEA's address and telephone number.

NON-PROFESSIONAL AUDITIONS: A TYPICAL SCENARIO

The following steps outline a common, practical audition format that directors use in school and community theatres; following the outline are some comments and suggestions.

STEP 1: Audition Announcement (Sunday)—An audition notice in the local press, probably in the arts and entertainment section, appears three days to a week before the auditions. Flyers are also distributed or posted about the same time. These announcements carry information with the title of the play, the producing organization, the number of roles for men and women, and the time and place for the auditions. Occasionally, the notices include the name of the director and a phone number for additional information. The press release sometimes includes such additional information as a plot synopsis and general descriptions of the leading characters. The auditions are scheduled somewhere between a few days and a week before rehearsals are to begin.

The director generally has some idea of the acting pool that will be represented at the audition and some anxiety about its size and quality. The director or other members of the producing organization make some discreet (or sometimes not so discreet) contacts with prospective actors. The director wants to be sure of seeing at least one reasonable prospect for each role, ideally two or more.

STEP 2: Open Auditions (Wednesday and Thursday)—The *cold reading* is the common audition format in the non-professional theatre. At the audition site, actors are given copies of the script to peruse while they wait. A stage manager or assistant takes names and phone numbers of the actors. Some will be reluctant to audition, claiming they have come "just to watch." Other representatives of the theatre are apt to be on hand to welcome those auditioning, and to encourage the hesitant among them to try out for one of the roles.

After the director has provided general information and background about the scene and the characters, two or three actors are asked to go up on stage and read a scene. Most of those auditioning sit in the auditorium to watch the others, occasionally responding approvingly to an effective or entertaining reading. Actors are called back to the stage to read other characters and to perform with other actors. Finally—usually at the director's invitation—the actors are allowed to read a specific character or scene until the process grinds to a close.

On the second night, the process is repeated. Some people return, convinced they were not at their best the night before for one reason or another.

STEP 3: Call-Backs (Friday)—By the third night, the director has eliminated some prospects, and others have reconsidered and withdrawn from consideration after hearing about the time commitment involved. Those called back will have been notified either by the posting of a notice at the theatre or by phone. One or two will invariably fail to show up, but one or two new faces generally appear. People are often persuaded to come by the director (or someone else involved in the production) to be sure that the roles can be cast satisfactorily. There is usually a certain urgency to such requests.

There are more readings from the script, this time much more purposeful; small groups read together, clearly representing some of the director's casting options. The director talks quietly and intently to one or other of the actors during breaks. At the end of the evening, the director thanks everyone and explains that the decisions will be very difficult, but they must be made right away because rehearsals begin the following Monday night.

STEP 4: Completing the Cast (Saturday and Sunday)—The cast list is posted at the theatre to be initialed by the actors. The stage manager calls people who do not come by. Most are delighted to have been cast and look forward to starting rehearsals. Almost invariably, however, problems arise. One or two actors may have to arrive at rehearsals late or leave early; some others may have conflicts that will cause them to miss some rehearsals. Most seriously, someone cast in an important supporting role might not think the smaller part worth all the sacrifices, and decide to "sit this one out." The director must then call the second choice and explain that even though another name appears on the cast list, the role is nonetheless "a perfect part for you."

When the group assembles for its first rehearsal on Monday night, the stage manager must read in the roles not yet filled.

NON-PROFESSIONAL AUDITIONS: SOME IMPROVEMENTS

The preceding process is familiar to anyone with experience in the non-professional theatre. Although generally a workable and fair procedure, it can be improved upon by a director who plans ahead. These may seem like small suggestions, but following them will result in important improvements.

Schedule the Auditions Early   Count on at least a week between the scheduled end of auditions and the start of rehearsals. Most non-professional auditions do not attract hordes of people so the director needs time to seek additional auditionees (if necessary) and to increase the likelihood of beginning rehearsals with a complete cast.

Choose the Appropriate Type of Audition   Select the material for the audition carefully. Although most non-professional auditions are *cold-readings,* other types are worth considering.
Alternatives include:

1. cold-readings
2. prepared readings
3. memorized monologues or scenes
4. improvisations
5. combination

The *cold-reading* is simple and fair. Because it is the best-known technique, it is usually the least intimidating. The *prepared reading*—assigning or giving a choice of a speech or scene for the actor to work up—and the *memorized* audition put more demands on the actor. Such strategies, however, can tell the director a great deal about the auditionee's interpretive skills and ability to make committed choices. The *improvisation,* on the other hand, is particularly useful when improv techniques will be used in the rehearsal process itself. This kind of reading can also give the director an insight into an auditionee's freedom of expression and range of movement or the ability to work with and respond to others.

The director must also be purposeful about *improvisations*. Work out a list of possibilities to suggest at the auditions. If you know what you want to discover with each kind of improv, you have made an excellent beginning. Several texts, notably Spolin's *Improvisation for the Theatre,* will be extremely helpful in developing your list of possibilities.

> For *cold-readings,* the director when possible should choose several short scenes involving each important character. It is good to limit most of these selections to those involving only two or three characters. This will allow the director a variety of choices in dealing with a large number of auditionees.

Prepared or *memorized* auditions should be assigned with an eye to discovering something about the actor's strengths if cast in a particular role.

Of course, the director may profitably employ a *combination* of these techniques.

Post the Notice Early and Have Scripts Available—Get the word out at least a week before the first audition. Scripts can be made available at the theatre, in school and public libraries, and other locations. The scripts may be supplemented by notes on each character (complementing the brief descriptions provided in the audition notice) to help the prospective auditionees understand the director's vision and expectations.

In addition, the theatre may find radio and television outlets willing to accept audition notices as public service announcements (PSA's) if submitted early enough. Cable-TV bulletin board services are sometimes available and effective. The director might also convince the producing organization to pay for small advertisements for auditions, even in the personal listings of the newspaper classified section.

> Public announcement of auditions—besides attracting people to the readings—also serves as advance notice for the performances and so can be seen also as promotion and publicity for the performances themselves.

Include Casting Requirements in the Audition Notice—The notice should specify the types of the people needed as well as any special considerations. These descriptions should be as liberal as possible to encourage people to audition, especially if the acting pool is not large.

Indicate Audition Requirements in the Notice—The director must not assume that everyone who auditions understands what to expect. Some of those auditioning will not know what they are getting into. Therefore, the notice should state clearly that actors will be asked to read from the script. Any other specific requirements also should be spelled out. For example, if the candidates are expected to sing, specify the groundrules—whether a song must be prepared, the availability of accompaniment, the requirements for sheet music or taped accompaniment, the acceptability of *a cappella* singing, and so on. Keep the notice informative but friendly and unthreatening; the aim is to draw the largest number of interested auditionees.

Organize the Process at the Audition Site—Auditioning can confuse and frustrate both the actors and the director. Neither is likely to do well if the procedure is not fair and efficient. The best way to avoid pitfalls is to set up a thorough, well-considered process. Some useful ideas in arranging the auditions follow:

1. *Have the actors log in on a sign-in sheet as they arrive.* Assign them sequential numbers.
2. *Have each actor complete an information sheet.* The primary purpose of this sheet is to identify and keep track of the actor. It also serves as a sort of resumé and can clarify and reinforce some expectations about the auditions and the rehearsal process. The sheet should give most or all of the following information:
   a) *Identification:* name, address, phone
   b) *Personal Description:* height, weight, age, hair, eyes, complexion, shoe, hat, suit or dress sizes, voice range or part (for singers)
   c) *Audition Restrictions:* an explanatory note, followed by the actor's agreement to be cast and to attend rehearsals and performances. For example, *"Actors will be cast at the discretion of the director in the best interests of the production unless otherwise instructed. If you wish to limit consideration to certain roles, you will be considered for no others. I AGREE TO ACCEPT ANY ROLE ____ or ONLY THE FOLLOWING _____. Rehearsals are regularly scheduled Monday through Saturdays from 7:00 to 10:30 p.m. for the period posted. You may be expected to attend all scheduled rehearsals. Please note any conflict(s): _____"*
   d) *Special Skills:* any performance skills that might be useful in the current production (or perhaps in the future)—musical instruments, dance, juggling, tumbling, etc.
   e) *Availability or Interest in Other Work with the Theatre:* publicity, stage management, technical, box office, and so on.

f) *Summary of Theatre Training and Experience:* need not be a highly detailed format; actors with a great deal of experience will communicate the essential facts; those without extensive backgrounds will not be put off by facing a number of categories that must be left blank.

g) *Director's Notes* (optional): Some directors prefer keeping audition notes separate (and private), thereby allowing the information sheet to be used as a resource for the theatre in other ways—recruitment of volunteers, for example.

3. *Insofar as possible, have the actors read in order of their arrival.* This poses no problem if you read each actor individually, but if you call them up in groups it may be necessary to juggle the order a bit to get the right mix of males and females.

> **At the first audition, take care to be equitable in the time allotted to each auditionee and the number of roles each is allowed to read.**

Listen to first auditions in groups of three to five people. By alternating selections and role assignments through a group of five, you can hear each person read twice, perhaps in two or three roles with two or three different partners. This gives you the opportunity to see and hear each actor in some sort of context. Time each group; a stop watch is very useful. By allotting about 10 minutes per group, you can effectively screen 100 people in less than 4 hours. A smaller turn-out permits you to give more time to each group or to have smaller groups.

4. *Have character descriptions available.* These may be written out and posted, or discussed in the director's oral comments at the beginning of the audition. Some people will not have prepared and will have very little idea about the characters they will read. Having a brief description available may not give anyone a genuine understanding of character, but it will probably save time.

5. *Post the list of readings for the audition.* This requires the director to make selections well in advance and to have extra scripts available at the audition site. Actors naturally feel more confident if they can look over the material before they actually walk up to the stage.

6. *Make it clear when the evening's audition is over for any individual.* Begin by explaining the process and the goals of this step in the audition process. If there are many roles to be cast and a great many people to read, it might be impossible to listen to everyone read for every role. In such a case, explain that you will be keeping the casting possibilities for each actor in mind throughout the process.

Some directors like to keep everyone around for the entire session. Others find it more efficient to dismiss each actor after one appearance, which may include the reading of several passages and characters. If the cast is a large one, you must decide whether to attempt to read every actor for each role that might be appropriate. If you have a large turnout, it may be better to save readings for specific characters for call-backs. In any event, make sure everyone understands the procedure. Remember, too, that if you remain to listen to one actor's "requests" to read specific characters or selections, you must be prepared to accommodate everybody who wishes to do the same.

7. *Keep to a realistic time schedule.* The time you allot for each actor will depend on your own preferences and the number of people auditioning. Do you expect five people to show up—or fifty? By making realistic projections about the turn-out, you can be much more efficient in dealing with the audition. Even so, be ready to adapt as the occasion demands: if you have 30 actors at a session and begin by giving each actor 10 minutes, you must either shorten the time per person, or face a five hour session—not counting breaks.

Be sure to take special situations into account when setting the schedule. Auditions for musicals (and other productions requiring special skills) are more complicated and time-consuming. Such auditions must also suit collaborators—the musical director and the choreographer, for example. The director might want all of these collaborators to watch the initial auditions together. Then, the follow-up auditions—acting, singing, dance—can be split up into three different rooms. The process will take time and may best be scheduled over two or three evenings. The director should then confer with the collaborators to discuss each prospect and outline a strategy for call-backs and final casting.

8. *Make the follow-up procedure clear.* The actors should know: a) if and how they will be notified, b) when and where the call-backs will be held and how they will be structured (some directors schedule appointments for the actors either individually or in small groups); c) what they will be asked to do (more cold readings, or something else).

Conduct Organized and Purposeful Call-backs—Use call-backs to get needed additional information or to reassure yourself of the validity of your impressions from the first audition. Call-backs allow the director to grasp the implications of the casting—to make sure the cast is balanced and credible both in terms of what the actors can do individually and how they will function as a team. In order to do this, you must have some questions or tests to try out during the call-backs. If an actor gave indications of any potential problems during the open call, those must be evaluated during the call-back. At the same time, it is patently unfair to expect an actor to perform beyond his or her limits. If the limitations are real, they must be dealt with or worked around. This is not to say that actors should be cast only for the abilities they can demonstrate before the start of the rehearsals. It is only to suggest the necessity of a *reasonable* expectation of success.

> It is valuable to assign a short scene or speech for the actor to prepare for the call-back, asking for attention to a specific element in the preparation.

By having the actor prepare for a call-back, the director can determine his or her willingness and ability both to respond to direction and to show potential and flexibility in the area of interest—vocal projection, dialect, physical responsiveness, emotional intensity, and so on.

Whenever possible, conduct call-backs in *depth;* have two or three possibilities for each role. This practice not only keeps you alert to possibilities, but also will prove valuable in the event the first choice for a given role is unavailable.

As mentioned earlier, call-backs are a good way to test the compatibility of the actors who must work together. For this reason, many directors call back several actors at a time in small groups to test their interaction and the suitability of their personalities, physical appearance, and vocal qualities in relationship to one another. For each actor and each group of actors, then, the director should have specific problems to resolve and a plan for resolving them.

Subsequent call-backs should be scheduled if needed, but should not simply by an excuse for indecisiveness because the process can be quite debilitating for the actors involved—especially in non-professional settings. For an actor trying to work in New York, the number of call-backs becomes something of a badge of honor, a way of showing that directors and producers are genuinely interested. For the non-professional, however, additional call-backs announced at the last minute may be taken as an indication that the director is simply not satisfied with the available acting pool.

Avoid Last-Minutes Surprises—Few things can be as frustrating or debilitating to director and company as having to change a cast that has only recently been announced. In some non-professional theatres, the experience of having an actor turn down a role after the auditions occurs all too frequently. The ethics of such action aside, the effects are intolerable. In most cases, the actor involved sees it only as a matter of private and personal convenience and gives no real thought to the position in which it places the director and the other actors and would-be actors. Communication is the best way to establish the groundrules for the audition.

> The director must make it clear from the beginning of the audition process that any reservations about casting or schedule conflicts must be made known—not held back until the casting decisions have been made.

The statement of availability on the audition information sheet (discussed earlier in this chapter) calls attention to the issue and requires a written response. This should help discourage any temptation to renege on a clear commitment.

It is wise to delay the public posting of a cast list if there are any doubts that a role will be accepted. Contacting the person privately is the best idea. The director (or assistant director or stage manager) might simply ask if the actor is committed to the production and is still available as indicated on the audition sheet. At this point, it is a good idea not to discuss a specific role. Having the word get out that the actor who becomes the *final* choice was the *second* choice is patently unfair to the actor and always bad for morale.

> **Like the lawyer who never asks a question without knowing the answer, the wise director never publishes a cast list without knowing it will be final.**

Before Rehearsals Begin—If there is a week or more before rehearsals actually begin, distribute scripts and ask the actors to begin their reading and study. If there is a longer period before the start of regularly scheduled rehearsals, and particularly if the actors must begin memory work before rehearsals start, consider having the firt read-through right away. Use the occasion to provide guidance on style, directorial approach, and characterization in order to keep each actor on the right track during the pre-rehearsal period.

End Note

Once the casting is completed, an entirely new phase of the process begins. All of the collaborators are in place, and the production is marked as entirely unique. For most practical purposes, the director is now committed to all the elements that will be employed in shaping the production, in transforming an abstract, idealized notion of what might be into a theatrical artwork. The process of putting all the elements together—the work of rehearsals—now begins.

So one must say that painting is both creative and responsive. It is an intimately communicative affair between the painter and his painting, a conversation back and forth, the painting telling the painter even as it receives its shape and form.

—**Ben Shahn,** *The Shape of Content*

10 REHEARSAL

All the director's skills are called into play during the rehearsal period. It is during this time that he or she functions in each of the three modes suggested by Stanislavski's advisor and collaborator Vladimir Nemirovich-Danchenko (in *Directors on Directing*, p. 119):

1. the *regisseur*-interpreter; he instructs how to play; so that it is possible to call him the *regisseur*-actor on the *regisseur*-pedagogue;
2. the *regisseur*-mirror; reflecting the individual qualities of the actor;
3. the *regisseur*-organizer of the entire production.

During rehearsals, it is essential for the director to be a creative artist—an interpreter and a responsive mirror. At the same time, he or she is called upon to be an executive—an organizer and manager. All too often, the desired balance between these functions gives way to an overemphasis on one or the other.

For example, on occasion one still hears the term "play practice" and thinks it naïve and quaint. But the underlying idea is more than semantic; it describes a fundamental attitude toward the rehearsal process. Some directors do, indeed, conduct "practice" instead of "rehearsal" by aiming only to have actors execute a prescribed directorial plan. The purpose and object of such an exercise is to construct a performance as the director envisions it after studying the text and formulating an interpretation. It neglects the *interpreter-mirror* functions of the director in rehearsal and emphasizes instead the *organizer*.

At its best, this approach to the process can be thorough and efficient. Clear goals are set, and the means of achieving them are laid out and carefully explained. Actors understand not only the individual tasks but also the total job before them. The approach is linear: Step A leads to B, then to C, D, and so on, until the production-structure is completed.

Such an approach is "practice" in the same way we speak of football or tennis practice. The objective and the shape of the play or the stroke is described, analyzed, understood, and *practiced* until it meets the prescribed standard. Then we say the practice has paid off: *We've gotten it right!*

We can describe this approach from another point of view as *architectural*. A production is built in steps according to a blueprint.

If, at the opposite extreme, the director assumes a purely *laissez-faire* approach to the rehearsal period (emphasizing principally the mirror function at the expense of the organizer), the results are sometimes exciting and energetic (especially for the participants), but rehearsals can easily become frustrating and wildly inefficient. The director who gets a marvelously inventive company can draw upon its storehouse of experience and creative resources to evolve a unique approach and method. While this *is* theatrical improvisation, it is also—by definition—undirected in the sense we discuss here. Most productions fall between the poles, neither dictated nor undirected. Creative directors aim to establish a *controlled, creative* environment. To distinguish this method of working from the *architectural* approach, we will describe this as a *sculptural* model.

The sculptor begins with the idea of making a piece and expressing feeling. The first step is choosing the material with which to work: clay, stone, metal. The choice affects the artist, the subject, the feeling, the very idea of the piece. Once the material is chosen, the artist must relinquish possibilities and choices offered by other potential materials and work within the range presented by the chosen one. For the artist, of course, this is a happy circumstance. The artist is eager to explore and celebrate the possibilities—not the limitations—of the chosen material. Ben Shahn, the celebrated painter, describes a similar process as it occurs to him in his medium:

> From the moment a painter begins to strike figures of color upon a surface he must become acutely sensitive to the feel, the textures, the light, the relationships which rise before him. At one moment he will mold the material according to an intention. At another he may yield intention—perhaps his whole concept—to emerging forms, to new implications within the painted surface. Idea itself—ideas, many ideas move back and forth across his mind as a con-

stant traffic, dominated perhaps by larger currents and directions, by what he wants to think. Thus idea rises to the surface, grows, changes as the painting grows and develops. (p. 49)

Both the painter and the sculptor are exquisitely sensitive and responsive to the materials at hand. Some unexpected element need not ruin the project. It might, in fact, suggest a new direction or a modulation previously unsuspected. For the classical Chinese calligrapher-painter, an accidental drop of ink must not be erased, but rather acknowledged and integrated into the total work.

These methods and attitudes suggest a combination of structure and creativity that may be of use in approaching theatrical rehearsals: first, a *matrix* to express both the creative idea and its potential form and, second, a *process* that allows freedom to respond to the material during the rehearsal process. "Let the work teach you" is sound advice. In speaking of the matrix, Suzanne Langer makes the point (cited in Chapter II) that the apparent restrictions of form are actually possibilities instead. "Creative accidents" happen to those who, by being prepared and disciplined, are free to respond to the energy of the moment. Arthur Ashe, the great tennis player, speaks of being "in the zone," a condition in which everything seems to fall your way. Directors are "in the zone" when—like talented athletes—they are so at ease with themselves and their task that, as they go about their work of directing in the creative mode, many problems seem to resolve themselves.

The rehearsal period, then, should be a balance of *structure*—an underlying design with a clear progression of steps leading to the performance—and *openness*—the ability to discover and explore new and unexpected possibilities.

The format assumes 24–30 rehearsals approximately 3 hours each. The serious non-professional production typically rehearses 5–6 days per week. Actors' Equity Association—depending on the specific contract—allows 7–8 hours per day for up to 6 days per week. In the week of an opening, one "10 out of 12" (a total of 10 hours rehearsal in a 12 hour period) is usually permitted. After 5 hours of continuous rehearsal a 2 hour break is always required under current Equity specifications.[1]

The Rehearsal Process
Part One: Read-Through and Discussion (2–5 sessions)

For the director and the actors, the read-through is sometimes routine, and the attitude is often cynical: "We read through the play so everybody knows how it ends." In the past—and in sometimes the present—the playwright or director reads the play to the cast, says a few words about intention or concept,

---

[1]Any director dealing with Equity performers should have a set of the current regulations covering the specific contract for that production. There are many contracts reflecting a variety of requirements and restrictions. Address information for Equity is found in Appendix D.

shows some designs, and waits until the next day to begin rehearsals. At the other end of the spectrum, we might find the director, and perhaps the playwright, sitting with the cast for several days—reading, discussing, analyzing. After this period, rehearsals move to the phase in which the decisions and agreements reached around the table are translated into action. The details of the staging remain virtually the only elements to be worked out.

Both these approaches to the first part of the rehearsal period have a certain value; yet they fail to provide the combination of structure and flexibility we seek. The first seems to deny the need for genuine collaborative exploration and discovery. The second is often so analytical and academic that the process smacks of a committee's compromise and consensus. Neither serves well as the sculptural armature or Stanislavskian "spine" that can begin to shape the essential elements of the production and yet still allow discovery and spontaneity.

Indeed, the read-throughs should be a joyous time of spontaneity, discovery, and interaction. The text of the play, the director's images and concepts, the designers' sketches, and the actors' impulses should all begin to mingle and meld. When a sense of openness and communication is established in these first rehearsals, we can be sure the production is on the right track.

Still, not *everything* is completely open to change. The director is faced with many more fixed parameters than the painter Ben Shahn describes. The first of these is the text of the play. If the play is not new and if the playwright is not present to participate in script changes, we assume the text to be the fixed core of the production. After the text, the director's notions about the *essential* aspects of the production form have the greatest stability. What we call the *matrix* marries with the text to shape a production. Still, even if the director's formative ideas remain relatively stable, they must be *flexible;* if they are not, the rehearsal process will lack that sense of sympathetic direction that makes guided creativity possible. Next, quite close in stability to the director's matrix (and intimately attached to it) comes the work of the designers. While acknowledging the possibility—even occasionally the desirability—of allowing designs to evolve in the rehearsal period, conventional practice and practical considerations demand certain decisions be made well before starting the rehearsals. Typically, scenic and costume designs are virtually fixed when rehearsals start; makeup design usually evolves throughout the rehearsal period (or should be) as the actors make their complex choices and discoveries; lights and sound fall somewhere in between as the needs of the particular production begin to unfold.

So, as the rehearsal process begins with read-throughs and discussions, all the collaborators should have at least an implicit understanding of the relative flexibility of the production elements. Usually the progression from *least* to *most* flexible looks like the sequence shown in the table on the following page.

As a practical matter, this sequence also reflects a fairly standard chronology in the preparation of a production of an extant script. It is not meant to be prescriptive, however. Under some conditions, it is quite plausible to see the actors' work as the basis for a production and the text of the play as one of the most fluid elements, perhaps even the last to be set.

Fixed	1. Text of the play (and the musical score)
—	2. Director's vision
—	3. Scenic design
—	4. Costumes
—	5. Actors' work (and musical arrangements)
—	6. Properties
—	7. Lights
—	8. Sound
Most	9. Makeup
Flexible	

What is essential, in every case, is that the director have some sense of what elements in the rehearsal are relatively fixed, even rigid, and what other elements must conform to or complement them.

These groundrules must be communicated to the company at the first read-throughs and discussions. But the director's attitude will be defined and redefined throughout the rehearsal process in responses to such questions as whether (or to what degree) the script may be altered to suit an actor or the audience's taste, whether the color of a costume should be changed at an actor's behest, or whether a staircase should be redesigned (perhaps even rebuilt) to accommodate an important piece of business developed in rehearsal.

D I S C U S S I O N

Project conditions in which the progression outlined above might be radically altered. List the sequences that might apply in the following circumstances:

A. An improvisational theatre doing *Macbeth*.

B. Peter Brook directing *Macbeth*.

C. You directing James Earl Jones in *Macbeth*.

D. A new comedy by a student playwright.

E. A new comedy by Neil Simon

FORMAT FOR THE FIRST READ-THROUGH

1. **Introductions:** If possible, the director should introduce each member of the company, acknowledging each person equally. Having the individual actors introduce themselves can be awkward and embarrassing for certain people, but is nonetheless an option.

It is important to have everyone involved in the production present at this rehearsal, not only to be introduced, but also to watch, to listen, and to begin to respond to the work of the others in the company.

This is, or should be, the first step in inviting a sense of *ensemble*. ("Ensemble" is a term often used loosely to connote some vague sort of bonding among actors in a company. As used here, "ensemble" means a group that functions as a *team*.)

2. **The Director's Statement:** It is important for the director to provide some sense of both vision and method. What is the point-of-view or image the production hopes to develop? What will make this production special? To what qualities of character and interaction should the actors be especially attentive? It is not necessary actually to state the directorial matrix itself. Rather, the director should attempt to *describe* what the matrix suggests—the created world and its attendant logic, and the *production* the director envisions. Elaborate commentaries or analyses can seem daunting and create the impression that all the important creative work has been done. Abstract concepts or visionary images must be handled with extra care because they might prove confusing, or worse, open the possibility of inviting opposing concepts or notions.

Description, on the other hand, tends to excite interest and open up a sense of possibilities.

In any event, the director must leave the clear impression that the production will be distinctive, that it will have a point-of-view. The director who defers to the notion of "letting the play speak for itself" runs the risk, as Peter Brook warns, of having the play "not make a sound at all." (*The Empty Space,* p. 35) Worse, such a statement gives the actors nothing to help them begin their explorations.

The director should also make a succinct statement about how the rehearsal period will proceed. If improvisation will be a key element for the first week, the actors must know it; if detailed blocking is to be prescribed, the actors should know that—and the conditions in which they might demur. The mechanical details of the rehearsals are probably best left for the stage manager to explain, as indicated below.

3. **Designers' Presentations:** For the *set design,* a sketch, rendering, or model is usually called for. A model—plain white or colored—can be extremely useful because it can communicate a sense of scale and dimension with great clarity.

For the *costume design,* sketches are standard and especially useful when fabric swatches are attached. The designer should alert the actor to any special considerations or problems, and be ready to cooperate in providing rehearsal clothes that might help in making the transition to the finished costume easier and more graceful.

For the *lighting design,* the presentation of light plots and hanging schedules is unnecessary. Although these are of little use or interest to the actors, an indication of color and a description of the effect and movement of the lights will help them grasp the intention of the design.

In *other design* and technical areas (properties, makeup, and sound) specific presentations are made only as necessary for a particular production. Often these elements are the responsibility of the set, costume, or lighting designer.

Even if—as often happens—the director is director *and* designer, everyone at the read-through is well served by a succinct discussion of the design elements.

|| **Every production has a designer whether or not one is formally designated.** ||

The director-designer, then, can present the design options and strategies by using sketches (however crude), photographs, paintings—anything that sets a visual image for the production.

4. **Stage Manager's Comments:** The stage manager executes many of the functions of the *regisseur*-organizer. The stage manager should lay out the plan and procedures for the rehearsal period, as well as the specific expectations for rehearsal discipline.

5. **Read-Through:** (For a suggested outline format, see Table 10–1.) Many possibilities for discovery and enrichment are lost by the tendency to make the read-through a performance. The director, the designers, the stage manager have all had their moments. The actors are now on stage, and they all want to establish credibility and confidence among their peers. Everyone wants to show "what they can do." This temptation is especially strong when members of the company have not worked together before. The director must try to reduce this pressure to perform if the read-through is to yield something of value and not become an empty ritual before getting to the "real work" of rehearsing the play.

TABLE 10–1

Suggested Format for the First Rehearsal (The First Read-Through)

1. INTRODUCTIONS—of all personnel, made by the director
2. DIRECTOR'S STATEMENT—a description of the proposed production, matrix
3. DESIGNERS' PRESENTATIONS—models, sketches, and samples
4. STAGE MANAGER'S PRESENTATION—rehearsal schedule, routine, expectations
5. READ-THROUGH—actors read the text in an informal, unpressured setting; emphasis on easy communication and clarity

Stanislavski and Boleslavsky both dwell on the absolute necessity of relaxation as a requisite for the actor's creative function. At a read-through, the subtle pressure to perform sets up inevitable tensions that dull the instincts and make spontaneity impossible.

Peter Brook observes with characteristic clarity: "Acting begins with a tiny inner movement so slight that it is almost completely invisible." (*Empty Space,* p. 99) That "tiny inner movement" is never so fresh, so intuitive, as at the read-through. The director would be wise, at this point, to set up conditions that encourage the actors to work without demands, without expectations, and without performance tensions. Also, the director and others need to be alert to the actors' instinctive choices and decisions. Brook's observation is again worth noting:

> In early theatre rehearsals, the impulse may get no further than a flicker—even if the actor wishes to amplify it, all sorts of extraneous psychic psychological tensions can intervene—then the current is short-circuited, earthed. For this flicker to pass into the whole organism, a total relaxation must be there, either god-given or brought about by work. (*Empty Space,* p. 99)

SETTING UP THE READ-THROUGH

How can the director help the actors toward a relaxed, creative read-through? First, the physical environment can be arranged to promote an atmosphere of unity and informal personal contact—not of a performance context. The most obvious and effective form is sitting around in a circle, with or without a central table. It is important that the arrangement create a *shared* atmosphere. Each actor should be able to see and hear the others clearly with minimum effort. In the case of very large cast, the challenge to the director is great. In such case, a wise tactic is to invite the cast to find the most suitable configuration for themselves.

After the company (including the designers and the stage manager) has settled into place, the director describes the goals and methods of the read-through. The following introductory remarks illustrate ideas and methods worth noting:

> "We want to read through the script now, but if we don't finish it tonight, we can at the next rehearsal. We will devote several rehearsals to read-throughs because that will give us a chance to feel our way through the play and to become bit more comfortable with what we're hearing from the play and from each other.
>
> "It's important for you not to begin too early to *act*. You are actors, and so the acting will come naturally. This time is for us to listen and to watch—even to taste and smell—what goes on when we simply let the play happen to us.
>
> "That's an important point, I think, to let the play happen to us. So get comfortable, but stay focused on what's going on. Don't project, okay? Ed is no more than eight feet from Donna, so neither one of them has to use much

voice. And don't feel you have to *make* this interesting or dynamic. If you stay tuned in, that's all we want. Later, I hope it will be interesting, even downright exciting, but now it's all right to be *simple, alert,* and *clear.*

"Make some mental notes as we go through. We'll stop a couple of times in the reading to discuss what we've discovered—especially things that might be unexpected or surprising.

"So let's begin with Act I. We'll skip the stage directions except in a couple of cases where I'll read them in. Remember now, stay with it, but don't force it."

The actors begin to read. What does the director look for? How does one recognize the "tiny inner movement?" Obviously, such a thing cannot be described precisely. We are speaking of an unexpected emphasis, a shift in rhythm, a surprising moment of warmth or coldness coming from actors who are at their ease and allowed to respond freely to a text and to each other.

Notice the adjectives—"surprising," "spontaneous," "unexpected"—tell us we are looking for something we do not *know* we know. Remember the metaphors of the architect and the sculptor. Both *know* their materials and their objectives. Each might be demanding, each a great artist. The architect, however, is more likely to use what is already known about a standard material to plan the work. The sculptor might find in material that seems to deviate from the standard an even more exciting creative possibility. One deals with material in a *prescriptive* way, the other in a *collaborative* way.

When the read-through ends, it is advisable to commend the cast and the designers on their work, and to summarize whatever of significance or interest has been discovered. Finally, give an idea of what might be developed or explored in the next rehearsal or block of rehearsals.

DISCUSSION

In the director's introduction to the first read-through quoted above:

1. What goals seem best served in the remarks and which ones seem slighted?

2. Towards what kinds of companies do the remarks seem suitably aimed? What kinds of actors or situations might require different emphases, specific changes either in tone or in the instructions themselves?

3. Suggest other strategies for using read-throughs creatively and efficiently.

SUBSEQUENT READ-THROUGH(S)

Although conventional practice is to have only one read-through, especially in the case of apparently straight-forward scripts, the director who *uses* more than one is often rewarded not only by the early discovery of unsuspected depths or variations, but also by increased efficiency in the remaining rehearsals.

For these reasons, the use of two or three read-throughs is a wise practice.

What to do in those rehearsals? Some possible approaches include scene objectives or descriptions rehearsals, character goals rehearsals, and "on your feet" rehearsals.

1. **Scene objectives or description** rehearsals employ an objective (e.g., to intensify Laura's feeling of isolation), or a description of title ("Laura's Retreat") for each French scene (marked by the entrance or exit of a character). Such a rehearsal technique does several things. For one, the device can be used to reveal dramatic structure and progression. Of equal importance, the designation of French scenes underscores the dynamics inherent in the entrance or exit of any character.

2. **Character goals** suggested at the beginning of rehearsal for each French scene can strengthen, clarify, complement, or alter the direction an actor seemed to be going in the first read-through. In this case, the director might suggest opposing or complementary goals to those the actor is using too glibly or in an unmodulated manner. An actor playing Laura in *The Glass Menagerie* with an unrelieved quality of extreme isolation from her mother might be asked to focus on the goal, "To make real contact with Amanda."

3. **"On your feet"** rehearsals put the actors in space and demand some sort of physical responsiveness. Occasionally, the actors find a moment of truth that illuminates a quality or relationship so clearly that it finds its way into the production. More likely, but of great value nonetheless, is the prospect that the director will find an intrinsic compatibility between his or her own projected staging ideas and images and those found by the actors' improvised blocking.

"On your feet" rehearsals can also help the director and actors to gauge the basic spatial relationships to be employed in the production. For this purpose, it is not necessary to lay out the groundplan precisely, only to respect the essential relationships of the scenic elements to be used on stage.

> **Whether the director chooses to use one read-through or a dozen, each rehearsal must have the clear purpose of exploration and discovery. The rehearsal that seems to be simply "filler" immediately becomes counterproductive.**

EXERCISES

1. Take an act from a play and mark the "French Scene" divisions in the margin.

2. Mark each scene with a) Scene Objective and b) Character Goal for each character.

The Rehearsal Process

PART TWO: BLOCKING (2–6 SESSIONS)

The part of the rehearsal period in which the production begins to take actual, physical, theatrical shape causes anxiety for beginning directors and experienced ones as well. Both the veteran and the neophyte perceive this period as a test—the first and perhaps the most critical time in which the director's ideas and craft are brought into the open. "What do you want me to do?" is a question that makes the director shudder. During the blocking sessions, this question carries a particular challenge quite unlike its implications in another phase of the rehearsals. The actor wants a specific response, not an explanation or an evasion. Worse, once that first direction is given, the director might be faced with that most awful of all conclusions: "This isn't working." Somewhere between the possible responses of "Do exactly what I tell you!" and "Do whatever you feel," lies that combination of structure and spontaneity we seek. An appropriate response at this point might be, "I don't know. Let's see if we can find out together."

Choreographers speak of "making a dance on the dancers." The notion is complex and elegant. The artist-choreographer is making an artwork based on a text (the music) but is challenged by, and must be responsive to, the possibilities and the limitations of the dancers through whom the choreographer's concepts must be expressed. In much the same way the choreographer works with dancers.

> The director should think and work in terms of *"making the production on the actors."*

A director who works out virtually the entire blocking plan of the production in pre-rehearsal sessions runs the risk of viewing that work as sacrosanct. Worse, the director can become so enamored of the achievement of *pre-blocking* that the preparation itself might end up neutralizing, or even eliminating, the creative contributions of the actors. If a director does extensive pre-blocking only to have *something* in the event nothing better emerges, he or she has wasted a good deal of time and energy at the very least and, at worst, communicated a sense of insecurity to the company. On the other hand, a director who leaves the actors more or less completely to their own devices in the blocking rehearsal faces the prospect of having the production generate no coherent point-of-view at all, or of having one imposed by someone else.

The director (standing, left) should be involved with the actors in order to shape the production effectively.
Play: *The Beggar's Opera* **Author:** John Gay **Theatre:** The Shakespeare Theatre at the Folger
Director: Gene Lesser (Photo by Joan Marcus)

Few directors have ever been more thorough and well-prepared than the late Alan Schneider, and few have been as artistically successful in delivering honest and well-crafted productions to the stage. No one was less tolerant of wasting valuable rehearsal time. Even so, in his autobiography, *Entrances,* he describes a remarkably relaxed, creative approach to blocking rehearsals:

> I consider the circumstances surrounding the scene, plan basic high points and essentials of position and movement, but encourage the actors to fill in and change things as we go along. This does not, however, mean that my preparation is any less extensive or that I necessarily accept the first thing that happens in rehearsal. On the contrary, I spend much more time reading and studying the script to discover the rhythms and subtext. (p. 142)

This is not at all different from the methods of the painter and the sculptor: a vision, a plan, and spontaneity.

DISCUSSION

Assuming a scale of 1 (the most authoritarian directorial posture) to 10 (the *laissez-faire*), rank the following situations. (You may assume 5 to be a condition of balance. The rankings need not go up and down the scale any farther than your judgment dictates. Make any qualifications you think are required in any case.)

1. You are directing *Charley's Aunt* for the local high school's senior class play.

2. An eminent British director will direct the Royal Shakespeare Company in a new production of *Rosencrantz and Guildenstern are Dead*.

3. A friend has asked you to direct the premiere production of her new contemporary comedy at a leading regional theatre, to be cast from the resident company.

4. The production stage manager of the Broadway production will direct a touring company of *I'm Not Rappaport* starring a veteran professional character actor.

5. You have been assigned to direct a production of *Miss Julie* in the theatre department of a large university. You have your pick of almost 100 actors, from M.F.A. acting candidates to undergraduate performance majors.

Why should the director be concerned with blocking? Why not let the actors do what they want? In acting school, this is a legitimate question, because scenes done for class are exercises to develop the actors' skills and sensitivities. In production, however, blocking serves two complementary purposes: *anecdotal,* and *aesthetic.* (It might be wise at this point to review the material in Chapter VI—The Director's Five Dimensions.) In dealing with these functions, the director must be *prepared* in advance and remain *alert* and *open* while blocking and refining the production.

As we saw in Chapter VII, the playwright posits certain physical actions and problems to which the director and the designers respond. The *anecdotal* function of blocking requires the director to integrate the text, the designs, and the actors to assure that characters can enter and exit appropriately—that they can mix their drinks, sit in their chairs, burn their letters.

> The anecdotal element is undeniable, indispensable to the clarity of the production. It tells *what's going on.*

But the theatre is obviously more than a medium of information. Every production creates—like it or not—a distinctive aesthetic statement. The *aesthetic* effect of blocking is often quite powerful in establishing the *qualitative* effect and ultimately the *meaning* of the production. Theatrical truth resides not only in the honesty and clarity of a dramatic statement, but in the distinctive way that statement is formed.

Now let us look at one approach to blocking that takes into account both the anecdotal and aesthetic functions of the work and creates that climate of controlled creativity.

PREPARATION

Text Requirements. Good groundwork for this step has already been laid by working through the Groundplan Design Checklist. Now this work is redefined by searching carefully through the play for *physical actions* required by the text, making marginal note or highlighting the text itself. Look for those things that are demanded by the action of the play itself. As we have noted, most acting editions contain stage directions recorded by a stage manager from an earlier production. These notes, often imperfectly recorded and sometimes incomprehensible, are best ignored. Mark entrances and exits and any other clear textual cues. These will represent some of the essential anecdotal requirements of the text.

TABLE 10–2

Preparation for Blocking

1. ANECDOTAL REQUIREMENTS: Marking entrances, exits, actions, props, and locations demanded by the text.
2. AESTHETIC CONSIDERATIONS: Defining qualities affecting the shape and coloration of each scene, expressed in terms of the visual and kinetic characteristic desired by the director.
3. VISUAL STRUCTURE: Creating a "storyboard" to visualize the beginning, end, and key moment(s) of each scene.
4. PRODUCTION CONTRACT: Establishing the style, vocabulary, and special characteristics of the performance during the opening moments of the production.

Because you have already developed a groundplan and a scenic design, you have already confronted some of the practical demands of integrating the text and the design elements. Still, it is good practice to review textual notations with the groundplan or model before you. In some instances, it is wise to have notes and sketches for costumes and props that have a particular bearing on your visualizations. This will give you a sense of how the necessary physical action of the play can move and the areas where it can take place.

> It is imperative at this point to remember that the *actors* will also make a contribution to this grand design. Do not try to stage the play without them; satisfy yourself instead that you are providing them with an environment in which they actually can perform the required actions of the play.

Mark one scene from *Miss Julie* (or another modern play) and *Macbeth* (or another period play) to note the anecdotal blocking requirements, using whichever method you choose. Note only what is required by the text of the play, not what is included in the stage directions unless it is essential.

Interpretive and Aesthetic Considerations. With the relatively few practical essentials of the blocking now established, you can proceed to explore some of the particular qualities you envision. Remember that your artistic decisions will affect the meaning of the production in a significant, even a profound, way. For each scene you are scheduled to block, prepare by trying to sense the visual or kinetic possibilities that best capture the theatrical *texture* or *feeling* you wish to express in the blocking. The result will be a complex of shapes, rhythms, and nuances—an aesthetic *preparation,* not a *prescription.*

EXERCISES _____

Using one of the scenes you worked on earlier in this chapter, apply the questions that follow to help define the qualities you seek in your staging:

Aesthetic Qualities in Blocking
Visual and Kinetic Possibilities

1. What specific *details* and what *qualities* does the matrix suggest?

2. Is the *scene* . . .
   agitated or quiet?
   horizontal or vertical?
   straight or curved?
   regular rhythm or staccato?
   smooth or rough?
   shared or dominated?
   close or far?

3. Are the *characters* . . .
   active or passive?
   hot or cold?

4. Is the *environment* (or any element) . . .
   active or passive?
   critical or neutral?

5. How do the qualities *change* or modulate as the scene progresses? For example, a scene might start out very quietly, then gradually (or suddenly) accelerate to a state of extreme agitation.

Here, the director creates a sense of unity among the characters by grouping them closely and providing them a single point of focus. Compare the composition and focus in this photo with the *Tomfoolery* scene.
Play: *Mother Courage*   **Author:** Bertolt Brecht   **Theatre:** The Williamstown Theatre Festival   **Director:** Gerald Freedman   **Set Designer:** Douglas Stein   **Costumes:** Jeanne Button   **Lighting:** Pat Collins   **Actors (l to r):** John Patrick Rice, Christina Zorich, Olympia Dukakis, Ray Virta (Photo by Teresa Snider-Stein)

The agitation apparent in this scene comes not only from the actors' facial expressions but from their body language and the director's control of composition and line.
Play: *Tomfoolery*   **Authors:** Tom Lehrer, adapted by Cameron Mackintosh and Robin Ray   **Theatre:** Theatre-Virginia   **Director:** Nancy Cates   **Set Designer:** Charles Caldwell   **Costumes:** Charles Caldwell   **Lighting:** Terry Cermak   **Actors (l to r):** Steve Liebman, R.L. Rowsey, Diane Pennington, Michael Calkins (Photo by Virginia Museum Photography)

6. What is the scene *like*? Does the scene's quality and texture call up an image that could be used accurately to describe the scene's character—not its story or symbolism, but the shape, sound, movement, and rhythm? Some of the discoveries you made in searching for metaphors and images as described in Chapter V will be immediately helpful in suggesting evocative ideas in your blocking.

Kinetic Mapping

Some of the most difficult images for many directors to establish are the musical and choreographic forms implicit in a scene. A literary analysis yields little of immediate or significant value to this effort. Listening to and watching the actors as they feel their way through the play and search for their characters, on the other hand, often *does* open up directorial possibilities in these areas. Identifying elements of exposition, rising action, climax, and denouement might indeed be useful in describing dramatic structure, as we saw in Chapter III, but it tells us nothing about how the scene looks, moves, or sounds until married to the actors' potentials.

A conventional graphic chart of dramatic action uses *labels* like these:

But if we abandon the labels and try to express the *feeling* rather than the *structure* of the scene, a much more fluid and expressive line results:

Now we can sense not only the scene's *quality*, but also design possibilities for movement and rhythm. The first part of the scene is smooth, rhythmic, low-profile; then it explodes into a frenzy of strong diagonals, cutting up and down, building to a crescendo, pausing for a moment, and finally falling away in a quiet, curved, easy motion. This *kinetic map* can guide the director in staging a scene.

In *Drawing on the Artist Within,* Edwards suggests that the very act of giving visual expression to thoughts and feelings is itself a way of knowing and of discovery; she calls these visual expressions *"analogs."*[1]

EXERCISES

1. Read through a scene until you have a good sense of its structure and feeling. Using a large sheet of paper (at least legal size) and a felt-tip pen, play through the scene in your mind and let your hand move the pen over the paper. Do not look at what you're putting on the paper until you finish the scene. Most important, don't try to guide your hand; let *it* tell *you* the kind of shapes it senses.

2. Do the exercise again with your other hand.

3. Review the scene again as in 1 and 2 with only the three or four key moments of the scene in your mind.

4. Use paper two or three times as large (newsprint is good) and a felt marker and try the exercises again.

5. Use two large sheets of paper and two different colored markers (one in each hand) and map each of two different characters in a scene. You may alternate the movement of your hands or not as the scene seems to dictate. Do not, however, look at the paper while you work. Let each hand work at reflecting the emotional states of each character.

Do not censor yourself by deciding these exercises "don't make sense." That is the idea: to get at feelings and responses that do not "make sense." Let these apparently random "doodles" suggest physical movement and emotional states. Rhythms and movements in space create tracings and patterns that, in art, reflect feelings and, ultimately, meanings. These sorts of exercises can suggest patterns that might influence your blocking or otherwise affect your understanding of the rhythms and emotions of the scene.

A musical conductor has a special brand of "emotional analogs" or "doodles" as part of the language used to communicate with the members of the orchestra (see Figure 10–1). Leonard Bernstein suggests "there are an infinite number of ways, for example of beating two, each way showing a different quality." (*The Joy of Music,* pp.131–33)

---

[1]To explore more of the implications and potentials of this technique, you would do well to examine chapters 8 and 9 of *Drawing on the Artist Within.*

VISUAL STRUCTURE

The final phase of preparation for this technique of blocking is the most important and most immediately useful. It involves the making of a series of images that resembles the *storyboard* of film and television. These images give the director the assurance of knowing the *essential* structure of the scene while allowing, indeed actually encouraging, spontaneity and discovery in the process of blocking.

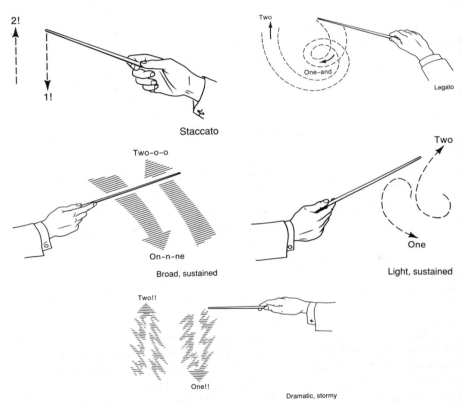

Figure 10–1 Musical Conductor's "Doodles"

In film and television, a storyboard is a device for visualizing and planning a scene or a series of scenes. Typically, it consists of a sequence of detail drawings resembling nothing so much as a comic strip (see Figure 10–2). The storyboard, then, is an outline of a visual structure upon which a scene is to be based. By employing a comparable technique, the theatre director can establish a structural outline for each scene to ensure a controlled direction for the blocking re-

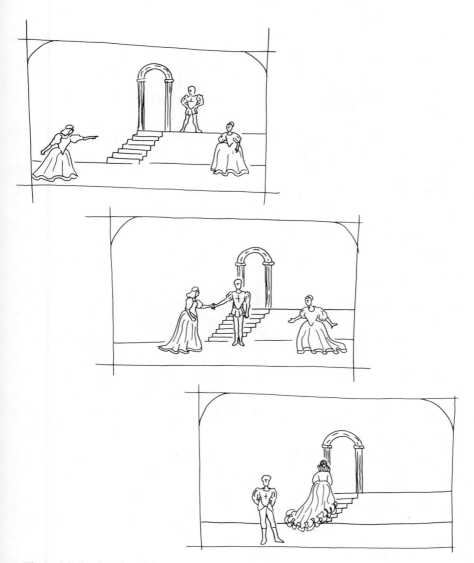

Figure 10–2 Storyboard 1

hearsals as well as create specific compositions to reflect the desired images for the production. The director's storyboard is for reference, not for presentation or discussion, and so should be done in a simple shorthand—with sketches of stick figures, marks on ground plans, or any other method that conveys the visual information convincingly but economically (see some variations in Figure 10–3).

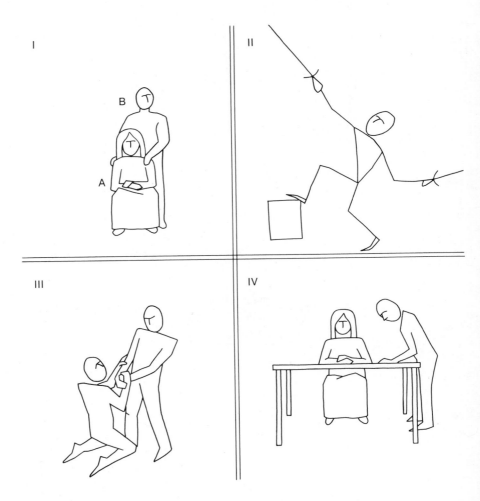

Figure 10–3 Storyboard 2

EXERCISES

Creating the Storyboard.

1. Identify the key moments in a scene. Include the beginning, the climax(es) or the most important moment(s), and the end of the scene. Note that although every scene requires at least three moments, there is no arbitrary limit.

2. For each of these key moments, create the composition that expresses the *feeling* you want that moment to establish. To create these composi-

tions, it is useful to work from the idea of making a photograph (or a painting or a sculpture) of the moment that expresses that feeling effectively.[2]

3. Make the storyboard by noting these moments and their compositions in your script using any of the methods suggested above.

THE PRODUCTION "CONTRACT"

The first few moments of any production present to the audience a set of terms to be agreed upon in the performance that follows. Those terms include the period and theatrical style of the production, an indication of how the design and technical elements will function, and how the actors will relate to their environment, their characters, and the audience. It is useful to view these terms as a "contract" between audience and production, and to give it special attention in preparation and execution.

What "terms" does the contract present? At the simplest level, the contract presents the theatrical environment. (Review the descriptions of the productions of *Hedda Gabler* detailed in the Introduction.) Each production contract is revealed as soon as the performance begins—when the curtain rises or the play is otherwise set into action. In those first few moments, the specific theatrical environment is presented and accepted. How the lights and sound function establishes another set of terms. After the actors enter and play their first few moments, the contract is usually complete. The audience is ready to accept virtually any terms clearly and effectively stated in the contract, including matters of style and theatrical convention.

As you can see, the production contract has little to do with the notion of "willing suspension of disbelief." We go to the theatre not so much "willing to suspend disbelief" as "eager to believe." Not so much to accept passively as to reach out for ardently. In the face of the audience's willingness to accept the truth of the stage, theatre artists must only play fair, by setting forth the rules of the game and abiding by them.

When the playwright or the director determines to undermine the audience's conventional expectations, the terms of the contract must be given special attention. The audience must be told they are in for something unexpected. But even the most convention-bound realistic staging of a routine commercial script inevitably establishes its own specific set of contractual agreements. The director conscious of this obligation is not only more apt to be effective in stating the

---

[2]As late as the early twentieth century, many dramatic productions actually used a convention called the *tableau vivant*—an image frozen in time, living statues in dramatic poses—immediately before the curtain fell.

terms for the audience, but also more succinct and effective in communicating with actors and designers preparing the production. Finally, keeping the production contract in mind usually results simply in a better opening scene in the production.

DISCUSSION

1. Describe in detail the opening moments of two productions you recall and the production contract offered by each.

2. Suggest specific details for the opening moments of a play of your choice in a way that defines the terms of the contract. See the descriptions of the productions of *Hedda Gabler* in the Introduction for some examples.

3. For any of the production contracts mentioned in 1. or 2., suggest an essential change and speculate on how it might affect the production as a whole.

ELEMENTS OF BLOCKING

Blocking is one of the director's primary means of expressing the *virtual life* of the play. It should never be considered simply movement to enliven a boring stage picture. It must come out of the impulses of the characters in the dramatic situation. It can be as blatant as a mad dash across the stage and a leap onto a high platform, or as subtle as a slight turn of the head (as discussed in Chapter XI on the "static" scene). In the early blocking rehearsals, however, the emphasis is on the larger movements, a process that can be thought of as "roughing-out."

The director must presume in creating the blocking that every movement, every action, is part of an overall pattern of **stimulus** and **response,** done in an appropriate **scale,** and conveying the desired **quality**. The stimulus provoking any action might be *physical,* resulting from a push; or it might be *reflexive,* reaching to catch a falling object; it could be *habitual,* pulling at one's ear; *emotional,* turning away from something unpleasant; or *deliberate,* deciding to leave before it is too late. Often, these responses are compound, and many are camouflaged. But without a stimulus, there is no response, no action. To complicate matters even more for the director and the actors, the responses vary in scale— in the size and intensity of the response relative to the stimulus and the context in which the action takes place. A simple action such as rising from a seated position can be a response of any single type or combination and can be expressed in any scale. In each, the same simple action will be fundamentally different even with the basic physical movement.

EXERCISES

Using any one direction that might be found in a script—entering through a door, sitting in a chair, rising, crossing left—try three or more variations on each of the possibilities below:

A. Change the *stimulus*.

B. Change the type of *response*.

C. Change the *scale* of the response.

COMMUNICATING THE BLOCKING

By the time you begin to work with the actors, you have prepared by deciding on the anecdotal requirements of the text, the physical shape of the playing area. You have clear visual images of the key moments in each scene and the potential rhythmic and movement patterns. The last critical element in the mix is the actors themselves. Use their instincts and impulses—those you noticed in the read-throughs and those you find now. These impulses will allow the play to come together, often seeming to fall into the forms and rhythms you have already sensed. There is no need for argument, or even for discussion now; you may simply nudge the production into life.

Begin by walking with your actors around and through the set, which has been marked out accurately by you or the stage manager. Refer to the set model or sketch to remind everyone of the world they will inhabit. Pay special attention to entrances, furniture, physical obstacles, and playing areas. Since you seldom will have actual performance elements to work on so early, make sure the rehearsal furnishings are as functional and appropriately scaled as possible.

It is always better for rehearsal furniture to take up slightly *more* space than the actual performance elements rather than less.

Next, assure everyone that you will be *roughing-in* the shape of the production and that some changes are to be expected if the work does not yield the desired effect. Make it clear that you will allow ample time for everyone to record all of his or her blocking in the script and for the stage manager to make comprehensive blocking notes in the prompt script. Ask that notations be made in pencil and that everyone has an eraser. Underscore the fact that the movement patterns established in these early rehearsals can indeed be changed if warranted. (See Chapter VI for blocking transcription methods.)

Usually you will want to suggest opening places to each actor in the scene, commenting briefly on the given circumstances of the opening. Then you can indicate movement to the actors as the scene progresses. Keep contact with the actors as you develop their changing relationships to each other and to the physical and emotional environment. The time allowed for the recording of blocking notes will interfere less and less with the implied rhythms of the scene as the actors warm to the process. Good actors seem to develop a technique like a "pause button" on a recorder, allowing an interruption in time for a notation, followed by an automatic "pick-up" of the rhythm and quality of the precise moment preceding the "pause." Use these moments to consider the possibilities of the next few action units or "beats" in the scene. Focus your attention on the scene and not exclusively on the text or your notes. Obviously, the director cannot watch the actors every moment during this period.

> The alert director will use the other senses as well—the sense of hearing, of course, and that indefinable but unmistakable "feeling" for the actors and the scene.

One "feeling" directors develop is sensitivity to fatigue. For both actors and director—not to mention the stage manager—blocking can be very tiring. An occasional few moments of relief from the concentrated work—even if it is not a "break"—can be very beneficial. Professional actors are attuned to the requirement of Actors' Equity Association for a five-minute break after an hour's work or ten minutes after an hour-and-a-half. These guidelines are reasonable even for non-professionals.

The initial blocking should proceed in relatively long spans before repeating a scene. This approach helps establish continuity and flow for director and actors. Every blocking rehearsal should, however, conclude with a run-through of the scenes done in that session. Such a review helps the director get a sense of the overall shape of the work and lets the actors and stage manager verify the accuracy of their blocking notations. Usually, some things will appear less than satisfactory, but unless those are going to have a clearly negative effect on later elements of the work, it is probably wise simply to note the fact and save the correction for a later rehearsal.

The scheduling of these rehearsals is especially important. Do the "roughing-in" blocking quickly if possible—a whole show in no more than four or five sessions, allowing time for a run-through at the end of each. You may find it difficult to restrain yourself from working out fine details of motivation and character at these rehearsals, but you must compare the undeniable satisfactions of that method with the disadvantages. For one thing, the time needed to work out the refinements will mean that longer and longer periods will pass before any given segment is repeated. Leaving parts of the show unrehearsed for several days is especially dangerous in the early stages. Things learned without the reinforcement of repetition are especially fragile. also, rehearsing different parts of the production to different stages of readiness can give director and actors a distorted view. *Keep all parts of the production on the same level of development.* It is better in principle to develop the different scenes and other production elements proportionally so that aesthetic and other considerations are perceived in their true relationships. As early as the blocking rehearsals, it is best to schedule no scene to be left alone longer than three or four rehearsal periods. Let a week pass before returning to the early scenes, and you will be discouraged to find out how much of the early work has simply evaporated. It usually helps to block the show in sequence, a process that also aids the actors and the director in grasping the structure of the show.

|| **Keep all scenes near the same level of development. Do not** ||
|| **have a polished first act and an unformed third act.** ||

The Rehearsal Process

PART THREE: DEVELOPMENT (6–10 SESSIONS)

It is important to concentrate on basics at this point. The actors need some of the time simply to run lines and blocking until they come reflexively, leaving the actors free to concentrate on intention and motivation. The director should structure the rehearsal period and the individual sessions to accommodate the actors' memory work and to clarify blocking, character relationships, and interpretive decisions.

Once again, try to rehearse the play in fairly large segments—seldom more than four parts. Ideally, this schedule will allow two repetitions of each segment per session—one a *work-through,* the other a run-through (sometimes a *stumble-through*). While the actors are still *on-book,* the work-through or *stop-and-go* is best done first in the rehearsal session. This can then be followed by the more or less uninterrupted *run-through* to solidify the earlier work and to put it all into a more coherent context.

Actors should aim at being *off-book* (with the stage manager [S.M.] or assistant stage manager [A.S.M.] prompting when an actor calls for a line, or when the blocking becomes confused). By the mid-point of the development period, the actors should begin working without scripts on between one-third and one-half the show. The remaining acts may then be scheduled for lines in the normal rotation of the rehearsal sessions. (See Sample Schedule, Table 10–3.)

Should the director schedule deadlines for being off-book or rely on the actors' initiative? This is a judgment that depends on the particulars of the situation. Although it is doubtless more in the spirit of trust and collaboration to leave line memory to the natural rhythms of the actor's own process, the director must motivate and encourage the cast to be off-book *midway in the rehearsal pe-*

TABLE 10–3

Sample Rehearsal Schedule

Week	Session	Rehearsal
I	1	Read-through; design presentations
	2	Read-through (character objectives)
	3	Read-through (on-feet)
	4	Block Act I, scenes 1–6
	5	Block Act I, sc. 7–8; Act II, sc. 1–3
	6	Block Act II, sc. 4–9
II	7	Work-through I, 1–6
	8	Work-through I, 7–8; II, 1–3
	9	Work-through II, 4–9
	10	Run-through (designers observe)
	11	Work Act I (rehearsal props and costumes)
	12	Work Act II
III	13	Act I (lines)
	14	Act II
	15	Work scenes TBA
	16	Act I
	17	Act II
	18	Run-through (lines Act II) [Set preliminary light and sound cues]
IV	19	Work Act I (costumes as specified)
	20	Work Act II (costumes as specified)
	21	Run-through (with rehearsal sound tape)
	22	Act I (no prompt)
	23	Act II (no prompt)
	24	Run-through
V	25	[*dry tech: level set, cue-to-cue*] Actors for cue-to-cue (costumes as specified)
	26	Tech run-through (costumes and makeup as specified)
	27	Full dress
	28	Full dress (preview audience)
	29	Full dress (preview audience)

riod (by rehearsal session 12–18 on our sample schedule). With a professional company, lines are assumed to be the actor's responsibility; seldom is a formal deadline noted. The same assumption should be made in other companies, but setting a fair deadline is a useful and conventional practice that virtually everyone accepts.

The first off-book rehearsal session might well begin with an uninterrupted run-through, allowing the actors to concentrate on their memory work and establishing with the prompter the "feel" of calling for lines and for other corrections. After this first run-through and a short break, the second half of the session can be devoted to working through the act in a stop-and-go format, with the director making suggestions and adjustments to the actors' work.

Subsequent sessions can reverse the order of work: first, a work-through using approximately two-thirds of the available time, then a run-through—exactly the process employed when the actors were still on-book.

The functions of the *development* rehearsals, then, are *memorization* (of lines, blocking, and business, with rehearsal props and critical costume elements a regular part of the rehearsal by this point), *clarification* (of intention and motivation), and *correction* (of obvious problems or flaws in the earlier work). Remember the production is still *developing;* it is not yet at performance level. By the end of this period, however, the director should feel assured that the basic shapes and movements of the production are coherent and effective in terms of both the anecdotal and aesthetic demands of the production.

The Rehearsal Process

PART FOUR: REFINEMENT (8–12 SESSIONS)

Once the production has been roughed-out, adjusted, and set, the next most demanding time for the director is the period of *refining* the work—adding telling details, fitting and polishing before setting the work into place.

Again, the metaphors of the sculptor or the choreographer are useful. Having roughed out a form in stone or clay, the sculptor steps back and tries to see what is there. The appraisal is followed by a breath—a sigh—before the work begins again in earnest. Hands work the tools, shaping the touches and details that give the material its surface and its life. The choreographer's creative rhythms are vitually the same—timing adjusted here, turn-out corrected there, lines of bodies and movements synchronized throughout.

The director, too, stands poised. The actors know what they are doing and why. Lines, blocking, characterization, and interpretation (for the most part) are well in hand. Allowing for adjustments to costumes, set, lights, and sound—and with a shot of energy from a friendly audience—the show could open and appear quite presentable. This is the point where many productions begin technical and dress rehearsals. It is a poor policy that often provokes the refrain, "We only needed one more week!" But the unhappy fact is that, unless the last few rehearsals are used creatively, that "one more week" probably would change nothing but the date of the opening night.

The director must plan on a block of rehearsals (between one-quarter and one-third of the total) *after* the setting of interpretation, lines, and blocking and *before* the final surge into technical and dress rehearsals—time to devote to refining the work and developing the final detail. Again, the director is concerned with the *anecdotal* and the *aesthetic* requirements of the production. In refining the work, the director can profitably re-examine those elements and evaluate them in the light of three factors:

1. the context of the action;
2. the implications of the action;
3. the structure of the action.
(See Table 10–4 for explanation.)

TABLE 10–4

The Refinement *Rehearsals*

Context of Action

ANECDOTAL: 1. The Stanislavskian *"given circumstances"* of each scene.
               2. The *antecedent events* of every entering character's immediate past.
               3. The *physical environment* as it affects plot and character.

AESTHETIC: 1. Relationship to *stage environment*—stage geography, body positions.
              2. Clarity and expressiveness of *stage pictures and movement.*
              3. Clarity and expressiveness of *performance sounds and rhythms.*

Implications of Action

ANECDOTAL: 1. *Meaning* of each action to plot and character.
               2. Each action considered in terms of its *logical conclusions and consequences.*
               3. Use of each important action (prop, gesture, stage area) adequately to establish *function.*

AESTHETIC: 1. *Expressiveness* of each action in terms of feeling.
              2. Each action considered in terms of its *expressive conclusion and consequences.*
              3. Use of each important action (prop, gesture, stage area) in *simple repetition or with modulations.*

This is another way of saying the director must step back from the work to see what actually is there and to see if the physical and emotional environment established has been appropriately explored. Are the actors aware of the implications of their physical and psychic surroundings? Has something been overlooked or not fully appreciated? A prop, for example, might have a special, subtle meaning for the character that has been lost or simply unsuspected. The same may apply to a sound or a gesture. The director can now view the whole work, looking for any element that has not been explored or developed to its potential.

In the same way, the *implications* of actions can be scrutinized to assess the validity and effectiveness of the choices made. Finally, the director can analyze the *structure* of each action to assure its logic and integrity.

Painters, designers, calligraphers, and graphic artists often step back from their work and squint to blur the details and allow only the basic design of the work to show through; or (as Edwards suggests in *Drawing on the Right Side of the Brain*) they turn the work upside down to get a true vision of the relationship of elements to each other and to the overall design. If directors cannot use that technique literally, they can apply the principle to their own work. The technique of "hearing with your eyes" and "seeing with your ears" can help the director isolate competing elements to judge the essential design more accurately.

"Hearing with your eyes" means that you block out sound in the rehearsal and concentrate only on what you are seeing. The technique is especially useful when either director or actors find a scene awkward or somehow underdeveloped. Without the support of the dialogue to explain what is going on in the scene, you are forced to judge if the physical reality of the scene—the way it looks and moves—is truly conveying the desired information and feeling. Do the compositional and kinetic images on stage truly say what you want? Do those images belong to the guiding metaphor of the matrix you have projected? In short, *is the scene beautiful?* If a soundproof booth with a good view of the stage is available, fine—but earplugs will do.

"Seeing with your ears" is easier since it calls simply for averting your eyes from the stage and listening intently, trying to detect nuances in pitch and rhythm, intensity and volume, all to discover if the sound of the scene is integrated and compelling—to *see* if your ears tell you the action of the scene is clear and effective. Using these simple techniques can be of enormous value in sharpening your sensibilities and making you more objective in evaluating your own work.

HINT: See with your ears. Listen with your eyes.

EXERCISES

1. In a restaurant, park, library, or other fairly public place, observe closely a conversation you cannot hear. Try to infer meaning and emotion or state of mind from what you see; relate the specific details or elements you have observed that led to your reactions and conclusions.

2. Listen to a scene on audio tape from a theatrical rehearsal, a television play, or an everyday conversation. Try to envision the scene with as many specifics as possible. Describe precisely the sounds of the scene that combine to communicate its particular quality.

Finally, because establishing a sense of continuity is important at this stage of rehearsal, it is wise to allow a whole act to run without interruption. In fact, it is good practice to prohibit prompting in the last few rehearsals prior to dress rehearsals and to require the actors to "cover" for any missed cues. This soon es-

What might be an Elizabethan stage translated into high-tech scientific statement of the universe, this moment might suggest high-pitched, random, metallic sounds—perhaps even electronic aural effects.

Play: *Frankenstein—Playing with Fire* **Authors:** from the novel by Mary Shelley **Theatre:** The Guthrie Theater
Director: Michael Maggio **Set Designer:** John Arnone **Costumes:** Jack Edwards **Lighting:** Marcus Dilliard
Actors (l to r): Stephen Pelinski, Peter Syvertson (Photo by Joe Giannetti)

tablishes a secure feeling of team-work and concentration. Notes taken by the director during the run-through can be communicated and worked through, if required, after the run-through. The stage manager or A.S.M. can post or hand out notes for each actor on missed or transposed lines.

The Rehearsal Process

PART FIVE: TECHNICAL AND DRESS (3–6 SESSIONS)

It is—or should be—something of a misstatement to speak of starting technical and dress rehearsals in the last week or so of the rehearsal period. This work actually starts with design conferences and develops along with the rest of the show during the rehearsal period. And so, when the time comes to introduce the physical elements of the designs into the production on stage, the step is a culmination, not a beginning.

Tech and dress rehearsals can be particularly stressful; the director must exercise organizational and managerial skills to assure both efficiency and the full integration and exploitation of the work of the designers and technicians. As the tech and dress rehearsals unfold, the director can re-apply the critical principles enunciated earlier concerning "refinements" (see Table 10–4).

EXERCISES _____

Assuming a specific theatre or company and your choice of play in each category, prepare a complete rehearsal schedule for one or more of the following:

1. a Shakespearean play

2. a contemporary Broadway comedy

3. a Chekhov one-act

4. a scene from a realistic drama

End Note

We began by saying that a production is an artwork. As such, it must incorporate every element into its overall design. Contemporary direction demands that every artist play an integral part in the process and contribute to the integrity of the work. When a director, designer, technician, or actor does not contribute fully to the process, or when some production element is not truly a part of the overall world of the play, the entire work is diminished. A set or a lighting effect can be beautiful and *seem* appropriate, but it is only decoration unless the director and actors *use* it. In the same way, actors must *use* their costumes. Makeup must *express* something.

Finally, it is up to the director to ensure that the production is entirely ready to open as scheduled. Only the amateurish fall back on the old saw about "bad dress rehearsals" and "good openings." That notion conveys an attitude insulting to the audience, the company, and the theatre. Good theatre comes from worthy materials combined with inspiration, craft, and hard work.

It was the leader's task to fashion a common language and a common point of reference with those whom he hoped to lead.

—**Harold Clurman,** *The Fervent Years*

11 DIRECTOR AND ACTOR

Between director and actor, the best relationship is one of genuine collaboration based on trust. That trust demands an implicit mutual belief in one another's honesty, respect, sensitivity, commitment, and craft.

As we have observed, the contemporary director's task requires a great deal more than working with actors. During the rehearsal period, however, there is no question that the director is intensely focused on the actors—individually and as an ensemble—and on efforts to understand, guide, and nurture their performances. This is the work that virtually all directors find most stimulating and rewarding—the best part of the job!

The task of the director in rehearsal is to establish goals and provide a context to inspire the actors' creativity, and to guide them in developing vivid and appropriate performances.

Several ideas need clarification here. It is not enough for the director simply to establish "context" and "goals." The actor must also be convinced of their rightness—their validity and feasibility. Furthermore, this conviction requires not only understanding and intellectual assent (which might in in some cases never evolve), but sympathy and commitment.

|| **The actor is out there on the stage at every performance, the visible symbol and focus of whatever is going on.** ||

Being on stage is a delicate and vulnerable position. An actor who places unquestioning trust in a director is not only in a position to accomplish his or her best work, but also in a position to be damaged. The actor's medium is self; trusting a poor director can result in a devastating blow to self-confidence, even to a career. Professional actors must try to maintain an almost impossible balance between the trust, openness, and sensitivity they need in the theatre and the hard-shelled professional callousness required to deal with a career. It is an awful, dispiriting dichotomy, and yet it is one actors accept in order to practice their art.

The director must be sensitive to this situation, whether working with trained professionals or rank beginners. Professional ethics demands honesty and integrity when dealing with any collaborator, and, most importantly, because of their special vulnerability, when dealing with actors.

One of the first things a director must establish with a newly-assembled company is the communication of a vision of the virtual world where the dramatic action is played out. The director certainly will not prescribe every step along the way. That, as we have seen, can be counterproductive. But the director must establish goals and a method for pursuing them. (It might be wise at this point to review some of the suggestions for structuring the first rehearsals outlined in Chapter X.)

Understanding Actors

Working with actors is almost always stimulating, and sometimes a little frightening. Good actors, experienced or novice, are subtle and complex people who work with internal and external resources of amazing variety and volatility. To do his or her best work, each actor has very special needs. One of the director's most exciting challenges is to identify those requirements and how best to meet them.

Understanding actors in their infinite variety is the work of a lifetime. The effective director must understand the actor's personality, temperament, and working methods—and then develop a vocabulary for each unique artist.

Every actor begins a rehearsal period with a fairly predictable set of admirable expectations in place. For each of these, there is invariably a corresponding anxiety. A director, recognizing this, takes the first step towards a genuine understanding.

PERSONAL SUCCESS

This usually means the fulfillment of personal goals in the creation of the character and performance of the role. Perception of success can be complicated by technical criteria, applying some new-found skill or extending one's range. Good actors are always in training, always looking for the "stretch" that means growth and maturity in the art of acting. Success inevitably means other things as well: having a generally pleasant experience in which one makes few mistakes; getting along well with the company; more and greater career opportunities; receiving some sort of validation from others. Probably it involves some of each.

The director must be aware of these expectations and try to provide for a positive outcome wherever possible. One thing the director can provide is *validation*. The actor wants assurance that the goals of the characterization and performance are clear and worthwhile, and that the method is effective. The director is in a position to provide this assurance, not by constant cloying praise, but by attention to the evolving characterization itself and to the actor's work in developing it. If the actor doubts the value or effectiveness of something, the director must be alert and prepared to respond.

> **The director must pay attention to the actors and communicate that attention and care.**

PEER COLLABORATION

Every actor expects other actors to share certain values and methods. Acting requires a generosity and tolerance towards one's peers, but these qualities are severely threatened when certain invisible boundaries are crossed. Directors should encourage every actor to work with the necessary energy and commitment. No actor should seem to be getting special treatment. Otherwise, a highly volatile situation can result in which rehearsing can give way to maneuvering for attention. Anyone in a position to make decisions about hierarchical matters— director, stage manager, wardrobe manager—must ensure not only that decisions *are* fair, but that they give the *appearance* of being fair.

The basic tenet of ensemble is *teamwork*. Teamwork means actors helping each other—*working* together but never *directing* one another. It is a fine distinction, but a critically important one: actors do *actor*-work, not *director*-work. When one actor senses another actor is trying to direct, the result is often resentment.

If this happens, the director must reestablish control of the situation immediately. Usually, this can be done by working through the scene with the actors and being very clear that the director is the arbiter. Occasionally, this might need to be reinforced by a private word from the director to each actor to restore the proper balance to the rehearsal atmosphere.

THE PRODUCTION

Most actors are aware that a good production honors everyone involved. Consequently, every actor in a show earnestly wants a success. This is the goodwill that every director should expect and count on. In the worst case, an actor can become so insecure that the best defense seems to be to undermine all expectations of success. An early symptom of this feeling of insecurity is an actor's concern with "the big picture." An actor beginning to feel insecure fixes on something to distract attention from his or her individual performance. In bringing the perceived shortcoming of "the big picture" to the director, the stage manager, or the other actors, the actor unconsciously seeks to distract attention from the actor-work (the individual performance) and to focus on director-work (the emerging shape of the production). Actors are programmed by training, tradition, and inclination to concentrate on their individual performances, and virtually everything they do reflects this natural bias. As a result, the director should at least examine the possibility that when actors express concern about "the big picture," they are actually communicating some of their own insecurity in the actor-work in which they are engaged. Actors who are confident, who feel good about their own performances, seldom express concern over "the big picture."

THE DIRECTOR

Actors' expectations of a director are amazingly varied. At the least, actors want the director to be competent and caring. But some actors want—need—someone to provide reassurance and validation. They want to be noticed, valued, pampered. Others, burned perhaps by a director's incompetence one time too many, want only to be left alone to do their work with as little intervention from the director as possible. All actors have strong ideas of the "right" way to approach rehearsal.

One of the biggest of all challenges is that the director must deal with these expectations, fair or not, in order to consolidate the acting company into a unit with shared objectives and methodology.

Even in late rehearsals, the skillful director must be alert to the emerging final shape of the production.
Play: *Tartuffe* **Authors:** Moliere **Theatre:** McCarter Theatre **Director:** Nagle Jackson **Actors (l to r):** Cynthia Martells, Robert Lanchester, Shirin Devrim Trainer (Photo by Randall Hagadorn)

Rehearsal Attitudes and Techniques

Rehearsals bring a myriad of challenges—from communicating with an actor to finding imaginative and productive ways to use time. In each case, as director you should begin by defining the challenge or problem at its basic level, then working through potential solutions in a systematic manner.

POSITIVE DIRECTION

Jed Harris, an infamous Broadway producer early in this century, told an actor on opening night to "eliminate all personal mannerisms." Another director, with the stress endemic to the profession, snapped at a particularly vivacious performer, "Don't do anything. Just stand there!" This sort of *negative direction* can lead to disaster. Poor actors, trying to figure out what they are supposed to *stop* doing, end up not concentrating on what they *should* be doing.

Positive direction, on the other hand, gives the actor something to *do,* which can automatically eliminate an undesirable element from the performance. Perhaps the most common example of this is the actor with problem hands. Actors who complain they do not know what to do with their hands are a constant frustration. Telling actors *not* to put their hands in their pockets, or *not* keep them behind their backs, of *not* cross their arms, aggravates the problem by increasing the actors' awareness and subsequent discomfort. The best solution is to focus attention on something else. If the actor's attention is focused on a task or point of concentration, it will be impossible for him or her to be distracted. If what to do with the hands is the problem, the easiest solution is to give the actor something to touch—a prop to hold, something to lean on, or anything to make physical contact with. Often, however, the point of concentration need not be physical. Sheer focus of attention can distract most actors from their feelings of discomfort. It is impossible to feel ill-at-ease if you are concentrating on something outside yourself.

> Minimize an actor's nervousness by using systematic warm-ups. Stress muscular relaxation and good breathing as discussed later in this chapter. Then suggest a strong focus of attention at every moment on stage—especially when the actor is not speaking.

Positive direction suggests *possibilities*. Since an actor should always be related to something in space and in terms of visual focus and concentration, the director can ask provocative questions: Where were you headed? Why did you stop there? What are you looking at? (You cannot look at "nothing" without considerable conscious effort. Try it. Even attempting to scan a blank wall will end with your eyes moving from point to point.) What is she doing with the paper? Can you hear the clock ticking?

When a director suggests an action to play and a clear focus of attention, many problems of actor discomfort will dissipate.

DISCUSSION

Here are some quotes from actors that exhibit a wide range of expectations and bespeak some potential problems. Try to understand the premise or attitude underlying the remark and suggest some strategy for dealing with it when it comes your way:

1. "The director is the enemy. If he'd just leave the actors alone, we could work this all out."

2. "She's directing pictures."

3. "Don't tell me that; let me find it for myself."

4. "It doesn't feel right," or "Why would she do that?"

5. "I hate to (or "I'd rather") do improvs."

6. "A concept director, uh huh."

7. "I'm saving it for the performance."

8. "I'm not warmed up yet."

9. "I'm working on that."

10. "I have to know what's going on in the scene before I learn my lines."

11. "My (Her, His) character wouldn't do that (say that, wear that)."

EXERCISE

Ask someone to stand in front of the group and be completely relaxed and natural. When the subject asks what to do, simply instruct the person to stand there while the group observes. With no clear action to play or focus upon, the subject will probably be ill at ease and try to cover the anxiety. After a while, ask the person to get his or her driver's license and return to the "stage" to read off the number of the license, the expiration date, or any other data. Observe the difference in the subject between this attitude and the previous one. The combination of clear directions and the use of the "prop" should have provided positively stated objectives and a physical focus for the performer.

ACTORS' PERFORMANCE PERSONALITIES

Just as every director tends towards either the *prescriptive* or the *laissez-faire,* so may every actor be considered fundamentally *hot* or *cool*. The particular degree depends upon the actor's personality, training, and experience. Successful actors from both ends of the spectrum give marvelously engaging performances, and no truly accomplished actor exhibits only one dimension. Some are characterized as cool because their work has a deliberate, detached quality, a sense of simply *permitting* others to observe and participate. Hot actors, on the other hand, work at high levels of energy and involvement. They are dynamic and strong personalities. They chafe against the confines of structure and predictability, *demanding* a response.

Neither type of actor is intrinsically better or worse. However, directors can find these categories useful not only for casting, but also for approaching the actors themselves. Knowing that the cool actor will tend towards quiet and modulated expression and the hot towards something open and expansive, the director is equipped to lead each in ways that recognize their inclinations. The director might build on the hot actor's ability to emphasize the dramatic moment and the cool actor's ability to penetrate an emotion or shading of meaning.

The director can also complement these instincts by suggesting hot character choices to the cool actor (strongly emotional, even violent motives or responses) and cool ones (thoughtful and introspective, even vulnerable) to the hot actor.[1]

Considering an actor's performance personality may also help the director recognize whether the actor is more open and fluent in hearing technical (external) or psychological (internal) language when dealing with character and action.

There is no one method, of course. In spite of the apparent continuing predominance of directors and actors who incline strongly towards the methods of psychological realism (especially in the United States), some find other approaches more congenial either through natural inclination or conviction. Jonathan Miller, the influential and successful British director, is quite outspoken about his preferences:

> "Nor do I want to hear actors' personal responses to the emotions they are depicting. I much prefer actors who simply, without having any feeling of it, just do it. The performer is a mimic who does something without feeling it. Now this is often condemned by actors who say, 'Well, then, it's purely technical.' Well, thank God it is! I only want an actor to be an accomplished technician who gives me the sense that I have seen something real." (*American Theatre*, p. 41)

Such an attitude runs counter to the ideas and methods of many successful directors, from Stanislavski to the present day. Still, it comes from one of many contemporary directors who have proved themselves in many different countries with plays from both modern and classic repertoires. This enormous latitude in approaches by successful artists suggests the range of possibilities open to the aspiring director. The best advice, however, is to remain as flexible as possible in dealing with actors and the related problems of theatrical collaboration. Actors—like any artists—must articulate internal impulses and feelings by technical means. All expression ultimately is technically framed, and without the ability to communicate effectively, the feelings and impulses are useless in the creative process. Miller modulates his radical hard line to some extent when he explains, "If someone gives an impression on the stage that they're being technical, what that means is that they're not being technical enough." We might add that the truth and validity of what is being communicated effectively must come from the actor's internal resources—emotions, psychology, experience, imagination. Something false or incomplete or inorganic, even if communicated effectively, is sure to ring false. And this is perhaps where Miller is heading.

|| **Technical clumsiness and lack of commitment is as much a fault as emotional dishonesty or superficiality. Either results in a poor performance; and that is always bad technique.** ||

[1]We discuss the use of "complementary qualities" in a broader sense later on in this chapter.

By staying alert to actors' personalities and methods, the director is best able to open the widest path of creative collaboration.

METHODS OF COMMUNICATION

There are obviously many ways to communicate with actors. Directors inevitably begin with the method they themselves have experienced in earlier productions. As one's experience and self-confidence grows, the options become more evident, as does the need for some special approaches to particular actors or unusual problems.

Actor Notes

The standard method of director-actor communication is detailed comments by the director to the assembled company after a scene or act rehearsal. Some actors jot down relevant comments for themselves during these sessions. Some directors actually distribute the written notes to the actors concerned, but this method requires more time and clarity of expression than most directors can muster in a darkened theatre during a rehearsal.

The type of notes the director gives at any rehearsal will vary widely, even in a single session. Since technical considerations of blocking, or the precise execution of a bit of business interacts with line interpretation and character relationships, overlapping is inevitable and welcome. Still, it is probably best to find a major focus for the notes at each rehearsal, depending upon your estimation of the show's greatest needs at the moment.

|| **Each rehearsal should have clear objectives and a feeling of progression.** ||

If you have assumed a set of objectives for each rehearsal unit, you have the beginnings of an outline to focus your notes. Begin each rehearsal segment by mentioning the main items on the agenda: memory work on lines and blocking the first time through, and working on problem areas in the second. At another point in the rehearsal schedule, you might announce the goal of exploring scenes to discover fresh reactions or new character relationships.

Rehearsals must always seem to be going forward, making progress and achieving growth. The notes should carry the clear sense of that achievement. Realistically, some rehearsals will lose ground. It is foolhardy to ignore such a state of affairs or to dismiss it. It is a fact of theatrical growth. Few things are more dispiriting to a cast than a director who ignores the problems exhibited in a rehearsal and blithely goes about proclaiming everything to be just wonderful. The problems should be acknowledged and turned to positive use.

As a rule, it is better to go back, if necessary, to correct a problem serious enough to distract or discourage the actors unduly. (Remember one of the actor's hopes and expectations is *to seem to be doing well,* in rehearsal and in performance.) The director will find times, however, when it is better to work around the problem rather than confront it. Yes, prod and challenge the actor when the sense of progress ebbs; but never allow a perceived obstacle to defeat the entire progress of the rehearsals. How? The skilled director may give notes suggesting an entirely different direction or response, an area as yet untouched or explored. As *positive direction,* this tactic can result in avoiding a problem by simply going around it. Often, after a short respite from the stress of trying to solve the problem, director and actors can return to it and find it no genuine obstacle at all. The release from the pressure of trying to solve the problem has allowed a solution to emerge.

Liviu Ciulei once admonished his actors by saying, "Don't obstaculate!" The stage manager learned he wanted them to stop creating obstacles for themselves. The director's English may have been corrupted, but his reasoning is flawless.

H I N T : The stage manager or A.S.M. can make a running list of missed or transposed lines for each actor who is "off-book." These notes can be distributed or posted on the call-board after each rehearsal.

Side-Coaching

This technique has the director working with the actors as they go through a scene or a moment. The method may be stop-and-go, trying to capture the perfect nuances in the scene, or the director may comment on the scene as it unfolds, deftly suggesting a different objective or a new approach or simply encouraging the actors as they work together. Work on individual scenes, after notes or as a regularly scheduled rehearsal, allows the director—often on stage with the actors—to make suggestions and adjustments to fine-tune the action or the characterizations.

When athletes or any other performers want to correct a problem or improve a particular aspect of performance, they invariably speak of "going back to the basics." In dramatic action, the same principles apply. In our discussion of action in Chapter III, we observed a structure of action as follows: *STATUS 1: STIMULUS → RESPONSE → ADJUSTMENT → STATUS 2.* There is a flow from one action or state of being to the next, and an analysis of any action will yield the same components. If you think of a dramatic beat as you think of any other action, as having a simple underlying process, you can approach it by analyzing it in precisely this way—clarifying or improving it by taking it one step at a time.

Good directors spend most of their time with actors. Some directors demonstrate; some discuss; some suggest. All try to inspire ease and confidence.
Play: 42nd Street **Authors:** Michael Stewart, Mark Bramble; music-Harry Warren, lyrics-Al Dub **Theatre:** Paper Mill Playhouse **Director:** Lee Roy Reams **Set Designer:** Robin Wagner **Costumes:** Kirk Bookman (Photo by Gerry Goodstein)

Another level of analysis breaks down the *response* step into its components as a coach might do while working with an athlete. It analyzes a physical action—particularly a violent one—into three parts: *setup, execution,* and *follow-through.*

Setup: This is the preparation, the shift that must take place to make the central action possible: drawing back a fist, aiming a pistol, cocking a bat. Define the given circumstances—external and internal. Has something been overlooked or, more likely, given inadequate focus or attention? Can something be altered that will make the completed action stronger or more subtle? (The scale and relative strength of any action resides in the contrast between the status at the beginning of the setup and the end of the follow-through. Moving these two poles farther apart will make the action stronger and more emphatic.)

Execution: What happens at "the moment" of execution? A blow lands; a trigger is pulled; a ball is struck. Is it a clear and appropriate action? Does it come from the setup? Should another expression of the action be considered? A bigger one? A smaller one? A different one? The execution must come from the setup and lead into the follow-through. If one element is changed, the others must be adjusted as well. (Think always only in terms of the characters and their situation. The action may have symbolic importance. It may connect with social issues, or validate certain psychological theories. But in the scene, it is an action performed by a character. One may infer other significance, but anything not immediately relevant to the character and the situation does not belong in the scene.)

Something must happen. It need not be a big or violent action, but something must take place. Some actors and directors (as well as some critics) suppose that nothing needs to be done, that the moment can take care of itself, that it should be left to the imagination of the audience. What these people probably mean is that there is no need to overstate such a moment or event. If so, no one can quarrel with that. Still, *something must happen.*

‖   Every human action has a physical expression.   ‖

It may be a violent contraction of the body and a gasp; it may be the utterance of a single syllable; it may be a change in the pattern of breathing. But rest assured, something happens.

In sports, this is often the moment of contact (hitting a baseball, tennis, or golf ball) or release (pitching horseshoes or shooting a basketball). In each case, the moment must be precisely defined, or "clean." In the theatre, the same idea applies. Each action performed by actors in a scene needs that same sort of "click." (Some actors, mostly British, speak of "pinging" or "ponging" a line or a scene. The terms apply to the quality of the execution. The "ping" calls up images of deftness and control, of light, objective precision; the "pong" a heavier, fuller, and more committed quality. These simple distinctions are useful because they call direct attention to the actor's execution of any action.)

Follow-through: What has happened? Which of the effects of the action—external and internal—are inescapable and which are merely potential? How has the action, the realization, or the moment affected each character in the scene? What are the visible, tangible effects? Dancers and other athletes know the importance of finishing an action. The follow-through is a necessary transition to the next action, but it also completes the execution by allowing the expended physical or emotional energy to reverberate, to dissipate, and to flow effectively. Just as the swing of a bat must continue after contact if the swing is to be effective, so too must the emotional swing of an actor continue. Coaches speak of hitting "through" the ball to avoid checking the swing before contact is complete. Actors must also finish a beat by playing through it to its natural conclusion before going on to the next setup.

For the same reasons that ballplayers must control their positions on the field and singers must control their breathing, actors must take charge of the emotional and technical shape of any scene they are playing. Without this command, the scene is, by definition, out of control; it may be exciting to perform and (occasionally) to witness, but without the proper discipline, it is unreliable. While spontaneity and inspiration are unquestionably desirable in a performance, the director must have a framework in place that not only allows, but encourages, controlled spontaneity in performance. Identifying and building on the structure of a scene or speech is one way to establish this control for the actor.

Signals

When the rehearsals have progressed to the point of run-throughs for polishing, some directors find it useful to establish certain signals to use while the actors are actually working on stage. Though not every director will find this technique appropriate, some will discover that a distinctive set of signals during the rehearsal can instantly connect with the part of the actors consciousness that monitors the technical aspects of the performance without interrupting the flow of the rehearsal.

The set of signals may consist of no more than three or four concise verbal or non-verbal sounds: a finger snap may direct the performers to focus their energies and concentration; saying "words" may indicate that vocal projection is dropping; "dress" will remind the actors to adjust for sightlines.

While signals can be a powerful and efficient means of communication, their use must be learned and practiced to avoid problems. True, a signal does engage the part of the actors' consciousness that monitors performance, but it must not impinge on the other levels of their concentration. Actors will be confused and upset by a signal if the lines or business of a scene are not under mechanical control (that is, are not reflexive). If the actors are "fighting for lines," a command to adjust some other aspect of the performance will simply be seen as an unnecessary and resented intrusion. Likewise, if the use or meaning of the signals themselves is unclear, the actors' reactions will be negative.

If you intend to use signals, establish some reasonable criteria:

1. Signals are a kind of side-coaching. Use them in the same way: to clarify and reinforce the actor's performance; to direct concentration and suggest adjustment, not to challenge or threaten.
2. There must be only a few signals—certainly no more than three or four.
3. The signals must be crisp, clear, and unambiguous. Nothing is more counterproductive than to have an actor turn in the middle of a scene and say, "Huh?"
4. Begin using the signals one at a time as soon as the actors are in control of their performances. If you are concerned about vocal projection, begin using the "words" signal while the actors still have books in hand. Relinquish its use while the actors are trying to set line memory—all their concentration will be focused on that single task—and resume, if necessary, when the memory work is firm. By this time, the early signals will probably have imprinted, and you will need to use them infrequently, if at all.
5. Be responsive to the rhythm of the rehearsal and the strength or fragility of the actors' control. When the actors already are working intensely, it is fool-

ish to ask them to concentrate. A rehearsal has a tone and a rhythm, and the director must not intrude on it to the point of destroying what the actors are working for.

Character Biography

The director may ask each actor to work up a biography of the character being portrayed. In educational settings, the biography may be written for the director's scrutiny, but usually it is simply thought through as the basis for one or both of the two applications noted immediately below.

Character Conference

Many directors find character conferences—meetings outside the regularly scheduled rehearsals in which the actor and director discuss specifics of a character's history and relationships—useful. Early in the game, character conferences can help make sure the actors are on the right track, and later they can help to clear up any misapprehensions or ambiguities.

Biographical Inquiry

In private as part of the character conference or with the company assembled, the director asks personal questions that each actor must answer in character. These questions need not be confined to areas clearly enunciated by the text of the play. The questioning should also search out bits of information that the character should know and be able to divulge. Facts about family, education, jobs, romances, and so on, are all fair game. The director should insist on specific details—drawn explicitly from the text or well-supported inferences made by the actor. In no case should the director settle for generalizations. Perhaps in no instance is this technique more useful than in period plays, where the tendency is for some actors to regard their creations as mere artifice without human dimension. Attention to the virtual biography of the character is obviously one way of making legitimate decisions about the manner of the character and even about the choices the character might make in the given circumstances. A reader or critic trying simply to understand the play might find it meaningless to quibble over the number of Macbeth's children. In contrast, the actor playing Lady Macbeth must play a scene (I, vii) in which she says:

" . . . I have given suck, and know
How tender 'tis to love the babe that milks me:
I would, while it was smiling in my face,
Have plucked my nipple from his boneless gums,

And dashed the brains out, had I so sworn as you
Have done to this."

The actor must play this moment specifically in terms of the character's inner life. There can be no equivocation. The verbal image demands a specific actor decision. Lady Macbeth nursed a baby and recalls the action. It cannot be generalized; she does not say "I am a woman and can imagine what it would be like to nurse a baby." She says, "I have . . . and know . . . I would . . ." Again, the *onlooker* may interpret the words on the page or in the performance and speculate about meanings and implications. The *actor* must play the moment, and in that moment, the actor's decision about biography will communicate something significant about the character.

To be neutral about the facts of a character's life, to attempt to "let the lines and the actions speak for themselves," is theoretically absurd and practically impossible when it comes to performance. Once again, the act is specific. A specific actor—impersonating the character, appearing in a chosen costume worn in a distinctive manner—speaks in a unique rhythm with a peculiar vocal quality, tone and inflection. She moves in a certain way, has a particular visual focus. All efforts to neutralize these elements are not only doomed to failure, they are counter to the very essence of acting.

Image Research

Ask actors to bring in visual images that they feel say something about their characters. Sources appropriate to the play in period or geography are obvious and useful, as are images that "look like my character." But you might also ask for images that simply provoke a feeling about the character or any element of the play. (See also the Chapter V discussion of "Other Art Forms.") These images can be shared with the company in periodic "show-and-tell" sessions, or labeled appropriately and posted on a *Resource Board* backstage or in the greenroom. The accumulation of these images serves many valuable purposes at once: providing historical research, sharpening powers of observation and a sense of form, and increasing the feeling of shared effort.

> Use a *Resource Board* to display images and information about the characters and the play brought in by the actors, the director, and other member of the company.

Sometimes, a director and actor can find an *immediate* use for images found in this way. In rehearsals for *Romeo and Juliet,* the actor playing Romeo and the director were frustrated in their efforts to stage the moments after the fatally stabbed Mercutio is carried off, leaving his friend on the stage. Wanting to express the overwhelming emotional impact on Romeo, actor and director searched for an honest and powerful way to fill the moments when Romeo is on stage alone. The director suggested that Mercutio's dagger be left behind (he had fought with rapier and dagger), allowing the actor playing Romeo a clear focus of his feeling. This proved helpful but still not quite satisfying. At the next rehearsal, Mercutio was carried off. Romeo picked up the dagger; his body twisted; he held the dagger in both hands behind his head. It looked as if he were pulling the dagger from between his own shoulder blades. The tension was electric. The moment was brief, affecting, and intensely personal; the character released his emotion in a swallowed gasp and collapsed to the ground. There was no mistaking the profound emotion of Romeo's reaction to the death of his friend.

What had inspired this potent image? Later, the actor explained it had come directly from a painting he had found depicting the martyrdom of Saint Sebastian. The agony of the Saint pierced by arrows, he revealed, felt to him to be a precise analogue for Romeo's sudden, deep agony.

"Secrets"

The director may ask an actor to create a "secret" the character knows and acts upon without divulging it in any way. In some cases, the director may actually suggest the specific secret to achieve the desired quality or modulations in a performance. The secret may be completely benign, or endearing—Romeo's fascination with his Juliet's eyelids—or it may be ominous or revolting. In rehearsing the character of the repulsively charming Nazi functionary, Bouller, in C.P. Taylor's *Good,* the actor playing the part of the middle-aged Fascist bureaucrat seemed almost mystically to capture his egregious, lurid manner all at once. A little sheepishly, the actor told the director of the character's "secret": under his tailored suit with the swastika armband, Bouller was wearing women's underwear!

Complementary Qualities

Good acting shows more than a single dimension of character, however powerful and compelling that one aspect might be. In any good performance, there is inevitably contrast and depth that makes the characterization all the stronger and more effective. A painter knows that to emphasize the dark, shadowy impression, the painting must include bright, light areas; that to bring out a specific color, the opposite color provides the most effective setting. That opposite color is "complementary" because it contains all the color the original does not. It is *complementary* because it completes the original by filling out all the remaining possibilities, *opposite* because it provides the greatest contrast.

The complexities of human life that the theatre depicts are richly textured. Patterns of behavior, personality, and motivation are seldom if ever one-dimensional. An actor working with the playwright and the director on the creation of a character is faced with the primary challenge of decision-making. Who is this character? What does he or she do? Why does he or she do it at all, and why in precisely this way? The initial answers to these inquiries tend to be monochromatic, the *what* and the *why* being satisfied with a single apparently adequate answer. All acting begins with this set of answers. These answers provide the "handle" or the "hook" the actor needs to build. The building consists in fleshing out—in adding dimension to—those initial impulses and decisions. It is a process of natural creative evolution for the actor, but sometimes it stalls.

|| **All good acting answers the *what*? and the *why*? of a charac-** ||
|| **ter. The best acting asks even more questions.** ||

One of the most useful actor coaching techniques is the use of complementary colors to enrich a characterization. Laurence Olivier, considered the finest actor of the twentieth century, was one of the greatest exponents of this technique. Showing the charm and sweetness of the great villains, the meanness and vitriolic temper of romantic heroes, and the feminine softness of the most masculine of adventurers, Olivier not only astonished audiences but thrilled them with the human dimensions of his theatrical creations. Almost any of his portrayals in movies or on video tape is worthy of study for this aspect of his art. Pay particular attention to his great Shakespearean performances: Hamlet, Richard III, Othello, King Lear.

Almost every aspect of any actor's performance can benefit from the consideration, at least, of complementary qualities: quiet moments immediately before or after a loud outburst, a sense of danger in a comic moment, a comic realization in a scene of pathos. As a rehearsal device, few techniques are as liberating and provocative as playing a character, scene, or moment with its complementary colorations.

Special Techniques in Rehearsal

Contemporary directors have developed many different techniques for using rehearsal time effectively and for leading actors towards achieving their potential. Following are some methods that have proved productive. Not all will be of equal value to any given director, or in every set of circumstances, but these techniques suggest something of the eclectic range of possibilities.

SET EXPLORATION EXERCISE

Once the set is in place, the actors should explore it completely to learn its technical quirks and possibilities, and to revitalize each character's familiarity and associations with the space and objects.

As mentioned earlier, as director you should explore the set at the earliest opportunity; then either you or your stage manager may lead the actors on a tour of the new environment to orient them to the space and to point out any potential problems with the set, especially those that might not have been foreseen during the rehearsals—a door, a step unit, anything that may be unorthodox or that requires special attention. Safety, needless to say is a prime consideration; nothing can be tolerated that may cause injury. The set should likewise pose no unnecessary performance difficulties; nothing should be present that unduly impedes the action or the actors. When moving into a new environment, many actors will suffer something of a crisis in confidence and concentration: everything seems to be consorting against them. Sometimes the problem is a physical fear—a platform so high that the actor feels in danger. Often, the set simply does not work the way the actor had hoped. In either case, the problem must be solved or the work of many rehearsals is threatened.

This problem cannot be treated as though it were frivolous or inconsequential. In some instances, the actor may have genuine anxieties amounting to panic. The problem should be addressed sympathetically but in a very businesslike way, assuring the actor that the trouble can be handled with special attention, or that something will be changed to circumvent the problem. After this reassurance, you should analyze the problem, dividing it into its components— step 1, step 2, 3, and so on—to turn a complex challenge into manageable units.

We should note here that difficulties in moving onto a set for the first time usually derive from unrealistic expectations. For this reason alone, the actors should be kept in touch with the design and technical elements that affect the work of the performance. The stage manager can be a valuable liaison for this work, taking the actors to look at parts of the set under construction. This simple step can avoid many frustrating and time-consuming problems later on.

ENCOURAGING RELAXATION AND CONCENTRATION

For actors, tension is doubly debilitating. First, it keeps the mind and body from working at peak efficiency, and second, it imprints actor tension on the character being portrayed. In rehearsal, the added stress of demands on memory and imagination multiplies the deleterious effects of tension.

Actors do well to emulate the techniques used by athletes to control physical tensions and focus concentration on the successful completion of the task at hand. While this is quite properly actor-work, the director should be able to recognize and be prepared to deal with problem tension. If the director establishes the importance of relaxation and warm-up exercises during the rehearsal, the effort will usually carry over into the performance. (Note: If rehearsals seem to take more than a few minutes to become productive, it is usually a sign that the actors are simply not prepared to start—that some are using the first part of the rehearsal period as a warm-up. Calling attention to the fact and ensuring that a rehearsal room is available 15–20 minutes before the start of the rehearsal is usually sufficient to communicate the groundrules.) Some directors include a formal warm-up session as part of the rehearsal routine and find this quite valuable. If suggestion does not yield the desired results or if it is part of the established routine of the theatre company, then by all means use a group warm-up.

The warm-up exercises should be efficient, purposeful, and brief—ideally around 10 minutes. Some actors are so convinced of the efficacy of warm-ups that they want to spend as much time as possible on them. It is not unknown to find actors reporting to rehearsal in a state of near exhaustion, smiling virtuously with satisfaction at their hour-long aerobic "warm-up." However, a sensible warm-up should focus primarily on loosening and stretching exercises for the large muscle groups, with special attention given the neck, shoulder, and arms, where tension regularly resides. The warm-up might consist of stretching, followed by tensing and relaxing the muscle groups. These steps can be finished by "loosening" exercises—vigorous shaking and relaxing of the arms and hands to let residual tension from the neck and shoulders flow out the fingertips. Simple vocal warm-ups are also important for most actors to relieve tension in the vocal mechanism. If the company seems lethargic, the warm-up session may end with something vigorous and oriented towards attention and interaction—tossing and catching an imaginary ball, for example.

The director, the choreographer, or any designated company member may lead the warm-ups. Alternating the lead among the actors from rehearsal to rehearsal can be used to involve everyone in the exercise.

COSTUME OR PROP EXERCISES

In addition to having awkward, unusual, and provocative props and costume elements available for regular rehearsals, the director may use props and costumes in a variety of creative ways.

1. **Establishing Attitudes:** Have the actor(s) create a new and specific attitude towards the item, and a special way of dealing with it that is appropriate to the character, the action, and the attitude. The actor might develop something like Judge Brack's habit of twirling his pince-nez (in the *Hedda Gabler* discussion in Chapter XII). Gaev in *The Cherry Orchard,* as mentioned, plays billiard shots as indicated in his lines. This type of imaginative exercise, using either a real or imagined prop, can help determine how an actor plays the scene.

Play: *Gringo Planet* **Author:** Frederick Bailey **Theatre:** Actors Theatre of Louisville **Director:** Frederick Bailey **Set Designer:** Paul Owen **Costumes:** Frances Kenny **Lighting:** Ralph Dressler **Actors (l to r):** F. Sanders, S. Hay, S. Hofendahl, A. LeFevre, D. Mills (Photo by David S. Talbott)

Play: *I'm not Rappaport* **Author:** Herb Gardner **Theatre:** TheatreVirginia **Director:** Terry Burgler **Set Designer:** Charles Caldwell **Costumes:** Catherine Szari **Lighting:** Jeff Stroman **Actors (l to r):** Ronald Hunter, Nick Smith

Play: *Passion* **Author:** Peter Nichols **Theatre:** The Williamstown Theatre Festival **Director:** Arvin Brown **Set Designer:** Michael Miller **Costumes:** Dunya Ramicova **Lighting:** Scott Zielinski **Actors (l to r):** Joyce Ebert, Caris Corfman, Frank Converse, Richard Venture (Photo by Richard Termine)

Actors confident in what they are doing are most likely to establish a sense of genuine communication. In these and other photographs throughout the text, note how the body language of the actors creates a subtle but telling statement about the characters.

2. Building Confidence and Expressiveness:

Some actors *wear* costumes; some merely *inhabit* them. Many actors are so frightened at the prospect of actually wearing period clothes that they are always uncomfortable in them. Practice, of course, is useful in and of itself. The imaginative and creative challenge in using the costume to make a statement can not only relieve some of the discomfort but can actually encourage the actor to use the costume creatively. A woman discovers that corsets and trains and bustles are not included in a costume to inconvenience her or to provide a silhouette that only an historian or a costume designer will understand, but to provide her with the means for discovering and expressing something essential about the character she is portraying. She will immediately grasp the fact that if Hedda Gabler is relieved of her corset and heavy layered clothing, the result is not only a change in the period but, inevitably, in the character as well.

> The ability to use a costume and its elements to *express* character rather than to *indicate* it is one mark of an organic and integrated characterization.

Perhaps no item of clothing is so consistently important as shoes. Shoes affect the carriage of the whole body (which interestingly, is called "attitude"). The actor's carriage while developing the "feel" of a role is a prime factor to be considered. Contemporary soft "athletic" shoes impart a bearing and overall feeling entirely different from the boots of the Cavalier period, and they can impress a physical quality on the character over a period of several weeks of rehearsal that will be virtually impossible to adjust in the few hours allotted to dress rehearsals. Even in contemporary plays, it is important to insist that actors wear shoes as close as possible in type to those to be worn in performance. Actual costume shoes are ideal and should be used if available. Indeed, everything mentioned concerning period or theatrical styles applies with equal importance to contemporary plays. Because we are familiar with contemporary fashions, we often overlook the fact that *every play is a period play* and that familiarity may often simply be an excuse for blindness—for not seeing clearly and responding to what is there.

3. **Exploring Possibilities:** Setting aside a period of time for improvised scenes or vignettes (in which the characters express themselves or simply meet and interact, using costumes and properties to the greatest effect) can prove a helpful and enlightening rehearsal tactic.

The director and actors should continue to explore the visual and the kinesthetic impact of the character's clothes and properties—their look and feel—on the lines of character development. Staying in touch with costumes and properties as they are being acquired or constructed is an invaluable aid. It sets up a creative dialogue with the costume and properties designers, and enhances the possibility that their creations become genuine artistic contributions rather than superficial additions to the production.

EXERCISES _____

1. Using a variety of hats and shoes (the actor's own or provided from stock), ask an actor to move around the room, sit, and try a variety of routine movements. Note any differences and ask how the different styles influence physical and psychological feelings or actions. Obviously, this sort of exercise may be extended to the use of other items of clothing, accessories, and properties.

2. Employ some simple personal props (items a character might carry about) and suggest the development of attitudes or feelings connected with each. See if the attitude can be detected in the way the actor deals with the object.

3. Now see if the actor can employ each prop in a way that deliberately expresses some attitude or emotional state. Look for combinations of object and action that are complementary, not merely arbitrary or self-conscious.

4. Demonstrate (without verbal explanations) some specific use of clothing or a personal "prop" you have observed offstage. The way people smoke, handle money, or adjust hair and clothing are good starting points. Take care to be accurate in your demonstration. Do not try simply to entertain, and avoid caricature.

USING MUSIC

Establishing a mood and a rhythm for a scene is a delicate and sometimes frustrating task. The director may be faced with conflicting actor energies as well as conflicting interpretations or "feelings." As a result, scenes sometimes do not come together; the actors hold onto their own internal rhythms, and the scene suffers. Using *music* to underscore the scene may often prove a valuable, sometimes even a miraculous, rehearsal technique.

The method is simplicity itself. Play a few bars of the chosen music just to establish it in the actors' heads, then call for the scene to begin. It may be necessary to side-coach at first, reminding the actors to let the music lead them. Eventually, you should notice some change as the music works its particular magic. If the method seems to have made an impression, it may be repeated to fix it in the actors' subconscious. Once this is done, the music can be used as a sense memory reference. The recall of the music should get the scene back on track, especially if the actors take a moment before the scene starts to refresh their memory of the rehearsal experience.

Of course, a production makes music inevitably as a result of performance tempi and rhythms produced unconsciously by the actors, the text, and the performance environment. Given this assumption, the director can identify and control the performance music by manipulating it either from within (by changing motivations, objectives, relationships) or from without (by changing phrasing, tempo, rhythm, or by consciously using a suitable musical score). Director Harold Clurman, in an effort to evoke a radically different characterization from actor Walter Matthau in *A Shot in the Dark,* asked the actor to choose a piece of "super-elegant" music to play for himself and learn to walk to. The result was an entirely new and completely realized character, as delightful as it was unexpected. (*On Directing,* p. 120) This technique is, of course, a variation on the *secrets* strategy mentioned earlier in this chapter.

DARK REHEARSALS

A "dark rehearsal" may be used either as a private rehearsal or part of a general rehearsal session. Its purpose is to alleviate performance anxieties and break down automatic or stereotypical acting. It can also be used to refresh actors' responses, to make them more truthful and direct.

The goal of the dark rehearsal should be like that of the first read-through: to set up an atmosphere where the actors can respond honestly and spontaneously. The director should encourage listening and reacting as directly as possible, using the lines of the play. The director should listen for nuances and discoveries that may have become lost or clouded as the rehearsals began to take a particular shape or direction. (It is also possible to use this same format as an environment for improvisations, thereby minimizing some of the pressure to perform or entertain that often characterizes such exercises.)

In one form, the room is darkened, and the actors sit or stand where they can easily be heard. There is no need for blocking or business. Then the scene begins, the lines being spoken quietly and simply. The director must establish the need for quiet simplicity before the session begins and reinforce it as the scene progresses if a sense of simple communication of idea and feeling gives way to line readings.

Another variation is to leave some light in the room and have two actors sit facing each other in the dim light. The same general instructions apply; only this time, some visual concentration is implicit. The proximity of the two actors, and the tight circle of concentration imposed by the dim lights, may well reveal qualities of the scene that had been overlooked or forgotten in the rush to "get it right."

Using very short scenes or segments that the actors have learned, try variations of the "dark rehearsal." Discuss the discoveries with the actors. See if the results of the exercise produce worthwhile results in terms of understanding or execution.

SPEED REHEARSALS

On occasions when the energy or concentration required in a scene begins to dissipate, a speed rehearsal can help re-charge and refocus it. Simply put, a speed rehearsal requires that everything happen at double-time. The actors speak and move as quickly as possible though still giving a complete performance. Alternatively, the speed rehearsal may be limited to lines, with the actors sitting around and speaking at the rapid tempo. This exercise forces listening and concentration as few other techniques can.

PRIVATE REHEARSALS

The normal rehearsal can become a sort of performance, no matter what precautions are taken to minimize that possibility. Inescapably, some people present will be perceived as judgmental. The stage manager, trying to keep blocking, lines, and business under control, seems acutely aware of mistakes. Other actors, sitting around waiting for their entrances, can appear anxious and critical. Designers who come in to watch a run-through to gauge the effectiveness of their own work may seem like outsiders—people from the world normally beyond the rehearsal hall.

When members of a company have worked together before and have developed a language and a set of expectations, these problems are not so acute. Everyone tends to know where they are and where they are headed. A newly acquainted company is an entirely different matter. There always seems to be something for everyone to prove. In most circumstances, initial anxieties will dissipate as the creation and collaboration goes forward—especially if the director takes care to establish a good working environment in the first rehearsals. Even so, there are times even in the most congenial of rehearsal environments when it is advisable to eliminate all outside distractions and tensions so that actors and director can work as freely as possible. This is where the *private rehearsal* comes in.

> **The private rehearsal is merely a session, scheduled or impromptu, involving the absolute minimum number of participants. Typically, this means the director and two or three actors.**

Some directors will choose to include the stage manager or prompter in the private rehearsal; some will not. Obviously, the decision varies with each situation, but generally, it is good to restrict the session to the director and the actors. The private rehearsal session may be used at any time, but it is most effective when no other rehearsal follows immediately; that is, for a full rehearsal session or as the last part of a longer session.

The main point of a private rehearsal is to work free from all stress and interference so that the actors and director can concentrate fully on the challenges of the scene. To achieve this, the director must be attentive to every element of the rehearsal. If performance anxieties begin to creep in, the director must put them to rest; if the actors' confidence starts to wane, the director must build it up. Using this approach, directors may discover the private rehearsal is one of the most effective techniques at their disposal.

Coaching Actors: Methods and Problems

THE DESIGN OF A ROLE

Every role, like every production, must have a design to give it distinction and structural integrity. Usually, this design is uncovered intuitively as the rehearsals progress. Sometimes, however, it is never discovered; or it is overlooked either because it is complicated, or because it is so apparently simple. In such cases, the director may help the actor by examining the design of the role as it is defined in the production.

A basic premise of drama is that every character has a life that involves reactions to changing circumstances. In its broadest application, this principle suggests that what a character is at the beginning of the play is different from what he or she is at the end. In some cases, the pattern may be circular, the character may "revert." But there must be change. No change, no life. This is true of the play as a whole, and it is true of each scene that affects the character. The movement of character through the play provides the basic structure for designing a role. Review the character analysis outline in Chapter III, especially the section on "Character Action."

For each scene or action involving the character directly or indirectly, the director and the actor must consider:

1. The character's attitude, situation, and objectives at the beginning and end of the scene
2. Important action in the scene
3. Important line(s) or sentiment(s) expressed
4. The emotional quality of the scene

This method may be applied to a single scene or to the progress of a character through the entire play. There should be pattern of change, growth, and evolution throughout each scene and an overall pattern throughout the play. If the actor cannot discover or express these adjustments, the exercise suggests its own solutions: awareness of the process of growth and change of the character.

FINDING THE VOCABULARY

In order to collaborate, the director must find a special vocabulary, arguably a unique one, to communicate with each actor. Many actors share terminology, but the director must be prepared to speak to each individual, at one time or another, in a special language. The director must discover or develop with each actor a set of cues to provoke the desired internal feelings and external expression. To complicate matters, actors must be helped towards developing their own language variations in order to communicate fully and effectively with one another. No wonder many a rehearsal period begins (and too many persist) as a Tower of Babel. Indeed, one of the hallmarks of a genuine ensemble or true teamwork is the shared theatrical and intentional language of the participants.

Analytical and Visceral Actors

Because each actor presents a unique case, it is impossible to identify all the dialects of director-actor language. There seem to be two general categories of actors, *analytical* and *visceral* (or *intuitive*), each requiring a special vocabulary.

The director learns that analytical actors (often "cool") like to talk about their work and themselves. While it sometimes may seem that such talk produces little difference in their characterizations or performances, these *analysts* do need concentrated attention and dialogue. Many have developed working methods that require some sort of intellectual validation or logical structure. The immediate and obvious tactic for the director is to concentrate on some of the discursive methods discussed later. Analysts are important to a director because they tend to insist on logic, a consistent pattern of facts and probability. A director who engages such actors can be sure of being tested on matters of preparation and consistency.

Useful as they are to any production, analytical actors can present problems: a narrow and unyielding literal-mindedness and a tendency to monopolize rehearsal time. The first exhibits itself when reasonable responses to inquiry or explanation provoke an apparently endless chain reaction—"If that is so, then what about . . .?"—or, worse, a confrontational response to every answer provided. Notice that there is a line between useful, thoughtful inquiry and discussion and the simply argumentative. In most cases, these problems are self-limiting, but each has the potential of becoming debilitating and counterproductive if the director does not recognize and manage the situation. The skillful analyst knows to back off when the questioning is irrelevant, no longer productive, or simply because the director does not have ready answers. The skillful director knows also that when the line is reached, either the focus of the discussion or the venue must be changed.

> **When discussion (between actor and director) becomes debate—a contest—or when the rehearsal time being used is not serving the purposes of the rehearsal schedule and the people assembled, it is time to end the discussion.**

If the actor's line of inquiry is neither essential nor relevant, you may be able to deflect it by suggesting a different objective or a variation in the given circumstances or motivation. The actor's question or objection is probably due to some niggling doubt or insecurity, and the change you suggest can alleviate the actor's difficulty by providing a fresh perspective. If this approach does not seem to work, another alternative is to change the venue—to meet with the actor outside of the rehearsal period to continue the discussion. This tactic usually does the trick. It gives the actor your complete attention, acknowledges the importance of the issues and concerns, and reinforces the sense of true collaboration. And it does not waste valuable rehearsal time.

In coaching the analytical actor, the director is wise to employ a considerable number of emotional and imagistic prompts. The actor who insists on extended intellectual discussion may be trying to avoid things that cannot be readily understood or controlled. Leading such an actor to respond to suggestions of images and emotions can provide a warmer, more spontaneous dimension to the work.

At the opposite pole stands the *visceral* or *intuitive* actor. The prototype is the performer who is all raw emotions and nerve-ends. Operating on instinct and energy, this actor wants to *do* it, to try anything even if it seems crazy. The director is never quite sure what will happen next. The actor demands stimuli, not explanations. This sort of actor (inevitably "hot") is intensely exciting to work with. But the director should be alert to some potential problems. Often, the actor's performance in rehearsal is so compelling that it is difficult to recognize its lack of richness and depth. The tactic in dealing with this actor is obvious. Emphasize structure, order, and control in your vocabulary and maintain a critical, analytical eye when observing the development of the character and its relationship to the rest of the production. Slow things down so that you can fully appreciate what is going on.

> **The analytical actor keeps you honest; the visceral actor keeps you alert.**

As mentioned, no one actor—certainly no good actor—is all analysis and no instinct, or the reverse. Virtually any cast of more than three or four will have a mix of the two types. You will find yourself evolving a preference for working with one or the other, but it is probably wise to seek a mix—in the individual actor and in the ensemble. This will help maintain a balance and depth in approaching actors and their work.

Actor-Director Language

To deal with actors, you need to know something about director-actor language. One type is *discursive*. Its vocabulary is based in facts and events, and it works in a logical and linear fashion. It is also one of the first methods a director will feel comfortable employing, because it is straightforward and objective. If you have explored the play in ways suggested in Chapter III, you have already learned some of the vocabulary necessary to communicate at this level.

1. **Discursive Coaching**—The main purpose of discursive coaching is to elicit, establish, and explore facts of environment, history, and biography and, ultimately, to deepen the sense of shared reality among the actors as they rehearse. These facts come from an analysis of the script and the special requirements of the production. They can give the performances a special definition and distinction. Below are some of the areas that may be explored in developing a director-actor vocabulary. Following each is an example drawn from Elia Kazan's notes (reprinted in *Directors on Directing*, pp. 374–375) for the original production of *A Streetcar Named Desire*. (The notes refer to the character of Stanley, played by Marlon Brando.) Kazan, along with other influential members of the Group Theatre of the 1930's—Harold Clurman, Lee Strasberg, Robert Lewis—have provided the most important models for this sort of coaching.

a. *Environmental*—The physical conditions surrounding or immediately preceding the event or action being explored. What are the physical facts of the given circumstances? What is the weather like? Was there a light on in the hallway? Was the coat comfortable? Have we really paid attention to the intended physical realities of the actual set, costumes, lights, sound, and properties? What about size, color, weight, contrast? ("Choose Marlon's objects . . . the things he loves and prizes: all sensuous and sensual—the shirt, the cigar, the beer [how it's poured and nursed, etc.].")

b. *Circumstantial*—This extends the consideration of surrounding conditions from external factors to actions affecting the mood and attitude of the character. Was the cab ride pleasant or hectic? Was the climb up the steps tiring? (A consideration of precisely this question gave a particular comic honesty and vivacity to Mike Nichols' original Broadway production of Neil Simon's *Barefoot in the Park*.) Did that tray belong to your mother? Is the phone call expected or a complete surprise? Is it louder of softer than expected? ("Stanley has got things his way. He fits into his environment. The culture and the civilization, even the neighborhood, etc., etc., the food, the drink, etc., are all his way. . . . The main thing for the actor to do in the early scenes is make the physical environment of Stanley, the props come to life.")

c. *Biographical*—The director and each actor should know the details of a character's life to the point of every critical scene. The biographical decisions must be consonant with the anecdotal information provided by the script and the controlling decisions of the production matrix and style. Pay special attention to events and relationships that might affect the actions or attitudes of the character in the play, but do not limit the biography to information that is obviously and immediately useful. In many cases, seemingly trivial or irrelevant decisions specify and illuminate aspects of character or action in vivid and surprising ways. (See "Biographical Inquiry," above.)

The teamwork of an effective ensemble cast requires an exquisite sensitivity of each actor to another.
Play: *Autumn Elegy* **Author:** Charlene Redick **Theatre:** The Williamstown Theatre Festival **Director:** Michael Montel **Set Designer:** Paul Feinberg **Costumes:** Sigrid Insull **Lighting:** Bruce Auerbach **Actors (l to r):** Ruth Nelson, E.G. Marshall (Photo by Richard Termine)

d. *Psychological*—Here we project the details of the character's inner life, most especially in matters of motives, intentions, and objectives. Appropriate questions to consider are those that center on the specifics of what the character wants and the degree of need or desire. ("STANLEY. Spine—keep things his way [Blanche the antagonist].")

e. *Relational*—This refers to the reactions and responses of one character to another—the interplay that defines each character in the light of the other. ("One of the important things for Stanley is that Blanche would wreck his home. . . . He's got things the way he wants them around there and he does not want them upset by a phony, corrupt, sick, destructive woman. . . . "Emphasize Stanley's love for Stella. It is rough, embarrassed and he rather truculently won't show it. But it is there. He's proud of her.")

2. **Non-discursive Coaching**—While a great deal of time and energy must be spent on the facts of character, environment, and action, creative directors invariably use of *non-discursive* methods to go beyond the facts and into form and subjective qualities. In the main, these methods provoke feelings and responses through *imagery* and *kinesthetics* (using movement and body position to discover the internal states of a character). Directors may use these techniques in either direct or indirect suggestion, or through improvisation. In any case, the aim is to discover attributes that do not yield readily to the methods of discursive analysis and discussion. Many of these imagistic elements you will have available following your search for images described in Chapter VI.

a. *Imagery*—While most language is filled with images ("You feel as if you're trapped here"), it becomes most useful in the director-actor vocabulary when the images are fresh and intimately connected to the problem at hand. An actor who is unspecific in a scene or moment can often be liberated by the suggestion of an animal image, for example. The image may already be there in the text, waiting to be called forth and applied to the particular case. In *True West*, playwright Sam Shepard provides Lee not only with a revealing speech about a fighting dog, but also with a notably useful image for the actor playing the role. The pit bull that Lee recalls so fondly is a breed that is stocky, quick, powerful of grip, and—most of all—notoriously tenacious and merciless.

The director, emphasizing this image to the actor playing Lee, suggests, first of all, a general quality of action and intention. A responsive actor will translate that suggestion into specific physical, emotional, and intentional qualities that affect posture, focus, and tempo-rhythms.

Even among the most hard-bitten "realistic" directors, the best use imagery consciously and effectively. Kazan himself describes Stanley in images of childhood, a "little tough-boy" who "cries like a baby." (*Directors on Directing*, p. 377)

Photographs, descriptions, and other records of Kazan's *Streetcar* show his directorial style marked as surely by conscious poeticism as by his more widely-noted "Method" attack on character psychology. In *Death of a Salesman*, Kazan demonstrated clearly the fact that, at its best, American Realism is far from a narrow slice-of-life; rather it finds its definitive directorial statement in a stunning combination of psychological introspection and graceful theatrical imagery.

One of the most influential of the Group Theatre/Actors Studio directors and teachers, Robert Lewis, sounds like anything but a hard-headed realistic director in describing his production of William Saroyan's *My Heart's in the Highlands*. "The actors were doing something real (offering gifts), but it was gradually seeming to be a tree that was flowering. Then, as they listened to the music, they started to hum and sway. and the whole effect became like a tree swaying in the breeze." (*Method or Madness,* p. 125)

The inescapable point is that imagery is a powerful tool for achieving the essential truth of character, action, and relationship that should reside even in the most naturalistic of treatments.

b. *Kinesthetics*—There is, in director-actor communication, a non-verbal mode in which the vocabulary is unusually direct and evocative. Calling this communication *kinesthetic* suggests that it works through the muscles, and is translated by the actor's instincts into character. Again, "Let the work teach you" is good advice for the actor as well as for the director.

In the early years of this century, the James-Lange theory was widely acclaimed for the idea that a person's physical state can influence internal attitudes and responses. Obviously, as we noted in Chapter IV and elsewhere, the external form of position or action on stage makes an inevitable statement of feeling and therefore meaning to those who observe it. These same external manipulations can affect an actor's exploration and understanding of character.

> **The director can communicate meaning—interpretation—to an actor simply by suggesting specific physical actions, states, or relationships.**

It can be interesting to observe the "ripple effect" of communication. In Athol Fugard's *Master Harold . . . and the boys,* the actor playing Willie is faced with the formidable task of being onstage throughout the play with relatively little to say and not much of apparent significance to do. While he is one of only three characters, little is known of him directly from the text; most information about Willie must be inferred and then communicated in ways that complement the main action. The characterization, then, must be complete and full but expressed in ways that allow the character to remain appropriately in the background.

At one moment, Hally, the young white boy, suggests that Sam, his black mentor, is guilty of "bigotry." Willie, also black, is cleaning the room at the time. The director and the actor have a number of choices. Willie can: 1) continue his work with no change; 2) pause for a moment without registering any other response, take a breath, and then continue his work; 3) pause and look at

The director must trust the actor's ability to suggest a full range of emotions from the subtle to the explosive.
Play: Master Harold . . . and the boys **Author:** Athol Fugard **Theatre:** McCarter Theatre **Director:** Jamie Brown **Actors (l to r):** Benjamin White (Photo by Randall Hagadorn)

Hally before continuing; 4) look at Sam; 5) stop the work and gaze at the floor for several seconds before going on to something else; or, 6) throw down his cleaning rag reflexively in disbelief. The possibilities are virtually endless. Each one inevitably makes a statement about Willie—his character and his consciousness, his relationship to the other characters, his place in this particular social order. Also inevitable is the "ripple effect" of each choice on the portrayal of Willie throughout the play. The character who does any one of these actions is significantly different from one who does another. The point is that the director can communicate with the actor using the vocabulary of kinesthetics, and that method is often more efficient and provocative than discussion or explanation.

c. *Improvisation*—Directors have strong feelings about improvisation, finding it somewhere between absolutely "indispensable" and "worthless." On one hand, directors argue that improvisation is one of the best and most effective ways of getting past the actor's conventional or overly intellectual predispositions. Besides opening the actor up to fresh discovery, the process of improvisation can build a sense of teamwork and pure creativity and provide new insight into material that has become stale or that refuses to develop. Other directors suggest that improvisation is an ineffectual and inefficient use of rehearsal time, arguing that the "improv" situation is virtually impossible to set up in a way that is at once to the point and still open to development and discovery. Besides, some actors have a genuine aversion to the whole idea of improvisation, and that attitude can doom healthy experimentation from the very beginning.

Improvisation as an actor coaching method for use in rehearsal does have some drawbacks. One of these can be the very enthusiasm of some actors for the process. These actors are generally good at improvisation and, unless controlled, can make the improvisation itself the point of the work rather than a means to an end.

|| **The critical issue in using improvisation as a rehearsal technique is the setup and definition of the exercise itself.** ||

First, the purpose and type of the improvisation should be established. Let us look at three possibilities:

1. *Anecdotal*—This technique involves the use of the characters, circumstances, and plot of the play; it usually consists of imposing some clearly defined changes.
The actors might be asked:

- to use their own words and personalities in a scene from the play;
- to change their characters' objectives;
- to play a scene that is referred to in the play but never played out;
- to improvise a scene in which the characters of the play behave in an unexpected way (the director might surreptitiously set up some unexpected turn of events with one or more of the participants to provoke a fresh response from another actor whose sense of participation has dissipated); or
- to perform a scene in an entirely different set of given circumstances from those in the play.

2. *Kinesthetic*—Unlike the more common anecdotal technique, kinesthetic improvisation tries to discover an appropriate physical reaction to a situation that the actor can use to induce the emotional state of the character. The technique presumes a vocabulary of physical reactions applicable to a range of emotions—that the body's response to being intellectually attacked, for example, is virtually the same flight or fight reaction felt by a person being physically attacked. It is therefore a variation of sense memory. The following guidelines (first published in *Players* magazine) are useful in developing this technique.

> The first step in this technique is to posit a key exercise for the scene. This exercise must be a physical task—a struggle, a contest, an expression of tenderness or affection, of dominance or hostility, or any expressive and meaningful action. This task or game is structured so as to give concrete form to the underlying emotional action of the scene. Sometimes it can be based on a verbal metaphor for what goes on in the scene. . . . The very act of structuring the exercise forces the director . . . and the actors involved to come to terms with

the specifics of the scene. . . . The very effort of performing such an exercise forces the actor to respond physically to what is happening. . . . The actor must learn to be alert to his physical responses—the muscular tensions, breathing, and rhythms of the body during the exercise—because some of these responses provide the raw materials that will later be selected and modulated for use in the actual performance. . . .

The use of the actor's physical experience in the exercise . . . consists simply of the controlled reproduction in performance of the appropriate physical responses found through experiment in the exploratory exercises. The actor makes his body work in performance the way he found it worked in the exercise. There are differences, of course. The visible external actions of trying to evade a head-on attack are different from those of trying to avoid an intellectual or emotional assault. But the covert physical responses are probably the same. The muscles tense; the covering [defensive] instincts are activated; the eyes and the rest of the body seek for an opening through which to escape or counterattack. The [improvisation] has shown the actor the response the body makes; the actor uses that response by introducing it into his performance. Whether the action is obvious to the audience or not is beside the point; the actor is engaged in a very real physical action. His muscles are appropriately in play or at rest. He is working within the bounds of a definite . . . scenario which his body has shown to be apt for the scene in which he is involved. . . . The actor [thereby] can achieve methodically that excitement and exhilaration that comes from an active and total participation in a scene. (Black, pp. 273–274)

EXERCISES

Cast two people as actors A and B in the following scene. They should know the lines without conscious reflection.

A: It's you
B: Good to see you
A: It's been a very long time
B: Not as long as you might think
A: Time's been good to you
B: I'm planning on even better
A: Let me hear from you soon
B: I can guarantee that

1. Provide two contrasting anecdotes for the scene. Each should suggest a clearly defined environment and character objectives. Do not concern yourself too much with biographical or plot information. The aim here is to discover some possibilities for this type of improv. Have each version performed and note the effects on the actors and the impression of each version.

2. Provide two physical metaphors for the scene, one in the form of a contest or struggle, the other of comfort or assurance. Let the physical ac-

tion commence; on your instruction, the actors will begin lines. In each case the action should take precedence for the actors' attention. Each line should be coordinated with the action, being spoken only when the opportunity presents itself. Do not allow the actors to speed through the physical action or to give it less than their full concentration and energy.

When the physical action is completed, return the actors to a conversational setting—sitting facing each other is an option—and have them play the scene using the physical scenario suggested by the action. This time the conscious attention should be on verbal communication, but the residual physical impulses from the exercise should be experienced again (in a kind of sense memory experience) and allowed to color the lines being spoken and the relationship of the two characters.

---

3. *Imagistic*—In this form of improvisation, the setup is defined by images appropriate to the truth of the scene, actions, and characters. As noted above in "Imagery," extended improvisations can challenge actors to call upon their intuitive creative responses.

In *True West,* two brothers, Austin and Lee, are clearly in conflict. To bring the reality of that conflict home, the director might suggest an improvisation based on a leading image from the play. Perhaps the contest between the two characters is best defined as a game. But what kind? A cardgame is one possibility drawn from the text. But the vitality of that image is questionable for most of the conflicts in this play; it is too thoughtful, subdued, too lacking in explosiveness. Golf is also mentioned prominently, but many of the same objections apply. The action consists of more or less violent confrontations throughout the entire play; the rhythms, the tensions, the *quality* of the game of golf has no relationship to the powerful emotional conflict between the two brothers.

> To be valid and successful, any improvisation must provide a structure that leads the performers in an appropriate direction and permits them to make discoveries within that structure.

The relationship in *True West* is closer to combat then to gamesmanship or strategy. *True West* contains several prominent images of dogs and coyotes, specifically Lee's self-identification with a fighting dog. If Lee is perceived as a pit bull, he can be put into the ring with his brother, Austin. Imagistically, Austin might be what?—a coyote, a poodle, a Doberman pinscher, a grizzly bear? Any of these would suggest a contest that is symbolically defensible, connected to the truth of the play through the text itself. Still, these are four distinctly different battles; each tactic is different, and so is the rhythm, the weight, the tempo, and the possible outcome. The images themselves might even change as the contest progresses, each brother evolving at given points in the struggle into yet another image. The director is on a good track with this image, but for the best results, the improvisation must be clearly and precisely defined before turning the two actors loose upon each other for the purpose seriously exploring the relationship.

OBSERVATION—THE "SAFARI"

In "Observation," a chapter in his book *Acting: The First Six Lessons,* Richard Boleslavsky responds to a question about what observation has to do with acting:

> A great deal. It helps a student of the theatre to notice everything unusual and out of the ordinary in every-day life. It builds his memory, his storage memory, with all visible manifestations of the human spirit. It makes him sensitive to sincerity and to make-believe. It develops his sensory and muscular memory, and facilitates his adjustment to any business he may be required to do in a part. It opens his eyes to the full extent in appreciation of different personalities and values in people and works of art. And lastly . . . it enriches his inner life by full and extensive consumption of everything in outward life. . . . We think that we see everything, and we don't assimilate anything. But in the theatre, where we have to recreate life, we can't afford that. We are obliged to notice the material with which we work." (pp. 97–98)

When an actor or a dramatic moment is stalled, when the character simply will not emerge with any sort of distinction, it is time for actor and director to go back to the source that Boleslavsky extols: close observation of human life and behavior.

> **Since everything we create comes from ourselves and our experience, we can only expect to expand our creativity by enlarging and refreshing our own storehouse.**

The actor can be sent on a *safari,* a deliberate search outside the confines of the rehearsal hall, to pick up and bring back bits and pieces of observed personality and behavior to incorporate into the character. Any place, any occasion, any person is fair game. Even the decision to look closely—to see truly what is there—will often prove a significant step towards putting the process back on track. Ask the actor to show what the safari turned up—perhaps a way to hold a glass, maybe a special little gesture, a posture, a walk, a rhythm—and ask to see it become part of the character. Often you will find a key to open many doors, but even if nothing immediately useful turns up, the hunt will have been productive in a new alertness and sensitivity that Boleslavsky, himself a great teacher of actors, describes so richly.

LINE INTERPRETATIONS

Although dealing directly with actors' line readings is a minor concern for most directors, it can seem enormously important, because disagreement always seems to focus on a question of basic interpretation. The director should try to keep the relative importance of a line reading issue in the proper perspective by handling it discreetly.

|| **There is widespread agreement that a director should not ac-** ||
|| **tually *read* a line to suggest meaning or emphasis.** ||

Some actors have accepted the idea that director's should never read a line as an inviolable tenet of the actor-director relationship. Often, when a director questions a line-reading, the actor will display signs of anxiety and tension. This should be a warning to the director *not* to give a line-reading. One can often avoid conflict by rephrasing the line—a conventional evasion that often side-steps potential objections. Paraphrasing is nonetheless an effective tactic when there is a misunderstanding about the meaning of the line. Paraphrasing becomes translation and explanation, and as such may solve the problem by clarifying the point of the objection.

We should understand how a line reading goes astray—at least to the director's way of thinking. Directors and actors diverge on matters of line readings for several different reasons: They do not agree:

1. on *meanings;* that is, on the understanding of the words or the syntax of the line—the intellectual content;
2. on *intentions, objectives,* or *subtext*—the emotional implications;
3. on *inflection, emphasis, tempo, rhythm,* or *melody* of the line—the *technical shaping.*

Often, of course, the three are intertwined.

First, there might be a different interpretation of *meaning.* The actor and the director might understand different things by the same line. Take an example from the prologue to Act I of Shakespeare's *Henry V:*

> Or may we cram within this wooden "O"
> The very casques that did affright the air at
>   Agincourt?
> Oh pardon. As a crooked figure may
> In little space attest a million,
> And let us, ciphers to this great accompt,
> On your imaginary forces work.

The actor and the director must reach an understanding on the meaning of the *words*. The "wooden 'O' " is, of course, the theatre, originally the Globe Theatre, believed to have been a wooden structure with open interior courtyard containing the stage. "Casques" connotes arrows and crossbow bolts. "Crooked figure" and "cipher" both refer to a zero in a written number. And "accompt" means, simply, "account." The meaning of the words poses no problems, then. The meaning of the structure is another matter. The actor interprets "Oh pardon" as a response to what has been said before: "Pardon us for trying to do this impossible thing." The "Oh pardon!" would be followed by a transition—an adjustment to the next beat or unit of thought or intention. The director, however, is convinced the phrase should be connected to the proposition that follows: "Give us the same freedom to symbolize events that you give to arbitrary numbers to represent actual quantities." In this version, the line is phrased, "Oh pardon [us] as a crooked figure. . . ." Either reading delivers an acceptable meaning, the first with a gently ironic twist and a bit of self-deprecation; the second, objective and positive in tone. In order to achieve the desired *inflection,* and with two acceptable meanings to choose from, the director and actor must decide on the *intention*—the tone of the line as it fits into the design of the entire speech.

How can they accomplish this? Probably the best way is to work through the *character,* to find a character objective that will produce the desired effect. This is precisely the method of motivation and justification that is obtained in blocking: if the character has to move stage right, one finds a motive for the move, not simply a technical requirement.

Paraphrasing is a relatively weak method for achieving the desired effect here, where the sequence of the words themselves is at issue, but other strategies can work from the outside in—from *inflection* to *intention* and then to *meaning.* A good grasp of the architecture of a line or speech enables the director to make these alterations through appropriate technical adjustments of volume, pitch, tempo, rhythm, timbre, and phrasing. In fact, the director dealing with the case above might have suggested that the actor try a new phrasing as a method for discovering the intention of the line. Perhaps the actor might try taking a short breath after "Agincourt"; or he might pause after that question and glance around at his surroundings *before* saying, "Oh, pardon." Technical suggestions like these are often very effective because they *lead* the actor to discover what the director wants in a way that is distinctively personal and based on the art and craft of acting. An added advantage is that the actor will often discover something richer in the process than the director had originally envisioned—pure artistic rapport!

Classical drama, conscious of the potency of form, offers innumerable examples of dramaturgical architecture. There is no better exemplar than Shakespeare. Consider this speech from *Richard III* (IV, iv):

Queen Margaret
[1]Bear with me; I am hungry for revenge,
[2]And now I cloy me with beholding it.

³Thy Edward is dead that killed my Edward;
⁴Young York he is but boot, because both they
⁵Matched not the high perfection of my loss.
⁶Thy Clarence he is dead that stabbed my Edward,
⁷And the beholders of this frantic play,
⁸Th' adulterate Hastings, Rivers, Vaughan, Grey,
⁹Untimely smothered in their dusky graves.
¹⁰Richard yet lives, hell's black intelligencer,
¹¹Only reserved their factor to buy souls
¹²And send them thither. But at hand, at hand,
¹³Ensues his piteous and unpitied end.
¹⁴Earth gapes, hell burns, friends roar, saints pray,
¹⁵To have him suddenly conveyed from hence.
¹⁶Cancel his bond of life, dear God, I pray,
¹⁷That I may live and say, "The dog is dead."

Assuming that we understand the meaning, intention, and general tone of this speech, let us examine its *structure* as a means of discovering an organic way to shape its meaning and help the actor perform it with the greatest effectiveness.

Lines 1 and 2 introduce the point of view with the repetition of "I"; the pronoun does not appear again until the two repetitions in the last two lines of the speech (16 and 17). In lines 3 through 10, no fewer than eight characters are mentioned by name, the word Edward occurring three times, pointedly contrasting "thy Edward" with "my Edward." The last name mentioned—the object of the Queen's hatred—is Richard.

Using the image of architecture, we might note a "build"—a rise of intensity and pitch—from line 3 to 4, 6, 7, 8, to a crest at the beginning of line 10— "Richard." Lines 5 and 9 support lines 4 and 8 respectively, and maintain the level already set. The climax or apex at "Richard" is held for an instant marking the beginning of a slow, rumbling descent that pauses after line 12's "send them thither." Then comes an unusual marker, the sharp contrast implied by "But" and a repeated phrase, "at hand, at hand." In the mouth of a Queen bent on revenge, this is not stumbling or searching for the right word; this is a powerful assertion of fact that falls to a brief stop at the end of line 13. In line 14, the fall becomes a series of short crashes increasing incrementally in force and tempo stopping only at the end of line 15.

Line 16 returns to the level of "Richard" in 10 and then crashes deliberately and ultimately with "The dog is dead."

The images we have noted suggest rising and falling volume, pitch, and tempo. Some of the phrasing and rhythm is implied as well. Timbre—the quality of the sound produced—may be inferred from the structural placement of the contrasting "Edwards" (the ironic tone of placing the voice in the head), the "Richard" (voice in the front of the mouth behind the teeth, a snarl), and finally "The dog is dead" (low and guttural, a growl).

This is precisely the sort of structural analysis we discussed in Chapter III, here being applied to a practical element of rehearsal. You now have at your disposal another tool with which to communicate with the actor, a set of images drawn from the structure of the character's speech: the vision of ascending a ladder, one deliberate step at a time, to find the object of her anger, then forcing him to fall under a series of rhythmic violent blows and to be crushed deliberately into the ground at the foot of a ladder.

EXERCISES

1. Try marking the speech above to indicate the structural elements. Use arrows accompanied by identifying letters—P(itch), V(olume), T(empo)—to indicate direction, curved or sharp lines moving horizontals to hint at rhythm, single or double underlining for emphasis, single, double, or triple slash marks for pauses to indicate phrasing, and marginal notes to describe timbre.

2. Use the same method to analyze another speech in a classical play. Read the speech aloud to help in your analysis, letting your intuitive responses lead your analytical method as well as the reverse.

3. Listen to a good actor perform a speech and try to mark the structural elements of the speech based on what you have heard.

4. Try the same technique with a good recording of a trained classical actor. One excellent resource for this exercise is John Gielgud's *The Seven Ages of Man.*

MEMORIZATION

One thing is certain: the willingness and ability of actors to master lines early in the rehearsal process is essential. A good director knows that if lines are not mastered, he or she has failed to fulfill the editorial function of the job and, worse, has not gotten to the very heart of the work.

Missed and paraphrased lines are no more acceptable on opening night than on any other night. Besides not giving the audience its due, poor line memory discipline undermines the rehearsal process.

|| **The director must be ready to insist that lines are memorized convincingly by about halfway through the rehearsal period.** ||

If memory work is not done early, the essential work of exploration and shaping cannot take place. We have already discussed the advisability in many situations of setting deadlines in the rehearsal schedule for being "off-book" (Chapter X).

Since line memorization is an objective fact, it represents a threat to the actor's credibility. As a result, actors have developed a repertoire of rationales and explanations for any shortcomings. Most of these explanations have some basis in reality, but they cannot be allowed to interfere seriously with the basic requirement of the rehearsal period; that is, to have line memory out of the way early enough to permit the important work of the rehearsal to be done properly. The director can help. Encouraging actors to run lines offstage is a technique that most actors respond to very positively. Having someone available to listen to lines is also a proven tactic. In both cases, the director (and others) contribute to getting the job done.

On some occasions, actors come ready with defensive tactics to cover themselves if the memory process does not go well. Let us examine some of the explanations frequently advanced by actors for not learning lines on time:

1. *"I can't learn lines before the rehearsals begin."* Although this explanation has a good theoretical basis (it might establish bad phrasing or interpretations before the direction of the production is well defined), it has been invalidated as a technical fact countless times. If the intervening time between the casting and the start of rehearsals is adequate, there is no question that a company can begin rehearsals effectively "off-book." To forestall any objection, schedule preliminary rehearsal sessions or conferences to set the actors on the right track in general direction and interpretation. Useful and applicable in many educational theatres, this approach can be used successfully when casting and preliminaries are done when a vacation or other hiatus comes right before the regular rehearsals commence. This requirement is common in many stock theatres where a show must be rehearsed and mounted in a very short period of time.

2. *"I can't learn lines until the blocking is done so I can coordinate the words and the action."* This is a very popular refrain, again with the ring of conviction and inevitability. While we grant that complete reflexive control of the lines is possible only with the integration of the blocking, this objection most often means that the actor does not intend to do any work on memorizing the lines until the blocking period is completed. Again, actors can learn lines quite authoritatively before the blocking is even begun, and such preliminary effort can pay off handsomely. Blocking and business can be learned much more efficiently, after all, if the *lines* have already been brought under control. In any event, the rehearsal schedule should allow a reasonable time for memory work; this allows the actor adept enough at memorization to wait for the blocking. Still, the director must make it clear that the work of the production demands line memory be completed within certain reasonable time limits and that it is up to the actor to meet that expectation.

|| Why is there no record of an actor ever saying, "I can't learn my *blocking* until I get my *lines* memorized"? ||

3. *"I just can't learn this speech* (or *scene* or *act*)." This is usually a different matter from the first two examples. Often an actor will confront a single block of lines that cannot seem to be memorized. Time and effort have been expended, but the lines elude the actor when the time comes to rehearse. When this happens, it is almost invariably a symptom of a deeper problem. Usually it indicates that the actor does not understand the speech or scene. Help the actor by: a) clarifying the meaning of the speech; b) examining its structure; and, c) using mnemonic devices.

Meaning (the literal and the subtextual) and structure (or *architecture*) are usually the keys that will make the speech cohere and allow the actor to commit it to memory with unexpected ease. If these method fail, using mnemonic devices ("hooks" that hang one word or phrase on another) can often provide a technical solution. *Hooks* gain some effectiveness from their novelty or even outlandishness. Far from distracting from the meaning, structure, or intent of a speech, they can serve to relieve the actor of the anxiety of "going up" and permit a much more complete and focused concern with the dramatic action being played out. Let us examine another speech from *Richard III* (spoken in III, vi by a character known as "Scrivener") and suggest some hooks for the actor who is becoming more and more tense and insecure in his inability to get the words of the first few lines of his speech all in their proper order.

> [1]Here is the indictment of the good Lord Hastings,
> [2]Which in a set hand fairly is engrossed
> [3]That it may today be read o'er in Paul's.
> [4]And mark how well the sequel hangs together:
> [5]Eleven hours I have spent to write it over,
> [6]For yesternight by Catesby it were sent to me;
> [7]The precedent was full as long a-doing;
> [8]And yet within these five hours Hastings lived,
> [9]Untainted, unexamined, free, at liberty.

Line 1 comes out on cue, but confusion sets in at line 2 because of the unusual terms and word order. "Set hand," it might be explained, means an established mode of writing, an alphabet; "fairly" means "clearly"; and "engrossed" means "written." Thus, the line translates, "Which in a standard alphabet is written clearly." "Set-hand" hangs together and so does "fairly is engrossed." Line 3 needs only the identification of "Paul's" as St. Paul's Cathedral. Since the transition in line 4 is problematic for our actor, who has difficulty coming up with "mark" to introduce the next thought, we might suggest his teaming St. Paul in the previous line with St. Mark. The director could even ask the actor to visualize the two saints "hanging together" after explaining that "sequel" denotes "sequence." Lines 5 and 6 are no particular problem except for the thought transition that might be helped by connecting the sense of "eleven hours" ago with "yesternight." If the construction, "by Catesby was it sent to me" is problematic, it could be helped by treating "by Catesby" as an oath. The "precedent" in line 7 can be corrupted into "present" (a gift) and connected to the idea of it being sent in line 6. These are only possibilities; the only real requirement is that the image or "hook" is vivid enough to be retained. Seldom are more than one or two hooks needed for any speech, but their judicious use can overcome genuine obstacles for the actor trying to "get it right."

Respect for the playwright demands that the goal of every actor is to learn the lines verbatim. With some plays and playwrights, any variation from the text is more serious (and noticeable) than with others. While in the stages of committing the play to memory, a certain amount of paraphrasing is inevitable. If the paraphrases are succinct, it is a sign the actor understands the intent and meaning of the lines at least. However, special attention should be given to correct the actor by giving line notes so the lines are not memorized incorrectly.

COACHING ACTORS AND TEACHING ACTING

It should be remembered that, strictly speaking, the director is *not* teaching acting. Unlike the acting teacher, who is trying to instill a sense of the art and the process of acting, the director is attempting to elicit the performance of a specific character from an actor in a particular theatrical context. The distinction may be a fine one, because alert actors are always learning their craft especially in a creative rehearsal setting. Three things, however, make the distinction useful. One, actors may well resent the attitude of superiority, however subtle, that such a *director-teacher* may exude. Actors are collaborators, not subordinates, in the creative process of rehearsal. The director's job may often require the exercise of suggestion, evaluation, and leadership to assure the suitability and complete integration of the actor's performance; but once cast, the actor's principal task is to *act,* just as the designer's task is to *design,* and the director's is to *direct.* Two, if the director undertakes to become a teacher during the rehearsal process, he or she loses some of the concentration and focus that director-work requires all by itself. Therefore, it is best to keep to the job of directing—that is already complex enough—and let whatever teaching function the job might entail happen as it might without conscious effort or resolve. Third, the actor who becomes a *student* in a rehearsal period is surrendering actor's responsibility to contribute creatively to the work of the production.

|| **At its best, the directorial function should seem effortless** ||
|| **and unintrusive—*direction by indirection.*** ||

The director should not be perceived as doing or inhibiting the actor's work, but rather seen as providing the conditions in which the actors can do their best. Direction should inspire a sense of positive collaboration. The ideal process results in an effective and coherent production in which all involved are convinced that the work came together from their combined efforts seemingly of its own accord.

ROUTINE AND THE DIRECTOR-ACTOR RELATIONSHIP

For the most part, theatre routine provides structures that make it possible to work productively and efficiently. There is the routine of the rehearsal period that we have already discussed, and there is the routine of rehearsing and performing that opens the door to imagination and creativity. For the actor, this kind of routine can be very reassuring; it provides a sense of stability and security that (paradoxically) promotes freedom and experimentation. In this sense, *theatre routine* is actually *professional discipline*. There is one level of that routine that may be called "performance discipline." Every production establishes parameters to keep each performance (and each performer) honest. These limits will vary widely from company to company and production to production. Take any two companies—say, the Circle-in-the-Square and the Performing Garage, both in New York City—and you may infer two radically different sets of standards. Even the same company will relax or tighten the limits depending on whether they are doing *The Good Woman of Setzchuan* or *Fool for Love*.

These guidelines usually evolve as rehearsals enter the final phases before opening. The actors and the stage manager (who oversees the company's performance discipline) must know how much freedom is allowed in changing the performance. Can the actors change timing, business, blocking, characterization, costume, lines? However the lines are drawn, there should always be *some* room for modulation and growth, for keeping the performance a vital and responsive creation. The natural evolution of a show in performance is a sign of its continuing viability and indicates the responsiveness and vitality of the performers. Deliberate alterations are another matter altogether. A conscious change in any aspect of the production that approaches the established boundaries of performance discipline should always be cleared through the director, if available, or the stage manager.

Peter Brook relates a charming story of Alfred Lunt, one of the most disciplined and creative actors of the American theatre early in this century. The actor had introduced in rehearsals a bit of business. He would take off a shoe, look for some irritant, rub his foot, and then replace the shoe. Brook reports that while on tour in Boston, Lunt asked him into the dressing room to show the director two small pebbles that he proposed to shake out of his shoe to add a fresh sense of truth and immediacy to the moment. When Brook encouraged him, the actor "looked delightedly at the two little stones, back at me, then suddenly his expression changed. He studied the stones again for a long anxious moment. 'You don't think it would be better with one?' " (*The Empty Space,* p. 105)

Even within the most restrictive of performance limits, the truly creative actor will find possibilities and inspiration. The director should never be afraid of the production "peaking too soon." That is only an excuse for a limited imagination.

End Note

A Cautionary Tale: In a theatre rehearsal scene in the movie *Tootsie,* an argument erupts between the director and the actor played by Dustin Hoffman. The director wants the character to move during a speech to accommodate audience sightlines. The actor perceives no way to justify a dying man making such a cross. Neither the actor nor the director will acknowledge the possibility of compromise. The rehearsal—and presumably the production—ends bitterly.

The comedy of this cynical little scene comes from the fact that the conflict is completely unwarranted. The director should know the actor's need is honest; the actor should know the director's request is reasonable. Both should know the solution lies in simple *collaboration*—the essential element of the director-actor relationship.

Every play and every performer poses specific problems and suggests specific techniques. Every production must be approached not theoretically but organically and specifically, and with as clear a perception of its problems as possible. Including the problem of rehearsal time.

—**Alan Schneider,** *Entrances*

12 SPECIAL STRATEGIES FOR STAGING

Using Arena and Thrust Stages

As noted in Chapter VII, arena (or "theatre-in-the-round") and thrust ("three-quarter staging") stages offer the director accustomed to a proscenium stage the opportunity to create a number of significant variations in tone, effect, and statement. One of the most attractive features of these stage forms, especially the arena, is their *intimacy*. This quality does not come from *proximity*, however. Most arena and thrust theatres retain a sense of intimacy although they are large and some seats are farther from the playing area than in many proscenium houses. The unique intimate feeling in these houses comes from essential three-dimensionality of the staging forms. Because the arena stage is viewed from virtually every angle, it offers an enhanced dimension of *depth*. As a result, every audience member senses the perspective of the other viewers and intuitively understands that the play is projecting outward in every direction, not

274

just one. This awareness alone gives arena audiences a greater feeling of community—of sharing the theatrical experience. In arena staging, the audience envelopes the action. From the thrust stage, the action invades or penetrates the audience space. In neither thrust nor arena is there the sense of formal separation that often characterizes the proscenium stage. The director, therefore, must be keenly aware of these phenomena and prepared to use them creatively.

The three-dimensional form of the thrust stage demands dynamic visual and kinetic compositions
Play: *Twelfth Night* **Author:** William Shakespeare **Theatre:** Alabama Shakespeare **Director:** Martin Platt
Set Designer: Rob Wolin **Lighting:** Karen S. Spahn (Photo by Scarsbrook)

THE MATRIX FOR ARENA OR THRUST STAGE PRODUCTION

The director must consider the qualities of depth and intimacy while evolving the matrix for an arena or a thrust stage production. Begin by visualizing the play in intimate and spatial terms, that is, a sense of the connection between the audience and the play sharing the space. The audience itself defines the production's length, breadth, and depth, and becomes a participant in it. Stay alert to this visualization while searching the play's text and context for provocative images. Be alert for any matrices that potentially complement or emphasize these intimate, personal qualities, and their possibilities for moving in three-dimensional space.

Theatrical Associations—Consider those periods and styles that convention- ally use non-proscenium theatres, especially styles in which the audience sur- rounds the performance, as with almost all European threatre before 1600, and some afterward. Look also for those modes that have an intensely *personal* per- spective; *expressionism* and many forms of *cinema* are useful examples.

Other Arts—Because arena and thrust staging are three-dimensional and fluid, you should give special attention to the arts that employ these qualities. *Sculpture* and *architecture* can be called on to enhance your sense of plasticity and spatial volume, and *choreography* to add kinetic form and fluidity to your staging statement.

Psychology, Rituals, and Games—Psychology is extremely useful because it personalizes action and emphasizes both the individual's emotional perspective and the relationship of characters. Some psychological theories employ images of territoriality or animal behavior—useful on any stage configuration, and es- pecially apt in the space-sensitive arena stage. Many of the available psychologi- cal models employ role-playing structures; these the director can translate from *psychological* into *theatrical* forms.

Many powerful rituals evolved historically in arena and thrust stage forms. Furthermore, since rituals usually denote a commonality of purpose and intent, the director can turn to ritual models to enhance the quality of *community* we observe in audiences at arena and thrust productions.

The resourceful director will note that some game images are more useful than others when contemplating a matrix for arena and thrust staging. Gener- ally, games that have distinctly three-dimensional movement patterns (for exam- ple, hockey and chess) and images of shifting dominance and subordination (for example, wrestling) are especially useful and provocative.

THEATRICAL ENVIRONMENT FOR ARENA AND THRUST

In creating a theatrical environment for either arena or thrust, the director must always consider the particular configuration of the stage. (Begin with the Set Design Checklist detailed in Chapter VII.) Because so little space is available for scenery of any sort, the scenic elements chosen must be especially effective. Definition of stage areas can be achieved by platforms, by indications on the floor (using rugs, for example), and by lights. Since there is little room for floor- standing vertical scenery, the treatment of the floor becomes extremely impor- tant. Obviously, a model is much more informative than a sketch or rendering when developing and communicating the design. Skilled designers and directors will include part of the audience seating in the model to help envision sightline problems with scenery, furniture, or actor placement. If the playing area is raised and the audience close to the action, furniture or other setpieces placed on or near the periphery cannot be very high. This sometimes means that tables and chairs and sofas with backs must be placed close to the middle of the space. In such cases, the director and designer must create a room or environment where such furniture placement is plausible and aesthetically pleasing.

BLOCKING FOR NON-PROSCENIUM STAGES

It is an obvious mistake to think of a thrust stage or a theatre-in-the-round as a proscenium stage viewed from different angles simultaneously. Yet, many directors proceed in exactly this way.

|| **It is far better to approach the direction of a play on a proscenium stage as if *it* were an arena than to do the reverse.** ||

The director is often tempted to approach a thrust as an exceptionally deep proscenium stage and an arena as a proscenium without an arch. These views not only invite a reflexive two-dimensionality, but also lead to the loss of marvelous spatial possibilities. Indeed, perhaps because it is typically a platform stage, the thrust is the most sculptural of all the stage forms. Actors move from the high relief of the scenic elements, emerging onto a platform and into the open space of three dimensions. The director who sits, literally and figuratively, directly in front of a thrust stage with little or no sense of the sculptural qualities of the space does the work injury and insult. The director should instead explore and celebrate the possibilities of this noble form as well as its potential to give a unique life to a great variety of plays.

H I N T : Remember: an audience member in an arena or a thrust stage performance *senses* what other members of the audience are seeing.

At the outset, the director must reject the notion that blocking is either impossible or irrelevant on a non-proscenium stage. It must be realized, however, that the kinetic and compositional principles *essentially* and *incidentally* differ from one form to the other.

In blocking action on arena or thrust stages, the director must move around the stage area. If the blocking is done in the theatre itself rather than in a rehearsal room, the director should take advantage of the opportunity by moving all about the audience space to get a sense of the visual and kinetic effect of the staging from different locations. Because many theatres of these types have steeply raked seating, many in the audience will have the feeling of looking *down* on the stage. The director must be aware of this perspective when blocking the show. As you become more sensitive to the space, you might find it possible—

Arena staging joins the audience and the actors in a communal relationship focused on the dramatic action.
Play: Inherit the Wind   **Authors:** Jerome Lawrence and Robert E. Lee   **Theatre:** Indiana Repertory Theatre
Director: Tom Haas (Photo by Tod Martens)

as some skilled directors do—to project yourself into different parts of the auditorium to view the action of the production from different perspectives without physically moving. Even then, you must move from one location to another to keep the actors alert to the audience's different perspectives.

Blocking for an Arena   The director encountering an arena stage for the first time confronts the immediate problem of *stage geography*. How do you give and record blocking when there is no proscenium arch and *two* centerlines? The director may use any system that seems efficient. There are many specialized ways to designate the stage areas. Two approaches to blocking vocabulary use the metaphor of the arena stage as "theatre-in-the-*round*": one suggests a clock face (directions given as "towards 12 o'clock," "towards 4:30," and so on); another uses compass points ("southwest," "north," and so on). These, like most other specialized techniques, tend to disorient most experienced actors (and stage managers). Even posting signs with the hours (or compass points) can confuse the company. In addition, such systems identify directions in which to move and not where to *stop*. Although it has serious theoretical flaws when applied to arena and thrust, standard proscenium stage nomenclature is probably the most comprehensible and efficient of all. It is true that an arena has no left or right, up or down, but the terminology is a serviceable fiction in recording blocking. The stage manager or prompter will instinctively sit somewhere along the line of view from the control booth. Designating that side of the playing area as downstage inevitably clarifies matters for everyone. There might be some disorientation still, but it is usually minor and short-lived.

If the stage has a number of set-pieces or other physical markings, it is possible, instead, to direct movement and place in relation to those markers ("towards the sofa," "away from the table," and so on). There are no rules, and there is no consensus. The director is free to communicate blocking by any available means.

Each stage configuration demands a unique movement pattern. As noted, the proscenium stage describes triangular patterns; the arena requires circling movement around an "X" pattern from corner to corner. For this reason stage center (also the center of the X) is the strongest stage position; it is the intersection of all lines of movement and visual focus. The ends of the X, marking the corners of the playing area, are the equivalent of the upstage areas on the proscenium stage—the weakest positions on the stage floor. Since these corners usually lead directly to aisles through the audience, these areas allow an actor to stand for some time without blocking audience sightlines.

Actors standing in front of people in the first few audience rows need not be a problem in an arena; audience members accept this as part of the production contract. Someone who sits in the front row a few feet (sometimes inches) away from the playing area expects some moments of obstructed vision. The director and the actors must be aware, however, that this tolerance is finite and must be carefully monitored. There are no absolutes, but ten to twelve seconds is about the maximum a viewer will accept without distress; if something crucial is happening that other audience members are responding to, the tolerance drops close to zero. Actors experienced in arena and thrust staging sense an audience member's discomfort and make adjustments accordingly. The director can alert actors to any situation that might be a problem, and instruct the actors to adjust accordingly. If the playing area is close to the audience, a small physical adjustment—perhaps even a simple shift of weight from one foot to the other—will accomplish the task. The farther away the audience is from the actor, the bigger the adjustment needed. As with any action on stage, these movements must be motivated; they must be in response to something going on. The director can put this requirement to good use—checking to see that the actors in the scene are alert and responsive. The director can also use the need to adjust for sightlines as a means to focus the actors' attention and to energize the scene.

How does an actor reveal a crucial prop to the entire audience? By using a technique similar to the one just described for opening sightlines. Suppose the actor must draw an important letter from his jacket pocket. On the proscenium stage, of course, only the view from the front usually needs attention. The actor moves downstage and takes out the letter with the upstage hand. On the arena stage, however, the actor and director confront several good choices: 1) the actor stands at a corner, facing C; 2) the actor stands C and holds the letter over his head (if such a gesture is appropriate); 3) the actor takes the letter out and makes a quarter to a half turn in response to someone or something in the scene; or, 4) facing one of the corners, the action moves the letter from one hand to the other, thus allowing the audience behind him to his left or right to see the important prop in quick succession. There are countless other possiblities, of course.

Such examples underscore ways that working in the arena (or thrust) can refresh and enhance a director's technique and imagination. The actor and director given the envelope to reveal on a familiar proscenium stage would probably choose something like the proscenium solution suggested above. On an arena stage, the director and actor are virtually *forced* to make the moment more specific.

> ‖ **Every challenge in creating a production should be treated as** ‖
> ‖ **an opportunity, not a limitation.** ‖

The relative two-dimensionality of the proscenium stage allows the director to establish relationships of one actor to another and to the environment through stage positions and body positions *relative to the audience viewing from the front*. On non-proscenium stages, this capability is gone. Up and down stage, left and right, have no such significance in a theatre-in-the-round. Remember, the audience is actually *seeing* things differently. For emphasis and control of focus, the arena director must rely more on *movement* and body positions *relative to one another and to the stage environment*. Actors must be always conscious of their relative positions, every one of which should be motivated and meaningful.

> ‖ **Arena directors learn to watch carefully and to keep their ac-** ‖
> ‖ **tors alert.** ‖

Directors working in arena stages also learn that vertical relationships assume a special importance. Sitting, standing, kneeling, using platforms and ramps: all of these are potent tools for blocking an arena production.

Coaching the Actors in an Arena—Arena production can be challenging and exciting for actors for a number of reasons. One that a good director will stress in different ways throughout the rehearsal period is the need to be *alive* in the performance at all times. This must be so, *not* because the audience is close, but because the sculptural and choreographic quality of a performance in the space means *there is no place to hide*. Some actors develop the bad habit on the proscenium stage of relaxing concentration and participation in moments when someone else has focus. The arena dictates that even subordinate characters in a scene are scrutinized for their reactions by those members of the audience who, momentarily, have no clear view of the principals. No matter what the role or function in a scene, the actor must be convinced that his or her character is the one everybody is watching. That awareness alone should stimulate the performance teamwork we characterize as *ensemble*. It is also a valuable lesson to apply to *all* productions—especially on a proscenium stage.

Blocking for a Thrust Stage—The practical problem of stage geography nomenclature is not an issue in thrust as it is in arena staging. The scenic wall that anchors the thrust platform correlates to the upstage wall of the proscenium stage so clearly that the vocabulary of proscenium geography serves easily and naturally for the thrust. The instinctive movement patterns sometimes echo those of both the proscenium and the arena. The dominant movement pattern on the thrust, however, is an "H" with a moveable crossbar.

Many thrust stages have aisles or tunnels for actor entrances and exits ("*vomitoria*"—from Roman theatre architecture terminology—or "voms") leading off the DR and DL extremes of the playing platform.[1] These stage positions offer the same possibilities as the corners of the arena discussed above. For this type of thrust stage, the dominant stage positions are along the centerline of the platform; the weakest positions are the ends of the legs of the H.

Principles of relative body positions and the importance of vertical composition noted for an arena apply as well to the thrust. Again, the director must guard against using the thrust as if it were a proscenium. Some directors play most of the important scenes close to the upstage wall. Many actors also find this a comfortable place to be because their instincts have been shaped on prosceniums stages, and walking out on that platform makes them feel exposed.

The creative director working on a thrust stage makes bold and courageous choices. Subtlety and implication are certainly possible, but they must be framed decisively. Even as nostalgic and poetic piece as *The Glass Menagerie* can work beautifully on a thrust stage; the characters and the atmosphere can be presented in the high-relief the stage permits. In presenting the production contract, the director should consider boldly establishing theatrical space by moving the action out on the platform at the outset.

> Thrust staging demands that the director establish a strong
> territoriality by using the space boldly. The arena requires
> concentration and specificity; the thrust mandates *authority*.

Coaching the Actors on a Thrust—The thrust stage is *aggressive*, even when it is used for light romantic or comic pieces. Its very shape *invades* the audience space. The name itself is assertive: *thrust*. Even the "H" movement pattern is strong—long straight lines and right angles. In no other form must the actor

---

[1]In some theatres, the voms are used also by the audience.

and director so clearly command the space and the theatrical event. This is not a stage for the timid artist. The director should begin by stressing the importance of the actor's presence and confidence. Some actors—both new-comer and veteran—find it difficult to stand out there on that platform, but the director must encourage them to "take the stage."

The director can begin the rehearsals on stage by having each actor walk out on the platform as if it belonged to them alone. Posture and body language must support each actor's assertion. Voice projection must also be clear and well-supported. Not every character is dominant, of course; but whatever the required characterization, it must be strong. No wonder the thrust stage is so adaptable to classic plays!

Encourage the actors to exploit these demands of the form. Look for clear acting choices supported by unambiguous execution.

Problem Scenes

Some types of scenes appear time and again, and each time they seem problematic. Often, a particular attitude or perspective is helpful when confronting the problem and, occasionally, some fundamental strategies require special emphasis when working through the difficulty.

> In every case, keep in mind the *meaning* and *purpose* of a scene; do not treat a technically challenging scene as one that must be outwitted or subverted.

THE ENTRANCE

Entrances should have conviction, effectiveness, and immediacy. Too often, though, they are awkward and seem to have no clear starting point. Entrances are seldom given the care and consideration they are due. Any entrance, because it introduces a new French scene, is a *marker*. It is the moment of transition between one set of given circumstances—whatever has preceded the entrance offstage—and those of the scene onstage. Let us look at the first entrance of Judge Brack in Act One of Ibsen's *Hedda Gabler* (Trans. Geir Jensen). Here is what the text provides:

> *. . . THE JUDGE is a gentleman forty-five years old. He is thickset, but well-proportioned, with flexible movements. Roundish face, noble profile, hair cut short, still almost black and meticulously done. He is dressed in an elegant walking suit, though a bit too youthful for his age. He wears pince-nez [glasses] attached to a string, which he sometimes lets drop.*
>
> JUDGE BRACK *(hat in hand, greets):* May one dare visit you so early in the day?
> HEDDA: One certainly may.

At the moment in the performance when the actor portraying Judge Brack first walks through the door, we as audience begin to receive countless impressions about him that inevitably color our later perceptions. We notice his reaction upon finding Hedda not in the drawing-room ready to greet him alone, but instead in the company of her husband and a woman the judge does not recognize. We notice several things: that he twirls the pince-nez a few times before deftly depositing it into his vest pocket; the friendly formality with which he acknowledges Tesman, Hedda's husband; his manner of kissing Hedda's hand; and the way his own and Hedda's expressions play off each other—so proper and mischievous at the same time.

The first entrance in the play, or the first entrance of any character in the play, must do more than establish a beginning point for the scene, it must begin to define the character as well. The actor playing this scene has not only established clues as to character and relationships within the first few moments following his entrance, he has done so by projecting a set of actions that precedes his entrance and gives the moment a particular quality. As Brack enters the room, he does not expect to find the others there. When he adjusts to this new reality, there is a shift in his manner, which Hedda notices. She is quite subtly but completely amused at seeing him put off his guard, if only for an instant, and he is aware of her reaction. This scene begins as a little game involving four people, but with only two players even aware that a game is going on.

Every entrance, then, has a basic structure containing three elements:

1. *The state of the character entering*—This is the result of offstage physical actions, internal states, and the character's expectations upon coming into the new environment.
2. *The moment of transition*—The character changes from one state to another.
3. *The character's new state*—This marks the adjustment of consciousness to the newly encountered conditions. This may be as simple as a physiological adjustment to different lighting or temperature or as radical as a complete reversal of urgent expectations—a great surprise calling for a complete reordering of behavior and priorities.

The "big entrance" is still with us. We treasure it in large scale productions like elaborate musicals, operas, farces, and suspense plays and other melodramas. Even in the staging of small scale serious dramas, however, we can find much to learn from the manner used by actors in earlier periods to make effective entrances.

Well into the twentieth century, an actor making an important entrance would take a step or two on stage, pause, and then complete the entrance onto the stage and begin speaking. The pause was critical. It gave the other actors onstage the cue to shift focus, and the audience the chance to identify the new personality on stage. (It also gave the chance to register appreciation for the actor with the desired entrance applause.) The structure of this sort of entrance is basically sound, although the mechanics and the motivation for making it have certainly changed. Whenever an entrance lacks theatrical or psychological effectiveness or credibility, imaginative attention to its three elements will usually show the way to improve it.

DISCUSSION _____

1. Suppose it was decided that Brack *knows* the other people will be in the room when he enters. What differences might this make when he does enter?

2. What does Brack's bit of business, twirling his pince-nez eyeglasses, tell us about his evaluation of the scene, his personality, or his sense of communication with Hedda?

3. Suppose the director suggests to the costume designer and to the actor that Judge Brack is wearing a new cravat or stickpin that he intends to show off to Hedda. How might this affect his entrance?

4. Suggest a different prop or costume element that would help the actor establish some quality or attitude as he makes his entrance.

EXERCISES _____

Try these entrances using a classroom or other meeting place. Each exercise should be very brief, lasting only long enough for the actual structure of the entrance to be completed. The exercises themselves should not involve talking. Discuss each briefly beforehand, concentrating on the elements of the entrance, particularly the moment of transition or adjustment. Ask one person to enter, using the actual given circumstances of the occasion, except as qualified in each of the following:

1. You are late after a serious warning not to be late again

   a. by 5 minutes;

   b. by 30 seconds;

   c. by 20 minutes.

2. As you enter, you discover

   a. this is the wrong place;

   b. the person you wanted to see is not here;

   c. someone you had hoped to avoid is here.

3. Moments before you enter, you discovered

    a. you have been given a new car;

    b. a loved one has a serious disease;

    c. you failed the last exam.

4. In the hour before you enter, you have

    a. broken up with someone important to you;

    b. been caught unprepared in miserable, rainy weather;

    c. been in aching physical discomfort.

5. The given circumstances are changed to a familiar private or semi-private setting. There is only one person in the room, and that person is

    a. unexpectedly remote—even hostile;

    b. someone who ordinarily would not be there;

    c. someone from whom you are trying to hide the purpose of your being there. (You must define that purpose or objective before you enter.)

THE STATIC SCENE

This scene is the bane of many directors, who cry "We have to get some movement in it, or it won't be interesting." Staging is often forced and obvious: crossing to the bar to mix a drink, crossing to the window to gaze out, or simply crossing up and back and back again. All this usually accomplishes is convincing the audience that nothing truthful is really happening in the scene. The static scene often functions structurally as exposition, giving the audience information it must have; but just as often, such scenes make important and moving revelations of character. In either case, the scenes function dramatically and should be staged truthfully, not as moments which need meaningless "business."

Assumptions

1. There is nothing inherently uninteresting about characters remaining seated throughout an extended scene, and there is nothing inherently fascinating about someone walking around during a scene.

2. Any movement (including physical movement) must be motivated. (See Chapters 6 and 10.)

A well-acted and well-directed scene will have life and energy even though the characters' movement is restricted.

Play: *A Life in the Theatre* **Author:** David Mamet **Theatre:** TheatreVirginia **Director:** Terry Burgler **Set Designer:** Charles Caldwell **Costumes:** Catherine Szari **Lighting:** Terry Cermak **Actors (l to r):** Ronald Hunter, Michael Lasswell (Photo by Virginia Museum Photography)

A Strategy

Stanislavski speaks of a "Circle of Concentration" in the art of acting—the physical limits of the actor's (character's) consciousness. The circle expands and contracts as attention focuses in on something and then is drawn outward to include something else. It is possible also to think of the *audience's* circle of concentration or of the director's control of a *focus of attention*.

In countless plays, two characters sit side by side or facing each other across a table and have a conversation. *Something* must be happening if the scene is dramatic, and yet no physical movement is required by the text. The actors and the director panic. The scene is dull, lifeless; nothing is happening! All efforts to create a believable cross to change the stage picture look like what they are: arbitrary, unconvincing, perhaps even desperate.

What to do? First and most important, the director must trust the scene. There *is* inherent dramatic action. Second, the director must find the potential theatrical movement in the scene. It *is* there, if for no other reason than the characters are alive and attempting to communicate.

The problem in this sort of scene is not a matter of "something or nothing," but rather a question of *scale*. Let us employ an image to deal with the problem. Suppose that instead of directing for the theatre, you are working with a movie or video camera. The scene will not work in a long shot, only in medium shots or extreme close-ups. You must zoom in so the size of the frame covers only 6 to 8 feet around the actors instead of the 25 to 40 feet defined by the proscenium arch. In staging the scene, this smaller frame defines *your* circle of concentration, *your* focus of attention. If everything happens within that frame, the surroundings disappear. You will have reduced the *scale* of the action to an appropriate size; and what were once perceived as small and inconsequential actions in the large frame will take on an appropriate magnitude and importance in the small one. When one character leans in across the table, she will have made a move halfway across the stage. When the other character turns his head slightly away, the gesture is dynamic and important. Now you may "block" the scene within this tiny proscenium opening with the same care and attention that you lavish on the physically large scenes, realizing that much of the "offstage" area is invisible to the audience if nothing attracts attention to it.

EXERCISES

1. Choose a scene in which two characters are seated throughout (perhaps the scene from *Our Town* between George and Emily at the soda fountain, or between Mrs. Webb and Mrs. Gibbs when stringing beans). Block the scene with the image of the close-up in mind.

2. Refine your staging by thinking in terms of opening up and closing down the frame, using timing, the physical positions of the actors, and their visual attention to control the audience's focus. Move from a medium shot (the two characters) to a long shot (including more than half the actual stage area) to a tight shot (one glass or a single bean, for example) and then back again. You might wish to "storyboard" this scene.

3. Take a piece of black card stock or stiff paper and cut an opening about 2" × 5". (See Figure 12–5.) Look through the opening without moving the viewing angle or distance and frame the scene as you wish to control it. Watch the effect this scaling down has on the relative size and strength of the blocking within the frame. Adjust the action of the scene if this new clearer perspective demands it. (As your experience expands, you will find yourself adjusting scale intuitively. Until then the framing device is an excellent aid.)

4. Observe the scene once again with the framing device, this time moving it in and out to frame the circle of attention demanded by your staging. Done attentively, this will indicate the effectiveness of your control of the scene.

THE PHYSICAL ACTION SCENE

If the "static" scene presents problems for the director because nothing seems to be happening, the "physical action" scene creates difficulties because *too much* seems to be going on. A physical action scene is, by definition, one in which a great deal of movement—usually complicated—is demanded by the text or the directorial matrix. Commonly, such scenes involve physical violence or farcical action.

Assumptions

1. There is nothing *inherently* exciting, effective, or dramatic about a great deal of frantic action.
2. Any movement (including *all* physical movement) must be motivated. (See Chapters 2 and 10.)
3. Any action must be *clear* to be effective as a dramatic element.

A Strategy

Simplify the action by breaking it down into its components. An outline for approaching this task can be found in Chapter 10, Chart 4, "Structure of Action." As noted, actions on stage (emotional 'beats' as well as physical actions) can be clarified and focused by counting the actor(s) through the following sequence:

- Setup,
- Execution,
- Follow-through.

Many violent actions can be staged effectively by extending or amplifying the *setup* and *follow-through* and concealing or camouflaging the actual *execution*. This technique is especially useful if the scene calls for an actor to be struck forcibly. In staging and rehearsing any stage action that is even remotely dangerous to a participant, special care must be taken in establishing and observing each step in the process. As further insurance, two tactics are useful:

1. Perform the action in extreme slow motion while talking through each step in turn. Gradually increase the tempo. Such routines should be rehearsed at every opportunity during the rehearsal period and before each performance.

‖ **It is impossible to over-rehearse a violent piece of staging or complicated business.** ‖

2. To control position when someone must be precisely positioned at the end of an action—especially when there must be a throw or fall—run the routine *in reverse* the first few times. This will help ensure that the steps in the process are clear and precise. The actor falling or being thrown about must be allowed to provide the motive force. (In this way, the actor is not at the mercy of another person's physical impetus, which may change radically in the tension and nervousness of a performance.)

H I N T : *The ability to perform complex physical actions in reverse or in slow motion ensures that the action is under the control of the participants.*

If many different actions must happen concurrently, structure each action independently, rehearse each one, and then begin the last step of putting the various actions together to make the complex action. If there is a battle scene to be staged, for example, begin by working with each individual set of combatants. Rehearse each fight independently; assign a geographical setting and a clearly established sequence for each (that is, define the space and time for each element). Finally, put the pieces together, adjusting as necessary. Of course, the focus of the final scene must be controlled. Again, it can help to use the framing device and keep in mind the camera metaphor.

THE CROWD SCENE

Like the physical action scene, the crowd scene seems to have too much movement to deal with. The staging challenges—and their solutions—are similar.

Assumptions

The crowd scene must have an underlying *image* that suggests structural simplicity, and a clarity enriched by the modulations made possible by the number of characters populating the stage. (For a vivid example, see Robert Lewis's anecdote in *Method or Madness,* 124–26.)

A Strategy

Again, the best approach is to divide the task into discrete units and move through the process one step at a time.

First, decide on an image for the scene. Is it to be the opening of a floodgate, an explosion, a race, or gathering clouds? This decision will define the *quality* of the scene and suggest visual, aural, and kinetic forms.

Next, divide the characters into groups based on their dramatic intentions or functions. Then, assign each group or sub-group an appropriate action and stage area(s). After the individual groups are set and rehearsed, assemble them and coordinate their actions. It is, of course, likely that some individuals or small groups will break off or merge with others, and this fact must be reflected in the initial setups.

Finally, after the group dynamics are established, attention can be turned to refining the group responses and punctuating them with actions of individuals.

THE ATMOSPHERIC SCENE

Strictly speaking, every scene is "atmospheric," but here we define it as a scene in which the atmosphere is *active*—usually mysterious, frightening, romantic, or poetic.

Assumptions

Theatrical atmosphere is defined by the sense elements of the scene: the quality of the form and color, the light, the sound, and the timing. All of these, of course, are abetted and amplified by the sensitivity of the actors in the scene to these qualities.

A Strategy

The director must have strong sense images to stage this type of scene. Heavy atmosphere is the result of things suspected and unspecified: moving shadows, unexplained sounds, patterns of light and dark, slow rhythms, sudden noises, distant sounds. All of these can contribute to the sense of "something out there." Lowering clouds, thunder and lightning are classic elements, because they provide all the sensory ingredients. On the other hand, a light, pleasant atmosphere shows everything; nothing is hidden or suspected. It is a spring day: the colors are vivid; the light is bright; the rhythms are vivacious.

The director must define the environment fully and look for ways to create and justify the atmospheric elements of the scene. Most important is having all the designers—set, costumes, light, sound, and properties—attuned to the atmospheric image you are trying to create. Prevailing atmosphere is a fabric made of many threads.

Chapter V provides some helpful guidance in the discussion of "Other Art Forms." With ideas based upon specific music or sound patterns or on visual images from design or painting (the Impressionists are especially instructive), you can then isolate the sense elements by "seeing with your ears and hearing with your eyes" (as discussed in Chapter 10).

For a definitive example of theatrical atmosphere, read Maeterlinck's short play *The Intruder* and be prepared to discuss the playwright's manipulation of the atmospheric elements in the play.

A QUESTION OF "STYLE"

Generally, "style" can be understood as the *manner* or *fashion* of presentation in the theatre. We ordinarily speak of two types of "styles"; *theatrical*—which comes from a particular view of the theate and the nature of theatrical creation—and *period*—in which the fashion of the day is translated into the theatrical fabric of the production. In the first, we speak of "Naturalism," "Expressionism," and "Symbolism"; in the other, of "Restoration," "Nineteenth Century," and "Elizabethan."

Assumptions

Style is the expression of a specific view of the world or art.

Without sympathy for and understanding of the view that provokes it, style is an empty, spurious thing—mere artifice without depth or significance.

The best expression of style in the theatre comes naturally and inevitably out of the created world of the production.

|| **Style is not imposed arbitrarily or superficially; it is organic and affects the total work profoundly.** ||

A Strategy

To create an organic, integrated style, the director must define the specific world in which the play takes place. Harold Clurman says, "To sum up: A particular rather than a generic style is what the director must achieve for each play. Generic styles only befit academe." (*On Directing*, p. 38) A production of *The Way of the World* with the dressings of the Restoration Period—the extravagant silks, the cosmetics and wigs, the fans, handkerchiefs, bows, and precious mincing manners—means nothing if the director fails to connect these elements to the world created within the production. The same may be said for a production of the same play performed in jeans and motorcycle gear.

Play: Twelfth Night **Author:** William Shakespeare **Theatre:** Alabama Shakespeare Festival **Director:** Martin Platt **Set Designer:** Stephen Found **Lighting:** Karen S. Spahn **Actors (l to r):** Stuart Weems, Jim Helsinger, Tad Ingram, Dennis McLernon (Photo by Scarsbrook)

Play: Tales of the Lost Formicans **Author:** Constance Congdon **Theatre:** Actors Theatre of Louisville **Director:** Roberta Levitow **Set Designer:** Paul Owen **Costumes:** Lewis D. Rampino **Lighting:** Ralph Dressler **Actors (l to r):** Edward Seamon, Jonathan Fried (Photo by Richard Trigg)

Play: JEKYLL! **Author:** James Costin **Theatre:** Missouri Repertory Theatre **Director:** George Keathley **Set Designer:** John Ezell **Costumes:** Vincent Scassellati **Lighting:** John Appelt **Actors (l to r):** Alan Brasington, Edward Conery (Photo by Larry Pape)

Every production's *style* should seem confident and inevitable. As these scenes imply, true style goes beyond conventional period elements and theatrical fashions.

> Neither stylistic orthodoxy nor audacity guarantees or invalidates a production. Either can be honest and effective—if the connections between the play and its *style* are honest and clear.

As we have seen, the world in which a play was written and the style in which it was first produced are not incidental factors. They represent powerful clues to the significance of a work, and to a myriad of other qualities implicit in it. A director who does not have a firm grasp of the original period and theatrical style of a Restoration Comedy is approaching the play with an unnecessary and unwarranted handicap. The honest director must find out, as fully and accurately as possible, *what* style affected the playwright's sensibility, and *how* the expression of that style influenced the communication of the sense of the play.

Clearly then, the directorial matrix must be profoundly connected to style. This does not mean that a matrix conceived and energized by a contemporary sensibility must be expressed in an overtly contemporary style. To the contrary, the expression of a contemporary vision in terms of a period statement is, in fact, a superb artistic goal. Done with vision and skill, such an achievement shows us the possibility of kinship and communication of artists across the centuries.

"Some styles just seem silly." Absolutely true. The mode of the nineteenth-century Romantic theatre strikes some as crude caricature. But we can be assured that the great actors and the audiences of the period would not have agreed, and how childishly touching might they have found the feeble, unconvincing efforts at the realistic *style* of our modern dramas.

"Some plays are just not believable. There's nothing to do but make fun of them." Putting genuinely poor plays to one side, we are more likely to find that the fault is not in the plays, but in our grasp of them. It is obviously our limited perspective that makes us reject Euripides' *Medea* or Racine's *Phedre* as artificial, arbitrary, and unconvincing, while letting us accept completely arbitrary, conventional devices in *A Chorus Line* or *The Glass Menagerie*.

> *Every* play is an exercise in style.

To some degree, every style is unique to the production it expresses. To master the challenge of "style," the director must comprehend the intellectual, social, and theatrical climate in which the playwright worked as well as the world in which the play is now being interpreted. Moreover, the director must master the inner life of the work being produced, must create a world in which the production style is not *laid on* but rather *grows out* of that life and that world.

Enriching the Staging: Patterns and Motifs

In directing any play, you are making forms you hope will communicate effectively the sense or feeling you have about it. You organize the material in a certain way to suggest relationships, rhythms, atmosphere, environment. *Patterns* and *motifs* in staging are primary instruments of the director's organization and communication.

Patterns and motifs are both designs composed of various elements. A pattern is a design structure made up of motifs repeated, reversed, or modulated in some way. A motif is an image that may exist in isolation or as a component of a pattern. A geometric wallpaper is a simple example. The pattern is the overall visual structure; a motif is the geometric shape that recurs throughout the pattern. In a director's hands, a pattern might be made up of an object or prop that appears in scene after scene. For example, in the Guthrie Theatre's 1980 production of *Arms and the Man,* director Michael Langham scattered chocolate creams for the characters to nibble throughout the production. And in the Arena Stage production of *Tartuffe* (a restaging in 1985 of the original 1984 Guthrie version), Lucian Pintilie had the character Flipote spill out a bushel basket of apples in the first scene—a vividly arresting image that formed part of the production contract. In subsequent scenes, apples reappeared inevitably as objects of temptation and desire.

MICHAEL LANGHAM
1919–
(Great Britain)

London and U.S. regional theatres: Old Vic, Stratford-upon-Avon, Folger. *Oedipus the King, Love's Labours Lost, The Merchant of Venice.* Served as Artistic Director of the Stratford (Ontario) Shakespeare Festival and the Guthrie in Minneapolis.

Langham's motif was drawn directly from Shaw's text. The protagonist, Captain Bluntschli, expounds upon his love for confections and the awful deprivation imposed by battlefield conditions. By planting them in this well-to-do household, Langham reinforces the comic contrast, using one of the very images the playwright calls up in a more limited context. One of the directorial statements becomes: "Peacetime is having all the chocolates you could want; war means doing without." The apples in *Tartuffe* are another story. Seeing the play in biblical terms of temptation, suffering, and redemption, Pintilie opens not with Eve's single piece of tempting fruit but with an entire bushel basket. Tartuffe enters not through the front door but from the very bowels of the stage, enshrouded in smoke and white-hot light, Satan himself—undisguised and unapologetic. As the plot moves forward, time accelerates. Orgon's Job-like torments begin in the world of Moliére but persist through the centuries as the play accelerates into the contemporary world. Tartuffe, the personification of evil, and the apples, emblems of temptation, persist.

In these two instances, a single prop is employed as a defining motif in the directorial pattern for the production. As any other important design element, the prop becomes a unifying device subtly linking scenes and characters together and taking on a peculiar quality and resonance. Used sensitively, a simple object can become an important expressive element in the production. However, it cannot be allowed to appear self-conscious, precious, or arbitrary. Its use must seem natural and inevitable within the world of the production. Otherwise, of course, it will appear simply to be a "bright idea."

Theatrical motifs emerge in the work of any director—whether or not they emerge deliberately or effectively. Joining pairs of lovers by means of color signals in their costumes has become a virtual cliché. Actors will often echo each other instinctively in the ways they perform actions—answering the telephone, writing notes, opening a door. These elements in turn establish patterns that may or may not communicate the desired effect. The physical staging of one scene may be repeated in another to suggest parallel underlying actions. For example, in *The Foreigner,* Owen tries, in a crude attempt at irony, to humiliate and discredit Charlie. By making the physical staging of this scene echo the earlier one in which Charlie first frightens Owen, the director can project a feeling of special satisfaction when Owen is outwitted. Or the staging may be deliberately reversed. If Owen physically circles the seated Charlie to mock the fellow he thinks is "dumb"; Charlie later can circle his tormentor seated in the same chair.

When repetition becomes obvious, by accident or design, it becomes comic because the mechanism shows, and human beings caught in a mechanical process are perceived as comic.[2] When the patterns are succinct and organic, they become an integral part of the created form and may be either comic or serious.

> **All artworks are formed through patterns of repetition and counterpoint, consonance and dissonance. Directing follows the same principles.**

Some directors will instinctively shy away from such an undertaking for fear of being found out, for being thought precious or pompous, or "technical." Again, it is the nature of theatrical creation that patterning is unavoidable. One need only attempt to direct a play—or even a scene—without a pattern or structure to discover it is a theoretical and practical impossibility. Instead, the creative

---

[2]Henri Bergson's classic essay, "Laughter," is an indispensable analysis of the comic and should be required reading for any director dealing with comedy.

director will attempt to learn more about imagery and patterns—in art and in life—and use these tools subtly and effectively in the making of productions.

EXERCISES

1. In your scenework, find ways to use an important element—a prop, a gesture, a movement, etc.—in at least three variations. You may employ simple repetition, modulation, or reversal.

2. Observe the pattern of a conversation in a public or semi-public place between two people. (If a videotaped recording of such an exchange is available, it will be useful to have as a reference for your work.) Pay close attention to body language, as expressed in sculptural and choreographic elements. Reproduce these patterns as accurately as possible using two actors. The scene may use spoken lines or simply be played out in pantomime with a silent dialogue, and need be only 30 seconds to one minute long. Do not invent, or try to improve on what you have observed.

3. Observe a movement pattern in a dance, either choreographed or popular. Translate the movement into an expressive scene or statement that you might term "realistic." Begin by noting the shape of the pattern, the feeling or impulse it communicates, and a natural relationship in which the same image is applicable. Maintain the pattern and gradually reduce the *scale* of the physical expression until it is acceptably *conversational* in its effect.

4. Find a non-representational painting with a strong composition in line or rhythm. Using one or two actors, try to translate the composition into a human context by using as much of the painting as you can. Project the results by suggesting a scene or situation that your resulting creation communicates.

5. Search through available pictorial sources and find 4–6 paintings or photographs whose *compositions* (not stories or themes or characters) can be used directly to create a storyboard for a short scene. Try to make the periods and styles of the paintings as different as possible. Use the resulting storyboard to stage the scene. You should try to reproduce the effect of each composition by following the structure of each picture carefully. The result you want to achieve is a scene which seems natural and unforced.

One way to develop your analytical sense is to look at the elements of your work—or of other directors—as pure form. When you watch a production, try to infer the matrix and the images that unify and inspire the work. Discover why a moment suddenly springs into life when a scene staged in measured rhythms in curved lateral patterns changes into syncopated straightline diagonal movements. Try to find natural ways in which each important prop or movement or sound is used more than once—either with simple repetitions, modulations, or reversals. In so doing, you are set to discover how to make every element vital and expressive as befits its part in the theatrical creation.

A work of art is either alive or dead. It is alive when the life in it to be expressed has found a body in the art involved, a body composed of its elements. Otherwise, whatever the idea, the result as a work of art does not exist.

—Stark Young, *The Theatre*

13 EVALUATING THE DIRECTOR'S WORK

Professional Evaluation

How do you evaluate your own directorial work and that of others? How can you sharpen your observation, your insights, and ultimately your skills and artistry?

First, if you are willing to bestow meaningful praise, you must also be capable of honest, civil, and *professional* criticism. One who is able or willing to praise or to criticize *only* is to be neither trusted nor believed.[1] This must apply especially to your own work. If you can only recognize its virtues, you will never see

---

[1]In this chapter we discuss serious, professional evaluation as distinguished from informal, social response to productions and performances. Backstage comments and offhand remarks are understood by everyone but the most rigid and unyielding of people as being *social and polite* remarks rather than professional pronouncements. In such situations, critical comments or bland, smirking compliments are simply rude and self-centered. One's *honesty* is not at stake in these cases; one's *manners* are.

it clearly enough to grow in your craft. If you can see only its faults, you will never develop the confidence to use your talents freely and imaginatively. Both extremes are untenable.

Still, the willingness to be honest and open in one's evaluations is of little value unless some kinds of reliable standards are applied. The first and most important thing is the power of *observation*. Although this is a matter of greatest importance, we can assume that few people actually *see*. What we hope to observe is a high degree of *craft* and a clearly defined *artistic vision*.

If we are honest, we will admit it as common to have work over-praised as it is to have it unfairly condemned. In this regard, amateur photography has many parallels with amateur theatre. People undertake each with a minimum of training and experience because it is possible to get recognizable results immediately. The photographer displays the snapshots proudly and the audience responds with approval. "Oh, I recognize that!" "Doesn't that look just like her?" Occasionally, the responses venture into the technical achievements of the work: "These are really sharp. That must be a good camera." "Look at those colors. They're so lifelike."

How much these comments parallel the judgments and standards applied to the theatre! To be fair, they are the only appropriate remarks in cases where the work has no goals beyond providing a diverting hobby, a creative outlet, or a means of pleasing one's friends. The serious photographer—assuredly the artist-photographer with professional pretensions—works at a different level of both craft and vision. It is fair to say that any serious professional artist actually sees the artwork differently from other people. The artist's eye interprets and translates what it sees in terms that are either opaque or irrelevant to those who do not share a similar background of talent, commitment, study, practice, failure, and success.

The eye of a layperson is influenced by entirely different expectations and criteria. Tonal range, selective focus, grain structure, composition, and contrast have nothing to do with the snapshot. Indeed, these considerations do not even engage the amateur photographer. The only thing that matters is whether or not the picture "comes out." The camera, film, and processing combination that accomplishes that end is the one that is kept. "Don't tinker with a good thing."

There are times, though, when a "snapshooter" reaches the point where the drugstore processing, the fixed focus camera, and the reliable results are no longer satisfying. But the next steps up the ladder towards becoming a world-class photographer are frustrating and complicated. Beyond the mastery of the technical challenges of f-stops and selective focus and reticulation and polycontrast, there is the even more demanding aspects of discovering and developing vision and style.

Theatre directors follow the same path. It is embarrassingly easy to direct a production that will please one's friends, or even a fairly sizable audience. On the other hand, learning the craft that will allow genuine artistic expression and growth demands commitment that few people have. As a result, many directors actually *choose* to remain at a fairly elementary level. Rationalizations abound:

"The work is popular." "The choice of the play is all that really matters." "Getting the right actors is the whole secret." And so on. If these statements seem to echo the claims of aggressively amateurish photographers, it is because the attitude towards the work is the same.

Developing Critical Standards

An ability to perceive and evaluate directorial work is indispensable to your progress as a creative director. The development of standards for judging director-work should be a high priority for you at this and every other stage of your training and development. One way to understand the underlying challenges in evaluating the director's work is to sharpen your objectivity, and one way to accomplish this is to observe art and audiences *outside* the theatre. At the next opportunity, go to an art museum when attendance is high. If you are alert to the comments and explications of the work on view, you will begin to see some of the challenges and frustrations involved in understanding an artwork and expressing those insights.

If non-traditional works are on view, disparaging comments will be easy to come by. "I could do that." "I wouldn't have that in my house." "It looks like a dropcloth." "What is that supposed to be?" "He (usually someone like Picasso, de Kooning, Pollack, or Stella) is a fake." And so on. If there are nudes, erotic or not, or parodistic works, you will doubtless hear negative comments about them—the merit of such subjects, or the artist's treatment of them, or their suitability for public support or display. As social mores change, these comments become more or less common—or loud—but they are always around.

If, on the other hand, the paintings are traditional in subject, theme, and treatment, you will hear completely different sorts of comments. "You can see every leaf!" "It reminds me of one we had like that at home." "Now that's art!" "Isn't it amazing they could do things like that back then?"

These comments betray prescriptive attitudes—aesthetic and moralistic—usually presumed by the critic to be shared by the rest of the audience. If we search for a more expert, or at least a more informed sort of comment, we are still likely to hear a discussion that moves *around* rather than *into* the work. Such talk usually focuses on anecdotes from the life of the artist or on the subject matter of the painting. Only occasionally will the discussion come to terms with the feeling expressed by the painting, or the way in which the artist manipulated the materials to make the painting what it is. Thoughtful practicing painters take a different tack. They speak of technique, of composition, of chiaroscuro, of "surface," and then of power, subtlety, passion. Essentially they look at the "how" of the painting, and then at the effects it achieves. Talk about the artwork centers on the painting, and not on peripheral matters. This perspective is shared by other media as well. In 1981, when many of the leading American film directors gathered to pay tribute to the inimitable Japanese director, Akira Kurosawa, they discussed at length some of the important challenges of their medium—shooting in the rain, editing, lighting concepts and execution. (Lillian Ross, "Kurosawa Frames," *New Yorker Magazine,* pp. 51–78) The "how" of the work was vitally important even to those film directors at the highest levels of commercial and artistic success.

When coaches or athletes or musicians call someone a "player," they are paying the highest sort of compliment by saying that someone *knows* the work well and has achieved skill in its execution. Having the skills—being a *player*—does not guarantee success of recognition or even solid achievement. But that very act of recognition does acknowledge the existence of a set of identifiable skills and the potential for their mastery.

Are there such skills in theatrical direction, and can those skills be recognized even in a limited sample of a director's work? The answer appears to be "yes." And yet few professionals and fewer critics seem able to discern those skills, much less to discuss the equivalent of the painter's *surface* in the work of a theatrical director.

As we have defined it, the director's work draws upon the script and subject matter as well as upon the actors, designers, theatrical space, etc., but it is different from any or all of these. And it is *independent* of the viewer's tastes. Creative directors, like other artists, must develop a vocabulary to discuss and evaluate their work. The ability to identify and apply standards is a valuable skill, but its mastery permits serious directors to develop their own *creative* skills. That is the point of the discussion that follows:

INTERNAL LOGIC

Premise: The production is a theatrical art-work and, therefore, must establish and obey its own rules and logic. While the playwright's text is usually the inevitable and vital element in establishing the character and framework of the production, its precise meaning and function is established by the director. This means that any production must be experienced and evaluated on its own terms and within its own self-defining boundaries. An axiom in painting has it that "the picture stops at the frame." This means that to criticize a painting because a tree is *not* shown is unfair to the work. In the same way, the mode or style of theatrical presentation is self-referring. It is as indefensible to denigrate an expressionistic production of *Miss Julie* for not being "realistic" as to devalue Segovia's rendition of a Bach prelude on the classical guitar because it is not played on the harpsichord.

This does not mean that the script is irrelevant. Far from it. It is usually, as we have noted from the very outset, the *critical* element of the director's material. What we *do* mean is that the text of the play does not prescribe the form or content of a given production. To attend a production with the notion that it *must* fulfill certain expectations is to deny the prospect of fresh theatrical interpretation.

But is this not the basic principle of criticism: that every play has requirements that *must* be satisfied? Mustn't Hamlet be indecisive, Macbeth ambitious, *Twelfth Night* light and frothy, musicals brightly lighted, Greek tragedies stately and majestic, *The Seagull* "realistic"? The answer in each case is a resounding "no." Each of these notions is based on an interpretation that *someone* has projected about the form and content of each play. Since the very purpose of production is to project an artistic vision, the observer who demands a certain interpretation as necessary, inevitable, and "right" is simply limiting the possibilities to what is already known—or what has already been said.

CRITICAL OBJECTIVITY

In analyzing and discussing directorial work, *professionals* should avoid violating the internal, self-referring nature of a production with prescriptions and prejudicial statements such as "The production should . . ." or "shouldn't . . . ," "too much . . ." or "not enough. . . ." Statements concerning the playwright's "intention" are presumptuous, and leave theatre artists no option but to reinforce the interpretations and standards of the observer.

In the same category is the use of previous productions and performances as standards against which to measure the work under consideration. The first production, the Broadway production, or the Royal Shakespeare Company's production is *not* the last word. Such productions may have been effective, powerful, and artistic, but none is truly definitive to the point of closing out all other options. If this were so, it would be an artistic contradiction in terms—an artwork that allows only one authentic interpretation.

Of course, comparisons can be useful in understanding or discussing a performance or design. We may, in fact, find more skill and artistry, or insight, in one production or performance than another; but to say that Derek Jacobi's playing of a soliloquy in *Hamlet* is inferior or superior to Richard Burton's is both superficial and patently absurd, because it tells nothing about either. The professional is interested in discerning and communicating *what* each actor did and *how* he did it.

Keep your attention focused on the production and not on your own personal responses and feelings. It is difficult to accept, but what we *feel* or what we like or dislike in a production is irrelevant to the value or the achievement of the production. To proclaim that merit is simply a matter of taste is to deny standards. If we evaluate any work in apologetic or aggressively subjective terms ("It worked for me." "I don't care. I liked it." "I wanted to see. . . ." "I didn't understand . . ."), chances are we are describing ourselves more than the work. While this may be fascinating for some, it is not to the point. To become a professional, you need not *like* everything of value and high achievement or *despise* everything that is cheap, easy, or vulgar, you must only *know the difference*.

Anyone is capable of liking or not liking something; a *professional* can make judgments about it.

Evaluation Criteria

If good directorial work cannot be recognized simply by a production using a good script with good actors and designs that ends up in a performance I enjoy, then how can it be done?

The production should be *beautiful* in the way it looks both from moment to moment and in its totality—in the way it sounds, and in the way it moves. By beautiful, we do not mean merely decorative, certainly not glamorous, but rather that the elements of the production are *composed and significant*. A good production is *designed* in every aspect. Its beauty lies in the relationship of the production elements and the integration of those elements to evoke meaning and emotional effect. Like the DNA model discussed in Chapter II, the production's beauty comes from the *unity* created by an essential connection of form, content, and feeling.

At the core of this unity is the *acting*. The power, effectiveness, and beauty of the acting—individual performances but most especially that of the *ensemble*—is the key to a production's validity and effectiveness. A wonderful production, however, goes beyond good performances to create the entire theatrical statement. In fact, the term "ensemble" can serve as the paradigm to judge the overall work of the director.

The Ensemble Production

"*Ensemble*" connotes a balanced relationship of performances within the company, which we earlier described as "team-work." Each actor assumes the authority and focus appropriate to the role as defined by the particular production scheme. There is no "star," no competition for attention, nothing to disturb the balance. We speak of *ensemble acting* when each performance complements the others, and each is in tune with the overall scheme of the production. This is precisely the aim of the contemporary director's work: to achieve excellence in individual and combined performances, and to extend that idea of ensemble to the entire production.

An "*ensemble production,*" then, is one in which all the elements work together in the same complementary fashion that we recognize in an acting ensemble. It is also, by definition, a "*beautiful production,*" in the way it looks, moves, sounds, and fits together to form the whole. To remove or alter any element, then, would be to alter—perhaps to diminish—the entire production, just as to change a performance in a beautiful acting ensemble would be to upset the balance and somehow change the effect of the acting.

What qualities identify an *ensemble production?*

There are three qualities of a director's work analogous to the actors' *ensemble* or the painter's *surface.* The ability to achieve and manipulate these qualities, *unity, shape,* and *imagery,* is the distinguishing mark of a director who knows how to use the medium expressively.

UNITY

Artisans speak of "fit and finish" and the "integrity of design." In direction, these qualities are expressed in the way various elements complement one another to create an impression of purposefulness and inevitability. Response follows stimulus; actions are completed; unresolved elements are purposeful. If one thing were to be changed, a whole chain of alterations would be required. Such a unified work might be described as "seamless." This is not to say that the result should be *simple,* but rather *integrated* and *organic.*

> **H I N T :** Look for the effect of a single vision guided by a single design.

SHAPE

In bringing any script to theatrical life, a director must give a structural principle to a production. Relationships, interpretations, themes—whatever we choose to call them—are expressed in the playwright's words (the given), and rendered in forms modeled by the director in collaboration with the actors, the designers, and technicians.

This directorial shaping is evident in the visual, kinetic, and auditory elements of the production, particularly in the complementary patterns the director has produced.

> **H I N T :** Look for directorial design and composition, for discernible patterns in the way the production looks and moves (actors, costumes, properties, scenery, and lights—even the curtain), to communicate a sense of purpose and feeling, and for a deliberate and evocative composition and use of sound.

Do not fall into the trap of sidestepping these issues by arguing that the production aims at creating a "slice of life," or "didn't intend to be artistic." These arguments beg the question. Practice, instead, analyzing life scenes or events as suggested in the exercises that follow.

Play: *Elmer Gantry* **Author:** John Bishop; music—Mel Marvin; lyrics—Robert Satuloff **Theatre:** Ford's Theatre **Director:** David H. Bell **Set Designer:** Marjorie Bradley **Costumes:** David Murin **Lighting:** Pat Collins **Actors (l to r):** Peter Lombard, Barry J. Tarallo, Tony Gilbert, Joe Barrett, J.K. Simmons, Casey Biggs, Sharon Scruggs (Photo by Joan Marcus)

Play: Jekyll! **Author:** James Costin **Theatre:** Missouri Repertory Theatre **Director:** George Keathley **Set Designer:** John Ezell **Costumes:** Vincent Scassellati **Lighting:** Joseph Appelt **Actors (l to r):** Alan Brasington, Edgar Meyer, Donald Christopher, Richard Bowden, Jay Karnes (Photo by Larry Pape)
Directorial design and shaping is evident in these scenes, displaying in each a unique statement of the director's vision.

IMAGERY

Unity and shape are essentially "craft" components of the director's work, much what brushwork and color are to the painter's work. These things enable the artist to create images. And it is through images that a production communicates.[2]

> We receive the artist's "message" through the experience of the artwork, but we cannot appreciate the artistic method fully unless we come to terms with the imagery.

To experience the *artwork,* total awareness of the imagery is unnecessary; to understand the *artistic process*—the *how* of the work—it is essential.

Inferring a coherent image matrix from a production tells you something about the director's work, certainly. It also sensitizes you, as an artist, to imagery in your own work. We need not be too concerned about giving the *right* answer to the question, "What is the director's matrix?". In an artwork as complex as a theatrical production, there is no single correct conclusion. Seeing Russian director Yuri Lyubimov's *Crime and Punishment* (produced at the Arena Stage, 1987), one might have said the directorial matrix was *"A nightmare of pursuit and persecution following a horrid act."* The created images of unmotivated lighting, of a free-floating blood-stained door appearing in scene after scene, of being stalked and entrapped by the mechanisms of society and its minions can all be interpreted as elements expressive of such a vision. This might or might not coincide precisely with the director's conscious decisions. No matter. The important thing is that Lyubimov's production—its created form—communicated a powerful image of a coherent universe.

YURI LYUBIMOV	Moscow: *Crime and Punishment, Ten Days that*
19 –	*Shook the World by John Reed, The Three Sisters.*
(U.S.S.R.)	Founded the Taganka Theatre in 1964; his personal style is strongly subjective and political.

In Chapter II, we discussed a *Black Mass* matrix created for Genet's *The Maids.* If you were to see that production and it was effective in communicating the qualities the director projects, the resulting images might be interpreted in

[2]We include, of course, the playwright's verbal images, which constitute a vital element of the director's medium.

terms of eroticism, funeral ritual, or perverted game-playing. That none of these is precisely what the director had consciously in mind does not mean that either the creator or the interpreter has failed. To the contrary, it suggests a richness and complexity that marks any serious artwork. It parallels, in fact, the interpretive process of a director dealing with a text. The director and the critical observer have many valid options because in each case the work is *expressive* rather than discursive.

EXERCISES

1. Observe two or three "scenes" in public or semi-public settings as if they were *theatrical events*.
   a. Since each scene is taking place within the framework of a certain time and place, some principle or motive holds the elements together. Which is this unifying principle?
   b. Describe the shapes and patterns produced in each scene in terms of the visual, kinetic, and auditory elements, and describe how the elements complement or counterpoint each other.
   c. What overall image or metaphor can best describe the *quality* of each scene?
2. Apply the same techniques to scenes from a play, a movie, or a television show.

Judgment and Opinion

As we have noted, personal tastes are most important to the person who has them and those who wish to cater to them. They are seldom reliable indicators of *quality* unless they are based on a standard of judgment that rivals or surpasses your own; even then, they are only *indicators* of quality. Millions of people seem to be inordinately fond of hamburgers and other "fast foods." There is nothing inherently wrong in that, but claiming a fast-food hamburger represents a high level of culinary achievement is patently foolish. If popular likes and dislikes were truly essential in determining quality, then we would be reduced to saying that a hamburger with commercial sauce on a soft white bun is great cooking, and that "sofa-sized paintings" are great art.

Judgment, however, is different from either taste or opinion. Judgment is based on a set of standards that takes into account the processes and the possibilities of the form. The subjective element does not disappear, but it is not the controlling factor. One sign of maturing critical judgment is the ability to acknowledge the excellence of a work one does *not like,* and the willingness to admit that one *likes* something that, frankly, is not very good (like our franchise hamburger). These positions suppose the existence of critical standards of judgment. It puts the onus on the object of the evaluation rather than solely upon the responses of the evaluator.

DISCUSSION

1. Discuss the comparison of the photographer and the director. How is what they do (and how it is received) different? Photography is dependent in large measure upon equipment. Does this fact weaken the analogy, or are there useful parallels?

2. Debate the premise "One who can praise or criticize *only* is to be neither trusted nor believed."

3. What are the hazards in being a self-proclaimed "perfectionist"?

4. Take a position on the following assertion and be prepared to defend it: "Since all art is subjective, opinion is the only valid way to respond."

5. Explore any distinctions between the term "opinion" and "judgment" as used in the discussion above.

6. Of what value to an understanding of a theatrical creation are the following sorts of comments:

   a. "I wanted to see . . ."

   b. "That wouldn't really have happened."

   c. "I didn't believe that."

   d. "It worked for me."

   e. "I had trouble with . . ."

Critical Questions

By now it is clear we are describing a two-tiered approach to the evaluation of directorial work. The first centers on the director's craft, and the second on the art—the creative or formative vision. Certain criteria are omitted completely. We do *not* address questions of intentionality, politics, morality, or social responsibility.

We confine ourselves to the *work* in terms of its quality and achievement as a piece of theatrical art, and to the director as a theatrical artist. To be an effective director, we assume, is to have something to express and the means to express it.

A masterpiece is a play that speaks across the boundaries of time and place because its true subject is the human condition. Such a play can live in our time when artists create the forms that give it life. **(Photo by Thomas Ramstorfer)**
Play: *Don Giovanni* **Author:** Wolfgang Amadeus Mozart **Theatre:** Boston Opera Theater, Plaza Media, Austrian Television **Director:** Peter Sellars **Actors (l to r):** Herbert Perry, Ai Lan Zhu (Photo by Ali Schafler)

> **A production devoid of directorial meaning or point-of-view cannot achieve a true theatrical synthesis. One that is lacking in craft and style cannot achieve theatrical effectiveness.**

According to painter Ben Shahn, "Form is the visible shape of content."

To evaluate directorial work, we must recall some premises with which we approached the director's task in the first place. We assume the director to be the artist responsible for the shape of the production. That shape proceeds from a *matrix*, which carries in it the meaning of the play. The director creates the matrix from a response to the script, using the created forms of the playwright, the creative contributions of the designers and the actors, and the theatrical space. Therefore, part of the director's work resides in the overall design and supervision of that work, its coherence and effectiveness. Those areas encompass the range of the visual, kinetic, and auditory elements of the production. The director then provides the design matrix, which establishes the interconnection of the acting, the movement patterns, the designs of the costumes, scenery, lights, and the music and sound.

In evaluating the director's artwork—the production—we raise critical questions:

1. Does the production communicate the image of a created virtual world?

Once the empty space becomes a stage, it becomes a world in which characters act according to the laws of the universe they occupy. The created world may or may not resemble the world outside; it must nonetheless establish its own distinctive environment, atmosphere, and universal laws. The created world should seem inevitable, possessed of its own internal logic to which everything must yield. In a universe created to be illogical (*Alice in Wonderland,* for example), real world logic is out of place and must be viewed and treated as an aberration. In a world defined as an environment of strict causality (like *Deathtrap*), cause and effect must operate with machine-like inevitability. Where conventional logic must operate within an arbitrary framework, that arrangement must have an unmistakable consistency (such as that required by A.R. Gurney's fanciful manipulation of time and space in *The Dining Room*).

The best productions create and project a specific environment and vitality while avoiding preciousness and self-consciousness. Peter Brook's *Carmen,* for example, was a fully realized performance proceeding from a clear and unequivocal vision. Brook deliberately avoided the traditional operatic trappings of the work and returned for his matrix to the story's novelistic origin.[3] The Royal Shakespeare Company's celebrated production of *Nicholas Nickleby,* under the direction of Trevor Nunn and John Caird, was a singular demonstration of the power of a vivid theatrical matrix in the hands of dozens of skilled artists working as a single creative entity. Creative excellence exists also outside such rarefied atmospheres. On Broadway, Hal Prince's work invariably has shown the American musical to be a treasure-trove of rich and varied possibilities. Alan Schneider could make theatre magic of "difficult" contemporary plays. Elia Kazan left a legacy of deeply felt, poetic productions that captured the play and his times definitively. And Mike Nichols brought intelligence and form to commercial comedy.

2. Does each of the elements of the created world complement the other, and does the result communicate an organic quality?

The production should seem to be the work of a single artist: the costumes enhance the actors, the lights harmonize with the sound, the actors with the set, and so on. This criterion presumes the levels of craft in design and execution are equal. Obviously, the production should achieve the highest level of quality available within the limitations and potentials of the materials at hand.

[3]As an example of the kind of work we have been considering, Brook's work violates one standard we have established because he restructured the elements of the opera's libretto (script) to suit his vision—as valid and evocative as that vision might be.

This standard presumes the director has used the best collaborators available and guided and inspired them to give their optimum effort. This means the best available actors, technicians, and designers—all doing their best work to support the director's production matrix. Most particularly, the criterion asks that the playwright's contribution—the script—be realized in an honest, cogent, and artistic manner.

3. Is every element of the work essential and every structure complete?

A production should possess an integrity that assures the *expressiveness* of each and every element. Anything in a production (from a bit of business to a costume or a sound cue) that is not connected to the matrix—the *core* or *soul* of the work—violates the integrity of the production, regardless of how well it "works." Nothing is forbidden to the artist-director embarking on a production *until the matrix is defined*. Thereafter, the choices must be related and integrated. The temptation to employ some element or device simply for the sake of its effectiveness in performance or its impact upon the audience is a symptom of poverty of imagination and invention.

Failure to fill out or complete some element usually proceeds from timidity, or a lack of technique, or both. A good director must be *fearless* in the pursuit of honest creativity. Too often, genuinely inventive directors stop short of employing a *theatrical* image structure and opt instead for a *literary* one; or they simply *suggest* an image and abandon it. While it is virtually impossible to *describe* just what talented, fearless directors can produce, we should always be on the alert. Once you have experienced several such productions, they will convey a coherence and fullness of execution you can use as a standard.

4. Is the production self-conscious or precious?

It is difficult not to be amused in a superficial way by the sheer cleverness and preciosity of some directors. We often see—on Broadway and regional theatres as well as in college and university productions—a kind of self-conscious preening that is often clever and sometimes engaging. Like junk-food, there may be nothing wrong with this sort of production if it is recognized for what it is. Campy productions are, in fact, as common as greasy fried potatoes.

Sometimes, however, precious productions are difficult to distinguish from audacious work. Critics and reviewers have as much or more difficulty making the distinction as audiences. Let Andrè Serban direct a lively, keen, and biting production of *The Marriage of Figaro* in New York and "serious" critics are struck with an inability to distinguish between genuine theatrical audacity and clumsy superficial nonsense. Serious theatre workers must learn to make the distinctions—to arrive at the point of being able to recognize the *artistry* in works they do not particularly *like* and the *clumsiness or dishonesty* in productions they actually *enjoy*. This ability marks the beginning of the maturation of taste and insight into the art of the theatre.

In evaluating any director's work—especially your own—you must return to two fundamental criteria:

- *The performance must be connected intimately and essentially to the text, not incidentally attached or overlaid.*
- *The elements of the performance must be so integrated that the full impact and meaning of each element cannot be expressed except in a complete performance.*

In short, if the production—either in whole or major part—shows a self-conscious reaching for *effect* or *titillation,* it is likely to fall far short of honest theatrical creativity.

End Note

To develop the sensibilities for the work of analysis, you must see many productions (the best you can find), watch them as a professional artist, and learn from them. As an aspiring director, you must learn to see *what* the director has done and *how*.

> **If you do not often see things in the work of genuinely good directors that you admire—even envy—and want to learn to do, you are either not seeing good enough work or you do not yet know what you are seeing.**

We are not speaking vaguely about an overall sort of quality of a production, but of specific things: how the director moves a certain scene in space; how a motif is laced through a production as an essential part of the performance; how the rhythm of the performance is built and controlled. When you can recognize these things, you are beginning to see past the veneer and into the technique that produces a work of art. Then you are on the way to becoming an artist.

APPENDIX

A

SCENEWORK: PRINCIPLES, GUIDELINES, AND SUGGESTIONS

Practice is as essential for directors as it is for musicians, painters, dancers, and tennis players. Understanding and insight, the ability to imagine, the desire to communicate feeling and meaning: all these useful qualities are mute without the skill to translate them into viable theatrical forms. Yet, the idea persists that all a director needs is to understand a text and cast good actors. If it sounds ridiculous to assert, "I am a wonderful musician; I just haven't learned to play," then how silly to think that all a director needs is one or two skills to create a complex artistic form.

If we agree that the director's job is to translate images drawn from a text into a theatrical artwork, then we should ask, is it possible to develop our abilities to create and translate images through systematic exercises? The answer is yes, and the process parallels the work in other disciplines—from writing and painting to dance and music.

Looking through this text, you find a number of exercises to develop your skills and sensitivities as a director. Obviously, though, you also need bigger, more demanding projects to exercise and synthesize your developing skills and insights.

If you have seen a great deal of theatre or have been around theatre production work for a time, you will be tempted to take on some fairly large and demanding assignments. No one can deny that some people learn to swim when they are thrown off the end of the dock into deep water. It is also true that some drown. The point is that no one ever became a championship swimmer—or director—by simply jumping in and trying to survive. Daring is important to both undertakings, but you are more likely to progress if you practice your "strokes" in a controlled environment if one is available. Swimmers do laps; pianists do finger exercises; singers do scales; artists do sketches; dancers do barres. Directors do scenes.

Scenes for Beginning Directors

TWO-CHARACTER REALISTIC SCENES

1. Selection—Each scene chosen for this level of work should involve two characters and be drawn from the modern repertoire, preferably contemporary realistic plays. Although some late nineteenth century works are suitable, the scene probably should not require the additional challenge of a period style. (If you choose or are assigned such a scene, you must be prepared to respond to the challenge and deal with the period.) The preferred setting for the practice scene is an interior, although this is not absolutely required. The scene should be between 4 and 8 minutes in length. If possible, it should present one or more complete action units.

Finally, you should approach the play in what we have called the *editorial* mode. The matrix you employ, therefore, should be drawn as directly as possible from images in the play, possibly from the scene itself.

Scene Selection

- Two (possibly three) characters
- From a modern "realistic" play
- Playing time between 4 and 8 minutes
- Single interior setting preferred
- One of more complete action units (See Chapter III.)
- "Editorial" mode

---

2. Preparation—You should prepare fully to work on each scene by doing a thorough analysis. Without such preparation, you cannot be assured of maximum progress in the work you do. In directing, as in any field, some people try to insulate themselves from failure by building in excuses at the outset. Directors must test themselves constantly, not look for a way out if things do not fall out right. Recall the Chinese calligrapher. A mistake is useful to an artist only if it is acknowledged and dealt with, and not simply covered up by excuses or rationalizations.

The scene must be approached as a *scene*—that is, as an *element* from a larger work—not as a complete play. Consider the scene in the context of the entire play, developing an appropriate matrix for the play based on the images you find there.

You may be required to write out some of your analytical work to demonstrate your mastery of the processes and your skill and insights in understanding the work at hand. At the minimum, you should write out a brief summary of your preparation to be used as a reference in the discussion of your scene presentation. In any event, keep a log of all your directing work, with notes on the following details to chart a record of your work and development:

DIRECTOR'S SCENEWORK LOG

PLAY: _____ BY: _____

SCENE: _____ TYPE: _____

STAGING: _____ DATE: _____

CAST: *Character*   *Actor*

REHEARSALS: *Total number:* _____. *Time (hours): Reading* _____;

Blocking _____; *Development* _____; *Refinement* _____. *TOTAL* _____.

Running Time of Scene (minutes): _____.

GOALS (Editorial Mode):   or   MATRIX (Creative Mode):

QUALITIES SUGGESTED FOR THE SCENE BY THE MATRIX:
  Visual:
  Aural:
  Kinetic:
 Specific Choices:

CHARACTER OBJECTIVES:

PROBLEMS/CHALLENGES:

GROUNDPLAN SKETCH:

DIRECTOR'S ASSESSMENT:
Achievements

Shortcomings

---

3. Rehearsal—Follow the same rehearsal format for a scene as for a major production; simply scale it to the scene you are preparing and the time available. Leaving out steps or trying to combine them will not allow a fair test of what you have learned. The amount of time spent in rehearsal should be scaled to the production: forty-five minutes to an hour of rehearsal for every minute of performance time. Under no circumstances should you schedule fewer than four separate rehearsals, even for the shortest scene. Seven or eight one-hour rehearsals over the space of a week to ten days is a reasonable average for a ten minute scene.

4. Method of Presentation—(The exact groundrules for scene presentation will vary, of course, from theatre to theatre and from class to class. The following are reasonable standards that seem to balance the need for a disciplined and creative format with reasonable technical restrictions.) The scene should be presented under *studio conditions;* i.e., the actors should be thoroughly prepared and have lines memorized. The props and setting should be taken from whatever stock is made available for the work. Props may be pantomimed, but any prop or costume element that is required may be improvised from what is available to you. In brief, the scene presented for evaluation should represent the level of readiness expected from a production about to go into technical and dress rehearsals.

5. Problem Scenes—You might be asked to prepare a scene of a certain type, presenting a specific problem to be addressed by you as the director and then discussed in class. In choosing such a scene, keep in mind that the designation of the type of scene is usually only a guide, not a hard-and-fast prescription. The scene chosen need fit only the spirit of its "type," not be the definitive example. In approaching the material, focus on making the scene vivid and true, not on illustrating a "how-to" for dealing with certain recurrent problems. If you do your work well, the result will be example enough for anyone.

The following list suggests scenes that present particular problems or issues that challenge the director's interpretive and image-making skills. Many of the challenges these types of scenes present and some of the strategies for dealing with them are found in Chapters XI and XII.

Expository: This type of scene is common, and frustrating. In older plays, especially, exposition was handled conventionally (as in the "French maid" technique Thornton Wilder parodies so deftly in *The Skin of Our Teeth* and Ionesco exploits in *The Bald Soprano*). Usually exposition occurs in the first scene, but it may be found anywhere in a text where it is necessary to communicate *information* to the audience.

In approaching such a scene, it is obviously important to get all the information across; but it is equally important (even for comic effect as in the two cases just mentioned) to give the scene a dramatic necessity, something beyond the mere recital of the facts. This usually means giving concentrated attention to environment, given circumstances, and character objectives. Look for and emphasize the stimuli that provoke the exposition. Define and intensify the *character's* urgency in communicating the information, rather than simply tossing off the scene as something that must be gotten out of the way. For example, in *Dracula*, by Balderston and Dean, a young maid is found alone in a room at night. She must speak a monologue that imparts a great deal of necessary information to the audience. But unless the production is presentational, the character is speaking to herself. Having the actor explore the awful fear that this young woman must feel in such a place and time is one effective way of giving strong emotional support to the lines that must be spoken: Mary is talking to herself to help assuage her fright. The scene now takes on an urgency that transforms the exposition into a dramatic necessity.

Static: A static scene is one that requires a minimum of physical movement. There are no drinks to mix, no closets to explore, no windows to peer through. Typically, such a scene involves two or more characters simply sitting (or standing) and talking. This is the case in Strindberg's powerful one-act play *The Stronger*, which is essentially a monologue addressed to a silent character seated at the same café table.

Action: This is a scene, in direct contrast to the *static* scene, that demands a good deal of physical action. Look at the scene in Shue's *The Foreigner* in which Ellard "teaches" English to Charlie.

Atmospheric: In a scene in which the atmosphere plays a prominent role, the *feeling* of the place and the time dominates. One of the definitive atmospheric plays is Maeterlinck's *The Intruder*. The director confronting such a scene should pay special attention both to the ambient sound and light and to the actors' timing.

Character Interaction: The director's choice and attention here should be focused on *beats* and *action units*. Close observation and side-coaching, with an emphasis on the stimulus-response process, is very important. Helping the actors focus their concentration and their ability to respond appropriately at the exact moment is critical. Appropriate scene choices are many and varied, but the scene between Laura and the Gentleman Caller in *The Glass Menagerie* is especially suitable, because the characters are so much in tune with each other's moods and responses.

Characterization: The choice of this sort of scene should derive from the inherent interest, eccentricity, or depth of the characters being portrayed. Again, virtually any scene is suitable, but the best are those with complex or unusual characters. The point of the director's work here should be to lead the actors to bring genuine observation into play and to integrate the elements of a characterization by means of a clear and imaginative biography.

SCENES FOR ADVANCED WORK

The type of scenes discussed below should be approached in the "creative" mode. The director should have a clear and effective matrix for dealing with the scene *as if it were being presented in the context of the entire play.*

At this level, you should start to be more assertive in your work. By all means, explore the associational methods outlined in Chapter V. Develop a matrix for the play that complements your image of the scene. If you have a strong impulse to do something "different" with the scene, then project a matrix for the play that will accommodate the statement you wish the scene to make. To do otherwise threatens the integrity of the work and your own progress.

Crowd Scenes: The crowd scene (See Chapter IX) can be defined rather arbitrarily as one with more than four or five characters on stage at any given time. A play like the American classic *You Can't Take It With You,* by Kaufman and Hart, provides many choices.

Period Scenes: These are, of course, drawn from plays demanding a statement of a specific historic period. Plays written before the late 1800's are the obvious source for material, but modern works set in pre-modern times are appropriate. Anouilh's *The Lark* or Robert Bolt's *A Man for All Seasons* are only two of many possibilities.

Non-Realistic or "Stylized" Scenes: Some plays present a clear and open challenge to the realist/naturalist mode. Any of the other "-isms" provide interesting challenges to the director trying to enrich a theatrical vocabulary. Brecht's *Good Woman of Setzchuan* is a good example. For this type of work, you should not overlook musicals and other works that are presentational in fact or in feeling.

Work on Imagistic Technique: Such work provides valuable exercise in the process of formulating and projecting a matrix. After directing several scenes or productions, you will want to expand your capabilities not only by working on different kinds of plays, but also by approaching them in different ways. Having chosen or been assigned a scene, you might concentrate your analytical approach on one of the methods you have come to rely upon the least. If, for example, you tend to ignore *scholarship and criticism,* you could deal with a challenging scene by concentrating on that approach. This is, after all, the same sort of idea we suggested to help enrich an actor's work, opening up a greater variety of approaches and techniques.

Complete Plays: The best plays for a director-in-training to start with are modern one-acts, such as those by Tennessee Williams, which are rich in environment and characterization. After doing one or two realistic plays, you may progress naturally to "style" pieces. Consider Chekhov's farces, Noël Coward's stylish pieces, or Tom Stoppard's and Christopher Durang's one-acts. In a different vein, investigate the short plays of Yeats, or Beckett, or Pinter, or the contemporary Europeans.

You will be tempted to start bigger. If you get the chance to direct a big play, try to resist unless you are certain it is something you can handle. When you decide it *is* something you can do, after all, then by all means, take it on. If you find it a wonderful and completely satisfying experience, then you are on your way. Good luck—and try to do good, honest work.

End Notes

Like any artist, a director must work constantly. Material is everywhere: an oil slick on a wet city street, a vagrant huddling in a doorway, the sound of locusts, a dance movement, Rodin's *Gates of Hell,* thunder. The director takes it all in; it is all material for reference and use. Working on scenes is a chance to use all these images thoughtfully and creatively. In the life of a director, such opportunities are rare, and the time is short. Dancers—great dancers, too—work out every day. So do other artists. They work not just to sustain a level of achievement, but to open up possibilities—what actors call a *stretch*. So it should be for serious directors and scene work. Since convention seldom allows young directors the opportunity for the kind of serious practice that other artists rely upon, you must seize every chance. Get all the practice you can—and make the most of what you get.

B

DIRECTING MUSICALS

Directing a musical requires a vibrant and imaginative matrix and great managerial skill. The music itself becomes part of the text of the play; it must be included in the director's formulation of the matrix and integrated into the fabric of the production. The addition of music and dancing usually requires additional collaborators: musical director, choreographer, and instrumental musicians. These people have specialized creative responsibilities the director must coordinate.

The Matrix for a Musical

Every musical is different. The matrix must reflect the play's unique character. Musicals share only one special ingredient: music. The power of music transports the drama (or the comedy) into another dimension, and so the musical—like the classical play—operates in an obviously abstract world. A world where people sing and dance their emotions is a place where arguments about "realism" no longer intrude. The created world of any musical is a place of heightened feelings and expression. As a result, musicals are naturally compatible with certain types of metaphors.

Story-telling Forms: In Chapter II, we mentioned Gower Champion's Broadway production of *Bye-Bye, Birdie* as an example of a matrix employing a "comic-book" metaphor. This is only one example in a wide range of metaphors useful for framing a matrix for a musical; the story-telling image encompasses the very bright and the very dark, the fantastical and the satirical. It includes fairy tales, folk tales, horror stories, science fiction, book illustration, comic strips.

Remember that an effective matrix must be more specific than the mention of a *type* of story-telling. Search through the possibilities until you discover something that catches the exact feeling you seek.

Theatrical Images: Theatre is another form of the broad story-telling genre and can provide particularly apt metaphors for a musical production matrix. Among the innumerable period and theatrical styles available to the director, ancient and modern *presentational* forms are often the most useful. The classic theatre has inspired contemporary musicals from *A Funny Thing Happened on the Way to the Forum* (Roman Comedy) to *Hair* (Greek Old Comedy).

> **A working knowledge of theatre history helps many contemporary directors produce lively and imaginative work—even in the most commercial of situations.**

Some successful directors of musicals draw their matrixes from cinematic forms, including specific movies or the style of a specific film director. Keep in mind that the most useful matrix will come often from a form not directly related to the play itself. Remember the advice in Chapter V: *"Do not consider the theatrical style for which the text was prepared or in which it is conventionally performed as a potential image for the production."*

The musical offers a director the challenge to rise to the level of the variety and energy of the play. Accept the challenge by being bold in searching for a matrix. But always maintain your respect for the play. A musical is, first of all, a *play* with a wide range of possibilities. Do not accept the conventional attitude that "It's only a musical." Rather, develop a matrix that provokes interesting creative choices and lets you and your collaborators create a uniquely effective production statement.

DISCUSSION

1. Discuss one or more "story-telling" metaphors (beginning with those listed in the discussion above) to be used in a directorial matrix for each one of the musicals in the following list that you are familiar with:

a. *Camelot*

b. *Guys and Dolls*

c. *Phantom of the Opera*

d. *Cats*

e. *The Robber Bridegroom*

f. *Little Shop of Horrors*

g. *Candide*

h. *Fiddler on the Roof*

i. *La Cage aux Folles*

2. List an appropriate musical/story-telling metaphor for other shows you are familiar with.

3. Mention and discuss potential theatrical period or style metaphors for the plays listed in 1. a) through i) above.

Auditions: Musical auditions require special planning and consideration (see Chapter IX). The fundamental requirements can be summarized as follows:

- The performers must know exactly what will be asked of them.
- The musical director and the choreographer must be given the opportunity to test each candidate's potential.
- The musical director and the choreographer must be carefully consulted at all steps in the casting process.
- The decisions on casting must rest with the director of the production.

Rehearsal Scheduling: A musical will require about 25% more rehearsal time than the same play without music. Depending on the complexity of the music and the production, the skill and experience of the performers and the other creative collaborators, this could mean a rehearsal period up to *twice* as long as for a non-musical production. Much of this time, of course, is given over to musical and dance rehearsals.

A skilled accompanist can be essential to the progress of musical rehearsals. The work requires skill, musicianship, patience, and endurance. Every experienced director of musicals knows that good accompanists are as valuable as they are rare.

> **HINT:** Coordinate the rehearsal scheduling with the musical director and choreographer and stay in touch with their progress at every stage of the rehearsal period.

Many directors find it best to turn over as many rehearsals as needed to the musical director immediately after the read-throughs. This time can be devoted to getting the cast familiar enough with the music to allow them to concentrate on the play itself as the rehearsals progress. The director must tell the musical director early on if there are any special considerations that might influence the singers (e.g., some groups may need to be separated on stage; some must be kneeling; and so on). Some musical directors prefer having the performers know all the lyrics before they begin *musical* rehearsals. This serves the function of allowing the actor/singers to concentrate on one thing at a time, in this case, the music itself.

The choreography presents a different set of scheduling problems. If the dance elements are to be integrated into the dramatic action of the play, they must seem to grow out of the scenes themselves. For this reason, the director and the choreographer must sometimes wait until a scene is blocked before attempting to stage the dance. This will allow the director and the choreographer to see the context in which the dance appears and will increase the likelihood of an organic flow from stage movement to dance. Of course, some plays have musical and dance numbers already set off from the dramatic action (e.g., *Gypsy* and *La Cage aux Folles*). In such cases, the choreographer can begin immediately to make the dances.

Astute directors of musicals deal with choreographers and musical directors much like they deal with designers. The director supplies images and an idea of the production's special character and requirements. For example, the dance may have to conclude in a certain stage location, or one character may need to seem uninvolved in what is going on. It is essential that these three collaborators understand their relationship to the production and to each other. Misunderstanding responsibilities and expectations can further complicate an already complicated task.

The Rewards

Directing a musical well is an enormous challenge. The director needs large measures of integrity, audacity, skill, energy, and diplomacy. If you have these things in good measure and can communicate your enthusiasm to your company, you have an excellent chance of directing musicals successfully. When you do, you will find few things in the theatre as immediately satisfying—even exhilarating—as musical production that goes well, and that applies equally to the big-budget Broadway spectacular and the junior class play.

C THE WORKING DIRECTOR

It is difficult to get work as a professional director, especially at a threatre with an established reputation. On the other hand, many less-glamorous or prestigious assignments go begging. If you are a serious director, you should set your sights and go about building your career systematically.

> **HINT:** The young director should take on as many directing jobs as possible to build practical experience and a good reputation.

Non-paying Assignments

It is safe to say that there are jobs for volunteer directors in every locale that has any kind of lively theatre environment. These can be excellent places to test your skills as artist, organizer, coach, and administrator. Typical of the organizations that welcome volunteer directors are:

- Small to medium-size middle schools and high schools
- Junior colleges and community colleges
- Recreation departments
- Civic groups
- Social clubs
- Arts councils or committees
- Community children's theatres
- Community theatres
- Employee clubs or centers
- Student groups
- Professional organizations

Often, such groups will have some sort of theatre program in place—or will at least have considered having one. Even if they do not, you should consider suggesting one. There are countless good reasons: making a cultural contribution to the community, fund-raising, calling attention to the organization and its programs, building camaraderie, providing a creative outlet for those involved, increasing public awareness of an issue. Any of these can be ample justification for sponsoring a theatre production.

If a theatre program already exists (as it might in any one of these organizations), contact the person in charge and make your interest known. Find out if a more formal application is needed; if it is, prepare an appropriate resumé and proposal, as discussed below.

Proposing a Production   If you are proposing to direct a play of your own choosing, make sure it is *appropriate* to the organization and its resources. The script should complement the organization's philosophy, objectives, and style; and the size and complexity of the production should be within the group's potential to produce successfully. Ask yourself the following questions:

1. Is the subject and style of the play suitable to the group's character and goals?
2. Can the roles be cast from interested members of the group, or will it be necessary to go outside?
3. Is there an appropriate space available for performance and rehearsals?
4. Can the design and technical elements of the production be completed in time to allow adequate tech and dress rehearsals? Who will take responsibilty for these functions?
5. Will you as director be allowed to establish rehearsal and performance discipline? Will the organization back you up?
6. What will be the strategy for promoting and publicizing the event? Who will be responsible?

HINT: Be open and clear about what is expected of the cast, the crew, the producing organization, and yourself as director.

When you have considered all these questions, you are ready to make a proposal. Remember, the production is for the *organization*—its members and supporters. With that in mind, present your ideas positively and enthusiastically. The thought, preparation, and excitement you communicate must convince everyone involved that the production will be a positive experience! Use your directorial matrix to communicate something of the production's special quality. It is your vision of what this production might be that will motivate and excite your future collaborators. (If the play is already chosen, you should nonetheless deal with all the questions above except the first. Try to understand the reasons for the choice and be prepared to carry through on the impulses that led to its selection.)

Holding Auditions—Review Chapter 9. Communicate as much as possible in advance about the auditions, the rehearsal process, and your own expectations about rehearsal and performance discipline. People not familiar with the demands of a production might not understand what is expected of them. You must tell them up front, or be prepared for misunderstandings and hard feelings. Do your preparation carefully—especially in dealing with questions 2, 3, 4, and 5 above.

HINT: If your *own* expectations of the actors are reasonable and clear, then *you* are not likely to be surprised or disappointed once the show is cast.

Rehearsing the Production—Prepare completely for your work as director, even if the play is short and simple. You, your cast and crew, and the producing organization are investing a great deal in the enterprise. If you are committed to the work, your chances of immediate success and satisfaction are greatly enhanced. So too, is your own opportunity for growth as a serious director. Do not give yourself any excuses for not doing your best work—no matter what the project.

Coaching the Actors—The difference between working with professional actors and beginners is largely a matter of degree. Beginners need *more:* more guidance, clearer choices, and more assurances. As you review Chapter 11, note especially the distinction between coaching actors and teaching acting. When you work with relative beginners, this distinction will be blurred, but it is still a good guideline. Every good actor learns something from every production. Be satisfied with that and allow the actors to learn what they can from the experience of working with you while you learn from working with them.

The company owes the production promptness, concentration, and commitment. As director, you owe the company a pleasant and satisfying experience. Many non-professionals reasonably expect their work on a production to be enjoyable. You should see to it that they are not disappointed.

H I N T : Make the work fun.

A pleasurable experience is the principal compensation for most of the people who are working with you. The biggest reward for everyone, of course, will come from doing the best possible production—exactly the same as it is with good professional actors. Make that the goal, but do not overlook the fact that people who are enjoying themselves in rehearsals are likely to be the most productive. Schedule the rehearsals conscientiously in order to waste as little time as possible. You might, for example, break the play down into French scenes to help schedule rehearsal time efficiently. Work hard when you're rehearsing, but allow time simply for *fun*. Everyone will soon get the message, and your job will be much easier and more effective.

Paid Assignments—Directing Jobs

There are four principal areas of employment for professional directors:

Commercial Theatres
- Single Production Companies (e.g., Broadway and Off-Broadway)
- Stock (present a series of plays in a season)
- Dinner Theatres (play and meal for one price)

Professional Not-for-Profit Theatres
- Regional (e.g., Arena Stage, Guthrie, Alabama Shakespeare Festival, TheatreVirginia)
- University Resident (e.g., Asolo, Yale Rep, Playmakers)
- Special Interest Theatres (new plays, ethnic, politically or philosophically committed: e.g., Playwrights' Horizons, Repertorio Español, Ontological-Hysteric Theatre)

Civic (Professionally Staffed)
- Community
- Children's

Educational (Usually those with schools or departments of theatre or drama)
- College or University
- Secondary School

Faculty positions for directors in educational theatres usually require an advanced degree or certification. College and university programs typically seek directors with an M.F.A. (Master of Fine Arts) or Ph.D. (Doctor of Philosophy). But, because the field is highly competitive, more and more schools are looking for directors (and teachers of directing) with advanced degrees *and* an extensive directing resumé that includes professional work. The few openings for directors in such listings as *Artsearch, Chronicle of Higher Education,* and the *Job Contact Bulletin* of the Southeastern Theatre Conference invariably specify "M.F.A., Ph.D., and directing experience."[1]

We are entering an exciting time for serious theatre directors. More and more, professional directors working in the regional theatres, and on commercial projects, are likely to have college or university training. Many of these same directors are finding engagements as guest artists in colleges and universities. At the same time, directors holding faculty appointments are working as guest directors in regional and commercial theatres. When the growing number of university-based resident professional theatres is added to the mix, the distinctions between directors (and other theatre artists) working in educational and professional venues are becoming blurred. Directors with professional skills and intellectual perspectives might soon become the rule in theatres across the country—a welcome and refreshing prospect.

Preparing Your Resumé—You should begin *immediately* to assemble a director's professional resumé and update it regularly. Applying for any of the professional positions listed (and some of the unpaid as well) will require you to submit one.

What should a director's resumé contain?

1. personal identification;
2. directing experience, showing the title of the play and the producing organization;
3. (optional) related experience (as assistant director or stage manager again with play title, theatre, *and* name of the director);
4. (optional) related skills (e.g., business manager, box office, promotions, publicity);
5. training or education (degrees, directing study, workshops);
6. (optional) names and addresses of references.

As your experience grows, you will probably choose to eliminate the optional elements, leaving the three essentials of a director's resumé to tell *who you are, what you have directed and where,* and *information about your education and training.*

DISCUSSION

1. Compare the fictitious resumés shown in Figures C–1 and C–2 from the standpoint of:

   A. information included or omitted;

[1]See Appendix C: References and Sources, for addresses for these and other references and services.

```
┌─────────────────────────────────────────────────────────┐
│                                                           │
│                   ROBERTA  BROADWAY                       │
│                      (Director)                           │
│    825 Sunset Drive                                       │
│    Meadows, TX 12345                                      │
│    (888) 555-6789                                         │
│                                                           │
│                REPRESENTATIVE EXPERIENCE                  │
│                                                           │
│    Director:                                              │
│                      UNIVERSITY                           │
│    The Boor by Anton Chekhov          Meadows State University │
│    Lady of Larkspur Lotion by Tennessee Williams    MSU  │
│    Talley's Folly by Lanford Wilson   MSU Experimental Theatre │
│                                                           │
│                      COMMUNITY                            │
│    The Real Thing by Tom Stoppard     Five County Players │
│                                                           │
│    Assistant    Director:                                 │
│                      UNIVERSITY                           │
│    Taming of the Shrew by Wm. Shakespeare   Dir: Beth Smith   MSU │
│                                                           │
│    TRAINING: BS in Theatre Arts (1988), Meadows State University; │
│       Courses at MSU in Basic and Intermediate Directing; Acting I, II, III, │
│       IV; Stage Make-up; Costume Design.                  │
│    RELATED EXPERIENCE: Business Manager, MSU Theatre 2 yrs. Proper- │
│       ties Master, Five County Players, 3 seasons. Stage Manager, Univer- │
│       sity and Community, 8 shows                         │
│    REFERENCES: Dr. Beth Smth, Chairperson; Theatre Arts Division, MSU, │
│       Meadows, TX 12345                                   │
│       Arnold Bland, Managing Director, Teen-Tent Music Theatre, Mead- │
│       ows, TX 12346                                       │
│       Doris Vernon, Arts Director, Central High School, Meadows, TX │
│       12345                                               │
│                                                           │
└─────────────────────────────────────────────────────────┘
```

Figure C-1: SAMPLE RESUME FOR A STUDENT DIRECTOR

    B. layout;

    C. overall impression or image.

2. Discuss what each director might have included, omitted, condensed, or expanded upon. (For example, the student director omits high school theatre experience; the professional director does not include college work.)

WILLIAM KALB
Director—SSDC

[212] 555-9876 (Service) [718] 555-5432 (Machine)

OFF-BROADWAY	
Bad Vibes by Charles Steele	Eastside Playhouse
Wonder Bread and Uncle Nat by Dot Ives	Cherry Lane Theater
EQUITY SHOWCASES	
Hamlet (with Ernest Frank)	Westside Rep
Girl Crazy by George and Ira Gershwin	Uptown Theatre Club
REGIONAL THEATRE	
Barnstorming Cincinnati by Ben Greet	Ohio Repertory Theater
Two Gentlemen of Verona	Bay Shakespeare Festival
STOCK	
Ten Little Indians by Agatha Christie	Lakeside Theater (NH)
Barefoot in the Park by Neil Simon	Lakeside Theater (NH)
A Thurber Carnival	Lakeside Theater (NH)
Camelot by Lerner and Lowe	Vermont Music Faire
Zippers! by Bill Kalb and Patrick Devon	Vermont Music Faire

TRAINING
Neighborhood Playhouse; HB Studios; BFA in Acting (1977), Peninsula State College (NY).

RELATED EXPERIENCE
Managing Director, Vermont Music Faire, 1981–84; Graphic Artist, Ampersand, Inc./George Nelson Associates, 1984–85; Computer Programmer, Denney Group, NYC, 1985.

Figure C-2: A SAMPLE PROFESSIONAL DIRECTOR'S RESUME

EXERCISE

Prepare a resumé that you could use in seeking a directorial assignment. Specify the position you are seeking and consider how the resumé might differ in applying for different directing jobs.

Supplementing Your Resumé—If you are fortunate enough to be interviewed for a directing job, you often will find it useful to have the following materials available for the interviewer:

1. Photographs: Two or three color slides (35mm) or prints (5 × 7 or 8 × 10 in color or black and white) of two or three shows you directed. If you use slides, have a good hand-held viewer available. Make certain the shots are of the highest possible quality and communicate an accurate sense of how the production looked in its best moments. Do not bring more photographs with the idea that you will overwhelm the interviewer, or that the pictures must communicate every important moment of the show. Even the most famous productions shot by world-famous photographers choose no more than half a dozen shots.
2. Reviews: One to three notices for one to five productions. Obviously, you will select only favorable ones, but if you have the option, select those that communicate the *feeling* and the *impact* of the production. Eliminate those that *tell the story of the play* or that are poorly written.
3. Releases and interviews: Two or three items that reflect your attitudes, ideas, or methods.
4. Prompt script: One example that shows your preparation and working methods.
5. Testimonials or references: Three of four letters or notes attesting to your special strengths and qualities. The best are from producers or other employers and theatre people of established stature (see "Hiring Standards for Directors" below).

Beginning a Career: Some Imperatives

Establish Your Reputation—Even if you have started only recently in the theatre, your reputation has begun to take shape. Choose projects and develop the methods and personality that help create the sort of reputation that serves you best.

> **For a director, reputation is the indispensable factor in getting work. Be conscious of creating and maintaining a positive professional image.**

Think of Yourself as a Director—Take stock of your abilities, interests, and potentials. Think seriously about the kinds of plays you respond to, the sorts of theatres that interest you. Work on your craft and your skills in dealing with actors and other collaborators. Being a director must become a crucial part of your life and personality. Look at things as a director, and before long, you will develop the habit of seeing things in directorial terms.

Consider Your Goals—Decide where you want to go in your professional and artistic life and keep those objectives in mind. There are no golden paths to success, but if you have an idea of where you are going, you at least can make informed decisions.

Cultivate a Positive Attitude—Some directors have gotten critical career opportunities because of their personalities.

|| **Few things are as valuable for a young director as energy, enthusiasm, and a positive outlook.** ||

Be Prepared—Read plays and history. Experience painting, sculpture, dance, and architecture. Go to the theatre to observe, then think about what you have seen and discuss it as a professional.

Treat Your Collaborators and Your Audiences With Respect—The modern director is one artist in a company of artists creating something for an audience. A director who understands this and behaves accordingly is much more likely to attract good collaborators and responsive audiences.

HIRING STANDARDS FOR DIRECTORS

Below, in descending order, are the criteria many theatres use in hiring a director for a single production. As you see, the standards are quite reasonable yet extremely difficult to satisfy. The ability to meet many of these criteria depends on your own first-hand experience and reputation. The priorities differ, of course, from position to position. A regional theatre seeking to employ a guest director will have a different set of standards from a college department looking for a teacher for basic courses.

Criteria for Hiring a Director

1. Seeing a production directed by the applicant
2. Enthusiastic recommendation of theatre where applicant has directed
3. Recommendation of actors or others who have worked with applicant
4. Applicant's resumé (where worked, types of shows, and regularity of assignments)
5. Applicant's personality and ability to communicate creative ideas and enthusiasm
6. Education or training
7. Related professional experience (as actor or stage manager, for example)
8. Personal and professional references of a general nature
9. Reviews and other documents
10. Scholarship and publication

PROFESSIONAL ASSOCIATIONS

In addition to the national organizations listed below, most serious directors belong to and participate in many state and regional organizations dealing with theatre, the arts in general, and related issues.

- *Actors' Equity Association* (AEA, Equity); 165 West 45th Street; New York, NY 10036; (212) 869-8530. Many directors belong to Equity, the theatrical union for professional actors and stage managers. Still others must deal with Equity, directly or indirectly, through contract negotiations and work rules.
- *Society of Stage Directors and Choreographers (SSDC);* 1501 Broadway 31st Floor; New York, NY 10036; (212) 391-1070. SSDC is the professional directors' union. It sets working rules and contract guidelines for many professional theatres.

PLAY SERVICES, UNIONS, AND JOB LISTINGS

Play Services

Anchorage Press; Post Office Box 80-67, New Orleans, LA 70182; (504) 283-8868.

Baker's Plays; 100 Chauncey Street; Boston, MA 02111; (617) 482-1280.

Dramatic Publishing Company; P.O. Box 109; Woodstock, IL 60098; (815) 338-7170.

Dramatists Play Service; 440 Park Avenue South; New York, NY 10016; (212) 683-8960.

Samuel French, Inc.; 45 West 25th Street; New York, NY 10010; (212) 206-8990.

Music Theatre International; MTI Enterprises, Inc., 545 Eighth Avenue; New York, NY 10018; (212) 868-6668.

Rodgers and Hammerstein Library; 1633 Broadway, Suite 3801; New York, NY 10019; (212) 541-6600.

Tams-Witmark Music Library, Inc.; 560 Lexington Avenue; New York, NY 10022; (212) 688-2525.

Unions

Actors' Equity Association (AEA, Equity) 165 West 45th Street; New York, NY 10036; (212) 869-8530.

Society of Stage Directors and Choreographers (*SSDC*); 1501 Broadway—31st Floor; New York, NY 10036; (212) 391-1070.

Job Services and Listings

Allen Publishing—Theater Guide; P.O. Box 2129; New York, NY 10185. (Useful listings of small and medium theatres; some details on salaries and fees for directors.)

ArtSEARCH; Theatre Communications Group, Inc.; 355 Lexington Avenue; New York, NY 10017; (212) 697-5230. (Employment listings include administrative, artistic, and education.)

Back Stage; 330 West 42nd Street; New York, NY 10036; (212) 947-0200. (Weekly paper with theatre, film, and TV information including casting and other hiring for theatres in and outside of NYC.)

Chronicle of Higher Education; Post Office Box 1955; Marion, OH 43306-1955; (800) 647-6969. (Features a large employment section for the full range of college and university departments, including theatre.)

Jobbank; National Arts Jobbank; 236 Montezuma Avenue; Santa Fe, NM 87501; (505) 988-1166. (Resource for theatre and other arts employment nation-wide.)

SETC Job Contact Bulletin; Southeastern Theatre Conference, Inc.; 311 McIver Street; Greensboro, NC 27412-5001; (919) 272-3645. (Employment listings for a full range of theatre jobs in the southeast and across the country.)

THEatre JOBlist; THEatre SERVICE; P.O. Box 15282; Evansville, IN 47716; (812) 474-0549 or (812) 479-2281. (National theatre employment listings.)

Theatre Directories; P.O. Box 519; Dorset, VT 05251; (802) 867-2223. (*Summer Theatre Directory, Regional Theatre Directory, Directory of Theatre Training Programs*).

Theatre Profiles; Theatre Communications Group, Inc.; 355 Lexington Avenue; New York, NY 10017; (212) 697-5230. (Detailed, comprehensive list of not-for-profit professional theatres across the country.)

GLOSSARY OF DRAMATIC AND THEATRICAL TERMS

Above In stage geography, upstage or farther from the audience.

Action Movement or progression of a play, a scene, or a character.

Aesthetics Theory or philosophy of art.

Analysis Systematic examination of the components of any entity—a scene, a play, a character.

Antagonist The opponent of the protagonist in a play.

Apron Part of the stage below the curtain line.

Arena A staging form with audience surrounding the action. Also called "theatre-in-the-round" and "central staging."

Artwork The product of a creative act.

Aside A line or comment that other characters in the scene are meant not to hear. Sometimes spoken directly to the audience.

ASM Assistant Stage Manager.

Atmosphere   The prevailing emotional or psychic quality of a scene.

Audition   The process of viewing actors to assign roles; *not* synonymous with "try-out."

Backing   Scenery placed behind doors, windows and other openings in the set to shield backstage areas from view.

Beat   A molecule of intention; the smallest unit of action.

Below   In stage geography, downstage or closer to the audience.

Bent Staple Set   A three-walled box set with returns DL and DR.

Bit   An action, a piece of business, or a special twist to a line reading.

Blackout   Taking all lighting quickly to zero, leaving the stage in complete darkness.

Blocking   The process of developing stage position and movement patterns with the actors.

Booth   The room or area from which the light and sound operators (and often the stage manager) run the technical cues for a performance. Also called the "control booth."

Border   Horizontal masking hung over the stage.

Box Set   A scenic enclosure, usually representing an interior room in a building.

Build   A stepped increase in volume, speed, or intensity.

Business   Any action performed by an actor—often involving a prop.

Call   Scheduled time for actors or other company members to be present and ready to begin.

Call Board   A board, usually at or near the stage door, where all official calls and other notices are posted.

Center   The middle of the stage or the playing area.

Center Line   A line from UC to DC from which lateral measurements are taken for scenery and furniture placement.

Cheat   To adjust stage or body position without taking focus.

Classicism   Associated with Greek and Roman drama and theatre.

Clear   A command to vacate an area and remove everything not nailed down, as in "Clear the stage."

Closed   Positioned so that the face of the actor or object is away from the audience.

Closed Turn   A turn that permits the audience to see as little of the actor's front as possible.

Company   All the people working on a production.

Context   Surrounding circumstances.

Costume Plot   A detailed listing of what each actor wears in every scene.

Counter   A discreet, complementary move made to adjust to another actor's larger and more important movement.

Cover   (1) To obstruct someone's view—usually the audience's. (2) To hide a mistake, as in a missed cue or forgotten line.

Cross   A move from one part of the stage to another.

Cue   A signal for a response.

Curtain Line (1) The demarcation on a plan showing the act curtain's position. (2) The last line in a scene or act—the *tag line*.

Cyclorama (Cyc) The upstage-most drop—framed or unframed—most often used as a neutral backing or for sky effects. It is often curved.

Direct Address In the presentational mode, the convention of acknowledging the audience and speaking to them in a straightforward manner.

Discursive A type of discourse that communicates information in a more or less objective fashion.

Dramaturg A literary adviser, researcher, commentator.

Dress Parade A review by the director and the costume designer of the cast wearing near-completed costumes.

Dress Rehearsal A rehearsal with the cast in costume.

Dress Stage Having the actors adjust positions to balance the stage picture and clear sightlines.

Drop A scenery element made of cloth, painted or unpainted, suspended from the flies.

Dry Tech Setting and running of technical cues without the actors.

Ensemble The company as *team*.

Entrance (1) Making an appearance onstage. (2) A door or other opening permitting the actor to get on the stage.

Environment Physical, emotional, social, and philosophical circumstances affecting action.

Exit Leaving the stage.

Exposition Information that must be communicated for the ensuing action to be understood or appreciated.

Expressionism A theatrical style usually marked by distortion of visual and aural elements and the objectification of characters through masks or other means. It aims at creating a semblance of *nightmares*.

Flat A unit of framed, cloth-covered scenery.

Flies The area above the stage where scenery can hang out of sight until lowered into sightlines.

Floorplan A representation of the scenery on the stage floor, drawn to scale.

Fly To use lines to pull scenery vertically out of sight.

Focus Visual or mental emphasis.

FOH Lighting instruments hanging *front of house,* that is, over the audience.

Follow Spot A powerful light that can be focused and moved about to follow a moving performer.

Forestage The apron.

Fourth Wall On a proscenium stage box set, the wall through which the audience sees the action.

Fractal Term from mathematical theory that describes the structure of things in nature and art achieved through repetition and modulation of patterns and motifs.

French Scene Designation marked by the entrance or exit of a character; every change of stage population.

Gelatine (Or "gel")   Color medium for lighting. Most color media today are plastic, but the old term persists.

Give Scene   To allow another actor to take focus.

Given Circumstances   Physical and emotional context in which a scene or action begins.

Gobo   A light pattern on stage, produced by a design cut from thin metal and inserted in a lighting instrument to project.

Go Up   To forget lines or business. Also "dry up."

Green Room   Traditional name for the area where the actors await their entrances.

Grid   Framework from which the hanging scenery is flown.

Groundplan   Floorplan.

Hold   Wait for something—laughter, an action, etc.

Impressionism   A style of production exhibiting intensely subjective elements in a generally soft and evocative theatrical environment—often in dreamlike and symbolic terms.

Improvisation   A rehearsal technique to discover something about a situation, a character, or a relationship through extemporaneous interaction.

In One   Stage area below the first set of wings, used in musical and variety shows for acts or scenes, allowing scenery upstage to be changed while the act is going on.

Instrument   Individual lighting unit, *not* a "light."

Justification   The reason offered for an action.

Lamp   The component of a lighting instrument that actually produces the light; *not* a "bulb."

Leg   A vertical masking piece placed L and R; may be framed or unframed.

Light Plot   Descriptive chart of instruments and their uses.

Magic "If"   Conditions of the dramatic fiction. An actor asks "What if?" in trying to grasp a character.

Masking   Flats or draperies that hide offstage areas from the audience's view.

Matrix   The director's image-model for a production.

Metaphor   A perceived likeness, usually between two apparently unlike things.

Mise-en-Scène   A production's total design.

Model   (1) A three-dimensional representation of a stage setting built to scale. (2) An imaginative or theoretical construct used to define and control a production's image.

Mood   Pervasive subjective quality of a scene or setting.

Motif   An image element that is repeated or modulated to form a pattern.

Motivation   Underlying force that provokes an action or response.

Naturalism   Theatrical style that attempts to reproduce life in all its detail. Emphasis is on environment and the impression of random behavior.

Neoclassicism   A period style, notably in the seventeenth century, that tried to re-create the dramatic and theatrical forms of Greece and Rome.

Objective   Character motive or intention.

Off   Away from stage center.

On Towards stage center.

Open Turn A turn that permits the audience to see as much of the actor's front as possible.

Pace The impression of a lively ongoing action, enhanced by a sense of things happening.

Pattern A image structure that exhibits relationships among the elements or motifs of which it is composed.

Pinging Playing a scene or exchange with a light, crisp tone and manner. "Ponging" connotes a heavier, more serious tone and quality.

Pit The area used by musicians between the front of the apron and the first row of seats; "orchestra pit."

Places Command to call everyone to opening positions for a scene.

Plant To indicate a prop or some business that will be employed more importantly later in the performance.

Plaster Line An imaginary line from the L proscenium arch to the R; used for measurements from the groundplan.

Portal A unit—often framed—of two legs and border.

Practicals Light sources seen on stage that are actually illuminated.

Presentational Performance mode or style that openly acknowledges the presence of the audience, usually by means of direct address.

Preview A performance with an audience before the official opening.

Producer The person with executive responsibility for the overall commercial aspects of the production.

Projection (1) Actor's technique of supporting the voice and enhancing articulation to ensure clarity and effectiveness in speaking. (2) A visual image projected with light.

Prompter Person who watches the script and gives actors lines as needed during the memorization period.

Prompt Side Traditionally, stage right, where the prompter was located.

Properties ("Props") Furnishings, set dressings, and actors' accessories. ("If it's not scenery and not a costume, it's a prop.")

Proscenium Line Same as "plaster line."

Protagonist The central character in a play.

Rake An angle or slope; especially a "raked stage."

Realism A theatrical style created in the late nineteenth century that tries to evoke an image of everyday life on stage.

Representational Performance mode that "represents" some view as self-contained on the stage and ignores the presence of the audience.

Return A scenery element—typically a flat—attached to the downstage end of a set wall or unit that runs offstage on either side of the stage as part of the masking.

Revolve Turntable.

Rhythm Pattern of sound in time; lilt or cadence.

Royalty Fee paid to the playwright to produce the script usually through an agent or play service.

Scrim Loosely woven fabric that is opaque when lighted from the front and translucent when objects behind it are strongly lighted.

Set   (1) Establish and fix as part of a production. (2) Setting.

Setting   Scenery; the theatrical environment.

Shift   To move scenery or properties from one position to another, as from scene to scene.

Sightlines   The lines of vision from the audience to the stage.

Soft Goods   Elements of scenery made of fabric and not permanently framed, as a drop or scrim.

Spike   To mark a position for a scenic element, usually with colored tape on the stage floor.

Static Scene   A scene in which there is little or no essential physical action.

Strike   Remove from the stage—either temporarily or (when the show closes) permanently.

Style   The manner of presentation; usually describes the conventional practice of a theatrical movement or historical period.

Subtext   The unspoken intention or motives of a speech or scene.

Symbolism   Late nineteenth-century style employing symbols to impart a sense of recognition and response.

Tableau Vivant ("Living picture")   A pictorial pose frozen on stage to underscore the significance of the moment or event—usually at the end of a scene or act.

Tag Line   The last line of a scene.

Take Scene   Assume focus or emphasis.

Take Stage   Command the space; take focus and move about freely.

Teaser   The first border—immediately upstage of the proscenium arch.

Technical Rehearsal   Rehearsal of technical cues with the actors.

Tempo   Rate of speed.

Thrust   Staging form in which the audience views the action from three sides; the fourth side allows a scenic wall or unit.

Tone   Overall quality of the experience or artistic statement.

Top   Exceed something in volume, speed, effect, intensity, or any combination.

Tormentors ("Torms")   The downstage legs immediately upstage of the proscenium arch.

Trap   Opening in the stage floor by means of a hinged or removable section.

Trim   Adjustment of a piece of flown scenery to its correct height and balance.

Try-out   Performance before an audience to test a production before its formal opening.

Turn In   Turn towards centerstage.

Turn Out   Turn away from centerstage.

Unit Setting   A set depicting two or more locales simultaneously so that action can move from one place to another without a scene shift.

Vomitoria   Tunnels, gates, or aisles in the audience space through which actors can enter or exit; from the architectural conventions of the Roman theatre.

Wings   Offstage space L and R.

REFERENCES

Books recommended for serious directing students and plays used as topics of discussion in this text are in **boldface**.

Theory and Criticism

Abel, Lionel. *Metatheatre*. New York: Hill & Wang Dramabook, 1963.

Bergson, Henri. "Laughter," in *Comedy*. Ed., Wylie Sypher. Garden City, NY: Doubleday, 1956.

Bernstein, Leonard. *The Joy of Music*. New York: Simon and Schuster, 1959.

Burns, Elizabeth. *Theatricality*. New York: Harper & Row Publishers, 1972.

Clay, James H. and Krempel, Daniel. *The Theatrical Image*. New York: McGraw-Hill Book Co., 1967.

Dürrenmatt, Friedrich. "Problems of the Theatre," in *Four Plays*: 1957–62. Trans. Gerhard Nellhaus. London: Jonathan Cape, 1962.

Edwards, Betty. *Drawing On The Artist Within*. New York: Simon and Schuster 1986.

———. **Drawing On The Right Side Of The Brain**. Los Angeles, CA: J.P. Tarcher, Inc., 1979.

Frye, Northrop. *Anatomy of Criticism: Four Essays*. Princeton: Princeton University Press, 1957.

Gross, Roger. *Understanding Playscripts*. Bowling Green, Ohio: Bowling Green University Press, 1974.

Hornby, Richard. *Script into Performance*. Austin: University of Texas Press, 1977.

Kerr, Walter. *How Not to Write a Play*. New York: Simon and Schuster, Inc., 1955.

Knight, G. Wilson. *The Wheel Of Fire* (4th edition). London: Methuen & Co., Ltd. 1960.

Kott, Jan. *Shakespeare Our Contemporary*. Garden City, NY: Anchor Books, Doubleday & Company, Inc., 1966.

Langer, Suzanne K. *Feeling And Form*. New York: Charles Scribner's Sons, 1953.

———. *Problems Of Art*. New York: Charles Scribner's Sons, 1957.

Meyer, Michael *Ibsen*. Garden City, NY: Doubleday & Company, Inc. 1971.

Shahn, Ben. *The Shape of Content*. Cambridge, MA: Harvard University Press, 1959.

Shank, Theodore. *The Art Of Dramatic Art*. Belmont, CA: Dickenson Publishing Co., Inc., 1969.

Sprinchorn, Evert. *Ibsen: Letters And Speeches*. New York: Hill & Wang Dramabook, 1964.

Watson, James D. *The Double Helix*. New York: Atheneum, 1968.

Woodbury, Lael J. *Mosaic Theatre*. Provo, UT: Brigham Young University Press, 1976.

Young, Stark. *The Theatre* (6th printing). New York: Hill & Wang Dramabook, 1966.

Directing Texts

Benedetti, Robert L. *The Director At Work*. Englewood Cliffs, NJ: Prentice-Hall, Inc., 1985.

Cohen, Robert and Harrop, John. *Creative Play Direction*. (2nd edition). Englewood Cliffs, NJ: Prentice Hall, Inc., 1984.

Dean, Alexander and Carra, Lawrence. *Fundamentals Of Play Directing* (4th edition). New York: Holt, Rinehart and Winston, 1974.

Dietrich, John E. and Duckwall, Ralph W. *Play Direction* (2nd edition). Englewood Cliffs, NJ: Prentice-Hall, Inc., 1983.

Glenn, Stanley L. *A Director Prepares*. Encino, CA: Dickenson Publishing Company, Inc., 1973.

Hodge, Francis. *Play Directing: Analysis, Communication, and Style*. Englewood Cliffs, NJ: Prentice-Hall, Inc., 1982.

Kirk, John W. and Bellas, Ralph A. *The Art of Directing*. Belmont, CA: Wadsworth Publishing Co., 1985.

Directors' Biographies and Commentaries

Bartow, Arthur. *The Director's Voice: Twenty-one Interviews*. New York: Theatre Communications Group, 1988.

Brook, Peter. *The Empty Space*. New York: Atheneum, 1968.

———. *The Shifting Point*. New York: Harper & Row, 1987.

Clurman, Harold. *The Fervent Years*. New York: Hill and Wang, 1967.

———. *On Directing*. New York: The Macmillan Company, 1972.

Cole, Toby and Chinoy, Helen. *Directors On Directing* (9th Printing). New York: Bobbs-Merrill Co., Inc., 1953.

Gielgud, John. *Stage Directions*. New York: Capricorn Books, 1966.

Grotowski, Jerzy. *Towards a Poor Theatre*. New York: Simon and Schuster, 1968.

Grube, Max. *The Story of the Meininger,* translated by Anne Marie Koller; edited by Wendell Cole. Coral Gables, FL: University of Miami Press, 1963.

Guthrie, Tyrone. *In Various Directions*. New York: Macmillan, 1965.

Hopkins, Arthur. *How's Your Second Act?* New York: Philip Goodman Co., 1918.

Jones, David Richard. *Great Directors At Work*. Berkeley and Los Angeles, University of California Press, 1986.

Prince, Hal. *Contradictions: Notes on 26 Years in the Theatre*. New York: Dodd, Mead, 1974.

Ross, Lillian. "Profiles: Kurosawa Frames," *The New Yorker,* December 21, 1981; pp. 51–78.

Schneider, Alan. *Entrances*. New York: Viking Penguin, Inc., 1986.

Wetzsteon, Ross "The Director In Spite of Himself: An Interview with Jonathan Miller," *American Theatre,* November, 1985; pp. 4–9, 40–41.

Acting and Actors

Berry, Cecily. *Voice and the Actor*. London: Harrap, 1973.

Black, George. "Physical Metaphor," *Players,* August–September, 1972; pp. 272–74.

Boleslavsky, Richard. *Acting: The First Six Lessons*. New York: Theatre Arts Books, Inc., 1933.

Chekhov, Michael. *Lessons For The Professional Actor*. New York: Performing Arts Journal Publications, 1985.

Cohen, Robert. *Acting Professionally* (3rd edition). Palo Alto, CA: Mayfield Publishing Co., 1981.

Delgado, Ramon. *Acting with Both Sides of Your Brain*. New York: Holt, Rinehart and Winston, 1986.

Hagen, Uta and Haskel, Frankel. *Respect for Acting*. New York: Macmillan, 1973.

Lewis, Robert. *Method or Madness*. New York: Samuel French, 1958.

Spolin, Viola. *Improvisation For The Theatre* (5th printing). Evanston, IL: Northwestern University Press, 1969.

Stanislavski, Constantin *An Actor Prepares*, translated by Elizabeth Reynolds Hapgood (22nd printing). New York: Theatre Arts Books, 1967.

———. *My Life in Art*, translated by J.J. Robbins, New York: Theatre Arts Books, 1924.

Design Theory and Practice

Barton, Lucy. Historic Costume for the Stage. Boston: Baker's Plays, 1938.

Corson, Richard. *Stage Makeup* (6th edition). Englewood Cliffs, NJ: Prentice-Hall, 1981.

Gorelik, Mordecai. *New Theatres for Old*. New York: Samuel French, 1952.

Jones, Robert Edmond. *The Dramatic Imagination: Reflections and Speculations on the Art of the Theatre*. New York: Duell, Sloan & Pearce, 1941.

Parker, W. Oren, Smith, Harvey K., and Wolf, R. Craig. *Scene Design And Stage Lighting* (5th ed.) New York: Holt, Rinehart and Winston, 1985.

Payne, Darwin Reid. *The Scenographic Imagination*. Carbondale and Edwardsville, IL: Southern Illinois University Press, 1981.

Russell, Douglas A. *Costume History and Style*. Englewood Cliffs, NJ: Prentice-Hall, 1983.

———. *Period Style For The Theatre*. **Boston: Allyn and Bacon, Inc., 1980.**

Simonson, Lee. *The Stage Is Set* (6th edition). New York: Theatre Arts Books, 1963.

General

Ardrey, Robert. *The Territorial Imperative*. New York: Atheneum, 1966.

Banham, Martin, ed. *Cambridge Guide to World Theatre*. Cambridge: Cambridge University Press, 1988.

Berne, Eric. *The Games People Play*. New York: Grove Press, 1964.

Bettelheim, Bruno. *The Uses of Enchantment*. New York: Knopf, 1976.

Brockett, Oscar G. *History of the Theatre* (5th ed.). Boston: Allyn and Bacon, 1987.

Hartnoll, Phyllis, ed. *The Oxford Companion to the Theatre*. London, New York: Oxford University Press, 1967.

Kitto, Humphrey Davy Findley. *Greek Tragedy*. London: Methuen & Co., Ltd., 1939.

Knight, George Wilson. *Principles of Shakespearean Production*. London: Faber and Faber, 1936.

Kott, Jan. *The Eating of the Gods*. Translated by Boleslaw Taborski and Edward J. Czerwinski. New York: Random House, 1973.

Kullman, Colby H. and Young, William C., eds. *Theatre Companies of the World*. Westport, CT: Greenwood Press, 1986.

Rigdon, Walter, ed. *Biographical Encyclopedia and Who's Who of the American Theatre*. New York: James H. Heineman, Inc., 1966.

Selected Plays

Chekhov, Anton. *The Cherry Orchard*. Trans. Michael Frayn. London: Methuen, 1978.

Dürrenmatt, Friedrich. *The Visit,* translated by Patrick Bowles. New York: Grove Press, 1962.

———. *The Visit,* adapted by Maurice Valency. New York: Random House, 1958.

Friel, Brian. *Lovers* (Part I: "Winners.") New York: Farrar, Straus & Giroux, 1968.

Fugard, Athol. *Master Harold . . . and the boys*. New York: Samuel French, Inc., 1982.

Garcia-Lorca, Federico. *Three Tragedies Of Federico Garcia Lorca*. Trans. James Graham-Lujan and Richard L. O'Connell. New York: New Directions Books, 1955.

Gardner, Herb. *A Thousand Clowns*. New York: Samuel French, Inc., 1962.

Genet, Jean. *The Maids* and *Deathwatch*. Trans. Bernard Frechtman. (6th printing, revised). New York: Grove Press, 1962.

Gray, Simon. *Butley*. New York: The Viking Press, 1972.

Ibsen, Henrik. *Ghosts*. Trans. Michael Meyer. London: Methuen, 1985.

———. *Hedda Gabler* and *A Doll's House*. **Trans. Christopher Hampton. London: Faber and Faber, 1989.**

———. *The Master Builder*. Trans. Kjell Amble. San Francisco: Chandler, 1968.

Kesselring, Joseph. *Arsenic And Old Lace*. New York: Dramatists Play Service, 1942.

Miller, Arthur. *Death Of A Salesman*. New York: Viking Press, 1949.

Pinter, Harold. *The Birthday Party* and *The Room* New York: Grove Press, 1968.

(Note: Dozens of Shakespeare editions are available with a wide variety of features to recommend them. Editions of the individual plays by Signet and Penguin are good values and size for production work.)

Shakespeare, William. *Hamlet*.
———. *Henry V*.
———. *Macbeth*.
———. *A Midsummer Night's Dream*.
———. *Richard III*.
———. *Twelfth Night*.
Shepard, Sam. *True West*. New York: Samuel French, 1981.
Shue, Larry. *The Foreigner*. NY: Dramatists Play Service, Inc., 1985.
Strindberg, August. *Miss Julie*. Trans. Evert Sprinchorn. San Francisco: Chandler, 1961.
Williams, Tennessee. *Cat on a Hot Tin Roof*. New York: New Directions, 1955.
———. *The Glass Menagerie*. New York: New Directions, 1949.

Index